Allegory and Ideology

Allegory and Ideology

Fredric Jameson

VERSO
London • New York

First published by Verso 2019
© Fredric Jameson 2019

Map in Chapter 3 reprinted with permission of *Financial Policy Magazine*, March 2, 2016.

The figures in Chapter 4 are reproduced with permission of Oxford University Press through PLSclear from Seth Monahan, *Mahler's Symphonic Sonatas*, 2015.

"Third-World Literature in the Era of Multinational Capitalism," part of Chapter 5, was published originally in *Social Text*, no. 15 (Autumn 1986).

Appendix A reproduced with permission of the University of Minnesota Press from the author's foreword to Algirdas Julien Greimas, *On Meaning*, 1970.

All rights reserved

The moral rights of the author have been asserted

1 3 5 7 9 10 8 6 4 2

Verso
UK: 6 Meard Street, London W1F 0EG
US: 20 Jay Street, Suite 1010, Brooklyn, NY 11201
versobooks.com

Verso is the imprint of New Left Books

ISBN-13: 978-1-78873-025-9
ISBN-13: 978-1-78873-045-7 (US EBK)
ISBN-13: 978-1-78873-044-0 (UK EBK)

British Library Cataloguing in Publication Data
A catalogue record for this book is available from the British Library

Library of Congress Cataloging-in-Publication Data
A catalog record for this book is available from the Library of Congress

Typeset in Minion Pro by Hewer Text UK Ltd, Edinburgh
Printed and bound by CPI Group (UK) Ltd, Croydon CR0 4YY

To
Phillip Wegner
and
Kim Stanley Robinson
for "mounting the stallion of reading"
and
in memory of
Masao Miyoshi and Hayden White

Contents

Preface: Allegory and Ideology	ix
1. Historical: The Ladder of Allegory	1
2. Psychological: Emotional Infrastructures	49
3. Psychoanalytic: *Hamlet* with Lacan	83
4. Musical: An Allegorical Symphony? Mahler's Sixth	119
5. Political: National Allegory	
A. *Third-World Literature in the Era of Multinational Capitalism*	159
B. Commentary	187
6. Poetic: Spenser and the Crisis of Personification	217
7. Epic: Dante and Space	251
8. Dramatic: *Faust* and the Messages of Historicism	287
9. Literary: Allegoresis in Postmodernity	309
Appendices	
A. The Greimas Square	349
B. Consciousness Explained Allegorically	361
C. Culture and Group Libido	383
Index	389

Preface: Allegory and Ideology

Some topics need no introduction inasmuch as they are already everywhere the object of dispute or simply because their relevance becomes obvious as soon as they are identified. Others, like this one, require some preliminary account of their significance in the scheme of things, as well as an indication of how they can best be presented. Sometimes an author does this by describing his personal discovery of the subject and its importance: I will not do that here.

But as my starting point in the ideological will seem partisan for some, idiosyncratic for others, and for still others simply old-fashioned, I will need to say why Ideology is none of these things and why it subsumes everything else in culture and the superstructures, assuming the position that religion once held for the first historians and cultural theoreticians of the West. And this will initially require us to identify one of the fundamental obstacles to grasping the centrality of Ideology, namely the conviction that there are areas of life, areas of activity as well as of thought, which are nonideological.

It is an illusion most easily entertained in moments of historical stasis, or at least in places in which ideological or class struggle seems to have been contained and reduced to manageable proportions. There is a certain parallel here with the history of linguistics and in particular with that of the tropes and figures. The study of these linguistic deviations was first made possible by the seemingly obvious (and logical) fact of the existence of a literal language the distortions of which could easily be identified. As tropology advanced, however, and became more secure in the possession of its instruments and analyses, the conviction that there was such a thing as a literal language became shaken and at length disappeared, leaving in its place a more generalized conception of Representation as such which is still with us and which remains the central mystery of this field or problematic. Is it possible, then, that naïve realism should find itself confronting the same fate?

As for what will come to be recognized as ideology, the exploration of non-Western social formations produced an explanatory concept, that of Culture, generally identified with Religion, in terms of which the deviations from the norm of Western society could be described, if not exactly explained. But in the course of modernization and secularization, when the variety of social mechanisms became comprehensible in economic terms as modes of production (historical materialism), and when religions themselves became the object of secular analysis as cultural or superstructural formations, then it became possible to grasp the relationship of culture or religion with their economic context, by way of the concept of Ideology—as what the Marxist tradition called *base* and *superstructure* (terms whose relevance is not particularly affected by their overfamiliarity or their frequent misuse either).

The usefulness, then, of a generalized notion of Ideology lies in its dual capacity to combine, I will not say the dilemmas of subject and object, or soul and body, but at least the controversies between materialism and idealism that turn on the objective functioning and history of the socioeconomic mechanism on the one hand and the construction of subjectivity on the other. We must credit Louis Althusser for having made an extraordinary beginning on healing this rift, this incommensurability of explanatory codes, with his notion of ideology as a mechanism whereby the conscious (and unconscious) individual biological subject situates himself or herself within the collective social structure: ideology as a kind of unconscious cognitive mapping.[1]

He did not, however, pursue this investigation into the historical realm, that is to say, into the processes where the transformations of subjectivity can be seen to accompany those economic changes in the history of the modes of production; he did not, in other words, inquire

---

1 Louis Althusser, "On Ideology," *On the Reproduction of Capitalism*, London: Verso, 2014, 171–207.

into the dynamics of what we may call *cultural revolution*, having been chastened, perhaps, by Marx's own explicit warning that "ideology ... has no history."² But this famous remark, read in its original contort, can be seen to apply specifically to what we would today call the *history of ideas*—that is to say, a history of ideologies or other cultural symptoms studied in their own right as autonomous phenomena. Just as today we would not study capitalism without taking commodity reification and its attendant subjectivities into account, so also—except for the area of religions as such—few would undertake an examination of what we still call non-Western cultures without any consideration of the mode of production of which they are both symptomatic and constitutive at one and the same time. Ideology, however, is the watchword for resistance to such disciplinary reifications, and it stands for the unification of objective and subjective fields into a single project, which, from that standpoint of the humanistic disciplines which is ours here, can perhaps best be defined as the examination of the construction and constitution of individual subjectivities and their susceptibility to revolutionary change.

This is then the larger context in which I propose to explore allegory as a fundamental mechanism in that process, in a project that on the one hand deals with representation as such, and on the other with History. But from both these perspectives a new problem emerges, which is that of narrative (and with it, the question of literature itself).

I have elsewhere proposed that we think of the *ideologeme*—the "elementary cell" or smallest possible intelligible unit of ideology—as a dual structure that can be approached from either side with quite different analytic equipment.³ On the one hand, the ideologeme is an opinion (*doxa* is a favorite theoretical term for this cognitive or pseudocognitive version), while on the other hand it can be articulated as a narrative. Racisms are the crudest and most accessible examples of this duality: "opinions" about the races being thinly disguised fantasies that express the fears and envies of individual and collective subjects in narrative form. Political

---

2 Karl Marx and Friedrich Engels, *The German Ideology*, Moscow: International, 1964, 42. As for the opposite number of the history of ideas, namely the history of technology, a significant note in *Capital* (London: Pelican Books, 1976, 286n6) complains of its woeful underdevelopment in Marx's own day, a complaint that must not be taken for an assertion of the autonomy of that "discipline" either.

3 See *The Political Unconscious: Narrative as a Socially Symbolic Act*, Ithaca: Cornell University Press, 1981, 29–33.

psychologists have never really been able to disentangle these twin dimensions of ideology by demonstrating the primacy of the one over the other; meanwhile, Enlightenment (insofar as one is permitted to evoke it historically as a tradition of some kind) has always presupposed the power of rational persuasion as a therapy for doxa in their cognitive forms. The roots of the narrative ideologemes in the form of this or that psychoanalytic primal fantasy have seemed a good deal less accessible, or at best, have seemed to take on purely personal and contingent forms. Althusserian analysis, however, drawing no doubt on Nietzsche fully as much as on Lacan, assumes a constitutive and well-nigh indissoluble link between the subject and narrative as such. The subject is somehow defined by its narratives of itself; and narrative in turn seems always to be wedded in one way or another to the presence of the subject, even when it is a question of the succession of "mere" objective facts.

This is where we find ourselves obliged to remember the classical opposite of the concept of doxa, namely *episteme*. To translate this second term simply as "knowledge" is to evade the whole confused and immemorial debate about science as such (its other possible translation). Marxism is certainly not the only philosophical system to have consecrated "science" as the way out of opinion, ideology, purely individual or idiosyncratic thinking, and the like. But I do like Althusser's definition of science as writing that omits the place of the subject;[4] and I appreciate the new representational problems to which this paradoxical formulation must inevitably give rise. Its great advantage is, of course, to have bypassed the question of truth (scientific or otherwise), or better still, to have delegated it to the existential realm, where it becomes a concept that can fight it out with older notions of "belief."

The Althusserian formula has yet another advantage, which we can dramatize by returning to Freud's notorious essay "Creative Writers and Daydreaming," an essay that most literary theorists deplore as the vulgar low point of psychoanalysis (literature as wish fulfillment) on a par with the most vulgar class-oriented Marxist criticism.

---

4 Louis Althusser, "Three Notes on the Theory of Discourses," *The Humanist Controversy and Other Texts,* London: Verso, 2003, 49: "We observe that the subject of scientific discourse ... is *absent in person* from scientific discourse, for there is no signifier designating it (it is an evanescent subject which is inscribed in a signifier only on condition it disappear from the signifying chain the moment it appears there— otherwise science slides into ideology)."

We can leave the matter of wish fulfillment, however, to the specialists in desire: what is most interesting in Freud's thinking here is his astute observation that the writer's fundamental problem lies not in his own wish-fulfilling fantasies, but rather in the reader's reactions to those fantasies.[5] Not only are we not interested in the wish fulfillments of other people, he tells us; the latter can strike us as positively repellent. (The relationship of this principle to political puritanism and the so-called "social issues" in American politics should be apparent.)

The author must therefore disguise his own wish fulfillments, his own personal stake in the story he is unfolding: and such mechanisms of disguise and concealment, of indirect forms of satisfaction, are at the very heart of the literary art, where they are generally obfuscated by questions of universalism, the human condition, the eternal story, and the like. The fact is, however, that this principle that Freud felt able to enunciate for literature is exactly the same as what Althusser formulated for science: the omission of the subject, the disconnecting of the individual subject from the narrative or the scientific-structural material.

Ideology is thus at the heart of all these issues: ideology not as the individual ideologeme or opinion, but rather as that intersection between the biological individual and the collective which is at stake in thinking, in literary expression, and of course in language itself (where the subject leaves its most visible mark in the shifter—the blank pronoun—that does double duty for both).[6]

Narrative analysis turns on the way in which ideology finds its fulfillment in temporal enactments of this dual subjectivity; what is called *Ideologiekritik* has for the most part concerned itself with the class content of its cognitive forms (as for example in Barthes's classic *Mythologies*). But insofar as class becomes visible and is affirmed in a self-conscious way (as a class-for-itself), it is perhaps as repellent for other people (other classes) as the individual wish fulfillment was on the

---

5 Sigmund Freud, "Creative Writers and Daydreaming," *Complete Works*, vol. IX, London: Hogarth Press, 1959, 152–3.

6 *Shifter* is a linguistic term for blank words—pronouns, temporal and spatial expressions like "here" or "now"—whose meaning "shifts" according to the situation or context: the "subject"—I—can thus be considered as a personal or existential reference and as a generalized linguistic function. It is also obligatory, today, to recall Nietzsche's warning: "I fear we are not getting rid of God because we still believe in grammar" (*Twilight of the Idols and the Anti-Christ*, London: Penguin, 1990, 48).

personal level. Both involve exclusions: the individual, by way of that brand he leaves on his psychological private property, on his ideational cattle (as William James famously put it),[7] excludes everyone else by definition; collective self-definition (by gender and race as well as by social class) excludes the other collectivities. In much the same way, then, the secret of class or group identification must be concealed; and, finally (coming around to our central topic here), it is allegory that often achieves this concealment most effectively, for allegory delivers its message by way of concealing it.

It is a process that can initially be dramatized by the way in which synonymy, homophony, ambiguity, polysemy, association, puns, *faux amis,* and the like—a whole materialist zone of that nonmaterialist collective dimension called *language*—offer the hinge on which local signifying systems (or ideologemes) are constructed.[8] For just as words are not the basic units of meaning, but rather syntax and sentences, so also there are no such things as ideas, if one understands by that word distinct and unrelated ideational entities: ideas are rather always elements in more complex signifying systems, whose most obvious mechanism—the binary opposition—is only one of the relationships that organize that cluster of themes we call a *meaning*. We have become accustomed to the notion that definition is negation, that identity is called into being by difference (and vice versa), and that what looks like an individual or autonomous meaning or idea always somehow includes its opposite. But as the Greimas square teaches us, a term has two

---

7 William James, *The Principles of Psychology,* Cambridge: Cambridge University Press, 1981, 317: Our distant or past selves "we shall imagine with the animal warmth upon them; to them may possibly cling the aroma, the echo of the thinking taken in the act. And by a natural consequence, we shall assimilate them to each other and to the warm and intimate self we now feel within us as we think, and separate them as a collection from whatever selves have not this mark, much as out of a herd of cattle let loose for the winter on some wide Western prairies the owner picks out and sorts together, when the time for the round-up comes in the spring, all the beasts on which he finds his own particular brand."

8 See Appendix A for a discussion of the functioning of the Greimas "semiotic square" and the way in which it generates seemingly distinct terms or ideas from the multiple meanings of their logical or semiotic starting points. For stimulating new experiments with the square, see also Phillip Wegner, *Periodizing Jameson: Dialectics, the University, and the Desire for Narrative,* Evanston, IL: Northwestern University Press, 2014, and *Shockwaves of Possibility: Essays on Science Fiction, Globalization, and Utopia,* Bern, Switzerland: Peter Lang, 2014.

opposites: its most vital and antagonistic polar opposition, and then that more passive and all-encompassing, uninteresting opposite or negation which is simply everything it is not. But these two very different kinds of oppositional terms then return on their starting point to transform it in its turn into two distinct meanings; and with that the whole complex dynamic of an ideologeme or signifying system is set in motion.

Yet it remains a static and unproductive motion, turning on itself very much like the rotation of the Greimas square, producing its various terms and identities in a revolving sequence, which marches in place without moving. It is at this point that the other face of ideology demands attention, the narrative one, in which the ideologeme in question is pressed into service of a properly ideological narrative. Which comes first, the narrative or the ideological "concept"? It is a very ancient question, if not an unresolvable one: thus, the Talmudic alternation between Halakhah and Haggadah (the Law and the Example) distantly reproduces this opposition,[9] as does the classic anthropological debate about the relative priority of myth or ritual; or indeed the more contemporary structural distinction between the synchronic and the diachronic. It is, however, a tension far more central to theology than to philosophy, insofar as the traditional vocation of the latter lies in the production of concepts as such, consigning narrative to such incidental uses as the Platonic myth or the contemporary ethical example or casus.

In theology, however, there is always a story to be dealt with—if nothing else, the story of Creation itself. The negotiation between this or that fundamental narrative or mythic history and its meaning of doctrinal content becomes therefore a far more significant field of debate and argumentation. This is why the allegorical process, which is in question here, receives its first impetus and its methodological development from the Talmudic tradition, and later on the Church Fathers, rather than from the philosophical schools that preceded them and on which they drew. My own use of the patristic and medieval system of the four levels[10] (explained in more detail in Chapter 1) can therefore be justified

---

9 See Haim Nahman Bialik, "Haggadah and Halakhah," *Revealment and Concealment: Five Essays*, Jerusalem: Ibis, 2000.
10 I have relied on Henri de Lubac, *Exégèse médiévale* (Paris: Aubier, 1959–1964), 4 vols., which usefully documents the distinction between three- and four-level allegories; and also on Jean Daniélou, *From Shadows to Reality*, London: Bloomsbury, 1960.

by this Benjaminian priority of theology over philosophy in narrative matters; and it is a scheme that will serve us well in ideological analysis as well. For the four levels essentially exhaust the various terrains on which ideology must perform its work. The first, literal or historical, level stands as the matter at hand, the thing demanding analysis—whether historical event (as in the Scriptures), text, idea, political debate, personality, ethical problem—whatever draws us up short as individuals and demands reflection and commentary.

The second allegorical or mystical level is then the secret or hidden meaning of that initial text, and this meaning is at one with the allegorical method deployed in order to reveal it (in much the same way as for Ibn Khaldun the other religions have separated revelation and miracle; only in Islam is the revelation—the Quran—itself the miracle).[11] We need not shy away from the use of the word *mystical* in this respect, for it can serve to remind us that *Ideologiekritik* is positive as well as negative and draws on a whole doctrine of group consciousness (*asabiyya*),[12] which is as restorative and ontological as the practice of suspicion and deconstruction with which Paul Ricoeur originally associated it.[13] The Marxist practice of ideological analysis is in other words also Utopian and draws up into the light not only all those features of class consciousness we wish to avoid thinking about, but also the thoughts and visions (wish fulfillments) that are designed to replace or displace them; it is a practice of allegorical enlargement rather than one of reduction, as its less consequential critics have always liked to maintain.

That enlargement will then, in the fourfold scheme of things, deploy the two prolongations of the initial interpretation, the two successive and related levels of individual and collective experience and history. What the medieval thinkers considered the moral level, or that of conversion and the salvation of the individual soul, we might well wish to interpret in terms of existential experience, the construction of subjectivity or the psychoanalytic. But just as in theology individual salvation is ultimately inseparable from collective salvation, so also for us today, and despite the distortions inevitably developed by an

---

11 Ibn Khaldun, *The Muqaddimah: An Introduction to History*, Princeton: Princeton University Press, 2015.

12 Ibid., 97–8.

13 See Paul Ricoeur, *Freud and Philosophy: An Essay on Interpretation*, trans. Denis Savage, New Haven, CT: Yale University Press, 1970, 32.

individualist consumer-oriented society, the very thought of the destiny of a biological individual is inseparable from that of the future of the species, in whatever collective form one chooses to imagine that. The final or anagogical level, therefore, classically reserved for the Last Judgment, is that of a kind of "political unconscious," that is, an often unconscious or merely implicit narrative of History as such, a collective and political narrative always latent in conceptions of our own personal destinies.

The terminology of the levels is useful in more than one way. Its principal convenience lies, of course, in the graphic and well-nigh visual way in which it permits an inventory of possible interpretations and as it were a concentration of a swarm of options into a few basic categories or reference points. The gaps between these zones, however, merit their own philosophical comment, for they constitute the empty spaces across which the attractions and repulsions (or identity and difference) pass. Such gaps thereby offer a convenient figure (in the absence of figuration) for the identification of incommensurables, as well as their differentiation. This is then the place to deploy a terminology I will not use frequently in what follows, but which must always be kept in mind as an interpretive resource and possibilities. For the gaps between the levels are the place in which libidinal investment takes place (to use a term first developed by Jean-François Lyotard): this concept designates a transfer of vital energies and of an almost obsessional attention from its source to another, less richly nourished area; or, if you prefer, and as the case may be, a distraction of one form of libidinal immediacy from its initial object to a less threatening or dangerous one. Such are the strategies and tactics of desire, as it seeks its satisfaction in what Freud might have called indirect means and byways: and interpretation, as the appropriation of an object of desire, quickly relearns the methods of its original nature. For ideology can also without much difficulty be transferred into the currently popular language of desire, these complex interplays and energy exchanges themselves offering an allegorical system of their own:

> terminologies of *Ideology* (the collective)
> terminologies of *Desire* (the individual)
> interpretive codes
> textual objects

(It will be objected that the very terminology of "investment" binds this particular model to a distinct historical social system. No doubt: but its displacement from one level to another as greed or social status are systemically transformed into different functions, and as futurity itself is modified, serves to foreground the analytic and historical uses of the allegorical framework.)

That these four allegorical levels can harbor many more implicit narratives—those of the material institutions, for example—is unquestionable, particularly in a highly differentiated society like our own. That the levels interact with one another in what are sometimes surprising and unexpected ways must also be foreseen, and I have borrowed Felix Guattari's term *transversality*[14] to designate particular examples of this process. That the levels can change places, and the text shift position into that of its own commentary, while the commentary then becomes a kind of text in its own right—that is also to be expected in a secular society in which nothing is endowed with indisputable centrality, and a multiplicity of interpretive options is virtually guaranteed in advance, depending on what counts as an event, a reality, or a text. With transversality, then, Guattari rewires the loose ends of the Deleuzian rhizome.

(This would be a moment for a digression—which I will only partially resist—on the dependence of the concept of transversality on the Deleuzian notion of the sedimentary levels or rhizomatic strands or lines of flight: these outline the program for a multiple set of parallel histories without any "ultimately determining instance" and therefore ultimately find their source in that war on Marxism or totality declared by Jean-François Lyotard. The multiple, yet somehow parallel but unevenly dated layer-chapters of *Mille plateaux*, are an extraordinary exercise in this aesthetic solution, while Manuel De Landa's *A Thousand Years of Nonlinear History* more openly betrays the parallelism, whose realization could not, however, be completed without the reunifying cross-flashes of transversality and reidentification.)

These allegorical propositions are hard to argue in any systematic way. The first chapter takes on the fundamental alternative to the

---

14 On Guattari's work in general, see Janell Watson, *Guattari's Diagrammatic Thought: Writing Between Lacan and Deleuze*, New York: Continuum, 2011.

fourfold system proposed here, namely the system of three allegorical levels that flourished in Alexandria around much the same time. This is not some mere numerological hobbyhorse but allows us to make some basic judgments on concrete interpretations as such, in particular, on those which promote what I would be willing to call the bad allegories of humanism and of the history of ideas (particularly when the latter is based on science). All are tripartite allegorical systems that with a little attention denounce themselves.

There follows a chapter on the historical concepts of the emotions, which are themselves allegorical systems and fundamental mechanisms in the construction of subjectivities: the essential theme here is, however, the relationship of such systems to the dimensions of their respective social formations and in particular to the forms of otherness to which they give demographic access: something particularly relevant in the era of globalization.

At this point, several chapters compare the multiple meanings of nonallegorical works (*Hamlet*, Mahler's Sixth Symphony) with the operations of officially allegorical structures (in Spenser, Dante, and Goethe's *Faust*). The aim is clearly not one of some liberal coexistence of interpretations but rather the structural mechanisms whereby the works either solicit multiple and incompatible readings or negotiate those already institutionally in place.

This is then the moment to offer a contemporary commentary on an older essay of mine that has raised a good deal of controversy: one dealing with national allegory as a form in which emergent groups find expression at the same time that they promote it.[15] The central category here, and in a good deal of my work generally, is the one already alluded to above: what Ibn Khaldun called *asabiyya*, or group or collective consciousness. It is to my mind the most basic political concept of all, both theoretically and practically; and allegory is one of the vehicles by which it can be tested and measured.

Finally, it becomes appropriate to confront the seemingly opposing realities of allegory as a literary structure (and even, in some cases, a literary genre) and allegoresis, as a conflict of interpretations that has no particular structural basis. The findings of our chapter on emotions will

---

15 See Chapter 5A. Fredric Jameson, "Third-World Literature in the Era of Multinational Capitalism," *Social Text*, no. 15 (Autumn 1986), 65–88.

be useful at this point, in mapping an analogous transition from emotion to affect; while postmodernity itself determines a shift from personification to process-oriented allegory, which demands a parallel critical and theoretical reorientation.

But there runs through the following chapters another perhaps less apparent argument, which may also be obscured by their length and their heterogeneous content. That argument follows population as its materialist theme, and can be said to propose a correlation, if not exactly a causal determination, between number and genre or structure. Allegory is not exactly a genre, but its initial existence as a fourfold structure certainly reflects the multiple classes and strata of the Roman empire, just as the Greek system of emotions reflects the far more limited dimensions and class structure of the Greek city-state. One of the stories the second chapter, on named emotions, tells is then the adjustment of a local culture to the dimensions of a universal political form.

The chapter on *Hamlet* does not reflect that kind of transition, but rather the contradictions of monarchy and of its attempt to resolve the problem of succession, just as the chapter on Spenser suggests the bewildering overlap of different kinds of space in an emergent maritime system of colonial control. Dante's fundamental structure is shown to project that attempt to think together the moral and spatial systems embodied in the struggle between pope and emperor implicit in that medieval alternative to kingship and the nation-state, which was the idea of empire itself: while Goethe's work can be grasped as that unsuccessful alternative to a national capitalism that was the "enlightened despotism" of a disintegrating feudal system. Empire in all these contexts means a political program designed to house enormous and multiple populations. It is then not surprising that its current form, globalization, should have been rebaptized Empire by some of its leading theorists, or that its culture should bear the marks of an increasingly abstract and quasi-statistical exchange system which can only conceptualize according to quantitative categories (in our final chapter, maximalism and minimalism).

This underground theme—the pressure of population on form and thought—might well bear as its motto a remark of Peter Sloterdijk quoted in Chapter 5: "people today are not prepared to coexist consciously with a billion other subjects."

I must finally thank Wendy Weiher and Eric Bulson for indispensable help in preparing *Allegory and Ideology,* which constitutes the second volume of the *Poetics of Social Forms.*

F. Jameson
Durham, NC
August 2018

1
Historical: The Ladder of Allegory

It does not seem wise to begin our presentation with the secret that allegory is itself allegorical: an interpretive virus that, spreading by way of its own propagations, proliferates and perpetuates itself until, in a kind of incurable interpretive frenzy, it becomes indistinguishable from the text and no longer visible to the naked eye. Yet allegory is also a surgical instrument and a diagnostic tool, by way of which the atomic particles of a sentence or a narrative, the most minute meanings and secondary connotations, are registered on the X-ray plate in all their guilty absence, in all their toxic participation. Freud showed us that our very dreams are allegories,[1] while the theologians of all the religions—great and small—read reality itself as an inescapable swarm of allegories with all the exegetical obsession of any garden-variety paranoiac. So we had better not begin by admitting that there is an allegory of allegory itself; that the allegorist, like the politician, is always corrupted by the power of his or her monopoly of interpretation; that allegory turns all books into a single central text; and finally that allegory goes hand in hand with secrecy, just as Umberto Eco showed that the whole point of language as such was not truth, but lying.[2]

---

1 What is called a dream contains (a) the literal level or dream protocol; (b) the raw material of the previous day and its surface "wish"; (c) an infantile desire from the earliest years; and (d) desire as such, "the immortal wish," as Freud calls it on the final page of his dream book.

2 Umberto Eco, *A Theory of Semiotics*, Bloomington: Indiana University Press, 1976.

It is always better, when confronted with so multifarious a term, to begin by identifying its various enemies, which is to say, its opposites. Maybe we can reduce them to two: the first condemns the multiplicity and dispersal of allegory with the unity of the living symbol. The second denounces everything cut-and-dried, abstract, desiccated in the allegorical narrative, with the concreteness of reality itself and the perceptual three-dimensionality of realism. (Erich Auerbach's *figura* was an ingenious strategy for combining both these onslaughts.)[3] Meanwhile, and characteristically, allegory turns against itself and indicts itself by way of a generic and pragmatic distinction between outright allegorical structures which have the objectivity of fixed forms and a multiple collection of seemingly random interpretations or readings now consigned to some general (and generally pejorative) category called *allegoresis*.

This final form of the dismissal of allegory as a dangerous contagion will be acknowledged in the last chapter of this book. The argument from realism, however, can be better undermined by history: for it presupposes a radical distance between meaning and empirical reality, and attributes to allegory a failed attempt to produce an impossible unification of these dimensions (which are ultimately those of thought and experience, or better still, of soul and body). But in an age that prizes difference and differentiation, heterogeneity, incommensurability, a resistance to unification, this failure cannot continue to be a reproach; and it is our fault then, as readers—perhaps as old-fashioned readers—that we fail to acknowledge the reality of the literal level of the allegorical text: this was not the error of the first allegorists, for whom that literal level was historical fact, to be respected in all its bloody triumphs and failures.

As for the symbol, however, it generated a historical debate in its own right in the Romantic period, on which it is perhaps useful to pause. Not that the Romantics themselves—whether German or English—were any too reliable in their promiscuous use of these seemingly contradictory terms. Nor was Wordsworth philosophically aware of the distinction between just that realism we have been evoking and the Nature of which his new style wished to be the symbol. But it was precisely that symbolism of nature and the natural which was itself profoundly allegorical. The bourgeois revolution—supreme event of the age and even, for

---

3 See Chapter 7.

Historical: The Ladder of Allegory

Immanuel Kant, of History itself, the seizure by a people of its own destiny[4] (and, for the bourgeoisie, the setting of limits for itself in the form of a written constitution)—finds its literary expression in the denunciation of the allegorical decoration and rhetorical embellishments of the poetry of the ancien régime, with its call for that plain style of American revolutionary clothing (Benjamin Franklin and the Quakers). That symbolic fashion, however, turned out to be not merely an epochal change in taste, but also yet another allegory for class: for democratic equality, without the flourishes or the rhetoric.

So we have here a first example of how allegory itself can be allegorical, when it is symbolic of an ancien régime and its class hierarchies. Its much-touted opposite number in characteristically Romantic symbols—Novalis's "blue flower," the simple-mindedness of Wordsworth's peasants, Schelling's call for a new mythology—when interpreted either historically, or in terms of literary history, in fact unmask themselves as so many allegories. However, the symbol as such—even when disguised under Hegelian trappings as "the concrete universal"—always marks the attempt at a flight from interpretation, from theoretical and historical understanding. It has at least that much in common with religion; and the conjunction of both in the person of Samuel Taylor Coleridge is no accident (although one would want to add that this personage—like Walter Benjamin in a later period—is an immense continent whose exploration is always rewarding, and whose flora and fauna are often in rich, genetically productive conflict with one another).

Meanwhile, if the revulsion from allegory has its historical determinants and its often-political meaning, it is well to remember that its revivals do as well. For the West, at least, the first allegorical stirrings are to be found around the emergence of sacred texts, or at least—in the case of Homer—culturally central ones, each one of which will in the modern period come to be identified as the Book of the World. We will examine Homeric allegory in a moment; but far more dramatic is the flurry of allegorization that accompanies the Pentateuch or the Torah down through the ages, in Jewish and Christian commentary alike.

As it is the latter, and the evolution of its doctrine of the four meanings or levels of scripture, that constitutes the axis of this book, it will be

---

4   Immanuel Kant, *The Conflict of the Faculties*, Omaha: University of Nebraska Press, 1979, 152–57.

worth recalling the dual function of allegorical interpretation in those initial centuries in which Christianity, following the strategic lead of St. Paul, prepares to become the universal religion of the archetypal Western world empire. On the one hand, a small Jewish sect needs to legitimize itself in the eyes of the non-Christian Jewish population by demonstrating the myriad and covert ways in which the Hebrew Bible announces the coming of Christ as its fulfillment—a word that plays a significant role in the allegorical theory elaborated in this process. Thus, to draw on a well-worn illustration, the historical (literal) fact of the descent of the Hebrews into Egypt and their subsequent liberation will stand as a figure for the death and the resurrection of Christ, an interpretation that by no means excludes other meanings and other kinds of allegorical interpretations of the same event.

Meanwhile, the new religion must also, at one and the same time, cleanse itself of any narrow ethnic or regional identifications and translate its foundational texts into messages that address the Greek-speaking Gentiles of the eastern Mediterranean. This is also achieved allegorically by sublimating and spiritualizing Jewish Law; to use its most famous problem as an example, the requirement for circumcision is transformed into a "circumcision made without hands, in putting off the body of the sins of the flesh by the circumcision of Christ" (Colossians 2:11). The physical act of circumcision is thereby figurally transformed and translated into a spiritual "circumcision of the heart."

Both of these aspects of allegorization—the typological one (proposing a fulfillment alongside its literal and prophetic enunciation) and the figural one (which seems to suggest a sublimation of the physical act into a ritual or in other words a symbolic and spiritual event)—can still be detected in the ideological function of modern allegory, where they can be identified as the revelation of a Utopian narrative of history on the one hand, and a construction of subjectivity on the other.

But at this point it will be desirable to return to origins in the elaboration of the ultimate fourfold system of allegorical meanings, considered as a ladder to be climbed rung by rung beginning with its simplest elements or forms.

◆

The term *allegory* is most often applied to what may be called a one-to-one narrative in which features of a primary narrative are selected (in the process rhetoric calls *amplificatio*) and correlated with features of a second one that then becomes the "meaning" of the first. The point-to-point allegory is then something of a reversal of the heroic simile, in which the epic poet (Homer, and following him Virgil and the whole epic tradition) embellishes a given action with a large-scale comparison:

> Now when the men of both sides were set in order by their leaders,
> The Trojans came on with clamor and shouting, like wildfowl,
> as when the clamor of cranes goes high to the heavens,
> when the cranes escape the winter time and the rains unceasing
> and clamorously wing their way to the streaming Ocean,
> bringing the Pygmaian men bloodshed and destruction:
> at daybreak they bring on the baleful battle against them. (Book III, 1–7)[5]

The comparison unifies the overall action of the multitudinous Trojan army charging forward, reducing it to a single sensuous feature, namely the war cries, before developing under its own momentum into a full-dress autonomous action in its own right: as though the very mention of the cranes evoked a whole dimension of being—their southern migration when winter comes, the perils of the journey, and the final murderous arrival, when the ferocious birds attack the Pygmies in their homeland on the other side of the world—a myth attested to in many different cultures. The simile, therefore, with a mind of its own, hones in on the bloody climax of a noisy and disordered clash, which it has first organized and aestheticized into the graceful figure of a single flight of birds. This parallel development cannot be said to produce a structure in which the meaning of one narrative is revealed in the form of a second one: at this stage, the movement is reversible, and the legendary story of the cranes can be said to be fully as much illuminated by its reversal of the Greek's invasion of Troy as in the standard reading, which, however, it revises into the inevitability of a natural and indeed instinctual impulse. The defending Trojans hate the Greek invaders as viscerally as the invading cranes hate the defending Pygmies; meanwhile, the stops and starts of the Greek invasion (assembling the allies, becalmed without wind in port, dissensions, leadership quarrels, and so on) are

---

5   Homer, *The Iliad*, trans. Richmond Lattimore, Chicago: University of Chicago Press, 2011, 117.

somehow themselves effaced by the identification with a well-nigh unconscious will to battle.

This two-level heroic simile must not, however, be confused (as it so often tends to be) with metaphor, with which it has only this in common: that when the latter is inspected in detail and considered to have distinct and separate parts and features—my love is like a red, red rose: what are its petals, its stamen, why red, what about its scent, and so on—metaphor tends to become simile in its own right. But the effect of metaphor, in a narrative, amounts to the latter's denarrativization: the horizontal momentum is disrupted, we pause on a vertical association and linger in some metaphorical perpetual present (or eternal present, out of time), which brings to a halt that onward rushing temporal momentum that the simile only tends to accentuate. Simile redoubles the power of narrative, while metaphor arrests it, transforming epic back into a lyric stasis.

In the structuralist period, such parallel structures began to be studied under the more neutral and technical term of homologies; and it was with the work of Lucien Goldmann[6] that this term at length achieved a general methodological acceptance, designating the search for some one-to-one correspondence between structures. In his most famous work (*The Hidden God*), Goldmann tried to establish a wide-ranging correspondence between the literary structures of Jansenist tragedy (particularly in Racine) and the social situation of the noblesse de robe as a class fraction doomed in its rivalry for class dominance with the "rising" bourgeoisie. The sociological diagnosis seemed original and profound, the method doubtful and unconvincing.

The conclusion to be drawn here is that an appeal to homology must always be a warning signal. The two-level system is the mark of bad allegory, insofar as it disperses the elements of each narrative line without reuniting them, at the same time opening a reversible correspondence between the two levels. Tragedy is Jansenist, but Jansenism is also tragic; meanwhile the component parts of each system tend toward autonomy and their own independent interpretations: Pascal's bet can be seen as a reflection on the future of his class but also as part of the development of probability theory in this period. Pity and fear are traditional tragic categories; but melancholy, when attributed to a whole

---

6 Lucien Goldmann, *The Hidden God: A Study of Tragic Vision in the* Pensées *of Pascal and the Tragedies of Racine*, London: Verso, 2016.

Historical: The Ladder of Allegory

social class and period, is a concept with rather more clinical and psychic connotations.

We may draw on a well-known modern example of this kind of two-level allegory for further demonstration of the limits that mar its form as well as its content—"defective content resulting in defective form," as Hegel famously put it. Albert Camus's *The Plague* has traditionally been read as an allegory of the German occupation of France during World War II, what Jean-Paul Sartre called "the republic of silence"; and much ink has been spilled in arguments about the adequacy of its representation of a complex human enemy as a nonhuman plague virus. In Camus's defense we may cite André Malraux's representational strategy of excluding from your cast of characters figures who, like the fascists standing in for evil, repel any form of empathy or novelistic understanding. (In his case, the figure of Ferral in *La condition humaine* then becomes an interesting problem.) But Camus's own work suggests a reading of *The Plague* as a more interesting experimental departure.

The undoubted distinction of the earlier works (*L'Étranger, Le mythe de Sisyphe, Caligula*)—Camus viewed them as a trilogy, all staging "the absurd" in different ways and from different generic angles—turned on a unique thematic contradiction between the meaninglessness of a life destined for death (what the existential philosophers called "finitude") and the experience of *bonheur* (a word a little stronger than the English *happiness*, I think).[7] The point is that the latter is not some pious hope or longing, but a real experience: yet it is an experience that can only be fulfilled in an absolute present, as in Camus' ecstatic evocation of the sun at Tipasa; while on the other end of the spectrum, absurdity is also a concrete experience, but it must be felt in that different temporal continuum of a past–present–future, what Sartre will call "the project," a life in time. The greatness of the early "trilogy" lay in its resolute option for *bonheur*, for the temporality of the pure or living present: *The Myth of Sisyphus* offers a handbook in achieving what its memorable last sentence invited: "Il faut imaginer Sisyphe heureux." Meanwhile, neither Caligula nor the Meursault of *L'Étranger* are adepts of the absurd, they are both in fact happy, in the peculiar sense with which Camus endows this word. Caligula has taken on himself the pedagogical task of

---

7 On the early work of Camus, see Alice Kaplan, *Looking for the Stranger: Albert Camus and the Life of a Literary Classic,* Chicago: University of Chicago Press, 2016.

imposing the lesson of the absurd on his subjects (by way of arbitrary death sentences) in order to teach them the experience of *bonheur* whether they like it or not; and as for Meursault, it has not sufficiently been observed that like some successful Sisyphus he is also happy and that the absurd must be imposed on him from the outside, by a death sentence passed on him for the wrong reasons by people who do not understand his life in the present, in other words by Caligula's subjects as it were, and as though on their emperor himself.

The extraordinary quality of *L'Étranger*, to be sure, lay in a uniquely mechanical decision, namely to have Meursault tell his nonstory in a nonnarrative tense, the passé composé, which, as with that "style indirect libre" which Ann Banfield memorably termed "unspeakable sentences,"[8] is never otherwise used in this narrative way. By way of language itself, Meursault becomes a strange kind of alien, catapulted into a prosaic world of humans living another temporality altogether: it is as it were a kind of science fictional estrangement effect, which can only be categorized in normal literary terms as a form of Asperger's syndrome, of an absolute absence in Meursault of anything like empathy with other ("normal") human beings. In that sense, indeed, the book's title, which has been variously translated into English as "The Stranger" or "The Outsider," might better have been simply rendered "The Alien"; and what happens to Meursault at the hands of the inhabitants of the planet on which he is condemned to live is not unpredictable.

But none of these remarkable formal solutions is appealed to in *The Plague*, in which Caligula's lessons are administered to the inhabitants of Oran in an already contingent, accidental, and indeed meaningless way: the epidemic is itself absurd avant la lettre and in advance, and fragile and ephemeral moments of *bonheur* reduced to mere psychological experiences. This is, if you like, an experiment in projecting Camus's unique temporal contradiction onto a realistic representation, which one must also call political insofar as its framework is essentially that of a collectivity.

This is why what in the trilogy had all the formal freshness of a genuine crux has here evaporated into sheer moralizing; the paradoxes of the great *moralistes*, from Pascal to Machiavelli, from La Rochefoucauld to

---

8 Ann Banfield, *Unspeakable Sentences: Narration and Representation in the Language of Fiction*, New York: Routledge, 2016.

Gracián, have here been drained of their savor and flattened out into academic philosophizing. The dualism of the allegory conceals a false premise, that the politics of World War II has something in common with epidemiology and quarantine: this may well have been the way the inhabitants of Algeria lived it. But the outcome, for us as readers, is a liberal humanism in which the two incommensurable dimensions of history and the body are illicitly identified. This is bad allegory at its most consummate. (Indeed, if one wanted to indulge the interpretive faculty by transforming this reading into the more complete fourfold system, it might not be too far-fetched to assign the medical diagnosis to our third, or "moral," level, while the fourth collective one could translate it precisely into that story of an alien lynched by a mob of incomprehensible humans hypothesized above. As for the text, perhaps the chronicler Rieux simply translates Caligula's unique character into a paradigm of disabused observation and wisdom, if not contemplative science as such while the besieged Oran is the figure of a closed community surrounded by even more incomprehensible adversaries, whether Nazi, Muslim, or toxic parasites one can never quite be sure.)

I will, however, suggest that this dualistic allegory is in fact more easily understood as a regression to mere symbolism; and that it is in fact the logic of the symbol—that Romantic conception which overwhelmed the older allegories at the moment of bourgeois modernity—which has usurped the more complex allegorical structure alone capable of doing justice to Camus's attempt to expand his insight into absurd experience out beyond its individual boundaries. *The Plague* offers at least this advantage, of allowing us to diagnose the ideological aftereffects of this reduction to symbolism and one-to-one allegory. They are humanism and (as we shall see shortly) the thematization of science. Indeed, I will go even further here and suggest that all such dual allegorical structures are essentially humanist in spirit and assert the meaning of their narratives to be an expression of the "human condition." In yet a different perspective, they all affirm the presence of meaning; and meaning always tends to affirm the existence of a human nature as a normative metaphysic (even when the larger nature into which it is inserted carries the meaning of "absurdity"). Homologies are always what we may term bad allegories, and they reenact those bad readings of Hegel in which opposites are always reunited into this or that "synthesis."

We may then also draw the provisional consequence that genuine allegory does not seek the "meaning" of a work, but rather functions to reveal its structure of multiple meanings, and thereby to modify the very meaning of the word *meaning*. It is indeed part of the contemporary critique of metaphysics (and of humanism along with it) to denounce the conception of nature as meaningful: an affirmation not merely of a meaningful system at work in the natural world, but also of a human nature as well, one which virtually by definition is normative. It will be clear, then, that this naturalization of both meaning and metaphor alike is the function of the symbol, as opposed to the allegorical structure.

I should add that as it is convenient to continue to use the term *symbolic* for figural moments in general, here I restrict the identification of such appropriations by the ideology of the symbol to the language of dualistic or two-level, point-to-point allegories, as distinguished from the multileveled systems we are about to confront. Still, confusion may also arise when we attempt to distinguish such complex allegorical systems as those of Bunyan or Kafka from the dual and oversimplified "allegorical" readings they have so often inspired. (Such readings or interpretations are indeed numerous enough as to seem to demand a fourfold allegorical analysis in their own right: this is then the moment to distinguish allegory from allegoresis and to affirm that the latter can also be allegorical in its own right—a regrettable complication that I return to in the concluding chapter.)

But the case of Kafka does suggest that it might be desirable to make a place for such a concept as the "allegorical frame"—a dual or metaphorical framework or setting in which a more properly complex (in fact, fourfold) structural development takes place. As a contemporary version of this structure, consider a remarkable and relatively recent film by Jia Zhangke, *The World* (2004), in which the setting seems to confirm a simple metaphoric identification of the "real" world of contemporary China with the Disneyland-type theme park which is its subject and which purports to register all the noteworthy "sights" of that real world around China (the Eiffel Tower, Angkor Wat, Stonehenge, and so on). Within this frame, however, which seems to convey the familiar message that late capitalism is a world of simulacra, a good deal else takes place "realistically"—complex social relations susceptible of a different kind of allegorical reading in their own right.

Historical: The Ladder of Allegory

To pronounce the word *fable* in connection with Kafka suggests not only the solution of the matter of bad or dualistic readings but also the transition to be made from these systems to the more conventional tripartite ones to be discussed in a moment. What will be absent from the fourfold system of interpretation as such, but what informs these two (dual and tripartite) unsatisfactory forms that precede it, is precisely a kind of pedagogical intent. Platonic myth can be added to the fund of examples here: not only does Plato's practice reinforce the development of allegory and interpretation in the philosophical and scholarly traditions that follow him, they set a stunning example of the strength of the two-level or dual allegory as a pedagogical temptation. This temptation is not only to be attributed to the institutional guild of the authorized readers and interpreters who practice it: it also accounts for the affiliation between the dual structure itself and the ideology of humanism with which we have associated it.

But there is also a way in which the question of pedagogy itself can provide the most plausible transition from the dual allegories in question here to the tripartite structures to be examined next. For pedagogy itself becomes a kind of third term, particularly when its seemingly objective and disinterested practice invokes the whole thematics of science and knowledge, which is, as we shall see, the central motivation and driving force of the tripartite scheme. Humanism or science? These two seemingly antagonistic "disciplines" (reflected in the very structures of the modern university system) are dialectically inseparable from one another, insofar as nature and human nature are part and parcel of the same fundamental metaphysic. This is what remains to be demonstrated in the next section.

◆

The tripartite allegorical scheme seems to have originated in the commentaries on Homer during the Alexandrian period (most notably by the Stoics); but the origins of the system probably go back much further in time, as is appropriate for the organization of culture around a single work which is then called on to answer a variety of questions to which epic narrative was never designed to respond. Unlike the later biblical commentaries, however, and particularly in the decay of paganism and polytheism, these questions turn out to be essentially cognitive rather than religious and prophetic.

Here then, we confront the Homer, not of the heroic simile, but rather of the interminable hand-to-hand combats and the numerous battlefield encounters as tedious as they are gruesome, which inspired Goethe to say that reading *The Iliad* was like being vouchsafed a glimpse into Hell. Battles, however, are frequent staples of formal allegories: Spenser and Goethe are full of them, as we shall see, while Dante is by the very nature of his climb spared the representational problem of warfare. Our reference here will, however, be the *Psychomachia* of Prudentius. One cannot say that either Homer or Prudentius finds any truly elegant solution to the representational monotony of the multiple hand-to-hand combats of such epic scenes (all the more reason to admire Virgil's artful variations on such obligatory generic episodes).

Homer was certainly a central or canonical text in antiquity, if not a sacred one: Alexander slept with the *Iliad* under his pillow, and the great age of the text itself, which, even if redacted under Pisistratus, breathed the air of an ancient lost heroic era, ensuring its binding authority for generations who interrogate it as you might consult an oracle. Unsurprisingly, then, the "interpretation" of Homer became a respectable practice and took many forms, among them not least the tripartite allegorical reading we mean to examine here.

Equally unsurprisingly, the most propitious sections of Homer for such reading will not be those famous dramatic moments of which Achilles is the protagonist, or in which Hector bids farewell to his tiny son ("terrified by as he saw the bronze and the crest with its horse-hair / Nodding dreadfully, as he thought, from the peak of the helmet"; Book VI, 469–70).[9] Rather, interpretation will be called in to wreak its wildest ravages in precisely those passages in which senseless slaughter rages, namely, the interminable battle scenes, the sequences of hand-to-hand combat.

What the tripartite interpreters found in such passages, however, was something more than a mere formal alibi: it was science itself, knowledge as such, but knowledge of a far more systematic and organized kind than the simplistic parallels of Camus's epidemiology.[10] For here the individual characters are called on to play their signifying roles; and in a reversal of what will later become the practices of personification, these mortal combats and duels will project their newly endowed meanings into outer and inner space, and become, although dehumanized, profoundly epistemological.

---

9 Homer, *The Iliad*, 183.
10 Robert Lamberton, *Homer the Theologian: Neoplatonist Allegorical Reading and the Growth of the Epic Tradition,* Berkeley: University of California Press, 1989.

Historical: The Ladder of Allegory 13

Homer's battle scenes now become symbolic of the passions (as later on in Prudentius) but also of the atoms as they form the very building blocks of the universe and in their attractions and repulsions make up the very fabric of matter. Greek atomism is indeed no doubt to blame for these exercises, for in its various forms a dialectic emerges in which it is the very notion of the atom itself that generates its own multiplicities: being the One, it can only reproduce itself as another One, which it must therefore repulse as nonessential, at the same time that its identity with itself necessarily attracts. The idea of the One therefore becomes inseparable from that of the Many, as Hegel demonstrated in the *Logic*.

Meanwhile, it is as a presage in that history of the emotions (to be examined in Chapter 2) that the various shapes and figures of the psychic battleground declare themselves, beginning no doubt with the four humors and their interactions and gradually perpetuating a more elaborate characterological chart and the rudiments of a whole psychology.

The two levels scarcely intersect one another, save as specimens of an atomistic thinking they both share and which at this stage is developed into more elaborate cosmologies and philosophies. But what is inadequate about this projection of twin "sciences" of physics and psychology onto what was for them a historical text is not the rudimentary nature of these two systems (for we still "believe" in atoms, and in the passions as well no doubt), but rather the way in which representation as a philosophical problem has been excluded from what is as objective as an astrological chart or a personal horoscope. It is this exclusion that makes them "defective" in Hegel's profound sense and which alerts us to the fundamental flaw in the tripartite scheme as such. Leave aside the question of fiction and scientific fact, as anachronistic in this period as it has come to seem ideological in our own, what the tripartite scheme omits is the process of interpretation itself; and insofar as allegory is itself allegorical, the peculiarity of this particular practice is that it in fact presents us with the strange case of a nonallegorical allegory.

The "defect" of the tripartite allegory can then perhaps be generalized: it lies in the utilization of this form of reading or interpretation for epistemological purposes, and it includes knowledge as such (science). In effect, it paradoxically confirms Croce's dogmatic exclusion of knowledge from the aesthetic (see Chapter 7) but in a way that would have horrified him, namely by identifying what is illicit in these allegories— as not the cognitive, but rather the expressive itself.

A modern example will perhaps strengthen this assertion, particularly one that stresses the unavoidably representational dilemmas confronted by language in the modern period and thereby implies the need for any adequate modern allegory to include the very problem of representation within its own structure.

This is indeed what seems to me at stake in philosophical or psychological works that attempt to deal with consciousness itself as a central problem, or in other words as an issue to be solved. Literature obviously has no choice when it comes to incorporating such specialized problems and must do so by way of the familiar techniques of internal monologue, *style indirect libre*, and so on. But philosophies are free simply to avoid the issue of consciousness as such, so that when, in spite of everything, they choose to tackle it head-on, the results can be enlightening for literary and linguistic study (even where the latter have already decided that such philosophical and psychological languages belong to literature in the first place anyway).

Among many other such philosophical attempts, Daniel Dennett's *Consciousness Explained* can serve to illustrate the untimely resurgence of the allegorical in the midst of a text ostensibly devoted to what the philosophers call "argument." Actually, analogies abound in this work, in which, for example, the notion of distinct mental functions so dear to Kant and revived by neurophilosophy takes the more "literary" form of "multiple drafts," in which we rewrite our experiences over and over again in a process that aims at describing the approximations of thought in terms of media reproduction, "knowledge" becoming simply the final or published version.[11] Here it is the multiplicity of the media (longhand, word processing, Internet publication, and so on), which offer a one-to-one analogy with the various states of consciousness to be unified in any satisfactory theory of the latter.

At this point, however, I need to lay my own cards on the table and to explain that for me consciousness is impersonal (in Sartre's and Husserl's sense)[12] but above all that it is unrepresentable, as Colin McGinn has powerfully argued.[13] We are in consciousness as the fish in water; we are

---

11 Daniel C. Dennett, *Consciousness Explained*, Boston: Little, Brown, 1991. See Appendix B for a fuller discussion of Dennett's thesis.

12 Jean-Paul Sartre, "Une idée fondamentale de la phénoménologie de Husserl," *Situations I*, Paris: Gallimard, 1947.

13 Colin McGinn, *The Mysterious Flame*, New York: Basic Books, 2000.

never, not even in the deepest sleep or coma, truly nonconscious, and therefore there exists no Archimedean point outside of consciousness from which we might adequately describe, let alone, explain it phenomenologically (and as for the brain, it must always remain the brain of other people or of the forensic anatomist). I am therefore disposed in advance to consider all theories of consciousness as literary exercises.

(This is then one of those problems that confirm one's conviction, not only that philosophy—call it theory, or simply thinking, if you like—cannot ever solve problems but only articulate them; but further than that, that its problems are of the type that must continue to be posed in full conviction that they can never be resolved: the subject–object problem is of this type, an antinomy that must be reenacted in every generation inasmuch as the reformulation of its impossibility will necessarily prove to be historically original and therefore operative. Historical failure is valuable because it is historical, not because it is a failure.)

From this perspective, it is thus of the greatest interest to find that, for his ultimate version of the multiplicity of mental functions exercised by "consciousness," Dennett has recourse to an extended figure, the crew of a ship. Full consciousness will then be a provisional, a temporary crisis state, in which these various functions are summoned to some supreme act of collective cooperation by the alarm signal of an "All hands on deck!"

It is an ingenious if profoundly allegorical solution; and we therefore find in Dennett's book yet another tripartite system in which the textual object—the undoubted existence of this mysterious thing called consciousness—is endowed with two parallel figurations: that of the media and that of the working collective, neither of which intersects, but whose "explanatory" combination, the tripartite allegory, confirms the essential humanism of this structure. It is, however, not necessarily an anthropomorphic structure: rather, it is an ideological one, in which structuralist and Nietzschean ideas of the syntactical tyranny of the so-called "centered subject" are refuted by this democratic image of centrality as a transitory moment, in which, as in the ancient polis, the "dictator" is summoned only to deal with a crisis, after which he is summarily dismissed or even banished. (That these seemingly complete thought-figures—the tripartite ones—could be enlarged to greater comprehensibility by simply adding a fourth term seems in principle possible if one is willing to change the whole tenor of the experiment.

Thus, the band of sailors would become a certain type of community, which would lend the momentarily emergent commanding consciousness a certain wish-fulfilling egotism.)

It is not necessary to underscore the kinship of this allegorical conception of consciousness with liberal American political thought in general (and with its internal contradictions). What I have wanted to argue here is that this judgment is not ideological and that tripartite allegory can rather be accounted a bad allegory insofar as it is incomplete. In the next section we will show how the fourfold system completes it in a way that utterly restructures the homologies of this incomplete form: suffice it to say for the moment that the latter lacks reflexivity (to use a term I dislike for philosophical reasons, as I will also explain). For the moment, it is enough to suggest that it is this very defect of the tripartite form that renders it apt for the generation of ideologies such as those of humanism and scientism. A contemplative stance is imposed on it by virtue of its very structure qua knowledge and can only result in the production of ideology as such, which is to say, of metaphysics or of what Heidegger called *world-pictures*.

◆

It is here, then, that some long-postponed numerological debate might be expected to surface. I have denounced the homological allegory: but surely, in order to reach four, it would be as easy to reduplicate its duality as it would be to add another level to the three of the tripartite alternative. Isn't some theoretical justification of fourness as a more adequately complete system required, along with a justification for the requirements of completeness in the first place? Cardinal numbers are meanings, after all, as the philosophers of number have assured us; and in this particular context, do we not have to take into consideration the claim of other numbers as well? Nobody has so far come forth as a defender of the five or the six, as far as I know: but certainly the seven has all the mystical significance one could wish for, and this despite the early theologians' assurance that, in a pinch, the seven could always be reduced to a four. As for the latter, I suppose that its reduction to a simple duality could be refuted by the Greimas square (see Appendix A). The fourfold is there shown to be not some replication of two simple dualisms added together, but rather a distinction between two kinds of negations, each one of which generates a different opposition of its own. These negations are not simple homologies of each other; they produce four distinct terms, and it is this set of four terms (and their own combinations) that is referred to as a *system*.

Indeed, having just expressed some doubt as to the relevance of science and truth in the tripartite system, I may now venture a naturalistic defense of the fourfold. In that spirit, it would be possible to evoke a whole acoustic system, in which a given note of the scale, functioning as a musical tonic, comes into the world with its own implicit (or unsounded) dominant, its tritone, the virtuality of its modulation into minor and major, along with a host of overtones and undertones, vibrations that imperceptibly accompany the central vibration on which our hearing and our perception is for the moment centered and whose logic extends over a shorter or longer period of auditory attention. So it is that for this bodily sense a whole elaborate system or auditory totality accompanies the attention to a single note: is this correlation of subject and object something natural (or in other words grounded in some deeper ontological relationship between the human sensorium and the physical vibrations inherent in our material universe)? Is it historical, so that the whole system is somehow modified when we pass from "Western" music or in other words from tonality back into the various kinds of modal systems in use in other cultures?[14] But could we not argue that both systems—the tonal and the modal—are natural and historical at one and the same time?

At any rate, such speculations are based on a conception of system that is not difficult to transfer to meaning itself, grasped from an essentially ideological standpoint. One might then construct an elaborate comparison (or indeed an "allegory"!) in which a term, a theme, or an ideologically charged word at once brings with it a set of unspoken relationships that organize our immediate attention and give value to a discursive sequence in which our starting point is confirmed, denied, qualified, modified, and so forth. The fourfold scheme would then be just such a system: one whose primary field of activity lies in ideology, but whose operations and effects are here deployed in the realm of narrative.

I will not expound this fourfold narrative system at any great length: its founders and practitioners (among whom Origen [AD 185–254] is

---

14 This was essentially Max Weber's argument in *The Rational and Social Foundations of Music,* Eastford, CT: Martino Press, 2010.

generally credited as its inventor) posited the events of the Old Testament as a literal text in which a different and future event was prefigured. Thus famously the descent of the Hebrews into Egypt, grasped as an event that really happened in history, is also read as a foreshadowing of Christ's descent, after his crucifixion and death, into Hell (where Dante will show the visible and cataclysmic signs of his passing); their exodus from Egypt then clearly prefigures the resurrection; and these twin events, taken stereoscopically, may also serve to characterize the wallowing of the soul in sin and earthly misery and its emergence into salvation by way of a radical conversion. At the same time, this earthly and individual parallel also prefigures the fate of the collectivity itself, which can be redeemed by the Last Judgment, or in other words, a wholesale spiritual awakening or religious revolution.

These distinct meanings—which can most conveniently be called *levels of meaning*—can then be schematically rendered, along with their theological names, as follows:

>ANAGOGICAL: the fate of the human race
>MORAL: the fate of the individual soul
>ALLEGORICAL or MYSTICAL: the life of Christ
>LITERAL: (in this case) the coming up out of Egypt

Now it will at once be clear that such "meanings," as they arise from level to level, are of quite different kinds, and more than that, that the transitions between them are quite different from one another. I have evoked the stereoscopic simultaneity of the relationship of the literal and allegorical levels, which Auerbach called *figural*; and in which they stand to each other as letter and fulfillment. But that rather academic relationship (signifier and signified) opens a rather different allegorical pathway than the prophetic one, in which the earlier event somehow "literally" prophesies the later one, or does so by way of the mediation of great prophecy and its lonely and legendary virtuosi. These two allegorical relationships are themselves allegories of rather different kinds: the one a figure of exegesis implying a priestly interpreter or scholar; the second a whole narrative of loneliness and persecution, of the Cassandra-like doomed warning and the great unheeded cry, verging on a curse: "Woe to the bloody city of Litchfield!" Here, then, we glimpse the truth of that paradoxical warning enunciated at the beginning of this chapter, namely that allegory is itself allegorical, that it contaminates its environment with a disturbing ferment.

Indeed it was to have been expected that the unique unity of any tripartite system (turning under its own weight from one configuration to another, without a center, doomed to fall out into a pair opposed to an excluded point) would face a different kind of structural danger when enlarged into a fourfold arrangement. For the latter, if not somehow internally reinforced, risks a disintegration into two pairs each of which seems able to lead a life of its own, and thereby to return us to the dualism we have spent so much time denouncing. On the one hand, the text and its allegorical interpretation, on the other the individual and the collectivity. Each of these pairs is fundamentally ideological when taken on its own; the bet of fourfold allegory lies in its promise to hold all four levels together in an original and somehow inseparable unity, albeit a unity of differences.

This dilemma emerges most vividly when we examine the quite distinct emergence of the third or "moral" level from the initial pair from which it emerges (and from their differences from each other, which is then quite "different" from this new "difference"). For it is not evident that the new level consists in any direct or immediate translation of either level into the psychic (or, I would prefer to say, the psychoanalytic) realities of the soul; rather, it is grounded on a properly symbolic relation between them. Conversion, therefore, would seem itself capable of being grasped differently according to the way that more fundamental relationship is construed. (Thus, in the limited possibilities already mentioned, one might imagine exegetical conversions of a more intellectual type being distinguished from prophetic or charismatic ones.) At any rate, this emergence of the moral level from the two initial ones is of a quite different type (the alteration offering a clue as to the origin of the twofold system described earlier and its radical insufficiency).

One may then suggest that later attempts to posit the practices of the soul, or in other words, the construction of subjectivity, as so many attempts to "imitate" the life of Christ (as in Thomas à Kempis's original version or in the Loyola spiritual exercises); can be understood as so many efforts to reconstruct some more direct and immediate signifying link between this third level and the second or allegorical one, without passing through the original allegorical structure or sequence.

With the fourth or political level, meanwhile, even more complex interrelationships come into play: for it is not at all excluded that this fourth or collective meaning might well overshoot the third or individualistic one and return to its immediate literal and historical model as the example of a whole people breaking its chains and seceding (whether literally or figuratively) from the repressive society in which it finds itself. And as for the second allegorical level as such, does it not itself already propose the possibility of a peculiar form of narrative extrapolation in which Jesus takes the place of the ultimate political prophet and assumes the role of his prototype Moses in that first revolutionary historical event which, now reversing its allegorical reference, rewrites the very life of which it was to have been the prophecy in a kind of retroactive potentiation? The purely moral level then would then come as a supplementary interpretative and individual commentary of a far more fully formed and fleshed out anagogical or collective meaning.

Such complexities and symbolic alternatives are then something like the Ptolemaic epicycles of the original levels, and explain the variants in which the original four levels are traditionally multiplied, where, for example, the Church fathers allowed as to how the life of Christ might also be reinterpreted as the life of the Church, thereby reinstating a historical institutionality along with law, obedience, and other hierarchical features not necessarily foreseen in the original paradigm. These "epicycles," as we have called them, are based on an original synonymy that makes for the richness of the scheme and will be reexamined in the conclusion in which the fourness common to both the fourfold scheme of the levels and the four basic terms of the Greimas square are compared and "reconciled."

It is no doubt possible, and even desirable, to grasp the fourfold scheme in its own historicity and its own immediate situation and function, something we have already sketched out for the patristic moment of a universalizing Christianity. Its revival here then clearly has its own political motivation as well, for on my reading the modern differentiation between public and private, between the logic of the collectivity or the mode of production and the existential life of the individual, is intentionally inscribed in its third and fourth (moral and anagogical) levels, which may be said to find their distinct dynamics in psychoanalysis and Marxism, respectively. As for the two fundamental levels on which the whole edifice is founded, we may say that the allegorical or

Historical: The Ladder of Allegory

mystical key—the interpretive code by which the reading of the literal level or "current situation" is governed—will vary ideologically. It would be ridiculous, for instance, to take anything like the life of Marx himself, however admirable it may have been, as a prototype of anything but the political intellectual; but, as with the "imitation" of Christ, there are certainly followers willing enough to find their spiritual models in the great revolutionaries or prophets of history, from Saint Paul to Trotsky or Che Guevara. Meanwhile, it matters very much whether this same fundamental allegorical level is grasped in terms of the dynamics of capitalism as it exists now or of some future mode of production, whether socialism, communism, or Utopia: that is, the very structure and function of the system changes depending on whether it is designed to elicit an analysis of the immanent laws of a world to which there is no alternative, or on the contrary to interrogate the signs of radical change and the foreshadowings of some radically different world to come. It seems possible that the allegorical level may also be read in terms of the medium by which it is transmitted, or, in other words, as a form of autoreferentiality.

At any rate, the two initial levels of an allegory form a dual narrative, which demands a peculiar and specialized kind of reading (Benjamin named it the *dialectical image*): we might call it a synoptic one, in the sense in which both narratives are to be attended to simultaneously. The older narrative retains its literal status, its events have really happened, they are not to be dismantled like so many hieroglyphs or esoteric signs. Do they lose their substance, waning into ghostly simulacra like so many prophetic dreams? It would seem not, for they constitute the history of the clan from which Jesus himself descends. Something similar can be said for Benjamin's reversal of the conventional historical framework, for whom the past erupts into the present and is reborn in it like a tiger's leap, the spirit of Robespierre reinvigorating that of Lenin, the spirit of Spartacus reborn in Che.[15] In the sense in which the New Testament fulfills the Old, it is the allegorical reading that somehow takes precedence over its literal foreshadowing; the older history was incomplete, the newer one is its fulfillment. (To be sure, Marxism certainly affirms something similar about those earlier revolts that

---

15 Walter Benjamin, "On the Concept of History," *Selected Writings*, vol. 4, Cambridge: Cambridge University Press, 2003, Thesis XIV, 395.

prefigured the revolutions of capitalism, while the older castes and hierarchies of domination are not yet the two modern dichotomous social classes even though they seem to foreshadow them.)

So even a reading of Christian allegory will seek to preserve the substance of the original or literal text, at the same time that it suggests reservations about the latter's conventional historiography, its system of representation, which omits the prophetic dimension and sinks back into mere chronicle. This very possibility, however, alerts us to the importance of the historical situations in which the practice of allegory is revived out of need, or on the other hand, discredited as a purely scholastic exercise.

◆

A serious revival of interest in allegory can be dated to the period of "theory" that set in after World War II (and when thoughts neglected, like those of Walter Benjamin's *Trauerspiel* book of 1928, came into their own); but the seemingly definitive end of allegory as a literary value was conventionally identified with the crisis of Romanticism. (Nor is it an accident that Paul de Man's idiosyncratic revival of the concept finds its authorization in that crisis point which inspired the work of Friedrich Schlegel, with Novalis and Coleridge, the most original thinker of the Romantic movement.) But on a more practical (and parochial) level, the already degraded form of allegory that is at that point definitively repudiated can be found in rhetoric and in the stylistic flourishes and decorations of the ancien régime, dismissed by William Wordsworth's manifesto for plain speech. This is itself an allegorical act: for such ornament is first and foremost to be associated with its related manifestations in all the other arts (architecture, furniture, fashion, painting, music) in an uneven or nonsynchronous development that extends across the nineteenth century all the way to the triumph of a literal-minded "realism" (and to Adolf Loos's manifesto, *Ornament and Crime*). But this stylistic revolution is best understood at its origins, when the decorative (hitherto associated with Baroque court culture)[16] is identified as a class language, and its symbolic denunciation and abandonment associated with the bourgeois Revolution itself. (I am fond of the example of the counterrevolutionary politics of the Parisian wigmakers, who stood to lose, not merely their application

16   See Chapter 8.

Historical: The Ladder of Allegory

of powder, but the manufacture of wigs themselves, in this not insignificant change in fashion and in taste.)

For the poets, and later on their interpreters (Schlegel and Coleridge can stand as the prototypes of both, including the trend toward a religious counterrevolution), what replaces allegory in its more fundamental structural sense is as we have seen the symbol as such. The allegorical includes differentiation in the form of the multiple publics it must capture simultaneously, the multiple languages it must coordinate; in a new period of class struggle, the symbol aims at a different kind of unison and a far more overt homogenization of its fundamental public (a context in which the word *hegemony* seems to impose itself). In the literary realm, this homogeneity is to be found in the emergence of the national language (and the elimination of the dialects), as well as the concept of a "national literature"—a new field which is not institutionalized until it finds its place in the new or modern university system, along with its belated invention of the "history of literature."

The role of the symbol in all this seems to me to be a complex and essentially negative one and to accompany the fate of the increasingly delegitimated "sacred text." The loss of the category of the canonical work can to be sure lead to the compensatory industry of producing new and "homemade" sacred texts and mythological systems, from Friedrich Schelling's call for a new mythology to William Blake's visionary production or William Butler Yeats's "visions." (In our time Jungianism has been the most successful popular version of this and the most instructive in its handling of the absence of the sacred text: it syncretically gathers within itself all the myths and religions of the past in an early version of ideological globalization.) But the more mainstream effort in promoting some new centrality of the sacred text in bourgeois culture will be the gradual emergence, in the various national traditions, of the ideal of a Book of the World (Mallarmé's *Livre*, Joyce's *Finnegans Wake*), which aims to perform many of the functions of the older religious text by substituting the emergent national collectivity for the older cult of believers.

No one denounced this general consensus on the desirability of the symbol more ferociously than Walter Benjamin:

> For over a hundred years the philosophy of art has been subject to the tyranny of a usurper who came to power in the chaos which followed in

the wake of romanticism. The striving on the part of the romantic aestheticians after a resplendent but ultimately noncommittal knowledge of an absolute has secured a place in the most elementary theoretical debates about art for a notion of the symbol which has nothing more than the name in common with the genuine notion. This latter, which is the one used in the field of theology, could never have shed that sentimental twilight over the philosophy of beauty which has become more and more impenetrable since the end of early romanticism. But it is precisely this illegitimate talk of the symbolic which permits the examination of every artistic form "in depth," and has an immeasurably comforting effect on the practice of investigation into the arts. The most remarkable thing about the popular use of the term is that a concept which, as it were categorically, insists on the indivisible unity of form and content, should nevertheless serve the philosophical extenuation of that impotence which, because of the absence of dialectical rigour, fails to do justice to content in formal analysis and to form in the aesthetics of content. For this abuse occurs wherever in the work of art the "manifestation" of an "idea" is declared a symbol. The unity of the material and the transcendental object, which constitutes the paradox of the theological symbol, is distorted into a relationship between appearance and essence. The introduction of this distorted conception of the symbol into aesthetics was a romantic and destructive extravagance which preceded the desolation of modern art criticism.[17]

But it cannot be said that, until after World War II, his voice was anything more than a decidedly minor protest.

At the same time, particularly as a reaction to the "religious wars" of the twentieth century, a multiplicity of worldviews (Heidegger called them *world-pictures*, Marxism *ideologies*) attempt to fill the vacuum of what is imagined to have been some more genuine collective belief or the "binding together" of religio. They then symbolically fight out real class struggles in the form of doctrinal disputes of all kinds, in a so-called relativism, which until recently has been protected and relatively

---

17 Walter Benjamin, *The Origin of German Tragic Drama*, trans. John Osborne, London: Verso, 1998, 159–601. Still, it is permitted to speculate that this diatribe may be a preemptive strike against critics of his early endorsement of a kind of language mysticism: why else would the Frankfurt group later press him so insistently to write a stern anti-Jungian critique?

neutralized by an unspoken confidence in the truths of "science": a set of operations able to withstand the skepticism of the philosophers (for Heidegger as for "Western Marxism," with its Viconian heritage, science is not to be counted as an essential "truth procedure"): until late capitalism unmasks them as so much "applied science" and instrumental activities. Science as a "worldview" has rarely nourished any would-be sacred texts, and when it does, it inevitably falls into the realm of an essentially allegorical practice.

And indeed, this fall from truth into allegory is the fate of most attempts, from Romanticism to the high modernist period, to produce a Symbol for a secular and relativistic bourgeois age. The meaning of such symbolic texts is itself allegorical, whether in an allegory of explanation (the psychic and collective life of the author) or one of structure (the raw materials of the work along with its formal solutions are themselves "symbolic" of history). But the analysis of such meanings, which comes into its own after 1945 and in particular after the abandonment of the various modernist adventures and experiments, is now called something else, namely *interpretation*; and when its allegorical structures become obvious and unavoidable, then it becomes identified as *allegoresis*, namely the reading of a text *as though* it were an allegory.

I have stressed the break of World War II in this hypothetical periodization (this disposable periodizing narrative) for two related reasons: first, because the collapse of the various nationalisms in that war relativized them all into so many ideologies and gradually revealed even the seemingly neutral one of political pragmatism and democracy to be a threadbare and increasingly transparent cover for the economies of late capitalism; and second, because in a few scant decades thereafter, capitalism itself discredited the nation-state and its hitherto vibrant nationalisms against the looming totalizations of globalization, for which no religions or ideologies yet existed. Marxism survived this generalized collapse as the only adequate theory of capitalism as such, even in its financial and global forms; but it has yet to invent a working ideology on the global level to replace the discredited options of social democracy and the party-state (for the good reason that a coherent form of world class struggle has yet to emerge from the transitional anarchy of this new and vaster horizon).

It is much the same when we come to so-called world literature: Goethe's well-worn term was meant to designate the variety of intellectual debates which became visible and available in the quite distinct historical situations of the nation-states that emerged after the revolutionary and Napoleonic transitions. No doubt, we also with this term attempt to do something similar in assessing those new multiple national, cultural, and literary situations to which we are today so fortunately, after the end of colonialism, exposed. But those situations are no longer the same; and in globalization we are confronted, not by difference but by identity, by a world of standardization and a domination by multinational capitalism to which no traditionalisms, "local cultures," "alternate modernities," "critical regionalisms," or multicultural variety can offer alternatives and whose structure is allegorically expressed by the hegemony of English as a global lingua franca at a moment when even the significance of the "literary" (and the older system of the beaux arts) as such is called into question by all kinds of new media.

This is then the situation in which allegory, having been discredited by bourgeois culture, reemerges as allegoresis in the dispersal of that culture and the relativization of its facts and its literal levels, its national and linguistic references, and the multiplicity of its historical situations and populations. Its renewal will be dramatized most conveniently by the account of the history of emotions outlined in the next chapter.

◆

Of the more ambitious revivals of allegory theory, de Man's and Benjamin's are the most notorious. I will say why I find neither as useful nor as stimulating as I would have wished. But first it is important to situate the destiny of allegory within that larger one of rhetoric as such, of which Roland Barthes and so many others have told the story.

As a species, rhetoric seemed to have gone extinct with the last original treatise written by Pierre Fontanier in 1821. For Barthes himself, the use of the characterization, in his classic early *Degré zéro de l'écriture* (1953), functioned as a historical foil to the emergence of style as a literary category after the French Revolution: before that, rhetoric, in the sense of public eloquence, was a universal value; after it, the private and individualistic conception of style displaced it as a literary practice. Barthes later reverted to the institutional or disciplinary use of the term, and his own idiosyncratic version of rhetoric is deployed in studies like that of *S/Z* (1970).

De Man's linguistics, and in particular his revival of the rhetorical tropes, is generally associated with a whole group of tropological analysts, in particular Hayden White and the Mμ group (*Rhétorique générale*).[18] But in my view, de Man's use of the tropes is only one feature of a more general and more systematic metaphysical system, in which language is posited—perhaps more for dramatic and pedagogical effect than as an evolutionary position—as an inhuman faculty as it were imposed on the human animal from the outside. This is then the underside of the structuralist "linguistic turn," too often grasped as a celebration of language, but which in fact grasps it as a profound alienation of our animal nature. Other theorists of the period, such as Jean-François Lyotard, concurred in de Man's affirmation that language is inhuman (or nonhuman, if you prefer), as does a certain period anthropology, best illustrated by the excruciating suffering Philippe Pinel's language teaching inflicted on the famous feral child of the Aveyron (an episode dramatized in François Truffaut's *L'Enfant sauvage* [1970]).

In reality, this rather science-fictional view of language served as a philosophical justification for de Man's critical practice, which aimed at showing that language, in the form of the tropes, always subtly or dramatically deflected and undermined conscious intention in such a way that in a sense we always say something other than what we mean, if indeed we say anything coherent at all. (As with Sartre, then, this means that sincerity—meaning what we say—is always in "bad faith.") This is the result of an extension of tropological theory beyond the merely figural and amounts to denying the existence of any literal or cognitive, referential language against which figuration could be tested or even perceived. Language then alone can be said to be "successful," if not authentic, insofar as it is designed to designate its own inner tropological dynamics and thereby to admit its own communicational or cognitive impossibility. It was this specialized autoreferentiality, indeed, by which de Man specifically designated literary language as such, as a kind of "allegory" of its own determination by its tropes. Whatever abstract philosophical objections may be made to this "system" (and whatever amateur psychoanalytic or biographical interpretations may be made of it), de Man's concrete literary analyses constitute

---

18 Paul de Man, *Allegories of Reading: Figural Language in Rousseau, Nietzsche, Rilke, and Proust,* New Haven, CT: Yale University Press, 1982; Hayden White, *Metahistory: The Historical Imagination in Nineteenth-Century Europe,* Baltimore, MD: Johns Hopkins University Press, 2014; Groupe Rhétorique générale, Paris: Seuil, 1970.

extraordinary critical performances (of which I would personally single out the reading of Rilke as the most successful); but they are only distantly reminiscent of the work of Jacques Derrida, or of ideological analysis either, although offering models of analytical rigor in their own right. It seems to me, however, that de Man's readings necessarily remain interpretations, even though their function is to destroy interpretation as such (which for him was "humanistic") and that they therefore yield to allegorical analysis (in our present sense). But it is equally clear that de Man's official concept of allegory, or even of "allegories of reading," has little to offer in advancing the project of the present book.

◆

De Man's implicit notion of autoreferentiality, however (presently unnoticed in a great variety of other methods in play today), deserves a more explicit discussion in any study of allegory. It was in reality already implicit in standard characterizations of the literary modernisms as *reflexive* or *self-conscious* (terms which deserve to be denounced in an intellectual culture for which the very concept of the "centered subject" or personal identity have become suspect). The mirror may have its place in Lacanian psychoanalysis and its theory of the Imaginary, but its mysteries are incomprehensible in any phenomenological account of consciousness as such (and I leave aside the rather petty objection that a text cannot be "conscious" in the first place, let alone self-conscious). That a text can refer to itself, however, and designate itself, seems to me a useful way of characterizing the crisis of Literature (and its very reinvention) in the era of advanced capitalism, where the status of a text needs to be specified in some way for its appropriate commodification. That mark or specification will be its self-designation or autoreferentiality, and in the modernist era it can take on the very value of a meaning. Allegoresis begins when this self-specification or "self-conscious" identification of the medium or media of the text becomes its allegorical level, so that its production becomes its own allegorical meaning, a process as varied in its outcomes as modern literature itself, or, if you prefer, as the various modes of expression—writing, artistic production, revelation, information, textual reproduction, or other conceptions of writing—permit. Such "allegories" destroy the older traditional structure of the fourfold system and substitute an interplay of lateralities or transversalities, for which the act of self-designation often seems a merely secondary or incidental afterthought or side product, but one which can, however, be an essential clue for the allegorist.

Perhaps another word is in order on the topic of the work's materiality. For many contemporary analysts, this emphasis on the henceforth mediatic status of the work (a newspaper serial or an Internet blog, a radio speech or a digital narrative) offers a more materialistic alternative to the old idealist conceptions of representation as meaning or narrative, as imaginary entities or constructed objects. Autoreferentiality would then be grasped as a material (and materialist) process, in which a given medium inscribes itself (as in Umberto Eco's classic essay on the way in which serializing form leaves its traces in the presumably "final product" of the published novel).

Still, this valorization of the materialistic may be premature. The younger Lukács was always impressed by a concept of the prematurely deceased art critic Leo Popper, for which the latter used the word *misunderstanding*. (In his early and late *Aesthetics,* Lukács retained this nontechnical term, perhaps out of reverence for his dead friend.) But Popper meant thereby something supremely technical, namely the incompatibility between two different approaches to the work of art. The first of this is that of the artist himself, who confronts raw materials and works with their specific properties: for this seemingly materialist activity we may perhaps substitute Freud's splendid word for the effectiveness of the raw materials from which the dream is constructed: he called it *representability*. The artist's assessment of such representability in his raw materials is then radically different, and indeed incompatible, with the critic's, with the reader's, with the literary scholar's; which is why the former so often heartily detests the latter and minimally holds them in contempt. For these consumers of the work, approaching it as an already completed object from the other side of the barrier of time and its production, read it as a kind of message: even Dadaist nonsense art is a meaning, and a slap in the face is a message. But what delivers this message is a completed gesture the artist is unable to see from his perspective, since he has been busy constructing it and has nothing to do with meanings or messages in the first place. Sartre liked the idea of a rug, whose underside is full of a chaos of threads that have no decorative relationship to the patterns on the other side (the meaningless sounds of the words that make up a meaningful poem, the verso of their recto).

The "misunderstanding" is then an ontological one: it can only be bridged by money and success, as when the producers of a film measure its viability, not by the reviews of the critics, but by its attendance and its drawing power. (It is true that the critics can be corrupted by the producers' perspective and waste their time in speculations as to the film's appeal to potential readers or consumers.)

It is conventional, if trite and embarrassing, to posit a third position as a way out of this unresolvable dilemma: a position above both that somehow reconciles them in their very incommensurability. But such a position does in fact exist, and it is that of history. The representability of the artist's materials is a social and historical one, and it depends on the evolution of society and the historical existence of the adequate raw materials themselves (in which, to be sure, are included personalities, feelings, character types, and the like). And as for the critic's interpretation, it is social and historical as well, inasmuch as its content is necessarily ideological. What is lost in this third position, however, is to be sure judgment itself and what is loosely called *value*. The third position (as in other contexts, including Hegel's and Spinoza's) has no time for judgment, it only contemplates the situation itself in all its historicity and necessity. It assesses the existence of the work, its possibility of coming into being, the fact of the taste and judgments of its consumers: all those things constitute the hands on the dial of history's clock; they yield a glimpse into the ontology of the work's present. The work's value is then no longer aesthetic in the restricted sense of aesthetic appreciation and consumption; it is symptomatic, it tells us where we stand.

As for Walter Benjamin, his "thesis" deploys allegory in a completely different way, one which comes closer to those (often very interesting) studies of allegory in specific writers, of which there is a welcome efflorescence today. But it does so by way of the mediation of a period concept, the Baroque, which presents rather different problems. Indeed, a long and obscure philosophical introduction to *The Origin of the German Trauerspiel* seems, in part at least, to attempt to theorize the dual status of the idea of the Baroque, which designates a specific historical period—running, say from the early seventeenth century to the mid-eighteenth (*Hamlet* prematurely dating from 1599, *Vierzehnheiligen* from 1743), and covering the entirety of the Thirty Years' War—at the same time that it seems to name a distinctive style not limited to any one

Historical: The Ladder of Allegory

period but perhaps more closely affiliated to that of postmodernity, as numerous current theories of the neo-Baroque argue.[19] At any rate, in the context of this particular work, allegory for Benjamin becomes restricted to a specific historical period, and, unlike that second Baroque—the spirit of which it is the letter—is not further generalized as a trans-historical structure.

Oddly, however, this analysis of the Baroque is limited to the second part of Benjamin's book, whose opening half turns on a theory of *Trauerspiel* (I have translated it as "funereal pageant" but the more literal "mourning play" seems to have become the accepted version), in a sharp generic distinction from tragedy. Everything points to the issue of tragedy as constituting Benjamin's deeper interest; early essays on the subject dwell, for example, on fate, on the role of silence in its noncommunicative speech, and on the fulfilled temporality of its moments, which are no longer those of Benjamin's famous "homogeneous time." *Trauerspiel* then, which certainly flourished in the Baroque period, but whose German specimens are greatly inferior to Shakespeare or Calderon, seems to have served as a mere pretext for Benjamin to return to his central interest in tragedy, whose contrast with *Trauerspiel* is perhaps closer to Michael Fried's distinction between theatricality and absorption than to the interminable debates about the difference between Shakespearean tragedy and that of the Greeks. At any rate, there is much useful incidental material in Benjamin's readings of these German plays (the opposition between the drama of the usurper and that of the martyr, for example), and much that is truly allegorical in our present sense.

But what Benjamin really wants to call allegory is baroque decoration, which either in its state of over-ripeness or as a litter of ruins is read as an expression of Melancholy (Dürer's famous engraving actually takes us back to 1514), of ephemerality and ultimately of death itself. It is a thematics very propitious for the interests of present-day trauma theory and much of the affect theory that develops out of it, but much less useful for structural generalization.

Meanwhile, Benjamin's later identification of a similar process in Baudelaire (including, to be sure, the omnipresence of *spleen*) essentially associates itself with personification, with the great capitalized

---

19 See, for example, Gregg Lambert, *On the (New) Baroque*, Aurora, CO: Davies Group, 2009.

forces of Douleur or Plaisir, la Vie, la Mort, along with all the accompanying swarm of lowercase reifications of Experience that are the signs and symptoms of the construction of a new kind of bourgeois subjectivity or *interieur* ("allegories are, in the realm of thoughts, what ruins are in the realm of things"). Unfortunately, it is this very identification of allegory and personification by Baudelaire himself that limits Benjamin's omnipresent use of the concept.

Indeed, one must be wary of reading Benjamin as a systematic thinker: in that, he was quite the opposite of de Man, who never composed a doctrinal treatise or exposition either, but who certainly had a theory. Benjamin had interests, but they were rarely philosophical in the disciplinary sense of the word. Meanwhile, his mode of writing, in which each sentence aims to be a complete aphorism in its own right, tends to disrupt the formation of systems and may well qualify him to stand as one of Alain Badiou's anti-philosophers. Adorno imitated him in this but nourished a professional philosopher's ambiguous and more purely philosophical distrust of systematic philosophy and wrote whole philosophical treatises on anti-philosophy as such ("negative dialectics"). Benjamin, however, was no philosopher; rather, all the while considering himself to be a literary critic (in a historical situation in which traditional literary criticism could no longer be practiced), he turned out to constitute a heroic precursor and role model for what followed philosophy and came to be known (inside and outside Marxism) as Theory.

Still, de Man and Benjamin share one specific relationship to the work of art, namely the insistence on the necessity to destroy it. It should be stressed that this is an aesthetic necessity: it is inherent in the reading process and all the more in that larger projection of reading and "understanding" which is interpretation (or in Benjamin's terminology, commentary and critique). To be sure, the valences of this process are antithetical in these two practices.

Deconstruction in general—whether one reserves this word for Derrida's practice or extends it to de Man's rather different commerce with the text—is always a hermeneutics of suspicion. The unity and coherence of the text is always an illusion to be undermined; and it is significant that de Man enthusiastically borrows Benjamin's own (rather theological) image to convey the violence of the breaking of the vessels. For him, however, the result is somehow always the same, never opening onto a variety of distinct historical situations in which the process is adapted. For what results from this therapeutic destruction is always the same fundamental discovery, namely that language is itself deceptive, illusory, and defective; that it always promises meanings, intentions, and coherencies on which it can never deliver. In a sense, however, the aesthetic already reclaims this discovery inasmuch as it points to its own mask, revels in its own fictionality, shamelessly avows its inauthenticities in advance. The work thereby deconstructs itself, as he pointedly reproved Derrida on their first textual encounter (the review of the *Grammatology*). Whatever the ultimate trend of his system, then, de Man cannot ultimately be judged to stand among the aesthetes in his critical practice, which always, beyond its promotion of the aesthetic mode over the cognitive or the communicational, keeps its eye on a kind of anthropological, if not exactly ontological, horizon beyond the individual work of art.

With Benjamin it is somewhat more complicated, if not indeed ultimately undecidable. It does not seem quite right to assign Benjamin a position within that hermeneutics of restoration, which is Ricoeur's ultimately religious version of a Utopian conception of the text's function; and this, despite Benjamin's flirtation with theology, but very much on account of his resistance to Heideggerian ontology. (Heidegger and Benjamin were virtually the same age and indeed classmates at one point.) To be sure, the Frankfurt School ultimately promoted a sanitized and secular version of "restoration," namely the notion of "truth content" (or *Wahrheitsgehalt,* on the order of Holderlin's *Gedichte*). But this mysterious (and I would argue, largely Platonic) conception also involved the breaking of the vessels and the disassembling of the aesthetic surface, however the constellations of "truths" or Ideas he might have retained. At the same time (and like de Man), something in the work (or in nature) abetted this critical process (for which Benjamin reserved the term *critique* in its Kantian sense), but in his case it was time and history, which gradually stripped context and content from the truth content and allowed it to become visible in its well-nigh eternal or at least ahistorical form. It is a position, however, which does not draw Benjamin any closer to the aesthetes; however, it may suggest philosophical preoccupations (which, to placate Gershom Scholem, he liked to call *theological*).

Still, both these theoretical positions, with their open invocations of allegory, insist on the question of the relationship of the latter to aesthetic judgment or values, something our very choice of texts threatens slyly to elude in the following chapters. I have indeed often suggested that in the dedifferentiations of postmodernity (or late capitalism), aesthetics has become an obsolete branch of inquiry (along with philosophy itself, I suppose); but one might just as plausibly argue that in a largely commodified and consumption-oriented world, everything has become aesthetic, and old-fashioned aesthetics disqualifies itself only in the sense of its universalization; questions of taste, judgment, beauty, and the like become the existential issues of at least the privileged segment of the world's population.

My general title suggests that whatever else it is, allegory has today become a social symptom: but of what? I tend to feel that allegory raises its head as a solution when beneath this or that seemingly stable or unified reality the tectonic plates of deeper contradictory levels of the Real shift and grate ominously against one another and demand a representation, or at least an acknowledgment, they are unable to find in the *Schein* or illusory surfaces of existential or social life. Allegory does not reunify those incommensurable forces, but it sets them in relationship with one another in a way which, as with all art, all aesthetic experience, can lead alternately to ideological comfort or the restless anxieties of a more expansive knowledge.

Above all, it will be said that the relevance of allegory is dependent on this or that dissatisfaction with what it terms the literal level, the surface of the text, history, as it simply consists in what Henry Ford memorably called "one damned thing after another"—in other words, the empirical. The historical question would then arise in connection with just such dissatisfaction, whether it is greater today than it was, and what can account for it.

I prefer, however, to move the interrogation one step back and to ground the rationale for allegory in the dilemmas of representation itself. This is to be sure a philosophical problem and a modern one at that; and inasmuch as most notions of representation (or their critiques) involve this or that mental distinction between a representation and the thing represented, it inevitably hearkens back to Kant and reawakens the distinction between a phenomenon (in effect, our subjective representation by way of the senses) and a *noumenon* (the famous thing-in-itself, by definition inaccessible to thought or sense

Historical: The Ladder of Allegory 35

perception), even if the problem of representation itself has been designed to discredit the classic Kantian solution. (Indeed, new versions of the problem have recently been placed back on the table by so-called speculative realism and object-oriented ontology, reawakened perhaps by the effacement, in this new "human age," of a natural environment by one of man-made commodities, Lukács's so-called "second nature.")

As I suggested earlier, however, it may be found more practical, in most literary versions of the subject–object dilemma, to replace the word *representation* with Freud's term *representability*, in which emphasis is placed, not on the unknowability or mystic ineffability of the object to be represented, but rather, the other way around, on the adequacies of language and the other media available to fashion a usable model of the object. This reversal has the additional advantage of bracketing metaphysical questions such as those of truth, and in particular of the truth of the representation and its adequacy with respect to the reality thereby designated.

The newer schools of thought believe themselves to have taken a mighty step forward, and indeed a world-historical one, when they affirm that their metaphysic has overcome both the epistemologically based systems and those aspiring to ontology and has replaced them with a return to the aesthetic, in the sense of poesis or making, of creation rather than of being or knowing.[20] For a postmodernity that revels in appearances—appearances without realities, copies without originals, *Schein*, semblance rather than truth, Deleuze's rather magnificent slogan "les puissances du faux," the appeal of the constructed rather than the Ding an sich—for such a perspective, the restitution of the aesthetic and its reassumption of its primacy as the crown of philosophy is a truly liberating prospect, which releases us from politics and history and for which the trivialization of art and the assimilation to the commodity form is not too high a price to pay.

I share some of this exhilaration but would only point out that the deeper meaning of this properly metaphysical discovery is not that of aesthetics but rather that of production: aesthetics is indeed the very allegory of production! It is constructivism that is at stake here in poesis

---

20 See Steven Shaviro's argument in *The Universe of Things: On Speculative Realism*, Minneapolis: University of Minnesota Press, 2014.

and not consumption. If the human age is to be celebrated, and the Anthropocene given its due, it is in terms of its production of reality and not its transformation into an aesthetic image. It is the perspective of human activity (*Tätigkeit*), of Marxist productivism, of the construction of nature as well as of human reality, that is the truly exhilarating vision: Fichte rather than the *Third Critique*! Sartre rather than Whitehead! Not for nothing did Mallarmé insist that aesthetics and political economy were two sides of the same coin, the coin of the realm, the ultimate prize.

Constructivism has the additional advantage of annulling the mystiques of the ineffable and their claims about the essential unrepresentability of objects, a mystique of the unknowability of nature and the world of being. Only professional metaphysicians need to "know" such things or to wallow in theories of their essential unknowability, issues we may thankfully surrender to the theologians, if any still exist.

The objects that theories of representation need to concern themselves about today are rather those which have their origins in human activity (something which can certainly include nature as it has been remade for millennia by human activity and even more intensively humanized in the century and a half since the invention of chemical fertilizer and the green revolution, and very much including genetic experimentation). The interesting problems and dilemmas of representation today then inevitably carry with them that other much maligned conceptuality that centers on ideas of totality rather than those of matter and being: on questions of systems that transcend not only our perceptual sense organs but also our more Kantian faculties of intellectual cognition and mapping. Not the knowability of things-in-themselves, then, but the functioning of airports, with their thousands of personnel and their intricately differentiated and synchronized processes; not the meaning of the laws of gravity and the speed of light, but rather the intricate and unimaginable networks of finance capital or of data systems, worldwide communications systems, and clouds rather than the contingencies of existence of the multiverse. These new posthuman environments are unknowable only in the sense that they are so far unrepresentable; and political questions about their expansion or their modification are inseparable from those—perhaps more artistic—omens of their representability.

The signal advantage of allegorical systems over symbolic ones is that they raise just such practical issues of representability, whereas recourse

Historical: The Ladder of Allegory

to the symbol and its impoverished systems of identification tends to efface the practical problems themselves and to substitute meanings for constructions, in the long run drifting toward the religious and the mystical, if not simply the humanistic.

It is important to grasp the political consequences of such a conversion of aesthetics into constructivism, for it returns us to a progressive Marx full of enthusiasm for the modernities of his day and the scientifico-technological advances of the future; and to a Faust who lives out Nietzsche's strong forgetfulness of the past and of guilt in the pursuit of new futures. We have to become aware of the degree to which radical efforts in the era of late capitalism have been conservative and traditionalist: Benjamin's watchword of revolution as the emergency brake on the train of history must not be thought as the final word of Marxism, nor should his denunciation of "progress" (whether bourgeois or social democratic) become a crippling limitation on some properly constructivist socialism. The political dialectic follows the classic scientific discovery of the "conversion of energy" as well as Marx's later discovery of "metabolism": *Umfunkionierurg* was Brecht's word for the transformation of all the unlovely advances of capitalism's universal accelerationalisms into humanizing achievements: the transmutation of ecological disaster into the terra-forming of earth, and of the population explosion into a genuine human age, an Anthropocene to be celebrated rather than caricatured in second-rate dystopias. Aestheticization can be energizing only if it becomes the allegory of productivity and radical constructivism; the social construction of late capitalism needs to be converted and refunctioned into a new and as yet undreamed of global communism.

◆

As for the philosophical issues posed by representation as such, my own feeling is that much of their seeming intractability is overcome by Hegel's notion of positing. Otherness is always essentially posited: the contemplative or cognitive stance itself necessarily posits the existence of an object over against itself; and it is at this point that the question of the status or being of that object—is it in our minds? is it out there, in an inaccessible reality?—arises. Indeed, this first dilemma is a self-perpetuating one, inasmuch as an answer that seems to draw the object back into its own field of perception then projects yet another vaster field of unknowability beyond that, which quickly becomes that of the

Big Other or of God as such. But it is from this initial act of positing, of separating self and other in the inaugural and purely epistemological stance, that the twin metaphysical dilemmas of idealism and realism arise: either what we call objects are in the long run phenomena, organized by our own mental functions, or, in a more naive realism, there is no such problem and that the real world offers itself to our cognition without afterthoughts, remainders, or backroom ontological mysteries. For the doctrine of positing, these dogmas are themselves generated by a false problem, namely that there exists a subject–object split in the first place, rather than a positing of that split which is itself a historical moment and a construction.

This is not to say that that historical moment is not still with us, and this is why it will be convenient to distinguish two moments in the emergence of an allegorical practice that must necessarily posit that gap from the outset, as an internal structural presupposition, rather than, as with some perhaps inexistent "naive realism," remaining unaware of it under the assumption that language functions and that our substantialist or Aristotelian–Kantian common sense is to be trusted without further philosophical hair-splitting or the exercise of logical paradoxes.

These two moments of our allegorical alienation are those of the emergence of the name and of the formation of ideological systems. Ultimately both moments converge, and the name is itself a word caught in its own systems and drawing their tangles with it in its affirmation ("I am Hamlet the Dane!").

Still, simple nomination—about which it is useful to remember that in French the name and the noun are a single word, *le nom*—allows us to pose the problem of substantialism, the Aristotelian ideology of the substance, of those separate individual things or items that make up the world and of which I am one. The name affirms this substantive unity of the so-called self, and this is why it can itself be characterized as a primal alienation. We are here in the realm of evolutionary stories (insofar as we all have names already), and of the story of some emergence of consciousness and of language as such from some primal swamp no one remembers and which is mythically expressed in the *infans* floating in a linguistic cloud of adult speech. This is the literary realm, so to speak, of psychoanalysis as well as evolutionary psychology, and Lacan conveniently narrates it in two distinct forms: the mirror stage, in which the infant posits its unity in the image of its body; and the repression by its proper name of the "subject-of-desire," which the name conferred by other people drives underground (the myth of the Unconscious). (The second alienation mentioned above, the systemic one, no doubt finds its Lacanian version in the relationship between my name and the so-called Name-of-the-Father or in other words between the Imaginary and the Symbolic; but this is a doctrinal development that does not seem relevant in the present context.)

What is important for our current discussion is the kinship between the name (or noun) and personification: the latter is so closely linked with allegorical procedures as to give the impression that it is in and of itself the very quintessence of allegory as such. When allegory as a literary form begins to lose its vocation and retreat into the past, thrust like some incomprehensible structure cast into the deepest shadow by the rising sun of the symbol and of symbolism, what can be most tangibly measured and demonstrated of this world-historical transition is the falling into disrepute of personification as such (discussed in Chapter 6).

For our immediate purposes here, however, emotions are a particularly rich field in which to observe these processes at work, and that for two reasons: first, because the line between the various named emotions and the local or historical theories or theoretical systems of emotions is at best a conjectural one; the reason for which constitutes our second and primary interest in them, namely that the emotions are already systems in their own right, and that the experience of one is always a kind of alternative in which others somehow implicitly propose themselves. In other words, the individual emotion is already in itself a system of oppositions, as I demonstrate in the next chapter. The named emotion affirms the substantive unity of a state of feeling and at one and the same time replaces that seeming "substance" in a relational field, which undoes its reification.

Emotions are, to be sure, not the whole of subjectivity or subjective experience: but the examination of their construction can serve as a particularly well-articulated laboratory in which to observe the historical construction of subjectivity itself. It is essentially an allegorical construction, and this constitutes one of the fundamental motivations of the present book and its relationship to the problems of History in general.

Several technical terms have already been mentioned in passing, and more will be encountered in what follows. Some preliminary clarifications will therefore be useful, and this is particularly the case when we deal in such diagnostic abstractions as alienation and reification. The becoming other of a phenomenon is governed by the first of these, which designates everything from property ownership (the alienation of a piece of land, for example) to a making strange in which we can no longer recognize what was familiar. What is less visible in this concept is the activity of several other movements of signification, such as the unity imposed by the very process of alienation: something withdrawn from me becomes in other words a kind of unity in its own right; it unifies what was hitherto disparate for lack of a general name, and only after it is thus unified can it be treated as a kind of object. In an age in which heterogeneity and difference are the watchwords, unity and unification are suspect operations, as they may well deserve to be; but for that very reason they deserve to be acknowledged as categories in their own right, which also exercise the attraction of a certain security and domestication. It is good to be able to name things, or so it would seem; and allegory preeminently participates in that process—particularly in its religious forms sorting things out into the ethical binary, the good and the bad—thereby bringing order out of the chaos of William James's "blooming, buzzing confusion," even when it might have been better to dwell a while longer in that state of productive uncertainty.

Unification, meanwhile, turns processes into objects, and with this moment we reach the term *reification*, a term which, as Mark Twain might have put it, is not always as bad as it looks. One of the fundamental differences, indeed, between Hegel's general philosophical values and those of Marx lies in the universal value the former attributed to objectification (it returns in Sartre's late version of the dialectic). Hegel's life ethic (if one wants to call it that), a stance he shared with Goethe, was that of perpetual activity, productive activity if one wants to move it closer to Marx's own practice. However, activity (*Tätigkeit*) in that sense always produces, and what it produces is then beyond the self; objectified, it has become part of the outside world, it is no longer an activity but a product, in short an object: the shoes made by the cobbler, the building erected by building crew (and their architect and manager), the pile of pages heaped up by the scribbler, whether philosopher or poet.

These can now belong to someone else; and it is at this point that Marx enters the picture—Marx, who has piled up enough pages of his own to have no doubt as to the value of sheer productivity, but for whom the final product will inevitably be alienated by someone else and become the property of another—the reader, hopefully, but also the publisher, and finally the monopoly that owns the publishing house, not to speak of the political movement itself. The product then undergoes its own sea change into a commodity, a process Hegel understood well enough on the conceptual level—the *Logic* is packed full of such transformations—but was unable to name or differentiate when it came to what he called *bourgeois society* (*bürgerliche Gesellschaft*, oddly translated into the Latinate English of "civil society").

Such objectification/reification is also to be considered an allegorical process, the alienation of an objectifying name and its transformation into an object of exchange. We do not often enough insist on the materiality of this process, which is certainly an objectification of spirit if you like. But it is also worth pausing on a less familiar Sartrean term, the *analogon*, to make a place for this dimension as well. The analogon can be said to be a bodily reminder inserted into a conceptual scheme: if the body is the primal source of later understandings (and misunderstandings) and furnishes the more tangible and material categories for use in the sublimation of our abstractions, then it will not be strange to find secret materialities at work in our most hyperintellectual thought processes (some of them returning in that odd physical and material analogies Herbert Silberer found at work in the infrastructure of dreams and fantasies).[21] Heidegger's sophisticated folk etymologies might also be cited here; he detects the still living presence of a primitive life far closer to Being itself stored up and sedimented within the shapes and the forms of sophisticated words and modern terminologies themselves, like a shadow of the Real.

But for us here, the analogon is something like the beat that attracts our attention within the regularities of musical or poetic meter: it concentrates attention and fixes the eye on one of the levels, even where it is not

---

21 Silberer was a sometime disciple of Freud whose experiments described the degradation of abstract ideas into images under conditions of lowered mental *niveau*: see, for example, Herbert Silberer, "Bericht über eine Methode," *Jahrbuch für die Psychoanalyse* 1, 1909, 413–525.

itself in play in the centrally signifying or allegorical one. The analogon in this sense, however, is certainly not limited to allegory: it is the hook that seizes one in a striking metaphor, Barthes' *punctum*, a bodily or gestural reminiscence, of which we are not necessarily aware but which catches our attention like a forgotten muscle. If not itself a rhetorical figure or *gestus*, it is surely a crucial mechanism in the operation of the tropes, a well-nigh physical sensation, a half-forgotten habit, noticed only out of the corner of our eye, which nonetheless grounds the conceptual flight of fancy and certifies the reality of the disembodied intellectual operation, that "tethers the balloon of the mind," as Yeats puts it.

What makes the concept of the analogon particularly useful for the analysis of allegory is the way in which it separates centrality from meaning in the fourfold system. It disrupts what seems to be a static and hierarchical arrangement, and alerts us to the possibility that, particularly in the modern era, where allegory has ceased to be an official genre in its own right, the levels may be rearranged and shuffled, their relations with one another altered, the inner generation of one out of the other restructured and *umfunktioniert*: so it is that the literal level may turn out to lie otherwise than in the text itself, or that the allegorical key may itself turn out to be allegorized and promoted to a different status altogether (the life of Christ, so to speak, becoming itself the content of a moral level and what is to be explained, rather than what explains, as might well be the case with those examples of the "imitation" of Christ referred to earlier).

It is clear enough that with the disappearance of the sacred text, and in a modern relativism, this reshuffling of the levels will in fact be an inevitable outcome, governed now less by a sense of what is orthodox than by what catches the eye, what focuses attention. So it is that where formal attention to the language of the text is demanded, as in style studies (and perhaps in so-called "surface reading"), the letter of the text becomes a new level in its own right, as when one listens for sounds rather than meanings (de Man on Rilke) or reads a sentence for its hidden syntax. These foregrounded properties then become a texture in their own right, which is substituted for the original, and the "literal" text has become a palimpsest.

And with this reshuffling, which sets one on a search for the "method" or ideology of the interpreter, another phenomenon appears which I call *laterality*, but which might better be associated with Felix Guattari's

Historical: The Ladder of Allegory

genial theorization of what he called *transversality*,[22] namely the sweeping shifts back and forth across the levels, in which the purity of the *isotopie* (see Chapter 6) is rudely interrupted by cross-currents of attention and of discursive semiosis. This need not produce official monuments like the heterogeneous forms both Northrop Frye and Mikhail Bakhtin tried to generalize under the term *Menippean satire*: transversality occurs in every living text as it opens itself to a reading by those multiple subject positions we are all as individuals. It is not that the mind wanders in such moments: it is the text itself that shifts back and forth across its multiple levels, distracted by the multiplicity of the meanings proposed there, unsatisfied with the official ones on offer, and with an insatiable curiosity for the other, more hidden and more precious ones, that "substantifique moelle" hidden away in the Silenus box which was Rabelais's term for his own allegories.

It would be fruitless and altogether undialectical and nonlinguistic to call all this ambiguity or even synonymity: in this respect Greimas's transformational scheme, whose very hinges turn on multiple meanings and associative word clusters, can stand as the hidden truth of those puns so dear to the practitioners of the structuralist period— conceptual puns, indeed, which like Geryon ferry us up or down to new levels of the figural structure. Transcoding plays its part here as well, in the way in which it wreaks havoc with the definitions of the philosophers and permits a wholesale alienation of older discourses by new and more imperialistic ideologies, just as the New Testament yearned to appropriate the Old in a hegemonic gesture of ecumenical tolerance.

Indeed, we periodize by way of just such allegorical transformations; and although only one moment of historical periodization is really significant in the present work—the passage from allegory to allegoresis—it may be permitted to say a word in favor of periodization as the fundamental act of historiography. But this must be staged in the right way, not on the basis of those homologies with a single homogeneous period, which Spengler indulged in such delicious detail, but rather, à la Foucault, on the basis of breaks and mutations, seismic shifts, catastrophic emergences, and welcome disintegrations. These will then be even and discontinuous, nonsynchronous as Ernst Bloch put it, in his

---

22 See Watson, *Guattari's Diagrammatic Thought*.

account of modern synchronicity;[23] and to search out such moments of radical change, from the minute to the cataclysmic, is today a more satisfying practice than the grand narratives and generalizations of yesterday's "history of ideas." The ontology of the present is an inventory of differences rather than identities.

In the present volume, with its long disquisition on named emotions, I have tried to offer the missing piece of the conception of affect I tried to stage in *The Antinomies of Realism*; so that it is the waning of named emotions and the suffusion of the void they left by nameless affect that (allegorically) underlies my present narrative of the supplanting of the official allegorical genres by new kinds of allegorical structures, a story that can also be told as the gradual replacement of personification by a language of affective sequences, a substitution of the substantialism of names and nouns by the relationality of qualitative states. Arnold Schoenberg's wonderful idea of the *Klangfarbenmelodie* comes to mind: a melody made up of a sequence of timbres and the material qualities of specific instruments rather than by the series of notes generally understood to constitute a theme or a musical "subject."

I will compare the elements and raw materials of allegory by a more general comparison, with what Lévi-Strauss called *pensée sauvage* (which has been mistranslated as *savage mind* in the standard English edition, which fails to render the adjective with its natural and spontaneous overtones, as in *grève sauvage* or *wildcat strike*; just as it ignores the pun in the French noun that designates both thought and the flower pansy). Lévi-Strauss meant this expression to mean something like a perceptual science, in which lacking the abstraction or the general term, his speakers simply chose one of its items to designate them all: a set which is part of itself, the name of a specific leaf doing double duty as the name of leaves in general. In this view, then, philosophy is the new discovery of abstraction and of general names as such, the Greeks being the inventors of this posthieroglyphic speech and thought. If pensée sauvage is the linguistic mode of so-called primitive peoples, then we are not, with Lévi-Strauss, that far from Vico himself.

Allegory is certainly not primitive in this pejorative sense; it follows abstraction rather than preceding it, and with theology develops the

---

23 See Ernst Bloch, *Erbschaft dieser Zeit*, Frankfurt: Suhrkamp, 1973.

Historical: The Ladder of Allegory

resources of the figural rather than of the philosophical; yet in its multiplicity it eschews an ultimate abstraction, very much in the spirit of pensée sauvage (and against the cognitive features harbored by the dual and tripartite systems). Allegory's theoretical revival, then, after the end of the philosophical system and of metaphysics, may well be less untimely than we might think.

◆

I will conclude this general account of the fourfold scheme of allegory by a word about its diagnostic function. It is not customary, I think, to recognize or acknowledge the structure of Alain Badiou's four "truth procedures" as an allegorical scheme.[24] Yet genuine allegory is a fourfold discovery process, which explores untheorized territory in familiar texts and finds in them new (as it were) electromagnetic spectra hitherto inaccessible to the naked eye. I believe that a useful version of the process can be found in the "truth procedures" if we take those (another fourfold) to constitute an allegorical operation. Science, politics, art, love—such are the "generic" zones in which these truth procedures operate, the latter consisting for Badiou in a fundamental "fidelity to the Event." The Event, like the life, death, and resurrection of Christ, is always in the past, which is why fidelity to it involves something like its reinvention in the present. I have found it helpful to juxtapose this "political ethic" with Walter Benjamin's historical materialism, which defines such an approach to the past as seizing

> hold of a memory as it flashes up at a moment of danger . . . Thus, to Robespierre ancient Rome was a past charged with the time of the now [*Jetztzeit*] which he blasted out of the continuum of history . . . a tiger's leap into the past.[25]

For Benjamin this authentic (yet intermittent) fidelity to the past is anything but nostalgic or retrospective: transforming a "homogeneous" continuity of time into the moment, the *Jetztzeit*, the time of the now,

---

24   For a more general view of Badiou, see my "Badiou and the French Tradition," *New Left Review* 102, 2016. I should add that I do not philosophically endorse Badiou's concept of the four procedures, which are here deployed simply as an illustration of the uses of allegory in philosophy (although I have no objections to them, either).

25   Benjamin, "On the Concept of History," 391, 395.

the *grand soir*, it affirms the existence of the Event in the present, incarnated and resurrected, fulfilled, while retaining the older theological figure. It thereby endows the resurrected Event with that supreme value that governs all four truth procedures and which is Innovation or the modernist "Make It New," as in Thomas Kuhn's conception of scientific history as the paradigm shift that breaks through "normal science" and changes everything. Benjamin's version has the merit of showing that it is only when the older Event, the memory of an Event in the past, comes as Novum or radical innovation (that is, as the New as such) that we can recognize the authenticity of such an operation and indeed grasp its significance.

The Kuhnian version then gives us a way of understanding why science itself can be counted among the Badolian truth procedures: this is not scientism (a rigorous observance of scientific orthodoxies) or some Western idolization of the scientificity of empirical facts, nor is it the promulgation of the "truth" of past doctrine; it is rather the passionate pursuit of revolutionary paradigm change, such as that embodied in Cantor's set theory, which indeed sets the standard for Badiou's other procedures. That of art is modernist innovation, the creation of new languages; that of politics as the emergence of new forms of struggle and new ideals of revolutionary transformation; that of love as the discovery of radically new experience in the place of the familiar words and names, the place of the incomparable as it supersedes fading memories of what is here reinvented as though for the first time. (The domain of love, indeed, is a rare concession of Badiou's system to what looks like individual or phenomenological experience; he would no doubt reply that Beatrice is not an individual experience, contrary to what the cover of his *Théorie du sujet* seems to attest, reproducing Henry Holiday's pre-Raphaelite painting of Dante's first meeting with her.)

It will thereby be seen that the four truth procedures are all in some sense "the same" and that the quest for and inauguration of the New in the form of the Event is what they all have in common, and what drives us forward in our rewriting of the four topics—politics, science, art, love—as so many versions of the endowment of Truth as such. But this is precisely why the whole Badolian scheme of things here is sometimes other than a mere set of homologies. Profoundly allegorical, it rewrites all these different materials and topics in the spirit of a single master-narrative that is common to all of them. Yet at the same time, the operation is a "discovery procedure" whereby new evaluations and interpretations are provided by the process of comparing the different generic narratives.

Thus, in his account of the eternal debate between Marxism and psychoanalysis at the end of *The Theory of the Subject*, Badiou not only affirms his allegiance to both traditions but also uses them against one another in an attempt to verify and evaluate their respective fulfillment of the generic "truth procedure." Rather than the old Freudo-Marxian attempts at this or that "synthesis" of two traditions, Badiou assesses their relative dynamics, the stages through which each dimension passes in its quest for truth, that is, in its saturation of the field of reality such that each one becomes its own Absolute, allowing us to affirm alternatively that everything is political or that everything is psychoanalytic. This final stage of saturation of Leibnizian "indiscernibility" is not the Truth but rather the sign that we are fully engaged in the appropriate "truth procedure."

What in fact happens in this specific confrontation is that Marxism or the political level is found to pass through a three-stage process on its way to fulfillment: first, there is the awakening to class; then the passage to action in the great insurrections; and finally the attainment of a kind of Platonic Idea of communism, the isolation of the authentic consciousness of the proletariat as such.

The properly allegorical procedure will then involve, not an imposition of these three stages on another dimension of reality (in this case, the psychoanalytic one), but rather an inspection of the latter to determine the completeness with which its development there fulfills the standard set by the political realm. It turns out that psychoanalysis only knows two of the three moments or stages in question: the discovery of the unconscious and then the turn toward the second topic (that of Eros and Thanatos, the so-called death wish). This movement is replicated in Lacanian psychoanalysis with first, the differentiation between the Imaginary and the Symbolic, and second, the turn toward the drive or "pulsion" in Seminar XI. But the third stage is lacking, and this absence very much corresponds to Freud's own hesitations about the "cure" ("Psychoanalysis Terminable and Interminable") and Lacan's own later doubts (which are inscribed in the theory of the Sinthome, the neurotic "complex" with which one agrees to live, or which one "chooses," to use the more appropriate Sartrean language). But what would some third moment turn out to be, on the psychoanalytic level?[26]

We can only conjecture the shape of this absence on the basis of the other truth procedures themselves. Whether that of science involves a development that can be readily theorized is unclear: it would certainly involve a transformation of the empirical facts into the kind of universality of which the Platonic Idea gives a figural hint: but presumably in the expansion and suffusion of mathematics and set theory throughout the Real we would eventually come upon something like Badiou's four truth procedures. As for love, its secrets are already revealed in Dante: a purely individual infatuation that is transformed into a universal love beyond all individuality.

The truth procedures then can be seen as Badiou's version of a logical differentiation between the particular and the universal and a narrative reinvention of some quasi-mystical journey from one to the other. That the whole scheme is an allegorical one is now clear in the way in which a single abstract progression is then projected onto its various levels and embodiments. The demonstration will also have driven home, I hope, the point that modern allegory involves a kinship between processes, unlike the personifications of classical or traditional allegory: it is the interechoing of narratives with one another, in their differentiation and reidentification, rather than the play with fixed substances and entities identified as so many traits or passions, for example, incarnated in individual figures all the way to the caricatural or the stereotypical. We will find ourselves reverting again and again to this insight: that it is the disappearance of personification that signals the emergence of modernity.

---

26   For new and unusual speculations on the matter, see Eric Cazdyn's *The Already Dead: The New Time of Politics, Culture, and Illness*, Durham, NC: Duke University Press, 2012.

2
Psychological: Emotional Infrastructures

It is a vast and ill-lit basement, intersected by pipes of all sizes, of various materials, in various states of deterioration, without obvious passageways and obstructed by tanks and storage containers of all sizes, each one of which, pipes and tanks alike, sporting dials and glass panels of equal variety whose registers, clocks, meters, thermometric pressure gauges, numerical scales, quadrants, warning lights, and calibrations are in constant surveillance by the innumerable historians in their white coats and checkboards, jostling one another as they jockey for a look or sneer at their neighbors. No one knows how many kinds of measurements are in play here, nor even the antiquity of some of the devices, each of which registers the variable rates of different indicators, such as water pressure, temperature, instability, consumption, luxury goods, life expectancy, annual film production, salinity, ideology, average weight, average heat, church attendance, guns per family, and the rate of extinction of species. Those who have concluded that these tasks are meaningless sit against the wall in various states of fatigue, others race frantically back and forth to invent a master statistic that might encompass all these random findings, while still others concentrate stubbornly on their own calculations and substitute their own algorithms which may or may not have any relationship to those of their neighbors.

None of them registers History directly, of course; it exists somewhere outside this basement or laboratory, and all the dials seem to record it in one way or another. You could certainly call it an absent cause (or an untotalizable totality) if you think it exists; but no one has ever seen anything but the gauges and their needles, the numbers and their rise and fall, which vary wildly and require separate monitors. Despite this, there persist the occasional joint cooperative efforts along with the most unsubstantiated generalizations and a tacit conviction if not a mutual agreement that there must be something or other out there.

In one of the smaller batch of instruments, something like the history of emotions is tirelessly grinding out its data and its findings, which its tenders consign to a variety of logbooks. This is a rather recent branch of activity, whose equally recent specialists have not yet united around the nature of their object of study.[1] Should one write the evidence up in the form of a history of ideas, such as the idea of love or the idea of emulation? Or is the material so culturally unique as to demand an indigenous term in its own right: or perhaps even a single category is inappropriate, insofar as "emotions" include things as different as pallor, moods, trembling, red faces, and manic depression?

By now, however, most seem to settle on words and names as a convenient starting point; so we will call them *named emotions*, just to be on the safe side. That way, we can begin with lists; and the lists show that some of these "emotions" have become extinct, and perhaps, like the blank spots in the table of the elements, others have not yet come into being. Do these lists form systems of some kind? It is tempting to think, as Aristotle seems to, that they are organized (mostly) in pairs of opposites; for systems begin with opposites and oppositions, while the latter, the names of the opposites, if suitably personified, could be expected to act out narratives of struggle or harmony, compromise or impotent rage—narratives at once allegorical in their very structure and thereby arriving at our topic directly without beating around the bush.

In any case the identification of an emotion with its name immediately raises a far less direct historical issue, namely that of hermeneutics. How do we know that the emotion Homer attributed to this or that hero or heroine (and which has dutifully been translated into its alleged equivalent in English) is anything like what we feel today? Or to take it

---

1   I have mainly relied in what follows, on Jan Plamper's *History of Emotions: An Introduction*, Oxford: Oxford University Press, 2015, which contains a useful bibliography of individual studies. The classic work on the subject is Harry Norman Gardiner, Ruth Clark Metcalf, and John Gilbert Beebe-Center, *Feeling and Emotion: A History of Theories*, Knoxville, TN: American Book Company, 1937.

from another angle, how do we know that the emotion referred to in some tribal language has any equivalent in our (American? modern? Western or Eastern?) psyche, except by asking in either one of our languages? But this could go very far indeed: it could raise serious doubts about my own immediate neighbor, while leaving me in complete confusion when confronted by those delightful structuralist hobby-horses which are the color scheme or the wine-tasting kit. It would not be very practical if emotion led us directly on into solipsism. But perhaps it is the very process of nomination itself that demands a closer look.

Meanwhile, for good or ill let us sort these terms out: those by which we name *emotions* seem to circulate on a different level than those reserved for judgment on them. The emotions or feelings would seem to stream along in an indiscriminate succession in which, like flowing water, they sometimes froth and sometimes stagnate, they overflow but also sink into the ground and dry up. One could imagine a sentient being whose life was nothing but a sequence in which bursts of anger punctuate fears and joys, shames and envies. Still, some of these will no doubt feel better than others, and here then glimmers the first inkling of what is not itself an emotion and what may well be called a judgment: the eudaemonic. And so, beyond the emotions and yet inseparable from them, there circulates a level on which things are not only judged to be good or bad but also pleasant or painful: are those judgments the same? They swell themselves out on the one hand into the very personifications of Good and Evil, while on the other side they get sorted out into body and mind, matter and spirit, meat and mental, material and spiritual, etc.: repression here beginning to play its part as training and habit, and shifting its identifications crosswise such that pleasure itself can become evil, while pain becomes a virtue and slowly some third position—apatheia—begins to swim into view. These are at any rate supplementary oppositions, which place the named emotions in specific and variable historical positions (for example, anger dividing into righteous and sinful kinds at one interesting moment of Western religious history). But these supplementary evaluations cannot simply be added in like a new ingredient; they must reorganize the named emotions themselves into new patterns and new oppositions.

Two distinct processes seem to be identifiable here: on the one hand, the nameless feeling is reified into the name for an emotion-event that repeats itself and that we recognize; on the other the names themselves are organized into systems of binary oppositions, which lend them that social meaning which Aristotle (for example) mapped out for his culture or mode of production. (We will examine his version more closely in a moment.) These systems of evaluation—cultural and historical—project a psychology, an ethics, and in many instances a set of religious estimations. But they are generally overdetermined by that more primitive opposition that classifies them as material or spiritual and that in some historical situations gives rise to a dual classification scheme in which the mental or spiritual "emotion" is doubled by a parallel corporeal version, which is not always the simple expression of the former but sometimes (as in Hobbes or the James–Lange theory) its reality. This is then a peculiarly complex situation in which the good–bad axis is overdetermined by a material–spiritual one.

Allegory can therefore be timely in two distinct moments: first, a situation of reification in which a name is conferred on a hitherto inchoate and unidentified feeling; and a second process in which a set of already named emotions is itself reorganized by one or more sets of evaluations—eudaemonic, ethical, religious, philosophical, or sociopolitical. But its forms and its X-ray work will not necessarily be visible in historical moments or historical societies in which these systems are as functional as common sense, habitual, needing no supplementary reinforcement. The two operations, however, mark a significant dividing line between the practice of allegory as a genre or fixed form and that of allegoresis as a mode of interpretation; about which I will argue here that these constitute a single story and not two unrelated historical episodes. The greatest and most distinctive works conventionally described as allegories, however—Dante, Spenser, and Goethe—are to be grasped from both perspectives, transcending genre on the one hand and proposing a unique practice of reading on the other.

But the essential dividing line between the two kinds of allegorical phenomena has its philosophical meaning as well: for the passage marks a vaster and far more extensive sea change from substance-oriented thinking and categories to that modern perspective often known as *process*, the passage from Aristotle to Hegel, if you like, or from realism to rationalism (to use Gaston Bachelard's formula): from a thinking in terms of object and what Hegel called "fixed" ideas to one of relationship and relativity, of situational concepts. Aristotle was a botanist and a biologist whose interest lay in an inventory of forms and types of objects: his fundamental category—the substance—still organizes the syntax of common sense and phenomenological experience to this day, and one can readily recognize it in those allegorical characters who wear their labels on their backs as they perform their interactions. What follows the reign of substantive thought is far less clear to anyone—post–Euclidean geometries, the dialectic, quantum physics, nonfigurative painting? But what is clear by now is that the initial interpretation of this epochal transformation as a prototypically modern "discovery" of self-consciousness or reflexivity, a radical move of thought from the objective to Cartesian and idealistic subjectivity, was incorrect, inasmuch as both objectivity and subjectivity itself are thoroughly disorganized by the antisubstantive transformation.

Indeed, did not Nietzsche observe that we would not get rid of the old substantivist metaphysics (including God himself) until we came to terms with the old grammatical first person and its "self"? Yet the "self" is another one of these allegorical objects that the analysis of allegory is likely to transform beyond recognition, an advance which will not be possible until we begin to think of the "self" as a construct and to acknowledge the allegorical nature of what may henceforth be called the *construction of subjectivity* as such.

This is no doubt a misnomer to the degree to which subjectivity (along with that elusive thing, the "self") includes consciousness; and consciousness is assuredly neither a thing nor can it be "constructed": here, as elsewhere, I follow Sartre's account of the latter as a not-being whose existence and operations are best characterized by Husserl's notion of intentionality, that is, as a being always "defined" by what it is not: consciousness is always consciousness *of* something.[2] This account leads me to adhere to Colin McGinn's extreme skepticism and to agree that consciousness can never be conceptualized: we are always within it, like fish in water, and from the inside it has no opposite.[3] We represent it to be sure, but in the most impoverished way, as a point or dot of light, etc.

The self, on the other hand, seems to be a kind of thing or being, and as such can be conceptualized (and has been) as well as abundantly

---

2 Jean-Paul Sartre, "Une idée fondamentale de la phénoménologie de Husserl," *Situations I,* Paris: Gallimard, 1947.
3 See Colin McGinn, *The Mysterious Flame: Conscious Minds in a Material World,* New York: Basic Books, 2000.

represented, nowhere more suggestively than on Proust's opening page, in which a familiar self, my private property of the day, is characterized as a kind of room whose objects, in their familiar places, remind me who I am and allow me to grasp my own "identity" as a kind of habit. But since that self always has a past, the contents of this room and its very shape and location shift bewilderingly around me as I wake up to the present, racing to take their now familiar stations like the objects in a Disney cartoon, who fall into place when I am fully "there" as though they had never moved at all in the course of a long and "unconscious" night.

To be sure, one can imagine variations on Proust's powerful representation, which depends on our life in dwellings and rooms: the desert, for example, or a dense forest through which a bewildered nomadic or schizophrenic self moves and wanders. But constructed subjectivity means that even Proust's more stable room has been laboriously, historically, furnished; its various items deliberately purchased if not found at random in flea markets; its space as furrowed as the path I follow to my favorite armchair, the light toward which I bend my head, or the blankets that warm me on a chilly evening. All of these items are so many names; and many of them are familiar emotions—the annoyance I feel when something doesn't fit or the pleasant anticipation with which I approach my window. "Knowing myself" in that sense means taking the familiar inventory of my reactions, the stations of my anger, the practiced caution with which I avoid unpleasant or painful thoughts, the Proustian reminder of my shopping list of loves and hates.

The self is thus an allegorical structure in its own right, peopled by names and emotions, which mainly sort themselves out into "named emotions." To be sure, it can be approached by other representational directions; but this allegorical one is perhaps the most travelled, and in any case one of the closest to me, its general form shared by my cultural contemporaries. So it becomes easier to understand why, at certain crucial turnings, allegory should propose itself as the most useful instrument of representation and the one most propitious to this or that pedagogy of change proposed by history itself: changing the furniture, tearing down a wall, reorganizing our daily life, and perhaps from time to time admitting a new feeling or two, a new name.

Nomination is a process for which the terms *alienation* and *reification* need to be invoked, although perhaps not this soon. Yet I will argue in what follows that an emotion can only be felt as such ("qua emotion") when it has been named: the opposite, perhaps, of the notorious James–Lange theory of emotion in which the experience is simply at one with its physiological expression. But the name is not the mind, not the spirit, not even cognitive: it is a reification by which inchoate "experience"—and even this way of putting it overlooks the fact that "experience" is after all itself just such a name and already does similar things to what it names in advance of their specific or specialized nomenclature—separated off from the stream of existence, lent specific qualities and attributes, made into a separate and individualized object of some kind. Schopenhauer expressed a profound insight when he observed that Kant's categories were lacking in the essential: a category of the object or thing as such.[4] But he failed to add that such a category is itself dependent in advance of the power of the name (or noun: the two words are significantly the same in French). Indeed, in Lacanian psychoanalysis the infant's name is one of the primal forms of alienation, which lifts the subject into the Symbolic Order, leaving its reality as "the subject of desire" behind it in what Freud would still have called the Unconscious. My name is how other people see me, and I spend incalculable energies in attempting to coincide with it and to knowing (impossibly) what they mean by it.

With nomination, we touch on a seam between mind and body that is less obvious, and more productive, than the traditional oppositions of matter and spirit (or life, or consciousness), and also, perhaps, a little more available to tangible analysis. This focus allows us to skirt the opposition of the inner and the outer more successfully (without resolving its dilemmas altogether), and it also helps avoid the irritating paradoxes which a constructivist approach always seems to exacerbate. The structuralists were fond of the phenomenon of color as it was modified historically and according to different cultures: for color offered the twin advantages of foregrounding its linguistic medium (language and its available vocabularies can testify as to the absence in a given language of this or that modern term, or the presence of adjectives unknown to us); and of systematicity, insofar as colors are always defined in systemic

---

4 See the Foreword to Arthur Schopenhauer's *World as Will and Idea*, New York: Dover, 1969.

pairings and distinctions from one another.⁵ (Wine tasting and its specialized vocabulary might have offered an analogous field of examination, except that its experiences are more reliant on testimony and more resistant to external testing procedures.) In the case of these systems, the old problem of subjectivity is never fully eliminated: does the other really have the same experience in his head, her head, that I do, and in any case what does "the same" really mean? Still, it is hard to devise satisfactory tests for the long dead, such as the ancient Greeks, or for tribes absolutely untouched by Western contact and contamination; and so otherness retreats into an even more inaccessible corner.

Such are the problems exacerbated by the analogous problem of emotions and their names; and Wittgenstein's denunciation of the pseudoproblem of private languages is of little help here. I believe that the notion of the construction of subjectivity is for the moment—although no doubt untestable and unfalsifiable—the most productive way of thinking about this problem, for it can include notions of habit as well as the various candidates for an "idea" of the self; it can subsume psychoanalysis (where in any case with both Freud and Lacan it was to all intents and purposes practiced avant la lettre, although with the omission of the key notion of "character" and character traits); it excludes the philosophically unresolvable matter of the nature of consciousness, which it simply presupposes; and it can lend itself to the most varied and suggestive thought experiments.

Such a working conception of the production of subjectivity will need to deal with (or name) several different kinds of procedure—differentiation and alienation; familiarity and omission or repression; association; taboo or reinforcement; and finally attention, that moment of what the rhetoricians called *amplificatio*—which we will find to be at the very heart of allegory as such.

But at its beginning, the name. Proust gives us an experimental situation, in his description of an awakening in which the surrounding object world of the self or room pass through multiple stages and embryonic positions until they reach that of the narrator's age and present location. So also with the inchoate, that illicit beginning of the beginning, the before of the very before itself, which as Kant taught us cannot

---

5 See, for example, Brent Berlin and Paul Kay, *Basic Color Terms: Their Universality and Evolution*, Berkeley: University of California Press, 1969.

be conceptualized, but which Hegel then taught us to posit as retroactively unconceptualizable. The word *inchoate* is itself already an illicit representation (it assumes a matter to be given form); and the dilemma governs both the emergence of individual consciousness and that invention of language at the "beginning" of human history.

But once we set foot in this moving stream which the very existence of language presupposes, a phenomenon becomes visible which we can speculatively theorize; and that is what we have been calling *nomination* or *the naming of a thing*: the latter thereby becoming distinguished from others (differentiation) and acquiring that identity of its own which the possession of a name presumably guarantees. But names—whether static nouns or dynamic verbs—inevitably bring a kind of repression with them: not merely the exclusion of any alternate way of framing the situation which other kinds of names might have provided, but also that distance between the name and the thing which we have observed Lacan to posit between the "subject" recognized by other people and taking his or her place in the Symbolic Order, and the "subject of desire" that sinks into what Freud called the unconscious (not to speak of the Real itself, or *das Ding*).[6] For emotions, then, we might also think of what Proust called the "intermittencies of the heart," in which the name comes loose from the experience it is supposed to identify, and we do not grieve "enough" (as Sartre will put it later on), the emotion-word fails to designate a plenitude of feeling, or else, as with Count Mosca's premonition of the word "love," it changes everything.[7]

Meanwhile the word for grief or love breeds familiarity and habit: the identity of the room's furniture, the names of its contents, gradually convince us that there is such a thing as personal identity, that we have a "self," which, thereby named, tends to do certain kinds of things and avoid some, while not even conceiving that there exist other selves whose possibilities we do not even suspect.

But there is a counterpart to this effect of habit (a pseudoconcept if there ever was one) and to the associations it seems to reinforce. Clues to this countermovement occasionally appear symptomatically in

---

6   Jacques Lacan, "The Instance of the Letter in the Unconscious, or Reason since Freud," *Écrits*, New York: W. W. Norton, 2006.

7   Stendhal, *La Chartreuse de Parme*, Paris: Cluny, 1940, Ch. 7, 153: "là, ou pendant le voyage, le hasard peut amener un mot qui donnera un nom à ce qu'ils sentent l'un pour l'autre; et après, en un instant, toutes les conséquences."

theories of the emotions where we would not expect to find them: such is for example, St. Augustine's positing of a concupiscence of the eye as a kind of passion in its own right.[8] We may call it voyeurism today, or stress the idiosyncrasy of the impulse in Augustine's own life (or even, as with Sartre and Lacan,[9] posit a drive to sight itself as a specific property of human lived experience); but it is surely surprising to come upon it in any conventional inventory of these inward "turbulences" Cicero called *emotions*. Meanwhile, "surprise" itself makes its appearance as a kind of emotion in Descartes's theory of the passions, where its very name— admiration—also powerfully underscores (by way of its etymology) the sense of sight as it seems to interrupt our normal thought processes and to focus our attention on an unexpected new center of attention (whether subjective or objective). Indeed, modern psychology calls this *attention* as such, without explaining it any better; and we may affirm in our present context that such a moment, by separating an object from its background and "foregrounding" it in a mesmerizing way, causing us to linger over it and to prolong its identity through passing moments of time—that such a moment very precisely constitutes that amplification or *amplificatio*, that heightening and differentiation, dishabituation and endowment with new value, that we will henceforth begin to associate with allegory.

This is the other face of nominalism: a process which as a cultural tendency Adorno systematically denounced as the contamination spread everywhere through capitalist modernity by empiricist "thinking": the taboo on the negative, the gradual retreat from the conquests of abstraction, the ever more peremptory insistence on the fact and the positivity of existence and reality alike and one which settles on measurability as a useful substitute for anything resembling the dialectic. Adorno's version of nominalism has the social and political advantage of excluding critique from those positivities, insofar as critique and the negative necessarily posit what is not there, what of the past or of the future may serve as the basis for a judgment on the status quo.

---

8   Augustine, *Confessions*, London: Penguin, 1961, Book I, paragraph 7, 28.
9   For Sartre, see the chapter titled "The Look" in *Being and Nothingness*, New York: Gallimard, 1943; for Lacan see the discussion of the gaze as an object of drive in *Seminar XI*, New York: W. W. Norton, 1981.

But perhaps Adorno overlooked a kind of dialectical pathology of nominalism, if not in some unexpected way a paradoxical cure for it, namely the intentness with which a fact may be obsessively received, until it becomes as it were a former fact, an item floating in the void and devoid of all context or ground—a thing whose very name, if it carries it with it, is transformed into that meaningless sonority only interminable repetition can bring about. The result is then that dissolution of *isotopie*,[10] which the analysts of traditional allegories underscored when they observed the profound breaks in realist continuity (and reading mode) caused, for example, by the appearance of Milton's Sin and Death or Dante's three ravenous beasts. Modernisms of all kinds have thrived on these "defamiliarizations" and breaks in niveau and reference; but allegory is not modernist in that sense (and modern allegory has a different dynamic, that of analogies between systems rather than the isolation of the individual object). And yet the phenomenon also can be construed as a kind of halt, or emergency brake, in the face of a colonization by nominalism of which realism can be a replication fully as much as a diagnostic. (A nominalist program that seeks to discredit these abstractions, which are the various systems of the named emotions, is what is referred to today as *affect*, a philosophical topic I return to below.)

As for the systems themselves, they come in the form of lists—generally of the basic or primary passions or emotions—which some theorists are capable of working up into a variety of "combinations," often on the basis of classificatory oppositions. (Hobbes, for example, produces a permutation scheme on the basis of the combination of a past–future axis with a motion axis, approaching–withdrawing.) The lists with which secondary and even some primary sources confront us are problematic to the degree to which what looks like a synchronic system can also be in part a diachronic one, that is, one in which the sequence itself projects an evolution of one emotion or passion into another one: so that the problem of comparing such inventories on the basis of what they select and omit is complicated by a dynamic inquiry into the type of feeling change or psychological mechanism their sequences

---

10   An *isotopie* can perhaps best be described as the uniformity of a given code within a more complex discourse, in which to be sure any number of isotopies interact or interrupt each other: a narrative isotopie might, for example, emerge briefly within an essentially cognitive discourse.

presuppose. The first problem will direct our attention to the personification of the various emotions, the second to what we may call *process allegories*, such as those deployed in Christian psychology around sin and temptation, or the therapy of salvation.

Perhaps some first step may be taken by the comparison of Western and non-Western classification schemes. The following table lists the classical Chinese view of emotions, as determined by the vital force (breath) of *qi*[11]; then the classical Hindu system of the rasas or "flavors" (*Bharata*)[12]; and finally the sequence laid out by Aristotle in Book II of the Rhetoric:

CHINA	INDIA	GREECE
Joy	Love (attractiveness)	Anger
Anger	Laughter	Friendship/Hatred
Anxiety	Fury	Fear
Pensiveness	Compassion	Shame
Grief	Disgust	Kindness
Fear	Horror	Pity/Indignation
Fright	the Heroic	Envy
		Emulation

The absence of joy or grief from the Aristotelian system has been much discussed (along with that of disgust or horror); the Chinese "pensiveness" is an unusual and idiosyncratic state by comparison with the other two schemes, while laughter (in the system of the rasas) is a welcome and humane addition to the collection (although its accompaniment by "heroic" attitudes may surprise somewhat, introducing a form of action into a generally passive-receptive series). These distinctions (Ute Frevert's "lost" and "found" emotions)[13] are of anecdotal cultural interest; and the English translations of the indigenous terms in question are obviously subject to the most strenuous etymological debate, which is more than likely to terminate in the conclusion that no English equivalents for any of the terminologies of the three foreign languages exist.

---

11   What follows is the standard list of the traditional "seven emotions" of Chinese medicine.
12   V. K. Chari, *Sanskrit Criticism,* Honolulu: University of Hawaii Press, 1990.
13   Ute Frevert, *Emotions in History: Lost and Found,* Budapest: Central European University Press, 2011.

What is more important in our present context is the fact that all three lists are mediated by a specific practical focus: indeed, even with the later passage of the philosophy or the emotions to the more purely physiological, it will ultimately be concluded that there exist no immediate descriptions of emotional phenomenology. The "phenomena" are in fact embodied names, whose realities always find themselves transmitted through this or that secondary code. Thus, the Chinese table of the emotions (or passions—the very alternation of these terms is a whole philosophical choice in and of itself) is an essentially medical enumeration. Indeed, it is incalculable to what degree the medical—most often in the guise of something like the theory of the four humors[14]—still subtends ostensibly nonmedical classification schemes. It would seem that the Indian classification also has its sources in medical lore and practice; but in the form of the rasas (or flavors) it is an essentially aesthetic scheme, which aims at classifying the aesthetic effects of various kinds of artistic performances, from dance to theater, from music to visual representations. As for Aristotle, as the very title of his treatise indicates, his is also a primarily practical handbook, destined for orators and designed to enumerate the kinds of rhetorical effects with which speakers have to deal and which they must learn to manipulate. Postponing any consideration of the Christian version of these psychic realities, we may then quickly summarize their modern forms, from the energy models of the seventeenth century onward, as so many physiological equivalents of the older passions, if not (as in Hobbes and in a different way, with William James) so many attempts to subsume the phenomenology of emotion under purely corporeal descriptions.

The seventeenth century broached the problem by positing a parallel between the two realms of thought and feeling (or thought and extension), by connecting them (as in Descartes) via the pineal gland; or by conferring on God the obligation to hold them together at every instant (as in Malebranche's "occasionalism"); by stoutly affirming the parallelism of the attributes (as in Spinoza); or by making a first heroic effort to subsume conscious experience altogether under the physiological movements and circulations of the material body (as in Hobbes, whose attempt simply reinforces the parallelism he wishes to abolish).

14   See Noga Arikha, *Passions and Tempers: A History of the Humours,* New York: Harper Perennial, 2007.

In the nineteenth century, however, Darwin effectuated a revolution no less significant than his theory of natural selection with his reduction of emotion to expression, achieved by way of that most ambiguous new technology provided by photography. The technological image now determines something like a return to older aesthetic systems such as the rasas, in this case by allowing culture to masquerade under the guise of a kind of materialist scientificity. (It is indeed this scandal of photography as such—the ambivalence between body and mind, the material image and its expressive meaning—which is responsible for the antinomies on which all "theories" of photography have come to grief.) But we might equally well blame Descartes (the first materialist philosopher as well as the first idealist one) for this slippage, inasmuch as his twin realms encourage that simulacrum of materialism indulged by Hobbes along with the idealism developed by the religious tradition. Such parallelisms can indeed be characterized as allegorical avant la lettre. As for Darwin, however, his "expressive" materialism celebrates its truly allegorical revels in the acting of nineteenth-century opera and in silent film, in which melodramatic gesticulation and facial contortion—particularly after Griffiths's invention of the close-up—produce personifications no less "spiritual" (or semiotic) for all their corporeal pretensions. The Darwinian table of emotions (codified by Paul Ekman)[15] reproduces many of the traditional items:

> Happiness
> Sadness
> Fear
> Anger
> Surprise
> Disgust

Yet now, in a kind of phrenological reversal,[16] the physical expression encourages a belief in the autonomy of the physiological; and we confront the James–Lange theory and its reanimation in contemporary

---

15 See Plamper, *History of Emotions*, 147–72.
16 See Hegel's thoughts on this allegorical pseudoscience in the phrenology chapter of the *Phenomenology of Spirit*, with its celebrated concluding sentence; "Spirit is a bone."

neuroscience, which reproduces all the older categories and assigns them to various parts of the brain, at the same time that it revives the older dualism of the concupiscent versus the irascible in the form of the cognitive versus the physiological. But by that time the formal link between emotion and personification had long since been broken off.

Indeed, what it is important to retain about modern theories of the emotions or passions since Descartes is the appearance of a new element, namely desire, which had not appeared in the abstract before, despite its palpable embodiments in drives like gluttony and sexuality. In the context of this discussion, we may hazard the hypothesis that it is the very concept of desire in the abstract which spells the end of allegorical personification and encourages the development of wholly new (and modern) kinds of metaphysics and conceptions of "human nature" (as well as of new kinds of allegorical structures).

But we have so far omitted the most momentous episode in the history of (Western) emotion, namely the Christian transformation of the classical emotional repertoire into the Seven Deadly Sins.[17] It is time to repair this omission, toward which Evagrius's initial list will make a beginning:

>Gluttony
>Fornication
>Avarice
>Distress ("lupe" or *aegritudo*)
>Anger
>Acedia
>Vainglory
>Pride

These initial eight will be reduced to the classical seven by Gregory the Great, who translated *lupe* into envy and combined vainglory and pride into a single psychic condition, moving it to the very top of the list of sins as such: not, however, before Evagrius had made his point. His foregrounding of the two great physical drives stands as a stinging rebuke to the pagans, none of whom would have considered either anything like a

---

17 I rely here principally on Morton W. Bloomfield, *The Seven Deadly Sins*, East Lansing: Michigan State College Press, 1952.

passion. We said before that what seemed peculiarly invisible in the pagan repertory, and thus decisively modern, was Desire. But here is the first form of desire, in its twin corporeal manifestations (with its more mediated form, greed, close on their heels).

It will be observed, quite correctly, that the theorization of the sins was inflected by its practical purpose, to serve as a guide for the anchoretic community which came into being after the gradual (and ultimately permanent) withdrawal of the present into the longest *durée* of all, the expectation of the Last Judgment. Meanwhile overdetermination must be invoked here; and the perpetuation of ecclesiastic property secured by priestly celibacy and the ban on the remarriage of Christian widows certainly play a role in early Christian asceticism; as does, in some broader view, the requirement that every new religion sharply distinguish itself in one decisively practical and stylistic way or another from its predecessors (monotheism, the ban on graven images, and so on). St. Paul's own personal obsessions are significant only insofar as they struck the right chord in this process of universalization and institutionalization. But modern scholars—the oddly mismatched team of Michel Foucault and Martha Nussbaum in particular—have also stressed the disciplinary functions of pagan philosophy, its emphasis on moderation and on self-control. I doubt whether consumer society today will find such recommendations timely or persuasive, except insofar as they are read into the more collective conservative agenda organized around the budgetary "virtue" of Austerity. But all this is to continue to read the historical and cultural conceptions of emotion in a narrowly moralizing framework, based on the life experience of the individual (for which they purport to offer rules of conduct). Whether we have to do here with the benefits of restraint, with the salvation of the soul, or with modern therapy, all such individualizing frameworks make for bad allegory and can be decisively put in their proper place by a juxtaposition with the great (political or collective) ethics of a Machiavelli, a Gracián, or a La Rochefoucauld.

In any case, I here propose a very different framework, which has to do with the construction of subjectivity and its eventual relationship to population and the Other (to which I return later). To grasp that framework more tangibly, we must now introduce the binary oppositions that play across the various tables of the named emotions and which unify them and secure their functionality. Such oppositions, which most often serve to sort the emotions out into the recommended and the taboo, are thematically numerous and not always even consistent with one another. But we can surely make at least one acceptable and pragmatic beginning with that between pleasure and pain, from which, in tortuous and devious ways, body and mind (or soul) on the one hand, and good and evil on the other, would both seem to derive. All three can be abstracted into the more purely formal classification of positive and negative; but as for content, only such notions as simple and compound, or the Stoic idea of a pre-emotion as opposed to the named emotion proper, are helpful in reconciling overlapping systems of judgments. In the long run, however, it is by adding in temporality that these still relatively static or structuralizing schemes can be developed (and in my current language that means moving from personification to narrative).

I have already hinted at the form problem confronted by any attempt to "represent" the emotion or passion in question, with which Aristotle will wish to associate an opposite number, a positive state if this one is negative, a moderate one if it is an excess, or even a threatening negation should it (more exceptionally) have some positive merit. But this is a strategy for evading the problem rather than confronting it (as can be seen from its final Christian form, in which the vices are all conveniently and symmetrically paired with their appropriate virtues). Unfortunately, as Bloomfield has shown, the virtues are an afterthought and were added later on, some of them having to be invented out of hand for the purpose (like "calmness" for the Aristotelian pendant to "anger"). Alas, the "turbulences" do not necessarily have any opposites, despite Aristotle's ingenuity; and it is at this point that temporality—or diachrony—comes to the rescue.

For as Bloomfield has also shown, Christian theology, whether knowingly or not, found a convenient substitute in the ancient Babylonian star journey, in which the soul moves from one distinctive position to the next: this means that classical anger (*orge*) cannot be neutralized by a nonexistent opposite but that it might well be redeemed by the appropriate modulation. Thus, the theologians deplored excessive, "unreasonable" fury, but were willing enough to allow that "righteous anger" ("righteous indignation") had its uses (particularly inasmuch as God very frequently found himself having recourse to it in his dealings with his creations). Already with Augustine, I believe, the negative and the painful turned out to offer positive incentives for the sinner who grows dissatisfied with his condition. Ultimately, and armed with the relatively new conception of Purgatory (Le Goff situates its invention and adoption somewhere between 1150 and 1200[18]), Dante was able to restore the narrativity of the Babylonian star journey on the successive shelves of his sacred mountain. It does not seem necessary to point out the obvious, namely that this narrativization of the formerly static emotions or passions makes a new and developmental if not evolutionary construction of subjectivity possible.

Still, for the modern West there persists an incorrigible temptation to return again and again to the distinction between philosophy and theology, between the Greeks and the Christians, or the secular and the sacred. One may feel that today, under current circumstances, the distinction is unhelpful and unproductive (religion being simply one more form of ideology). Or one may feel, as I do, that since Lévi-Strauss and *La Pensée sauvage*, we ought to be capable of including the "perceptual science" of the latter, which does not know abstraction, as well as the purely figural thinking of theology, which does not know the literal, in the house of philosophy itself (unless it seems preferable to tear the whole building down to make way for shopping malls full of Adorno's non-negative commodified empiricisms). Indeed, does not something similar seem at work in the wholesale displacement of the named emotions by a generalized *affect*?

At any rate, even to understand this latest development, it may well be preferable to start again at something like a beginning, namely with Aristotle's treatise on emotion, the *Rhetoric*, in order to try to determine where sin and guilt found their way into it in the first place. Heidegger called this great handbook of the emotions and how to address and use them the first great "phenomenology of everyday life."[19]

It is therefore all the more striking that it should begin its inventory in the same place at which the *Iliad* itself began, namely with anger. Sing, goddess, the wrath of Achilles! And no doubt, of all conceivable emotions, anger is the most dangerous and antisocial, the boiling point of everything that must be contained, repressed, and disciplined for a collectivity to function. Anger is the source of all rebellions, revolutions,

---

18 Jacques Le Goff, *The Birth of Purgatory*, Aldershot, England: Scolar Press, 1990.
19 Martin Heidegger, *Sein und Zeit*, Tübingen: Max Niemeyer, 1957, Pt. 1, Ch. 5, 138.

revolts, and even of crime; and there is a sense in which virtually all of the so-called negative emotions (Spinoza's sad passions) find their path way back to it in one way or another. Indeed, anger is itself revealingly self-referential: appropriately enough, Prudentius's allegorical figure of anger reaches a point in its fury at which it destroys itself.[20] All historical systems of the emotions or passions have had a practical interest in theorizing anger and in finding the most manageable place for it, in determining the ways in which it can safely be diverted or used, if it cannot be extinguished.

As we have said, Aristotle's method insists in pairing opposites in an inconsistently dialectical way: sometimes they are genuinely antagonistic terms, such as hatred and friendship; and sometimes they are simply complementary excesses that can be avoided by steering a mean between them and choosing moderation. In this sense, Glenn Most's brilliant reading of the *Iliad*,[21] in which Achilles' twofold wrath (which targets Greeks and Trojans alike) is "cured" by the final experience of pity for Priam, does not square with the Aristotelian system, in which *pity* (if that is the right translation) does not quite work that way, and its opposite, *indignation*, is to be found in a different place from anger.

To be sure, the Aristotelian list presents many other anomalies for the modern reader: love, for example, does not seem to be an appropriate example of emotion for Aristotle, nor sexual desire either. Grief is altogether omitted from this system, as from ancient Greek psychology in general; while hate finds itself paired with anger in an interesting but uncharacteristic way. Anger, he tells us, is being aroused by individuals, while hatred is in contrast destined for groups, collectivities of a more general and abstract character. It will be said that as a psychology the *Rhetoric* is meant to offer practical instruction in public speaking and that attacks on individuals need to be staged rather differently than denunciations of whole groups or classes. Yet a good deal of purely

---

20 Prudentius, *Psychomachia*, vol. I, Cambridge, MA: Loeb Classical Library, 1949, 288–91: "Wrath is beside herself and casts away the luckless ivory that has been false to her, the token of honor turned to shame. Afar she flings that unwelcome reminder, and wild passion fires her to slay herself. One of the many missiles that she had scattered without effect she picks up from the dust of the field, for an un-natural use. The smooth shaft she fixes in the ground and with the upturned point stabs herself."
21 Glenn Most, "Anger and Pity in Homer's *Iliad*" in *Ancient Anger: Perspectives from Home to Galen*, eds Susanna Braun and Glenn W. Most, Cambridge: Cambridge University Press, 2004.

psychological theory seeps through these suggestions, and I will draw two kinds of lessons from them at this point. The first has to do with the relationship between Aristotle's theory of the passions and the structure of the social formation—the polis—in which he conceptualized them; while the second bears more directly on the continuities as well as the modifications that led historically from this classical system to later, medieval views on the matter.

Let us look again at these concepts. Even the description of anger is completely alien to the contemporary reader: Aristotle defines it as the reaction to a "slight," an offense, an insult (implied as much as articulated). But is this what I feel when I am unnecessarily clumsy or fail to put something together according to the directions on the box? Is this exactly what is involved when I find someone else incompetently making a mess of a perfectly simple job?

There is even more to it than that: "anger may be defined as an impulse, accompanied by pain, to a conspicuous revenge for a conspicuous slight directed without justification toward what concerns oneself or toward what concerns one's friends."[22] The word *conspicuous*, several times stressed, is important insofar as it signals the necessarily public nature of the slight (and its public reparation). But what is even more striking is the affirmation of an inextricable relationship between anger and vengeance, not particularly evident in our modern examples but clearly enough central (if not obsessive) in all the classics from Homer to Shakespeare, where the Elizabethan obsession with revengers' tragedies of all kinds is even more pronounced than in Greek tragedy. Is this to be read as an inexpungeable trace of the old, omnipresent lex talionis, softened in capitalist times by the "douceur du commerce"? At any rate, both these features raise suspicions, not only about the nonsubjective nature of Aristotelian emotions (his analysis did after all focus on their uses in oratory and public deployment), but also about the radical differences between this supposedly democratic Athenian society, this citystate or polis so universally admired by our Western political theorists, and the dynamics of our modern world.

The crucial clue is given in the following offhand remark of the Stagirite, part of a well-nigh dramaturgical exploration of the situations

---

22 Aristotle, *Rhetoric*, trans. W. Rhys Roberts, New York: Dover, 1954, Book II, 2, 1380.

in which anger arises (and can be subdued): "We are not angry with people we fear or respect, as long as we fear or respect them; you cannot be afraid of a person and also at the same time angry with him."[23] This will surely be felt as an odd view indeed, until we begin to appreciate to what degree Aristotle's system, and Greek or at least Athenian society generally, is criss-crossed and saturated by yet another fundamental binary opposition we have not yet mentioned: that of social hierarchy and the all-embracing contrast between high and low, between those above me in the social scheme of things and those below. Indeed, on closer inspection everything seemingly random or empirical about Aristotle's selection of emotions for his basic list falls into place around this fundamental opposition. We cannot be angry with people above us, people we respect or fear: indeed, a slight administered by one of them is much more likely to arouse fear than it is anger. It is around this axis that the systematicity of Aristotle's theory of the passions is organized, an axis that accounts for the peculiar and rather for modern tastes offensive account of pity and also for the terminal position of emulation, which sums everything up (and is virtually positioned as a kind of variation on envy): the imitation of my betters, the rivalry with my equals, the unremitting competition of this society, which Pericles praises as "rash" and "reckless" (in Nietzsche's translation) and for which David Konstan's characterization seems rather mild:

> the world that Aristotle evokes in his account of the emotions is highly competitive. It would appear that the Greeks were constantly jockeying to maintain or improve their social position or that of dear ones, and were deeply conscious of their standing in the eyes of others. When ordinary people stepped out of the house and into the streets of Athens, they must, on the basis of the picture Aristotle draws, have been intensely aware of relative degrees of power and their own vulnerability to insult and injury.[24]

In fact, this is a truly terrifying view of a social formation that has aroused admiration at least since the Renaissance and has been for many

---

23 Ibid., 1385.
24 David Konstan, *The Emotions of the Ancient Greeks: Studies in Aristotle and Greek Literature,* Toronto: University of Toronto Press, 2007.

cultures the very image of an ideal communal organization and of egalitarian social relations (save for women and slaves). But it was René Girard who reminded us (from the most intelligent conservative standpoint) that it is the most egalitarian societies that are the most rivalrous, the most litigious, and the most given to competition for status and prestige, and thereby to the central passion of envy, with its accompanying violence. (Indeed, I am tempted to rewrite Aristotle's emphasis on revenge very much in that spirit.)

We also tend to forget Hegel's insistence on the contradictions of the polis: the famous Antigone chapter of the *Phenomenology* does not take sides between the family (the clan) and the state but rather charts the irresolvable structural tension that will spell the end of both and accounts for the disappearance of the Greek world organized around the city-state. (In his *Aesthetics* it will live its demise in satire and laughter and in the transformation of the Olympians into sheer caricature.) It is the political form of the city-state (whether it be Athens, the Italian communes, or Rousseau's Geneva) which knows an absolute structural limit—one historically transcended by the unique promotion of one of them into that structurally very different social formation which was Rome, or Empire as such, a form now projecting a new universal religion (which ends up turning the pagan gods and personifications into so many demons).

Here we reach the vital center of this whole argument: the constitutive relationship between the system of emotions and the social formation itself. The face-to-face Utopia is a suffocating society, in which everyone knows everyone else and the citizens (the males) live in public at all times. Social life is a perpetual judgment: everyone is judged (seen) at all times and at all times judges everyone else. Not even friendship (a kind of truce, a sham equality) is free from its imminent danger. Only modern aristocracies, modern ethnic groups, or Barbara Rosenwein's "emotional communities"[25] can use such intimate group structures positively, but they do so primarily as a defense against that larger form which is the nation-state.

What takes the place of the city-state in the ancient world—the universal Empire—is a rather different kind of equality, that of the

---

25 Barbara Rosenwein, *Generations of Feeling: A History of Emotions, 600–1700*, Cambridge: Cambridge University Press, 2015.

subjects in the face of that lone supreme Subject who is the emperor (until his structural place is taken by God himself). The stifling otherness of the polis—fantasized as a homeland by the modern metropolis—gives way to a different kind of permanent judgment in the desert wastes of the anchorites; and the Aristotelian (and Stoic) systems are transformed into the various systems of sins that no antique "virtues" can redeem. It is a transformation that takes place as it were behind the back of the Empire and its legions and bureaucrats; the foundational assassination of Julius Caesar is in reality fulfilled by the execution of Christ in a properly allegorical procedure.

This momentous transformation can best be measured by three fundamental developments. The first, already touched on, is the substitution of a ubiquitous and internal Other, whose presence is the source of tireless observation and judgment, for the suffusion of otherness and judgment in the daily life of the older city-state. This internalization will bring subjectivity into view as something like an autonomous space in its own right: not the habits and customs we attribute to premodern peoples and their externally observed behavior, but rather a space of what we like to think of as self-consciousness or reflexivity in which self-judgment is always possible, bringing relativism with it, and in which, virtually for the first time, the construction of subjectivity can itself be witnessed in action. Virtually all theories of modernity—most of which, as I have tried to show elsewhere,[26] fail to acknowledge their own representational dilemmas—turn on the emergence of individuality, self-consciousness (Descartes), Western humanism, and the like in ways that are no longer satisfactory in the context of globalization. If I locate the infrastructural preconditions of this contemporary construction of subjectivity in population, this has little enough to do with sheer number, or with universality either as a logical category, but rather with the cultural diversity confronted by a "democratic" religion (or an imperial ideology). Allegory is itself a first sign and symptom of such radical cultural differences as it seeks to reconcile Judaic, Roman, and many other mentalities and to invent transcoding systems capable of accommodating them. Theology itself, as a figural system, is an attempt to

---

26   See Fredric Jameson, *A Singular Modernity,* New York: Verso, 2013.

construct "hegemonic empty signifiers" able to achieve something similar on a vaster scale.[27]

The second significant feature of the process will then involve the adaptation of the older classical systems of emotions to the new framework, something that includes two fundamental steps or stages. In the first stage, the classical oppositions between pleasure and pain will be sublated into that between positive and negative, and virtually all the codified or named emotions will be revalenced into negative quantities and marked as sins. The process underscores the function of taboo in the construction of subjectivities, which, as with toilet training in individual psychological formation, must necessarily rely on exclusionary violence (inasmuch as pleasure is not natural but learned and positive incentives are thereby "unnatural" and derived or secondary supplements). But what must be underscored in the present context is that for human animals, language learning is the primary form of such violence; and we have already insisted on the way in which naming is a first form of alienation. The emotion in question is thus disciplined first and foremost by its endowment with a name, which marks its difference, separates it off from the phenomenological stream, and thereby opens it to judgment, evaluation, and taboo. Aristotelian society was in that sense "other-directed" and reinforced its emotional systems by shame and by social hierarchy; the new imperial world system must, however, revise these names into a set of sins, in which internal guilt can be called upon to reinforce some more external policing system.

But there is yet another peculiar feature of "anger" as a named concept which has significant consequences in a different direction, namely for the transition to properly Christian systems of emotion as well as the dawning gap between the Aristotelian and the Stoic views on emotion and what is to be done with it. The Greimas semiotic square[28] (which ultimately derives from Aristotelian logic in the first place) is useful at this point: the crucial clues as to the difference between the systems of emotions of the various cultures (or historical periods) can generally be found in their omissions, in the absences of the positions one would

---

27 The term is that of Ernesto Laclau and Chantal Mouffe, in *Hegemony and Socialist Strategy: Towards a Radical Democratic Politics*, London: Verso, 2014.

28 See Appendix A.

Psychological: Emotional Infrastructures

expect them to fill (such as grief, in the Aristotelian table of the elements), and in the new functions for which such additions or blank spots prepare them. The Greimas square is an instrument for detecting such gaps or absences and thereby for preparing a comparative superposition of systems, as one might lay one transparency upon another.

The square had as its philosophical (and linguistic or semiotic) intent the enlargement of the starting point of structural linguistics in the simple binary opposition—one of those luminous principles about which it can be said, like the Cartesian cogito, that its conceptual productivity depends on being able to get out of it in the first place. Now, in its more elaborated form in the square, we find two distinct binary oppositions set in relationship with one another (not unlike Louis Hjelmslev's analogous four-term system) in such a way that the ambiguities of a given term become its field of exploration and expansion, rather than its breakdown in confusion.

The semiotic square in other words disambiguates by way of two distinct negations, the one specific, the other general. (That their logical nomenclature should be the contrary and the contradiction, respectively, in the reverse of a modern dialectical terminology is little more than an annoying technical problem.) An initial term, in other words, will stand in an inextricable relationship of negation and definition with a specific opposite number, at the same time that in a more general way its meaning will be generally cordoned off from everything it is not. It seems appropriate to reserve the term "binary opposition" for the first of these negations, which is more generally social and situation-specific, X and anti-X, for example; while the second is the simpler yet more generalized negation, namely non-X:

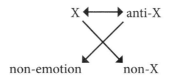

What happens in the missing fourth position, which ought to be labeled *non-anti-X*, is the speculative moment of this analysis and involves, as we shall see, an interpretive leap.

The relevance of this seemingly overcomplicated apparatus becomes clearer in the context of the topic just raised, namely the position of anger in the Aristotelian system of emotions. For in light of the Greimas square it will immediately be clear that what is anomalous about anger is that it has no binary opposite, something no doubt as exasperating for Aristotle as for us, inasmuch as his preference lies in the sorting out of emotional phenomena into just such pairings. To be sure, he supplies a term for the missing "emotion"—*praotes*—a word whose translation poses well-nigh insuperable problems. Liddell and Scott propose *soothing* or *taming*, but these words are dramatistic, as Kenneth Burke might say: they inevitably suggest a whole impersonal scene, in which one person tames or soothes the affected party (two quite different operations, one might add). A standard translation of the *Rhetoric* proposes the term *calming down* but that also, in its evasive wavering between transitive and intransitive, does not seem to be any more adequate for Aristotle's requirements here (why not call it *pacification*?). In the most admirable and extensive book on the Aristotelian emotions, David Konstan follows this usage, finally, however, proposing an alternative in one of Hegel's favorite words, *satisfaction*: but that is a good deal more than a mere translation, it is a whole philosophical program in its own right and not necessarily to be attributed to Aristotle.

One sees what the translators—and indeed, the philosopher himself—meant by these various attempts (the Greek word is itself a kind of translation in its own right): the opposite of *anger* is *no longer being angry* or perhaps *not getting angry in the first place*. In short, it is not an emotion, it is simply a state of nonanger, and, as essentially privative, to be ranged among all the other feelings and emotions to be dropped into that particular non-X box. But it is not an anti-anger, as *serenity*, for example, might be: but *serenity* already has its own opposite, which is surely something closer to *worry* (the Heideggerian *Sorge*).

This is then the moment to turn to our other missing term, namely the fourth one, or in other words *non-anti-X*, or in other words something that is neither anger nor its mysterious opposite. I believe that what emerges at this point is not the absence of anger but the absence of emotion altogether, and that the distinction marks the watershed between the two lines of Graeco-Roman ethics, which may be identified as the Platonic-Aristotelian and the Stoic, respectively. For the former, dealing with the emotions, which they called *passions* (Cicero calls them *turbulences*), meant finding or inventing a. harmony among them, as the Aristotelian search for a "mean" may already have suggested. Thus the solution to the problem of finding an opposite for anger will involve a kind of splitting of the thing itself and a reorganization of the opposition around that between justified or righteous anger and a type we moderns might characterize as irrational.

But the Stoic "solution" is quite different: it involves the attempt to rid oneself of emotion or passion altogether: not the management of anger, its domestication into a tolerable and even socially useful kind as opposed to a destructive force, but its thoroughgoing elimination in the name of *apatheia*, the absence of all emotions (and perhaps a more meaningful candidate for the proper use of a term like *serenity*).

There is, however, another way of looking at all this. We have hitherto restricted ourselves to logical categories; it will now be more productive to rethink the problem in terms of Gestalt psychology, where a figure (or form) is in general opposed to a "ground" and where we may observe the beginnings of a more properly allegorical process. For in order for anger to constitute a distinctive figure in its own right, it will require a neutral background; just as the experience of anger will only be consciously and dramatically perceptible when it erupts against a background of calm (of a momentarily Stoic apatheia).

At this point the investigation turns into a representational problem: how can an emotion like anger best be staged? In a struggle with its opposite number? Or against the background of a lack of feeling? (The classic situation will obviously be one in which Nestor, or some other equally wise counselor, urges calm and moderation on his angry colleague, Achilles or Agamemnon, gripped by an uncontrollable rage.)

To put it another way, do we always feel emotion? Is emotion a permanent feeling-tone of human life, whose contents are in constant flux and modification, but which persists in one form or another throughout the waking day? Or are we mostly in a state of mild and reasonable activity or contemplation which is merely from time to time interrupted by those overwhelming perturbations we know as the emotions or the passions? To put it this way is to see that the first alternative confronts us, not with "normal" human beings, but rather with a pathological individual at every moment caught up in drama and in obsessive self-absorption and immoderate feelings: someone with whom, as they say, it would be difficult to live.

There is a kind of claustrophobia about such an existence, in which emotions succeed each other without a pause, and in which it becomes difficult to distinguish or even to represent them with any specificity, unless, indeed, one invents a new name for the whole series, for the flow itself, taken not as one distinct emotion following another, but rather a pathological process in its own right: a single overwhelming feeling or character trait, which can only be observed and represented by contrast with that "ground" that is the feeling tone of "normal" people. Strindberg was surely the epic poet of such a pathology, of which Nuri Bilge Ceylan's film *Winter Sleep* gives a recent representation. It is most often, however, to be found in the battle of the sexes, as in Albee's classic *Who's Afraid of Virginia Woolf?*; but Ceylon's figure is more reminiscent of Dostoyevsky and old man Karamazov.

Meanwhile, it certainly seems possible for the "ground" itself, that absence of emotion against which the specific emotion is perceived and registered (and recognized by name), to turn into a kind of emotion in its own right, at which point it can itself be openly diagnosed as a pathology, an indifference of the type identified as depression, if not as that melancholy which has taken such a central place in affect theory. The "ground" then, the nonemotional background against which the individual emotion is itself perceived, is an ambiguous space that can be foregrounded in its own right under certain circumstances (those of daily life, ideology, social formation) when it is not simply attributed to other people as they form a kind of objective background to my own subjective "stream of turbulences."

There will be more to say about this, but for the moment I want to suggest that it is the perception of the emotion as such, as it is observed in its eruption against the background of that peaceful void of the nonemotion generally, that is also the very emergence of allegory. The emotion—anger, say—is already allegorical in its own right, insofar as we perceive it as a separate entity and (what is even more important) ratify that perception by endowing it with a specific name (in other words, the word *anger*).

In a sense, then, the formal problem of some neutral ground against which to identify the (now allegorical) emotion is at one with the moral or psychological therapeutic question of a cure for the emotions or "turbulences" generally. Aristotle's problem—finding a specific opposite number to the named emotion called *anger*—has morphed into the more general one of a relief from emotions altogether, a state not available in the Aristotelian system but which the Stoics found themselves able to name *apatheia* or *ataraxia*.

The real question lies here: whether we experience emotions all the time (such is, I think, the premise of affect theory), or whether we are normally free of emotions in such a way as to undergo their intermittent ravages as a genuine event, as a specific and distinctive experience that can be described and theorized. The adherents of moderation suggest that we cannot do away with emotions altogether but must find some way of living with them and of minimizing their harmfulness; thus, for example, they do not recommend doing away with anger, which can be righteous, as we put it, but only of avoiding its excesses. And of course the insistence with which, following Aristotle, I have stressed the emotions of the citizens of the polis gives us another, different but analogous, and equally inescapable picture of a reality we can never escape, and in which we can never hope for some absolute freedom from incessant reactions to our social world.

Stoicism, meanwhile, would seem to offer the hope of a place outside the social world in which a certain relief is at least momentarily possible, dependent on our moral outlook, from a system of emotions which is an uninterrupted series of reactions to those omnipresent others who constitute the polis as such. This is the sense in which Stoic psychology can be seen to reflect the vaster social space of the emergent Roman world that eventually replaces the network of the closed city-states in which Aristotelian psychology was at home.

And this is also the moment to affirm the fundamental argument in play here, which has hitherto only sporadically surfaced: the identification between the system of emotions in question and the structure and dimensions of the collectivity in which individuals feel and identify them. Just as in a simpler world, radical differences were evident between the psychology of country people and those of the big city with its anonymity and labyrinthine space, so now one can observe a transformation of the psychology of the citizens of the city-state, as they were codified by Aristotle, and those that emerge from that unique city-state which supplants the Greek (and Alexandrian) system and whose imperial universality eventually endows itself with the elaboration of a new kind of universal religion. The stifling Greek social life, subject to an uninterrupted sociability that inevitably stimulates that continuous irritation of the individual psyche we interpret in a stream of recognizably modern "emotions" now slowly gives way to a cosmopolitanism and a stream of anonymous encounters only comparable to Georg Simmel's descriptions of the modern metropolis as a set of continuous stimuli that can no longer be handled by classical methods.[29]

The new universal and imperial religion will come at the problem (which is in reality one of cultural revolution) in a different way from the Stoics, who promised their elites the possibility of temporary withdrawals and intermittent relief. It will rearrange the relationship between traditional psychology and those other systems of judgment and classification that are the separation between the physical and the mental (body and soul) and the axis of pleasure and pain, thereby allowing a negative judgment to be extended to all the "turbulences" indifferently, in that codification of emotions as sins we owe to the great Evagrius in the declining years of the fourth century AD. It is a genealogy which explains why the so-called theological virtues, which endow the sins with a well-nigh Aristotelian opposite number, have initially nothing to do with this first system but are, scholars tell us, a later grafting, which clearly presents practical and pastoral (even, as with Dante, poetic) advantages, but which is scarcely intellectually rigorous at this point in the transition.

Meanwhile (and this is the crucial development), a new foyer of otherness is created—one that can be international and universal by way of the omnipresence of God—to replace that inescapable and implacable permanent process of judgment and the struggle of reputations in the classical polis. The Greeks had a diffuse system of friend and foe, of superior and inferior, to organize their subjectivities so as to create value and make evaluation possible. Now, however, a disembodied witness, an omnipresent Other, can replace all those immediate judgments and make possible the prolongation of this hitherto far more immediate and social system of emotions even in the desert and its unpeopled wastes: the desert now becomes the theater and the locus of the intellectual capital city of this Roman world, Alexandria, which, neither Jerusalem nor Rome, houses that fundamental struggle between Greek philosophy and Judaic religion that will transform the subjectivities of the ancient world.

The judgment of God, then, permits a new kind of introspection, in which I can follow his inventory, as in a mirror, of my inner events and

---

29 Georg Simmel, "The Metropolis and Mental Life," *On Individuality and Social Forms*, Chicago: University of Chicago Press, 1972, 324–39.

gradually experience them in some new and interiorized form. The codification of the emotions as sins now for the first time allows a characterology to appear, a synthesis of the Aristotelian system of emotions and its counterpart in physical doctrine, most notably that of the four humors. Now for the first time a table of figures becomes possible in which physical and physiological positions combine with emotional dominants and subordinates to produce caricatural stereotypes of the various structurally possible configurations of the social world. Allegory is reborn with this possibility of a systemic review of social positions; linking characterology with external class and geographical (ethnic) positions, it releases that flood of images which organizes our social experience from Theophrastus to the modern ethnic hatreds and racisms. The inner register of possible sins, which constructs a new and interiorized subjectivity, then links up with external features to make a daily mapping of social experience possible even at the scale of worldwide cultural stereotypes.

Now I have dwelt on this historical transition so insistently for a reason, which has to do with its analogy to contemporary developments. The supersession of the polis by the empire presents many analogies with the vaster scale of the contemporary supersession of the national by globalization. The forms of experience of the nation-state were, to be sure, in many ways as oppressive as those of the polis, imposing an oppressive national identity on its subjects but at the same time releasing an extraordinary flourishing of cultural speculation and production. Today, it is the national formative limits that risk dissolution in the newly global reorganization of capitalism, which threatens to invalidate all the categories of national modernity and national modernism and to transform them into new social and psychological formations we can today only imperfectly imagine, but of which the Soviet revolution and the new images of socialism that emerged from it remain a significant anticipation, as does religious revival and religio-political rivalry on a world scale (Alain Badiou's identification of Saint Paul with Lenin is here symptomatic): both in some sense foreshadowings of the standardization and universal commodification of the world market.

As for Stoic apatheia, it survives at best in the concept of a state of grace, or in some "third" state of consciousness beyond the physical and the mental alike, which—paradoxical anticipation of Joachim's tripartite history, Spinoza's third kind of knowledge, or even of the Hegelian moment of the "speculative"—Origen already posits as an ultimate term of the purification of the soul.

This glorification of a salvational lack of feeling as some virtually unattainable perfection of spiritual development will have already implicitly transformed the earlier static or synchronic systems of emotions into a new kind of dynamic one, most dramatically in Dante's version in *Purgatorio* (as opposed to the eternally static rings of *Inferno*). Dante went on to try to project a hierarchy of perfectabilities in *Paradiso*, but other forms of a pure or purified consciousness are also conceivable (as most famously with the Cartesian cogito). What is then novel is this reorientation of the universal scheme in a temporal or developmental (even historical) direction.

As for the various systems of the emotions themselves, we have previewed their attempts to move toward a kind of materialist monism earlier in this chapter. This spells the end of personification, whose ramifications are dealt with later in this book. It also has the result of restructuring the structural system of the emotions in several consequential ways and in particular in generating the same kind of high–low bifurcation to be observed in the modernist moment of literature, in which an elite or experimental high literature separates itself from a lowbrow entertainment production organized by a nascent culture industry.

On the more noble, philosophical level, the waning of the named emotions has had rather different and sometimes quite unexpected results. Affect theory is surely in one sense a predictable reaction to the psychological materialism and monism set in motion by Hobbes and culminating in cognitive brain study. Dialectically, it is less surprising that these two seemingly antithetical research interests of affect and physiology should combine in various proposals for this or that specific linkage. Nor can it ultimately have been any great shock to neutral observers to witness a resurgence of the old materialist–idealist debates today, at a time when the older idealisms and spiritualisms have virtually disappeared.

What is symptomatically more interesting is that return to a Kantian problematic (and even an improbable revival of Whitehead!), which has been publicized under the slogans of "speculative realism" and "object-oriented ontology" and which offers us a "democracy of things" in which humans and inanimate things are dealt with as equals, and Nature and whatever you want to call its opposite (consciousness? spirit? life?) are no longer divided along subject–object lines. The connection between affect theory and this new turn toward objects and the inanimate is described thus by one of its most astute commentators:

> the thing withdraws into its network, luring me into the shadows, and it bursts forth in a splendor that dazzles and blinds me . . . The "lure for feeling" [Whitehead] is anything that, in some way, works to capture my attention. It may entice me, or incite me, or seduce me, or tempt me, or compel me, or even bludgeon and bully me . . . things *proposition* me or . . . they offer me certain "promesse de Bonheur" (Stendhal).[30]

For a more dispassionate observer (for whom philosophies, as indispensable as they are in articulating new feelings and relations to a historically world, are still essentially *symptoms*), the new philosophy reflects the coming of what Wyndham Lewis used to call "the human age," that is, the obliteration of a former nature by man-made objects of all kinds (very much including the information technology which constitutes a dialectically new stage in this humanization). The commodity world having become a "second nature" (to use Lukács's formulation), we rightly now obscurely feel that we are, in some way, among ourselves: this is then some final stage of reification (a word the object-oriented philosophers ought proudly to reclaim), in which we may expect all the old systems of emotions to play some part, just like the attraction–repulsion formula dramatized by Shaviro above. But affect theory has the advantage of overruling the distinctive bundles of particulars and characteristics mobilized by the emotional systems, in favor of flows and unarticulated rising and falling scales that dissolve the hitherto named moments into a multiplicity of feelings it is both impossible and unnecessary to name or to differentiate.

Yet from a historical perspective the ontological debates are irrelevant: if nature has changed and become absorbed by technological humanization, the possibility was already there, in nature itself. If human nature changed again (say around 1980), then the new changes

---

30 Steven Shaviro, *The Universe of Things: On Speculative Realism*, Minneapolis: University of Minnesota Press, 2014, 53–54.

were also present *in potentia*; and in any case, there is no such thing as human nature and probably no such thing as nature, either. But in place of the idea of a global transformation of the world of objects into so many sentient beings (along with the call for a concomitant adaptation of our subjectivities), I would propose to substitute a postmodern Malthusianism, in which it is the immense and inconceivable proliferation of otherness in our now unrepresentable "globalized" species population which takes precedence over and indeed subsumes all these other undeniable developments. This is the context in which we may eventually expect a new table of emotions and of their names (or their un-naming) to emerge.

3
Psychoanalytic: *Hamlet* with Lacan

Hamlet continues to inspire new mysteries in postmodernity: the modernist "conflict of interpretations"—each one trumpeting its own "method" (which is to say, its ideology)—giving way to a legitimation of multiplicity, which is less relativistic than it is consumerist: we revel in their styles and pause only to wonder what it is about this peculiar object that arouses so many different readings in the first place. The variety of approaches has thereby been turned into a new problem in its own right—sheer quantity itself inspiring a new and qualitative question. The older readings themselves are by now effortlessly assimilated into so many master-codes, from the humanist to the historicist, from the psychoanalytic to the theatrical-performative: what now demands interpretation is the structure or "dispositif," which encourages so many distinct and seemingly disparate libidinal investments (to use Lyotard's excellent expression).

This development already gives Lacan's meditations on the subject a certain priority, whose experience with psychic investments left him with a most convenient key or master-signifier, namely Desire itself[1]: even more conveniently, it is a usefully empty signifier. What do all these interpretations want? Or rather, reversing the question, what do they think *Hamlet* wants, and why does its "desire" so effectively capture their

---

1 The fundamental discussion of *Hamlet* is to be found in Jacques Lacan, *Seminar VI, Le désir et son interprétation (1958–1959),* March 18 and April 8, 1959.

attention? As our fourfold scheme of allegory certainly presupposes various kinds of libidinal investment, perhaps it can say something useful to this question.

I.

The first two levels posit a text and its "mystical" or allegorical meaning. But as we have here an only figuratively "sacred" text, along with a surplus of spiritual meanings, modern allegory often tends to reverse this order, turning the text itself into a "meaning" for this or that "context," which has become a literal level in its own right. Thus, an allegedly historical reading of *Hamlet* proves on closer scrutiny to be an operation in which Shakespeare's play is itself taken to be a symptom (or interpretation) of a historical narrative now posited as the true or literal level of events: we claim to be using history to understand *Hamlet*, but in fact it is *Hamlet* we are using to understand history, that is to say, to construct a historical level or narrative in the first place. This slippage, this insensible shifting of levels in which the object of interpretation has changed places, is characteristic of much of modern allegory, owing to the disappearance of any universally acknowledged master text such as Homer or the Scriptures; but as for the history involved, I think it simply most often means "modernity," that is to say, the transition from feudalism to capitalism, or the emergence and nature of this last; and *Hamlet* is no exception.

Brecht thought it was about militarism, as his magnificent sonnet suggests:

> Here is the body, puffy and inert
> Where we can trace the virus of the mind.
> How lost he seems among his steel-clad kind
> This introspective sponger in a shirt.
>
> Till they bring drums to wake him up again
> As Fortinbras and all the fools he's found
> March off to battle for that patch of ground
> "Which is not tomb enough . . . to hide the slain."

> At that his too, too solid flesh sees red.
> He feels he's hesitated long enough.
> It's time to turn to (bloody) deeds instead.
>
> So we nod grimly when the play is done
> And they pronounce that he was of the stuff
> To prove "most royally," "had he been put on."[2]

But we can just as easily construe his meaning—shorthand for the Thirties but also for the long Cold War—as feudalism, and even more narrowly as late feudalism, namely that strange and unclassifiable moment of the absolute monarchy, a moment that could just as easily be seen as the climax of the feudal system (liege lords, feudality, loyalty to the great clans) as on the other hand the laborious attempt to overcome its anarchy in national unification. From that perspective, the fundamental task of the new absolute monarch (amply represented in Shakespeare's own history plays) was to subdue the warring feudal barons and, in a grisly reversal of Freud's own myth of the primal horde, to castrate them all: Rossellini's grand vision of *La Prise de pouvoir de Louis XIV*, indeed, demonstrates the enactment of that program, which turned the great nobles into drones by forcing them to leave their estates and to live all together in a Versailles in which they are little more than the slavish ornaments of a richly overdressed personnel. Marc Bloch's classic book on feudalism, indeed, detected two contradictory systems at work in the catch-all term: on the one hand, the system of loyalties that link liege lords and vassals within the clans of feudal nobility, on the other, the relations of exploitation between landlord and serf.[3]

Given these ambiguities, we may be entitled to introduce a third one involving a doubtful etymological relationship of the "feudal" with the feud as such, thereby staging the entrance of the first of our interpreters, René Girard, whose version turns less around his influential theory of mimetic desire than on that of the essentially religious recourse to an external mediator.[4]

---

2 Bertolt Brecht, *Collected Poems, 1913–1956,* London: Liveright, 2019.
3 Marc Bloch, *Feudal Society,* London: Routledge, 1962.
4 René Girard, "Hamlet's Dull Revenge: Vengeance," *A Theater of Envy: William Shakespeare,* Oxford: Oxford University Press, 1991.

Girard's historical imagination is stirred, above all, by the interminability of the great blood feuds of the ur-historical tribal world, as documented by Jules Henry in his *Jungle People*:[5] blood feuds between tribes (which are not yet even clans in our modern sense) that last for generations, the original slaying to be repaid now lost in the mists of time immemorial. This dizzying nightmare of history, which suddenly sparks the prophetic impulse in a thinker already equipped with his master theory of mimetic desire (that is, of the dependency of the human being on the model of the Other's desire), now unexpectedly casts a garish new light on Shakespeare's play, the final form of the so-called revenger tragedy, and a tale of the blood feud scarcely sublimated by the attribution of it to royalty itself.

We may omit for the moment the ethical controversies to which this view of *Hamlet* inevitably gives rise (and which Girard himself revives): namely, the immorality of the assumption on which it seems based, that it is right and proper for the offended party to kill the offender. Girard thinks that Shakespeare's play was written to disprove this uncivilized assumption by way of a bloody object lesson. Bernard Shaw thought something similar before him; but 'tis no matter. For us here and now the essentials lie in the breakdown elements of feudalism: on the one hand, the residual memory or legacy of the great clans, memorialized in feuds and familial or dynastic competition (for Girard, indeed, this particular original sin is even to be detected in the aggressivity that individualism and social equality brings with it, the aggressivity of a well-nigh Lacanian mirror stage)[6]; and on the other hand, the generational dilemma of the feudal primus inter pares, the questions of royal succession and of the authority of usurpers: a dilemma that cannot be solved by pure reason, whence Hegel's transformation of sovereignty—the monarch—into a mere empty unifying point.[7]

This is not a matter of the older biohistorical criticism, in which current events or people in the author's life are laboriously identified in

---

5 Jules Henry, *Jungle People*, New York: Vintage, 1964; and see also, more notoriously, Napoleon Chagnon, *The Yanomamö*, Belmont, CA: Wadsworth, 1997.

6 Lacan's mirror stage explicitly includes aggressivity: see "The Mirror Stage as Formative of the *I* Function as Revealed in Psychoanalytic Experience," *Écrits*, trans. Bruce Fink, New York: W. W. Norton, 2006.

7 G. W. F. Hegel, *Elements of the Philosophy of Right*, ed. Allen W. Wood, Cambridge: Cambridge University Press, 1991, n. 281, 323.

a kind of one-to-one allegory in the works as such. What is at stake rather is the ideological confusion of contradictory categories within the "political unconscious" of the contemporaries (author and spectators alike). This does not mean that some of the situations in the work may not reproduce historical memories in a suspiciously analogical way: thus, in his little study *Hamlet oder Hekuba*,[8] Carl Schmitt reminds us that the situation of a king murdered by a queen's lover who then assumes his throne already took place in reality some twenty years before Shakespeare's play in the neighboring kingdom of Scotland (Mary Queen of Scots and Bothwell). But for Schmitt this is worth mentioning, not because it is supposed to have suggested his plot to the dramatist (who was in fact using an ancient story already recently revived in more or less contemporary form by Kyd): but rather because it supplied the answer to one of the lasting problems about Shakespeare's version: why the Queen's innocence (or guilt) is not satisfactorily resolved in the play itself. For Schmitt the answer is clear enough: to declare Gertrude innocent is to offend Elizabeth, who put her real-life counterpart to death; to declare her guilty is to offend the sovereign's most likely successor, the son of the lady in question (and future patron of Shakespeare's company). To leave the matter unsolved is then the best part of valor and an uncertainty that can only heighten the suspense Shakespeare necessarily needs to infuse into his remake of this now familiar old play.

Carl Schmitt borrows Benjamin's distinction between *Trauerspiel* and *Tragödie* (they were mutual admirers) and reverses it, locating the binding nature of tragedy, as opposed to everything *spielerisch* in the *Trauerspiel*, in the way in which through it history "intervenes" in the aesthetic. For the Greeks that "history" was what we call *myth*, and it carried the conviction that the events in which those legendary gods or heroes were inextricably involved were historically archetypal. In modern times, it is the relationship of *Hamlet* to the "tragedy" of the Stuart family—the execution of Mary Queen of Scots, the accession of James I/VI, in other words, the historical core of Shakespeare's play— which for Schmitt demonstrates a different relationship between the Elizabethan public and "current events" than in our own time, or with the Greeks either.

---

8 Carl Schmitt, *Hamlet oder Hekuba*, Düsseldorf: Klett-Cotta, 1956.

Although Schmitt and Girard both indulge in tirades against the contemporary taboo on biographical criticism, Schmitt wants this exercise to be something rather different than the hunting of sources and models in the archives (what he calls "das Bildungswissen um die Geschichte, das bei den Zuschauern vorausgesetzt werden kann," the historical knowledge that can be attributed to the spectators), but rather an intervention of History itself that gives the public sphere a "common present of time" and that might better be described as a kind of decisive breakthrough of "real" history. It is not therefore a matter of some one-to-one matching of fiction and reality—a superficial kind of topical allegory which can perhaps best be dispelled by thinking of history, not in terms of individual characters and models, but rather in terms of the tragic situations themselves.

Schmitt's conception of the aesthetic function of history—"der Einbruch der Zeit in das Spiel" (his subtitle: the eruption of time itself into the "play")—has indeed something in common with Benjamin's more convulsive and revolutionary notion of the breakthrough of the past in moments of need, that "Jetztzeit" or time of the Now, in which ancient Rome "erupts" into the present of Robespierre's revolution.[9] If so, then Schmitt's interpretation would have to be reread in terms of the deeper categories at work in his correlation of "current events," namely that of sovereignty and usurpation—those at play in his fundamental notion of the "state of exception." In Benjamin, too, the usurper is the secret truth of the Sovereign: for him the inner movement of the "Trauerspiel" (the "funereal pageant") revolves around the triangular relationship between the roles of Usurper, Martyr, and Intriguer.[10] We will see later on that these roles are scarcely absent from *Hamlet*: if Claudius is the obvious candidate for the part of usurper and tyrant, there are also more secret and subterranean readings whereby Hamlet himself occupies all three positions as well. At any rate, categories of our political unconscious such as succession and usurpation are what are profoundly unsettled by certain kinds of representations as well as certain kinds of events; and these are in any case, like all purely political

---

9 Walter Benjamin, "On the Concept of History," *Selected Writings*, vol. 4, Cambridge: Cambridge University Press, 2003, 395.

10 Walter Benjamin, *The Origin of German Tragic Drama*, trans. John Osborne, London: Verso, 1998, 65–74.

categories, internally contradictory ones, subject to slippage and contamination; they are related to what are supposed to be more private or subjective categories, such as incest, marriage, the paternal function, and so forth; and when the two shift, there is a shudder in the world, like the premonition of an earthquake, or like the body's spasm when an elevator falls. It would then preserve Schmitt's commitment to history if we added the specification that this categorical reflex must first be glimpsed in this or that contingent historical event—an assassination, a scandal, a run on the market, the emergence of a new national enemy— before the literary work can then appropriate its deeper experiential content.

This kind of historical criticism is then very different from the kind that searches out topical and historical models: it is a deductive process that moves, step by step and by logical exclusion, and demonstrates what the play is not. What such procedures can do by way of suggesting what the work is and means is simply to deploy current events as symptoms—Elizabeth's hesitations about the choice of her successor (like Hamlet's own procrastination), the question of succession and usurpation raised both by the Essex rebellion and the eventual accession of a foreign monarch: these are so many signs of a profound categorial uncertainty aroused by the contradictions of the late-feudal system itself and of the structural incapacity of the dynastic institution to resolve the generational problem, the dilemma of time and change itself.

As for the revenge format, here indeed we can return to René Girard's anthropological diagnosis and indict the early feudal clan system for this particular structural contradiction, which provides no solution save for a power rivalry and an internecine violence which will inevitably end up producing a centralization in royalty that undermines the system itself (much like monopolies under capitalism).[11]

Hamlet thus can be seen to emerge from a twofold situation that combines the contradictions of both feudalisms, the early rivalry of the clans, the later primacy of the monarch. It activates the conscious or unconscious uncertainties that haunt both, addressing its categorial

---

11   Margaret de Grazia thoroughly explores the archaic, unmodern sociopolitical background of the play in *Hamlet without Hamlet*, Cambridge: Cambridge University Press, 2007. We will come back to regression in a different context at the end of this chapter.

anxieties not as its central thesis but rather as the raw material of its affective mood and as the narrative possibilities of its *Darstellung*. The political level of the text—clearly essential to the theatrical conventions of this genre—is thus not thematic in reference, but rather the secondary expression of deeper collective anxieties about the structural contradictions of the political arrangements of this historical society: here ideology is not the taking of a position on those problems (for example, whether Shakespeare was a Catholic sympathizer or a patriot) so much as it is the dawning confrontation with infrastructural contradiction as such.

But none of this does much to explain why *Hamlet* is so joyous a play, in the sense in which Deleuze uses the word (for which "life-enhancing" would be an adequate substitute only if we understood life as the heightening excitement of the present moment). Empson once explained the density of Shakespearean language by the need to keep the actors interested and to fuel debates and discussions in the green room.[12] It is a welcome and materialist perspective—let us say theatrical-materialist— with which to restore all the "material causes" also at work in *Hamlet*'s place in history, now grasped as the history of the theater: the excitement of the audience is then stirred and aroused by this heightened intensity on stage, which results from the possibility of playing the roles in a variety of different forms and styles, so different from the naturalist assumption that there is just one way of doing it, namely the correct one. Here, in some first approach, we may revive the disagreement between Schmitt and Benjamin and contrast the former's commitment to history with the latter's insistence on the thematics of *Spiel* or play, as it surfaces in the name of the genre (Benjamin wants to distinguish his *Trauerspiel* sharply from an older *Tragödie*) and reaches a climax in Schiller's aesthetics (for Lukács a prefiguration of Marx and disalienation). While Benjamin's conception of Tragödie is nowhere fully expounded—it has to do with fate and silence and emerges from myth as history—it is much clearer that for him the Baroque (whose distinction from the medieval is to be found in the absence from it of the transcendent in a still nonsecular age) grasps history itself as Nature, eternally recurring in its rises and falls, the successions of its dynasties, in which death and

---

12 William Empson, *Seven Types of Ambiguity,* New York: New Directions, 1947, 46–47.

resurrection are seasonal and only the span of a baroque ceiling or sky conveys the heavenly (even the idyll or the shepherds' play "sows history like so many seeds in the earth's motherly soil").[13] For such an aesthetic of immanence, even the formerly tragic is little more than the seasonal passage of the generations, and we catch a glimpse of this nonclosure of the eternal at the end of *Hamlet*. So the "mourning play" will in fact be a playing with natural symbols and recurrent ornamentation: nature is here ornament and profusion, and even the ever-changing stream of named emotions (which we are tempted to assimilate to some postmodern play of affect) confirms Schiller's famous cry about the plants and animals of the natural world: "They are what we were!" In that case, we scarcely need to play at being them. Trauerspiel thereby completes its vocation to treat human history like the "history" of nature, to modify the stunned silences of humans in the face of destiny (tragedy) into the hapless baroque contemplation of the transience of all things.

II

This is the aesthetic recovered in Lionel Abel's unjustly neglected classic, *Metatheater*,[14] in which *Hamlet* becomes a play about acting, and thereby, in its reflexivity, the first truly modern drama and one radically distinct from Greek tragedy (spectacles of cruelty, Nietzsche said, fit only for viewing by the gods). *Metatheater* thus ranges itself alongside all those other theories that combine a thesis about the impossibility of tragedy in our time with an account of the radical difference of modern or often simply realist or bourgeois drama; in doing so, it becomes, in spite of itself, a theory of modernity as such and yet another periodizing and narrative version of the twice-told tale of modern individuality, with this difference, that: it is practical, and that its thesis is neither "performative" in the abstract-linguistic sense nor *Spiel*-oriented in the

---

13 Walter Benjamin. *Selected Writings, Volume II, Part 1,* Cambridge: Cambridge University Press, 1999, 237.

14 Lionel Abel, *Metatheater,* New York: Hill and Wang, 1963. "Hamlet is . . . a man with a playwright's consciousness who has just been told to be an actor . . . he is the first stage figure with an acute awareness of what it means to be staged . . . After *Hamlet* it would be difficult for any playwright to make us respect any character lacking dramatic consciousness." (47, 57–58).

anthropological, but finds its evidence on the stage in the acting itself: and not merely in that openness of the role to multiple interpretations of which we have already spoken, but in the delight of the physical bodies under the lights, making their faces and belting out their lines. We are thereby already in Brecht (one of Abel's prime exhibits), save that here the medium does not here lay out the message ("now from this side, now from that"), but as in its classical formulation, finds it in its own medium: Hamlet is a man of the theater, a producer and director of productions, besides being a madman who acts out his various fantasies. Meanwhile, king and queen famously have their official roles to play; the court is necessarily a place in which etiquette and intrigue require gestures rather than realities. "Sincerity" is in any case a romantic offshoot of this dramatic "insincerity," along with the close-up and method acting; and only Sartre's philosophy (omnipresent in Abel) risks the view that everything we feel and do is acting in the first place. So the stage shows us not rage or jealousy, hesitation, anxiety, love, admiration, confusion, loyalty, fear, or euphoria, but rather the acting out of all these things. In that sense, Hamlet's famous madness, which might have been "real" in Kyd's lost first version, is here patently a simulation that can stand as the very symbol of this meta-acting that characterizes the play as a whole—with this reminder, that just as Hamlet himself occasionally shades over into real delirium, so, too, the reality of all those emotions enumerated above also tends to show through more immediately from time to time. For the acting of them must be given its content by the things themselves: we are not yet in any thoroughgoing phantasmagoria or play-within-a-play (the Romantic emblem—*The Prince of Homburg!*—of that meta-distance from the role under discussion here).

I imagine that for whatever reason—maybe the political situation ruled out anything too close to power for comfort—Shakespeare was confronted with the demand for a remake of an already well-known play, which he had to liven up and modify for commercial purposes. Already the revenger's tragedy itself was old stuff, and Kyd's madman was easily transformed into someone pretending to be mad, but at the same time eluding the easy judgment that he was simply an intriguer in Benjamin's sense, out for power in his own right. From the modern distance of existentialism we can see why "power," the succession, being crowned Hamlet II, means lapsing into being: becoming only that, once and for all, and for good, losing the satisfactions of multiple possibilities—what Goethe and Coleridge thought of "hesitation"—by choosing one of them definitively. Acting, then, becomes the nonpsychological, nonsubjective vehicle for such an allegedly psychological state, which is in fact an ontological one. Hamlet can for the moment be everything and anything, but at the price of being nothing at all (which is no doubt the definition of the actor in the first place).

What is clearly central in this performance of metatheater is the critique of expression as such, a category which is still, at its outer limit rhetorical and at its ideological heart a belief in the existence of a true inner emotion that can be externalized. The player king's famous account of Hecuba's grief is then the definitive enactment of the latter kind of acting and Hamlet's response an implicit designation of the constitutive difference between such rhetorical expression (at its best in Greek tragedy in the form of silence) and this role-playing of it.[15] Meanwhile the distance from the content will not be demonstrated within the character as such (although it is itself acted out in Hamlet's soliloquies); rather, it comes out best in the dialogue, the interplay between the characters, each of whom necessarily has a role to play with respect to the other. The transitional nature of the play is then underscored by this survival of the feudal or courtly role as such, at the moment in which it is becoming a role to be enacted; and the slippages within Hamlet's own expressivity (and to a lesser degree those of Polonius) are to be explained by the constitutive uncertainties of their respective roles (for example, whether Hamlet is an heir to the throne, a son, or an avenger). Here, if we might be permitted a crude and peremptory interpretation, the play serves as a diagnostic symptom of that genuine historical transition which will ultimately "resolve" the feudal contradictions described above: it does not represent them, nor does it express them formally or thematically, but rather designates their effects, in this fluidity of the social roles which evolve and then dissolve in this transition between the two moments of the feudal system.

As for the language itself, Frank Kermode has given us at least one unassailable standpoint in his identification of hendiadys as the

---

15 This is a version of the debate about the "sincerity" of the actor, which rages from Diderot and Brecht to Stanislavski and method acting.

fundamental trope of this play at least, if not of Shakespeare's style in general.¹⁶ Richness then is guaranteed by the overflowing of every named phenomenon into two distinct substantives, which are both the same and different all at once: "the windy suspiration of forced breath" can then be taken as a purely rhetorical figure and exaggeration, or as language's own demonstration of its distance from the object and its capacity to revel in that distance and the differentiations it permits. In a Bakhtinian way we may glimpse here, in the carnavalesque opening and momentary window of Elizabethan style, a moment of freedom between the scrawny emergence of syntax in the Middle Ages (see Auerbach)¹⁷ and the codifications of the baroque era, the counterreformation's dual reforms in terms of Spanish exuberance or French classical discipline. But here this possibility is dependent on the dual ancestry of the English language: its simultaneous Latinate and Germanic roots, which give us two of everything, rather than Heidegger's Germanic Ur-purity or the mongrelized Latin proliferation.

I hesitate to attribute to this constitutive duality the two moments of feudalism designated above, although it should be noted that Kermode himself makes the connection between the trope of dualism and the proliferation of doubling that runs through the play's action and characters. We will, however, certainly encounter such duality on the psychic level as well. For the moment, however, this trope can be considered as an operator of multiplicity.

We must not be too dogmatic on the matter of a philosophy of number. Certainly dualisms have often been signs of closure. But in this case it seems to me that the doublings encourage proliferation; while, if anything, Flaubertian or indeed Ciceronian triplication shuts a sentence down more irrevocably than any multiplication of dual alternatives ever would.

The opening of the language, then, its distance from itself and its object, encourage an immense variety of affect that is a source of this theatrical jouissance to which we alluded above. Not emotions but moods are developed and encouraged here: not Hamlet's anger or his

---

16 Frank Kermode, *Shakespeare's Language*, New York: Farrar, Straus and Giroux, 2001.

17 Erich Auerbach, *Mimesis*, Princeton: Princeton University Press, 2013. I argue in Chapter 7 that Auerbach's fundamental subject was the relationship of the development of syntax to what he called realism ("earthly realism," the realism of the "creature" or the created).

foreboding, not the King's guilty suspicions, not Ophelia's pity or the Queen's rueful hurt, but rather the moods, melancholia, euphoria, eagerness, fury, insolence, disdain; these affects course through the scenes, as it were, spurring its heterogeneity of sheer difference into a succession of tones and keys. "The observations are suggested by the passing scene," as Hazlitt put it,[18] "the gusts of passion come and go like sounds of music borne on the wind." Nor are the characters in any way fixed or monologic in their psychology (Hazlitt again: "Shakespeare was thoroughly a master of the mixed motives of human character"), and each one, as the occasion demands it, can momentarily constitute a vehicle for affective variety—Claudius with his kindness to the deranged Ophelia, the senile Polonius with his spymaster's lucid cunning in the instructions on his son's surveillance, the Queen herself, only occasionally given over to concern for her son in a moment of distraction from courtly festivities. All of which is an excellent and far more comprehensive equivalent for that more restricted gamut of repartee of the fool (le fol, the Renaissance madman), which was not only a staple of the time but also, one can surmise, the part an earlier Hamlet played in the lost first version. To the degree, however, to which this conception of reflexivity as a kind of ontological playacting becomes the narrative of modernity as such, this interpretation can be seen to constitute yet another allegorical level—perhaps, insofar as modernity (and its reflexive individuality) is the dirty little secret of so much historiographic periodization, a new and more satisfactory historical one—but one which has the advantage of illustrating itself in the variety of acts and gestures on stage before us in their form rather than their content.

And this very range is what opens the spectacle up for investment in the psychoanalytic sense, a flow of time and temporalities as varied as a Mahler symphony, and which stimulates Lacan again and again to express his admiration for its useful variety:[19] this "tragedy of desire" (271) is a veritable "phenomenology" (355), "une sorte de cartographie de tous les rapports humains possibles" (449), "comme une plaque tournante où se situe un désir, où nous pourrons retrouver tous les traits du

---

18 William Hazlitt, *Characters of Shakespeare's Plays*, Lexington, KY: Create Space, 2011; page references in text.

19 See note 1; page references to the 2000 noncommercial edition issued by L'Association freudienne internationale.

désir, c'est à dire l'orienter, l'interpreter dans le sens de ce qui se passe à l'insu d'un rêve pour le désir de l'hystérique . . .!" (315). But here, with the indication of a form that fulfills the fundamental structuralist demand for exhaustive permutation schemes, we pass over into the third level of our allegorical system, namely the moral level, or what corresponds to the situation and experiences of the individual subject.

III

I will not here recapitulate the development of the specifically Freudian interpretation of *Hamlet*, which begins, as is well known, with the famous footnote in the first edition of *The Interpretation of Dreams* (where the Oedipus complex is first, with a suitable discussion of Sophocles's play, described and named)[20]: it finds its fullest development in Ernest Jones's article on the subject (later expanded into a book-length study).[21] I should add that Lacan had the greatest respect for Jones, as for many of the first generation of Freud's disciples: the notion of the phallus as primal signifier along with that of aphanisis as the fading of desire (and in Lacan, the fading of the subject as such) are both attributed to Jones. But it would be dishonest not to admit that it is the Oedipus complex which has become the most boring theme of traditional Freudian literary criticism (however much we might still, unlike Deleuze and Guattari in their *Anti-Oedipus*, believe in it). Lacan maintains it along with castration as such: and at that point, as with the classes and class struggle in the most ingenious "Western" or Hegelian neo-Marxist interpretations, the postcontemporary reader may well feel that despite appearances all this is simply more of the same tired old stuff. On the other hand, if we turn the Lacanian castration complex into a mere figure of speech, where the "phallus" simply means the feeling of personal autonomy, strength, renewed identity, and so forth, then one passes just as surely into revisionism as do those post-Marxists who dispense with class and class struggle altogether. The alternative to this postmodern "exhaustion of the raw material" would seem to be the

---

20 Sigmund Freud, *Die Traumdeutung* (*erste Ausgabe von 1900*), reprinted in Frankfurt: S. Fischer, 1999, 183.

21 Ernest Jones, *Hamlet and Oedipus*, New York: W. W. Norton, 1976.

equally unenviable (more Foucauldian) conclusion that even tired old stuff can be true, but then in that case perhaps it is unnecessary to have it repeated. At any rate, in what follows I try to avoid this dilemma by concentrating on what Lacan does say specifically about this or that feature of *Hamlet*; an allegorical level does not need to be systematic or even coherent, it is one code in a larger scheme of things.

This rather pragmatic if irresponsible view is then confirmed by Lacan's own methodological remarks:

> In many works, searching from this viewpoint for this or that trace, for something that can give you information about an author, you practice an essentially biographical investigation of the author himself, you don't analyze the meaning and significance of the work as such. And the meaning that for us takes center stage in *Hamlet* is what gives it its structural equivalence with that of *Oedipus*. What allows us to examine the deepest level of this intrigue, what allows us to structure a certain number of problems, is not this or that passing confession. It is the whole, the articulation of the tragedy itself, that interests us and that I am trying to underscore. This works by way of its organization, by what it constructs in the way of superimposed levels within which the specific dimension of human subjectivity finds its place. And it is by way of this machinery, or if you like by these supports and bearers—to metaphorize what I'm saying—by way of the necessity of a certain number of superimposed levels, the depth of a room, of a hall, of a scene, that a depth is provided within which we can most fully pose our problem, which is that of the articulation of desire.[22]

The seemingly offhand remark about "plans superposés" is the key here, not only for Lacanianism as such, but also for our allegorical framework: levels no doubt, but above all spatial discontinuities as in the cinematic depth shot. These are related but discontinuous dimensions, which will ultimately in Lacan take the form of the orders (Imaginary, Symbolic, Real) or later on the rings and knots of the final period. Yet even before that, the Unconscious itself—however it may be imagined (or not, since strictly speaking and literally it cannot by definition be

---

22   *Écrits*, March 18, 1959, my translation.

imagined at all)—is in absolute discontinuity with the conscious subject, whether in its Freudian or Lacanian forms. Modern allegory then emerges from this strange situation in which somehow discontinuous realities must be placed in contact with one another, and the incommensurables somehow function concurrently.

This makes, then, for an appropriately discontinuous discussion of *Hamlet*, in which the fundamental "diagnosis" (we have seen hysteria briefly rear its head a moment ago, but obsessional neurosis will not be denied its rights either) must not be allowed to supersede other traits or comments, which in principle bear in a more general way on the matter of desire as such. (Indeed the *Hamlet* seminar is formally entitled "Le désir et son interprétation.")

"Qu'on me donne mon désir!" cries Lacan at the opening of one of the lessons. Desire, indeed, has often been grasped as a Lacanian "master code" or interpretive theme (although it is clear that even if it is, it is certainly not the only one); we need first to look at this term more closely. To characterize *Hamlet* as a tragedy of desire, or even the tragedy of desire, as Lacan himself does, is no doubt to confirm this impression. I will for the moment argue against it by suggesting that "desire" in the Lacanian formulation has no content, and that a master interpretive code (normally the second line on our fourfold scheme, and in Christianity, the life of Christ) is constituted by the way in which it translates its objects or texts into this or that specific narrative content or demonstration about last things, metaphysical truths, the nature of reality, and so on—whether that be existential angst, the human condition, class struggle, the Oedipus complex, the self-designating structures of language, aesthetics itself as such—in short, any transcendental or extratextual thematization (of which religion is of course a fundamental paradigm).

Linguistic reification is to be sure a subset of the general reification process inherent in market society, one evidently greatly amplified by information technology, where it reinforces the structural property in language itself that seeks to slow down its own temporality and to organize it into islands of names and nouns. (French has but a single word for both: "le nom.") Philosophers have identified reification under a variety of terms and descriptions, and the word itself has become an example of its own meaning, a class of which it is itself a part, being itself a reified slogan connoting a specifically capitalist form of commodification. Deleuze's idea of the speech as a "mot d'ordre," which must be seen against the background of his general linguistic pessimism—see the tirade against conversation and communication, in *Cinema II*—may also be taken in this spirit: it means "slogan," but the political content is perhaps better grasped by translating it as "party line."[23] Here a theory of linguistic reification becomes a party line, and its presence can be detected in Foucault and Derrida as well, in their very different guises.

Indeed, we may attribute a theory of linguistic reification to Lacan himself insofar as the latter's predilection for -isms and named thought systems stands as a fundamental example of what he termed *university discourse*.[24] De Man has usefully rebaptized it as *thematization*, underscoring the way in which, as in the reappearance of tones in atonal music, such reified terms tend to organize discourse around themselves and to transform a formal linguistic process back into a kind of content, or ideology, or metaphysic. For these three things are in reality the same phenomenon, and all of them the result of reification.

Linguistic reification may indeed be seen as a fundamental feature of the Lacanian system, insofar as its "structuralism" (often taken by the uninformed as the usual glorification of language as some ultimate "determining instance") in reality expresses a deep sense of the form-creating damage done by language to the prelinguistic and on the way in which the "signifying chain" is somehow the scar of a wound it has itself caused. The word in Lacan—which is always the word of the Other—is (following Sartre) a traumatically alienating shock from which one does not recover.

But here, in the context of a conception in which desire is not only unrealizable but ultimately unformulable, the reproach of a master code loses much of its force. What is dialectical about Lacanian desire is that it can be specified as this or that longing for a specific object, but also as its own absence, as the mere will to desire as such, to feel desire in general. Meanwhile, it can also accommodate the experience of a fading or eclipse of desire, and to be sure, it can also lose its individual reference, its

---

23 Gilles Deleuze, "Postulats de la linguistique," *Mille Plateaux*, Paris: Minuit, 1980. "C'est toute conversation qui est schizophrénie, c'est la conversation qui est le modèle de la schizophrénie, et non pas l'inverse" (*Cinema II*, Paris: Minuit, 1985, 299).

24 The theory of the four discourses, in *Seminar XVII*, trans. Russell Grigg, New York: W. W. Norton, 2007.

identification with my "self" and be projected out into the ill-defined labyrinth of the Desire or the desires of an equally ill-defined Other or others; while in the late period, beginning with *Seminar XI*, desire slips into a different kind or concept altogether, namely "drive" (in French, *pulsion*) refashioned out of Freud's infamous and enigmatic "death wish." (At that point, one might be tempted to shift positions—like the Ghost's voice under our feet—and to affirm instead that it is in reality not desire, but the Other that constitutes Lacan's master code.) From his interpretive perspective, then, Lacanian desire is not merely desire or nondesire, it is also not-yet-desire, as Bloch might put it, it is even someone else's desire; the desire to desire; maybe even the desire not to desire. So this thematization is less a code than it is a philosophic injunction to raise the question of desire and its nature on the occasion of a text, rather than a readymade thematics into which to translate a given text.

The argument obviously omits a fundamental connotation of this term, which is its sexual undertow; and we do not need Freud to observe that sexuality is the inevitable tenor of this vehicle, however muffled or mute; and that if we really wanted to avoid those questions (they at once turn metaphysical in the conceptions of human nature they cannot avoid raising), it might have been better to substitute something else, such as the concept of lack or the concept of loss (I will not enter the polemic around these two rivals), both of which are of course absorbed into the larger and more capacious Lacanian abstraction. Still, I have already observed that we cannot remove the sexual, orthodox-Freudian underpinnings of Lacanian psychoanalysis without turning it into one more relatively revisionist philosophical or metaphorical system among others. But is not this the Gödel's Law of all philosophy, that at some point we inevitably reach an hors-texte, a forbidden transcendental signifier, which is to say, the temptation of the metaphysical, of some "theory" of nature or of human nature? (We also remember, however, that in Lacan's formulation there is no metalanguage.)

But what is Hamlet's desire? We are meant to assume a fairly normal (which is to say, functioning) pretraumatic state of things: a student life (Lacan thinks he is about thirty, and so does the gravedigger), having an affair, if not simply a courtship, with Ophelia. (The question of her virginity seems to be one of the more minor cruces of *Hamlet* exegesis.[25]) The clinical developments begin with the death of the father and the queen's remarriage, which, as the first monologue so classically expresses it, issue in the twin effects of mourning and melancholia, very much in the spirit of Freud's famous essay, which, as Alexander Welsh points out, is probably more relevant to *Hamlet* at this stage than Jones's amplification of the famous footnote on the Oedipus complex.[26]

Two primary questions must guide us in this very provisional attempt to organize Lacan's *Hamlet* observations into a study of the play itself. They have to do with the inevitable matter of Hamlet's procrastination (Lacan likes this "pregnant" English word), and that of tragedy as such and the play's relationship to it (or not). This second theme may seem to be a more specialized literary topic, raising as it seems to do the definition of literary genres: but Aristotle's formulation had all kinds of collective and political implications, while the issue of the possibility of modern tragedy has been widely debated and also bears on political life. Meanwhile, as we have seen for Benjamin and for Carl Schmitt, the nature of tragedy and of its opposite, the *Trauerspiel*, is central, and not only to their discussions of *Hamlet*.

The Benjaminian alternative, however, with its component *Trauer* (melancholy), points us in a direction in which the question could have a more than literary significance for psychoanalysis as well. Freud's famous essay "Mourning and Melancholia" figures prominently in any number of contemporary theories (most notably for Derrida) as well as in Lacan's reading of *Hamlet*. In addition to being a question of rituals (which figure prominently in Freud as social mechanisms for completing mourning, as well as in the scene of Ophelia's burial and the doctrinal discussions around it), the analysis of both mourning and melancholia designate a blockage of desire by the loss of the loved object. In the case of Hamlet, however, the situation is even more complex: his initial melancholia emerges with his mother's remarriage, that is to say, with the Queen's absence of mourning, which somehow interrupts Hamlet's own. The revelation that his father was murdered then frees Hamlet from mourning by giving him a task and a new goal (that of

---

25 William Empson, *Essays on Shakespeare*, Cambridge: Cambridge University Press, 1986, 105–7.

26 Alexander Welsh, *Freud's Wishful Dream Book*, Princeton: Princeton University Press, 1994.

revenge); while as we shall see, the mourning for Ophelia (also already a lost object) dispels the block on Hamlet's energies and releases his capacity to act. We will return later to the question (appropriate in any discussion of classical tragedy) of the meaning and effects of the play's dénouement.

As for procrastination, any number of significant "revisionist" discussions of this traditional Hamlet interpretation—pioneered by Goethe and Coleridge—have long since marginalized this theme, not least by pointing out that none of the contemporary audiences had any great problem about Hamlet's alleged delays. The crucial scene here is the decision not to murder Claudius at prayer, which what we may call Empsonian theatrical materialism chalks up to the need to provide a five-act play. Meanwhile other, more moralizing revisionists, from Shaw to René Girard, have wondered whether "procrastination" did not in fact reflect serious "modern" doubts about the very ethics of premodern revenge as such. Does the perspective of desire have anything new to add to these multiple perspectives on an age-old theme, which sociologically, with Goethe and Coleridge, reflected the emergence of the modern intellectual and his differentiation from the political "man of action"? (Goethe, to be sure, as virtual prime minister of the little principality of which Weimar was the capital, incorporated both functions, as did the Faust of Part II.)

At the least, the focus on desire breaks up this theme of delay and forces us to inquire into the circumstances of each of its alleged instances. Violence is in any case a confused ideologeme, and the stabbing of Polonius or the dispatching of Rosencrantz and Guildenstern provides as little evidence of Hamlet's capacity to act as the hesitation before the kneeling Claudius demonstrates his innate characterological irresolutions. But to put all this in perspective, we must return to the essentials of the Lacanian diagnosis. For Freud and Jones, to be sure, the case is clear enough: Claudius has succeeded in doing what Hamlet unconsciously desires, namely to kill his father and marry his mother. Claudius is therefore a kind of alter ego (although of a different kind than the imaginary figure of the Lacanian mirror stage, embodied in Laertes and perhaps even more distantly in Fortinbras): he has, to put it in Lacanian terms, had the jouissance that is forbidden Hamlet, the confusion of desires then falling back on Hamlet's relationship to his mother, whom he must dissuade from that very jouissance in which he (or his unconscious) wishes to substitute himself for Claudius. This is then a double bind, in which at one and the same time he finds himself defending the sexual taboo—in the person of Claudius—which he himself longs to break: a psychology of puritanical repression with which we are only too familiar in the modern day politics of repression.

Our approach to Lacan, however, must start from the premise that *Hamlet*'s interest derives from the protagonist's simultaneous embodiment of the two great variants of neurosis in the Lacanian diagnostic: hysteria and obsessional neurosis. They can succinctly be described and differentiated as follows: the hysteric "desires to desire," he or she does not desire or does not desire enough (the dream of the butcher's wife),[27] desire is itself a problem for this subject. The subject of obsessional neurosis, on the other hand, by neutralizing or occluding desire, wonders whether he or she is alive or dead: not desire is central here, but rather time as such, and a perpetual scrutiny of it. I tend to associate this neurosis with that *Sorge* that Heidegger, following *Faust II*, placed at the heart of the human condition but which we do not properly understand, I think, unless we translate it as worry rather than the more noble-sounding Care. The obsessional neurotic's problem is then this constant worry about a time seemingly empty of a desire that he does not in fact want to experience in the first place. Why? Because it is the desire of the Other, in both senses of the genitive, objective and subjective: it is a desire for the Other, but it is also (in a Girardian mimetic sense) the Other's desire, rather than his own; and indeed, the Other's desire for him, the infant, a desire that is terrifying by virtue of its all-engulfing power.

In this description, however, it is to be noted that the gender of the Other has imperceptibly changed: the masculine or paternal character of the Other has subtly given way to the demands of the maternal Other, primordial, and earliest in time and in the infant's experience. This gender ambiguity in the Lacanian category of Otherness is indeed an interesting originality that we cannot pursue any further here. But it offers the opportunity to restate briefly the fundamental outline of Lacan's theory of desire as such. Desire arises in the gap between need and demand, that is, when the nameless bodily urges of the infant are doubled by its helpless realization that only the Other can supply the

---

27 "Dream of the Smoked Salmon," *Standard Edition IV*, 147; Lacan, *Écrits*, Paris: Seuil, 1966, 622.

lack. Desire is thus always desire of the Other, in the double sense of the genitive: the Other, following the hideous apparition in Cazotte's *Diable amoureux* (a monstrous camel's head that addresses the stentorian question to the protagonist: "Che vuoi?" "What do you wish?") is both subject and object of the infant's own interrogation, which is also to say that the Other is the same as language, the Other is the Symbolic Order or at least its source and guardian. (The Sartrean trauma of the other and the structuralist primacy of linguistics are thus here united.) Yet this intersection of the question to the Other and the prelinguistic (and preunified) body designated by the enigmatic "graph of desire"[28] in which two vectors cross in opposite directions—confluence, Lacan says, of the synchronic and the diachronic, and a kind of psychoanalytic version of the mysteries of the hermeneutic circle—will have yet another, even more mysterious consequence that seems to me less than adequately mapped out by this complex graph (which also includes, as a subepisode the mirror stage and the emergence of the ego), and that is its sedimentation in the primal fantasy:

$$\$ \lozenge a$$

Here a barred subject, the subject of the unconscious, stands in relationship (the lozenge $\lozenge$, Fink tells us, can mean "envelopment, development, conjunction, disjunction ... but is most simply read 'in relation to' or 'desire for'"[29]—a most dialectical relationship indeed) to the little a (or o), the object of desire. Is this primal *fantasme* a narrative or even the cell of a narrative? Does the subject stage itself as an imaginary spectator from the outside to this scene (not exclusively the primal one, I think)?

Insofar as the fantasy of desire is inspired by what was one of the basic texts, not only of the whole structuralist period but of Lacan's own work as well, namely Freud's little essay "A Child Is Being Beaten," we may hazard a few additional conjectures on the relationship between this characteristically Lacanian *matheme* of the primal fantasy and narrative as such. What comes into play in Freud's essay, indeed, is the way in which the unconscious fantasy of the beating constitutes a structural permutation scheme where not only the positions but their very

---

28 See *Seminar VI*, November 12 and 19, 1958; and also "Subversion du sujet et dialectique du désir" in *Écrits*, which is a kind of summary of the Seminar itself.

29 Bruce Fink, *The Lacanian Subject*, Princeton: Princeton University Press, 1995, 174.

functions change. (To be sure, Freud's text bears officially on the problem of perversion, that is, on the missing third possibility in the catalog of neuroses I have given above; but the essay has most often been read in recent years in purely logical or formal, "struturalist," way.) In the original system, with its three logical permutations, the initial fantasy specifies simply that someone (the father) is beating a child to whom I am hostile. In the second configuration, I am being beaten. In the third, there is simply an unidentified beating taking place. For narrative purposes, I will add a fourth possibility (it is in a sense already implicit in the third one), namely that I myself am doing the beating, which would place me in the father's position. All of which means that these "I"s and "me"s are not identities but subject positions, including the neutralized possibility of the purely contemplative spectator viewing all this from the outside. The scheme not only literalizes the concept of a "subject position"; it also recalls those "learning plays" of Brecht in which the actors take all the successive roles in turn in the rehearsals, now heroes, now villains, now secondary witnesses, and so forth. Indeed, it is just such a permutation of roles that the character named Hamlet is called upon to play in his drama, and Lacan will be helpful in allowing us to specify that these roles seem principally to be divided into those of his two fundamental neuroses, hysteria and obsessional neurosis. That the hysteric's search for desire opens the whole gamut of possibilities for Hamlet's languages, affects, gestures, and intentions has already become clear; and the dialectic of hysteria also ensures the alternating moments in which desire is missing and the subject somehow blocked or split, in its "fading" or its castration.

But it is the situation of obsessional neurosis that will for the moment be more productive, for this neurosis is a temporal one, and it means, among other things, that the subject is always "on the time of the Other," his temporality running by the other's clock, his appointments set by the other's schedule, and so on. But this then casts a whole strange new light on the premise of the revenger tragedy as such. We have said that Hamlet is in mourning, and indeed in deep melancholy, by virtue of the superimposed death of his father and remarriage of his mother. The ghost, however, now places him unexpectedly under an injunction that ought to offer the relief of action in the paralysis of that complex mourning, but which in fact complicates it by placing Hamlet under the injunction of the Other. For it is the Father, not Claudius, who is the Other here (and in general), Claudius being, by virtue of the Oedipus complex itself, Hamlet's alter ego. Whatever the truth of the ghost's narrative, it is into Hamlet's ear that its poison is filtered. Hamlet's situation before that was a relatively simple dynastic one: as the legal heir, he needed to decide whether to escape the king's present jurisdiction and to claim the throne in his own right. The shadow of the Fortinbras narrative is there to emphasize this narrative option, in however minor a key; the redeparture of Laertes to his Parisian university drives home another version of the same option.

Now, however, a different Law and a different injunction completely transform what amounts to the very same choice by depriving Hamlet of any freedom of decision in the matter (we must here recall how threatening the desire of the Other is for the subject in the Lacanian scheme of things). More than this, the ghost's peculiar insistence on the mother's exemption from this revenge (whatever political motives Shakespeare may have had to insert it, following Schmitt's ingenious conjectures) is clearly itself a reinforcement of the Oedipal taboo: do not touch the mother. She belongs to someone else (to the father).

Indeed, Lacan's reading of this climactic scene is one of the most remarkable in the whole Seminar. He notes the febrile excitement and intensifying energy with which Hamlet urges his mother to cease all sexual intercourse with Claudius—itself a rather remarkable moment in world literature, as he notes. (Surely this is a quintessential expression of that sexual disgust and revulsion which T. S. Eliot found so inexplicable in this play and in Shakespeare generally.)[30] But even more significant is the collapse of this excitement after the second appearance and intervention of the ghost: a veritable withering and shriveling, as Lacan puts it. After the ghost's warning—the reappearance of the Oedipal father and the threat of castration—Hamlet gives in: he withdraws his absolute demand for Gertrude's renunciation and weakly asks her to reduce her indulgences of Claudius and to moderate her own desire and participation ("and that shall lend a kind of easiness / to the next abstinence"). Here more than anywhere else in the play, Hamlet's own "desire" finds itself rebuked, and the strength of this interpretation is that it can be acted out and realized on the stage. It then casts a retroactive light on

---

30 T. S. Eliot, "Hamlet and His Problems," *Selected Essays*, New York: Harcourt Brace, 1950.

Hamlet's behavior with Ophelia, which has left many respectable critics indignant, but which amounts to a systematic attempt to extinguish "normal" desire for an acceptable object in the light of this "unnatural" revival and reawakening of all the unconscious thoughts that center on the mother.

But then if this is what the emphasis on desire amounts to in Lacan's reading, we need to be more attentive to the ebb and flow of energy itself: when is it aroused, so often in manic form? When does it suffer the kind of "dégonflement" Lacan so perceptively diagnoses in the scene we have just imagined? The arrival of the players is a particularly interesting moment, for Lacan sees in it the momentary chance for Hamlet to occupy the role of the artist and creator, the space of a kind of sublimation that if only for the moment lifts the psychic asphyxiation to which his desire is subject. ("You could, for a need, study a speech of some dozen or sixteen lines which I would set down and insert in it, could you not?" [Act 2, Scene 2].) It has always seemed strange to me that few critics have wondered what those lines actually were and whether—given the interruption of the performance—the actors ever get to speak them. Most conjectures assume that they consist in an attempt to underscore the relevance of the older repertory staple to the current situation, particularly in the account of the murder itself and the peculiarity of its method, the pouring of venomous liquid into the ear (no doubt an Italian inspiration). Instead, the exegetic focus has mainly turned on Claudius's peculiar inattentiveness: why not break things off during the dumbshow, when the very nature of the murder is out in the open for all to see? Was Claudius distracted, or did the murder itself (whose commission is acknowledged by his own outburst) perhaps not take that particular form at all? I believe that the speech of some dozen or so lines had nothing to do with the murder (or indeed with the ostensible aim of this "mousetrap"), but rather with the queen's second marriage, about which notoriously the player queen "protests too much": these lines testify to Hamlet's obsession and document his unconscious hesitations about the rival and alter ego he finds in Claudius himself. Killing Claudius would in that case amount to a kind of suicide and thereby justify the famous soliloquy on this subject, otherwise interpretable as a merely existential interpolation.

As for Claudius's reaction, Lacan seems to me extraordinarily perspicacious in identifying the moment in which he does recoil in surprise and horror from the theatrical spectacle: it is the moment when Hamlet explains the change of title and the transposition of responsibility for the crime from the king's brother in the original to his nephew in this new acting version. The old version suits Hamlet well enough, the change (which he deliberately points out) makes its relevance even more obvious. But look at this change from Claudius's perspective. Who is his nephew? And what is this king's current anxiety?

In fact, Claudius is living in a different plot than that of Hamlet himself: beset in his newly acquired sovereignty by potential enemies on all sides: Norway as well as Hamlet, and later on the Polonius clan and the mob as such; the formerly adulterous relationship—indeed the murder itself—being the least of his worries. The designation of a nephew as a regicide then has for Claudius a very different meaning than it does for the nephew himself (leaving aside the fascinating matter of uncles and nephews inherited from the power relations of the earliest matriarchies).[31] No wonder it is at this point that he cries out in alarm and halts the production.

There follows upon this interesting mismatch—treason along with artistic satisfaction—what is certainly the most probative scene in the play when it comes to the theme of procrastination, namely Hamlet's postponement of his vengeance at the very moment, not only of the snapping shut of his mousetrap but of the greatest vulnerability of Claudius himself, unguarded by any of his retinue. I think we must simply conclude that what this scene proves has little enough to do with theological motives (whether Claudius will in this case still go to Hell or not), nor with any secret moral scruples about the ethics of revenge itself, à la Shaw or Girard, so much as it is a demonstration that Hamlet is not really interested in killing his father's murderer and that he sees no real gratification in it. It does not, in Lacanian terms, really correspond

---

31 If we push a little further here, following distorted unconscious anxieties, not only with succession, but also with the generations and the very continuity of history itself, the uncle becomes a figure of matriarchy, of which anthropologists today tell us behind its Utopia of a feminine non-power lies the authority of the mother's brother. In that cases, and on this level of the allegorical primal fantasy the adulterous union of Claudius and the queen dissolves into a matriarchal power structure, a kind of regression into that earlier mode of production which preceded the patriarchy of the murdered king—a fantasy in which Utopian desire mingles disturbingly with Oedipal loyalties and sexual confusion becomes the very element of political doubt and ideological hesitation.

to his deepest desires; it is not what he really wants—even though we do not wish to suggest by those words that he actually knows what he really wants. It is indeed the strength of the Lacanian perspective here that the "tragedy of desire" it emphasizes is not the failure of desire, let alone its disappointed fulfillment, so much as it is the very search for desire as such. The scene dramatizes the problematization of desire, the mystery not of its fulfillment but of its very content.

Now we come to another of Lacan's great insights, which has to do with the astonishing recovery of Hamlet's energies in the grave scene, another of what Lacan calls the "phallophanies" in which phallic power, personal identity, and the capacity to act are unexpectedly reborn.

The grave scene is distinguished by two new characteristics that seem to have little enough to do with the revenge plot. First of all, it stages a first substantive confrontation with Laertes, Hamlet's boyhood friend, whose "activation" as an actant now for the first time reintroduces the theme of the mirror stage with a vengeance. Hamlet's unconscious identification with Claudius remained within the Symbolic Order and in particular the Oedipal triangle and resulted from the usurper's assumption of Hamlet's position within that triangle, as the adversary of the father and the suitor to the mother's attention and affections.

Laertes, however, is Hamlet's double, his mirror image, and thereby the operator of a self-construction, in which narcissism is difficult to disentangle from aggressivity. This particular rivalry is thus Imaginary and involves what can be termed *ambivalence*, to distinguish it from all the other dialectical varieties of identity and difference that flourish throughout this play. The possibility of an antagonistic relationship to Laertes is then what enables the reassumption by Hamlet of an ego, a self, a personal identity (to use the pop-psychological language current today): "What is he whose grief / Bears such an emphasis? . . . This is I, / Hamlet the Dane." But this is the very assumption of that alienated thing, the name, which reinserts the "subject of desire" back into the alienating social network—as royal, dynastic, son, and heir—as precisely those false identities and mythologies of the self from which the Ghost's message had so traumatically separated him. This assumption of the alienated name is the moment in which Hamlet passes from hysteria—desiring to desire—to obsessional neurosis, being on the time of the other, the false time of the social and court of ritual. The speech in the grave then begins by denouncing Laertes and ends up assuming the latter's rhetorical emotions for the speaker himself. It would be worth exploring further the way in which (as in the player king's Hecuba declamation) rhetoric, bombast, the mere expression of an emotion whose very existence is in doubt, is foregrounded and not so subtly identified and denounced as bombast by contrast with the symptomatic glimpses through a different kind of language of affect as such, of nameless foreboding. ("Thou wouldst not think how ill all's here about my heart. But it is no matter.")

This preprepared Imaginary role of an active self or subject is then reinforced by what happens on the level of desire, and that is the death or neutralization of the "objet petit a" or in other words, Ophelia herself. Now that she is dead, this desire is no longer embedded in the Oedipal entanglements that unexpectedly came to smother it and can be given full-throated expression (without consequences).

But it would be wrong (in my opinion) to see this upsurge in Hamlet's energies as a sign of that renewal of self-confidence and phallic power that will lead him to his final "règlement de comptes." For the sloppy denouement is in reality nothing of the kind; and it tends to reconfirm the Benjaminian position on the *Trauerspiel* as opposed to Carl Schmitt's affirmation of true historical *Tragödie*. What Lacan points out is significant indeed, namely that this final duel with Laertes, from which the settlement emerges and all secrets are revealed, is not Hamlet's act at all, but rather his service in a role Claudius has planned for him: by which I mean not so much conspiracy as rather feudal duty. Hamlet, says Lacan, is "le champion de l'Autre": already reset to the clock of the Other, Hamlet now shows himself willing to do battle for his mortal enemy the usurper—the King—thereby remaining even more deeply mired in his feudal and familial subalternity. It would then be tempting to say that it is rather Laertes who defends the cause of a dead father, were the situation not so artfully confused by Shakespeare as to make even the deeper motive of the encounter (death of Ophelia? death of Polonius?) indeterminable (the ostensible occasion being a mere *Spiel* in Schmitt's dismissive sense). This ending has nothing of the tragic climax we find in *Lear* or *Othello* (*Macbeth* and *Coriolanus* are clearly separate cases): it is simply an accidental massacre, and the deeper aesthetic satisfaction can only lie in the succession of Fortinbras himself, which fully reconfirms the contingency at the heart of dynastic logic as such, as much to his own amazement as that of the spectators on and off stage. This is satisfying because it proves what the Lacanian reader will have already anticipated, namely that there can be no satisfactory conclusion to a drama, let alone a tragedy, of desire; and that the return to dynastic thinking then appropriately confirms this impossibility, while at the same time allowing the whole complicated matter to be shut down.

But at this point another dimension of the Lacanian system proposes an explanation: Laertes, as we have said, is a character who has emerged from Hamlet's mirror stage, so to speak; his activities are therefore firmly fixed in the Imaginary order, whereas the family situation ultimately belongs to the Symbolic. As I understand it there can be regressions of a familial signifier into the Imaginary realm—indeed, there can be a whole range of permutations in the way in which these three orders offer perspectives on one another[32]—but the promotion of a mirror figure to Symbolic status seems a good deal less likely.

What this means is that the whole bloody denouement has in fact been played out on the level of the Imaginary, whereas the proper conclusion to Hamlet's Oedipal dilemma would require a Symbolic resolution. This reading of *Hamlet* would then seem to be a reversal of the great allegorical triumph of the Symbolic over the Imaginary in Lacan's *Seminar on the Purloined Letter*. Here in *Hamlet* it is the Imaginary that blocks access to any Symbolic solution (whether in the form of some true revenge or of a conversion of the mother figure, perhaps even of a renunciation of the Ghost's command altogether). The sense that the denouement is cobbled together, in haste and without any genuine necessity, is thereby both explained and justified: we are meant to be unsatisfied as the very recognition of our fixation in the Imaginary sphere.[33]

---

32 Slavoj Žižek projects a suggestive permutation scheme for the Lacanian orders ("The Imaginary with a Symbolic emphasis, the Real from the vantagepoint of the Imaginary," etc.): see *Organs without Bodies: Deleuze and Consequences*, Oxford: Routledge, 2004, 102–3.

33 The Lacanian interpretation finds some confirmation in Walter Benjamin's reading of *Hamlet* as Trauerspiel: "The death of Hamlet, which has no more in common with tragic death than the Prince himself has with Ajax, is in its drastic externality characteristic of the *Trauerspiel*; and for this reason alone it is worthy of its creator: Hamlet, as is clear from his conversation with Osric, wants to breathe in the suffocating air of fate in one deep breath. He wants to die by some accident, and as the fateful stage-properties gather around him, as around their lord and master, the drama of fate flares

But perhaps a short coda is necessary here in order to trace the loose thread of Horatio's charge ("to draw thy breath in pain to tell my story"). Empson might well observe that this is a charge to the public to come and see the play again and to the actors to continue to want to perform it. But there is here a generic twist as well, which bears on the issue of what we may call transitional narrative structure. Under the practiced direction of Henry James, the novel in its most fully developed form was able to deploy a new kind of dual perspective that critics since have baptized "Irony." This is to say that the novel, in its construction of bourgeois subjectivity, was able to bring us close enough to the inner life of its individual characters, both to lock us into their subjective blindness and to deliver us from it all at once. Irony in the novel means a commitment to Densher's subjectivity, a lack of distance from it, a veritable immersion, such that if and when we are brutally torn away from that spell we can see that the whole plot of *The Wings of the Dove*, which he himself simply lived as his own life, was in reality, when seen from the outside, a sordid matter of extortion and prostitution. This is a complex effect that depends on two related social developments: the one, an increasing autonomy and isolation of the individual subject (so-called individualism), and the other a well-defined multiplicity of social interrelationships organized into so many externally named situations.

The ultimate import of such irony is of course political: in principle, it should make it possible for the reader to take a dual perspective, inside and outside, on subjective ideology and on a historical totality in which such ideology and experience are seen to have an altogether different meaning and value. It is rare enough that literary works reach this level of effectivity; more important for us here is their relative scarcity—but now for technical reasons—in drama as such, where identification with the individual protagonist is nowhere near so absolute as to enhance the shock of withdrawing from it. But when we reflect on *Hamlet* in this

---

up in the conclusion of this *Trauerspiel*, as something that is contained, but of course overcome, in it. Whereas tragedy ends with a decision—however uncertain this may be—there resides in the essence of the *Trauerspiel*, and especially in the death-scene, an appeal of the kind which martyrs utter." (*The Origin of German Tragic Drama*, London: Verso, 1998, 136–37.)

The reading suggests an interesting kinship of Benjamin's foundational opposition (Tragedy/mourning play) with the Lacanian distinction between the Symbolic and the Imaginary.

context, we see a latency of the novel form, as well as the absence of its realization. I have already touched on Claudius's sudden alarm at the identification of the player villain as the King's nephew. With a little further effort along these lines, a completely different narrative—that of Claudius himself—seems on the point of emerging here. In recent memory, indeed, the heir to the Nepalese throne, presumably in some fit of derangement (not unlike Hamlet's own?), entered the royal dining room and assassinated the entire royal family before taking his own life. Is this not the objective tale of Hamlet as it will reach the public, if Horatio does not tell the "true story"? That Hamlet includes this possibility without developing it can then be for us the sign of its unique historical situation, on the cusp between two worlds. And with that possibility we have in fact arrived at the fourth level of interpretation, the analogical one, or that of the political destiny of the human race, of human history as such.

That level is in fact what Jean-François Lyotard once famously named a *grand narrative*, or in what has been called in another context that of *philosophies of history*.[34] Lyotard only indicted two of these, which he identified as the Marxist narrative of the inevitability of socialism and the "liberal" narrative of emergent freedom (Francis Fukuyama's "end of history" or the universal triumph of "democracy," understood as a representational political system). These particular visions may not really be narratives at all, although they do certainly touch on the destiny of the human race, and are allegories of what is on the other levels a narrative structure. That they are also ideologies is something Lyotard did not seem to want to stress, inasmuch as his "postmodernity"—an end of history in its own way—also included an equally banal ideological stereotype in its own right, namely the infamous "end of ideology."

I believe, however, that underlying the concept of postmodernity is yet another "grand narrative," a more fundamental one, which Lyotard failed to see and denounce. For both of his candidates are in reality narratives of modernity, and it is modernity that we must identify and denounce as the single great philosophy of history or ideological grand narrative if we wish to be consequent with Lyotard's program. He was himself, as his aesthetic writings made clear, preeminently a modernist in taste and character; and there can be no doubt that for all of us who

---

34 Jean-François Lyotard, *The Postmodern Condition*, Minneapolis: University of Minnesota Press, 1954.

have been formed by modernism in the arts, the indictment of the concept and the ideology of modernity is a peculiarly reflexive and self-critical process.

In that spirit I would argue that the historical meaning of *Hamlet* is also modernity. "The unity of the personality has been recognized as illusory since Shakespeare's *Hamlet*," remark Adorno and Horkheimer in passing.[35] The offhand reference marks the play as a fundamental break, standing as an index of modernity as surely as all the other famous "beginnings" (such as Descartes or Galileo, Luther, the French Revolution), something one would not think of saying about *Lear* or *Othello*.

This inference then becomes far more consistent with Lionel Abel's conception of metatheater as acting and reflexivity, as the reflexive transformation of classical spectacle: and is probably implicit in most of the polemics around modern tragedy, when they do not include Shakespeare on the other side of that particular grand divide. For the grand divide that is constitutively a necessary component of any ideology of the modern is probably also very much a structural feature of everything Lyotard would have been inclined to subsume under the category of the grand narrative as such.

Yet the permanence of this latent obsession with modernity may be detected in other kinds of debates about *Hamlet* and tragedy. So it is that the distinction between Tragedy and *Trauerspiel* that is the occasion for the Benjamin–Schmitt debate may itself be complicated by a third possibility. For Schmitt himself explains that his dissatisfaction with Benjamin's classification of *Hamlet* as the paradigmatic *Trauerspiel* (along with Calderon's *La Vida es sueño*) lies in fact in the exceptionalism of the English situation, which does not evolve into those continental absolute monarchies which furnish the raw material for Benjamin's "funereal pageants." For Schmitt, the emergence of absolutism on the continent is to be explained by the unresolvable religious and confessional civil wars to which feudalism was unable to put an end: absolute monarchy—Hobbes's *Leviathan*—comes into being with the vocation of repressing these bloody struggles. But England in the Elizabethan era moves in the very different direction of maritime empire. (It will be

---

35 Theodor Adorno and Max Horkheimer, *Dialectic of Enlightenment*, Berkeley: Stanford University Press, 2007, 126.

remembered that Schmitt's *Nomos der Erde* is something of a revision of Mahon's doctrine of land versus sea powers.) The maritime expeditions begin as commercial ventures, which develop into imperial enterprises and the emergence of industrial capitalism (raw materials from the colonies, foreign markets, and so on). For Schmitt, then, the tragedy of *Hamlet*, associated in his mind with the Stuart dynasty and in particular with James I, lies in his (and their) erroneous belief that they represent absolute monarchy in a situation in which it is utterly out of place.

We can retain Schmitt's historical framework while replacing his own interpretive conclusion. In that case, *Hamlet* would be some third kind of text, unclassifiable generically at this period, but which points toward that eventual dominant generic expression of (Anglo-American) capitalism which is the novel; and indeed most of the innumerable interpretations of this play (probably not excluding this one) can be seen in effect as writing "the novel of Hamlet." But the novel is the quintessential expression of modernity (itself an ideological substitute and idealized image of capitalism as such): Bakhtin indeed thought that the novel was always the sign and expression (the symptom?) of emergent modernity. Thus, from another more roundabout direction, the debate about Hamlet's tragicality also resolves itself into a disguised or distorted meditation on modernity as such.

But we have not yet considered the most curious theory of modernity of them all: Lacan's version. Like the others, it turns on the matter of tragedy, and indeed like that of Freud himself, and Jones, on the structural differences between *Oedipus Rex* and *Hamlet*. Freud famously pointed out that of all the males in the world, Oedipus alone did not have an Oedipus complex, in this quite unlike Hamlet. But this is not the fundamental distinction, for which we must scan the rest of the *Seminar* on desire, in particular asking ourselves how to account for Lacan's peculiar fascination with a certain type of dream.

This particular one comes from Ella Sharpe,[36] but there are other examples throughout Freud's writings and indeed in the course of Lacan's own *Seminars*. It is this: a son in mourning once again sees his dead father in a dream and talks to him: "but the father did not know he was dead." The rest of the dream has to do with the guilt of the son, who had hoped for the father's death during his lifetime (ostensibly owing to

---

36   Ella Sharpe, *Dream Analysis,* New York: Brunner/Mazel, 1978.

the painful illness to which he succumbed): but this guilt does not seem so startling in the Freudian-Lacanian context as the father's nonknowledge. What can this last mean? It is this odd intervention of an alien note into the dream consciousness that is somehow for Lacan constitutive. His further exploration of paradoxical negatives makes this clearer: the pleonastic "ne" in French, for example, which must grammatically accompany an affirmation in which, however, it strikes a kind of minor self-contradictory note; in English the famous double negative, forbidden by schoolmasters. Fink ingeniously proposes another English version, far rarer, perhaps, than the French: it is the "but" of hesitation and reversal: "Not but that I should have gone if I had the chance."[37] Fink goes on to gloss this peculiar grammatical event as follows:

> A conflict seems to be played out in such expressions between a conscious or ego discourse, and another "agency" which takes advantage of the possibility offered by English grammar (and French grammar in the case of *ne*) to manifest itself. The other agency, this non-ego or unconscious "discourse," interrupts the former—almost saying "No!"—in much the same way as the slip of the tongue.[38]

(And we should here parenthetically recall Lacan's remark about Shakespearean puns and wordplay—as with the gravedigger scene if not the preciosity of plays like *Love's Labour's Lost*—as a half-open door that gives the unconscious greater access to verbal expression.)

The unconscious cannot say no, Freud taught, but perhaps this is the exception that proves the rule: it can say no in conscious discourse, and it does so in the way we have been outlining, hereby opening a space for itself in our waking life, as the father who does not know (that he is dead). What is the relationship of all this to modernity? On a popsociological level, this unknowing father is of course the waning of the paternal function socially and historically, as the Germans have lamented since Mitscherlich's famous book.[39] Even Marcuse deplored the end of the old authoritarian father, insofar as it excluded the option of Oedipal

---

37 Fink, *The Lacanian Subject*, 39.
38 Ibid.
39 Alexander Mitscherlich, *Auf dem Weg zur vaterlosen Gesellschaft*, Gütersloh: Bertelsmann, 1963.

revolt. On a level of social opinion, Lacan also seems to have sympathized with this line, and in general, in the later *Seminars*, also alluded to a kind of historical retreat or waning of the Oedipal situation.

Yet in any case there is a paradox here, inasmuch as the Ghost, in *Hamlet*, knows that he is dead (and can recite the details of his own murder), whereas Laius, long forgotten, presumably does not. But this is to misunderstand the very function of a ghost, who is par excellence a figure who remains, who fails to realize he is dead and to disappear appropriately, who taunts the living with his ongoing half-life and inspires them (as in Ella Sharpe's dream) with the consequent guilt.

When a Greek dies, he's dead, to paraphrase Gertrude Stein. The implication in this Lacanian designation of *Hamlet* as dawning modernity, and the emergence of the Unconscious as something palpable if not yet theorizable, is that it portrays a father who does not know he is dead. On the appropriate level of allegory—that of the anagogical, or world history, the analogy would be that of an old order incapable, as the Stuarts were, of acknowledging their obsolescence, of realizing that they were dead. Perhaps our own moment of late capitalism is in a similar situation, of denial and rebirth.[40] At any rate, it becomes clear that on this level the fascination of *Hamlet* lies in just this allegorical staging of the misrecognized emergence of what has over and over again been identified as modernity.

And if this chapter had been entitled "*Hamlet* and Allegory," we might have ended this way:

>ANAGOGICAL: transition to modernity (capitalism)
>MORAL: acting (in metatheatrical or Brechtian style)
>ALLEGORICAL: Lacanian (names, hysteria, obsessional)
>LITERAL: the (old) dynastic text

---

40   Gramsci's famous diagnosis is often quoted: "The crisis consists precisely in the fact that the old is dying and the new cannot be born" (*Selections from the Prison Notebooks*, New York: International Publishers, 1971, 275–76).

4
Musical: An Allegorical Symphony? Mahler's Sixth

The premise is that we cannot have allegory without first having narrative; and therefore that before we can identify an allegorical activity at the heart of music, we must first show that its effects are also narrative ones. We may leave program music and tone poems aside here, despite Gustav Mahler's flirtation with them in his early works and his formative companionship with Richard Strauss,[1] one of their most notable practitioners: the term *ekphrasis* (description), which rhetoric uses to distinguish an essentially picturesque discourse from narrative, also paradoxically presupposes the possibility of musical narrative for its own elaboration in the first place. (We must also entertain the possibility that the tone poem is simply an example of bad or tripartite allegory, something that cannot be pursued further here.)

That there can be bad allegory in the area of musical interpretation must also be admitted; in the following, for example, no less an authority than Richard Wagner, himself one of the sources of late nineteenth-century program music, offers this account of what is for many people one of the most sublime pieces of music ever composed, Beethoven's Opus 131, the C-sharp Minor Quartet:

---

1 Charles Youmans, *Mahler and Strauss in Dialogue,* Bloomington: Indiana University Press, 2016.

The lengthy opening Adagio, surely the saddest thing ever expressed in notes, I would term the awakening on the dawn of a day "that in its whole long course shall never fulfill one wish, not *one* wish!" Yet it is at the same time a penitential prayer, a communing with God in the firm belief in an eternal Good.—The inward eye then also glimpses an appearance only he can recognize (Allegro 6/8) and in which longing has turned to a play of melancholy captivation: the most private fantasy awakens in fond memory. And now (with the short transitional Allegro moderato) it is as if the Master, mindful of his status as an artist, set about his magical work: this reawakening power unique to him he now (Andante 2/4) trains on the fixation and establishment of a single graceful figure, in order to experience again and again that holy testimony to the most primordial innocence—in ever changing and unexpected metamorphoses illuminated by the prismatic and eternal light he trains on it turn after turn.—And now we seem to see him as in his deep inner satisfaction with his own power he gazes again at the outside world (Presto 2/2): it stands before him again, as in the Pastoral Symphony, all lit up with his inner creative joy; it is as though he hears the very sounds of appearance itself, which, alternately ideal and material, moves before him in a rhythmic dance. He gazes at life and at the same time (short Adagio 3/4) returns in memory to that first moment when he began to make this life come to dance: a brief yet gloomy reminiscence, as though he were once again sinking back into the dreams of his own soul. One glimpse was enough to disclose the very inner essence of the world; now he wakes again and arouses the strings to a dance such as the world has never heard before (Allegro finale). This is the very dance of the world itself: the wildest desire, wails of pain, love's transport, the utmost bliss, grief, frenzy, debauchery, suffering; all this shuddering like lightning, rolling thunder, and high above it all the colossal Virtuoso himself who masters everything and charms it, leading it imperiously from whirlwind to whirlpool, and to the very brink of the abyss—and then he mocks himself, for all this magic was little more than a game.—And night beckons him. His day is done.[2]

I must confess that one is stunned by the philistinism of this "allegorical reading." Leaving aside the narcissistic evocation of the genius and his

---

2 Richard Wagner, *Beethoven*, Leipzig: Elibron, 2005, my translation.

transcendence of an essentially Schopenhauerian world of suffering, one asks oneself for whom this little fairy tale is meant: an essentially stolid bourgeois public in need of help in approaching this complex work, or other (presumably) more sophisticated performers for whom its practical, pedagogical usefulness will surely be limited? Like all Wagner's prose writings, his short Beethoven essay is meant to serve a purpose in proselytizing for his own work and reception and can certainly be seen as a (rather awkward) move in training his future public to grasp his own music dramas as the logical heir to Beethoven's absolute music. Wagner's appreciation of the late quartets and his championing of what were (and remain) difficult, even inaccessible works coincides with his composition of *Die Meistersinger*.[3] Indeed, a certain influence of Opus 131 has been detected in the Prelude to Act III of that opera, so that it is appropriate to juxtapose this Wagnerian narrative with a far more critical and jaundiced view of the same musical text than Wagner's storytelling resumé. This is then Adrian Leverkühn's narrative of Wagner's Prelude:

> How stupid, how pretentious it would be to ask: "Do you understand that?" For how should you not? It goes like this, when it is beautiful: the cellos intone by themselves a pensive, melancholy theme, which questions the folly of the world, the wherefore of all the struggle and striving, pursuing and plaguing—all highly expressive and decorously philosophical. The cellos enlarge upon this riddle awhile, headshaking, deploring, and at a certain point in their remarks, a well-chosen point, the chorus of wind instruments enters with a deep full breath that makes your shoulders rise and fall, in a choral hymn, movingly solemn, richly harmonized, and produced with all the muted dignity and mildly restrained power of the brass. Thus the sonorous melody presses on up to nearly the height of a climax, which, in accordance with the law of economy, it avoids at first, gives way, leaves open, sinks away, postpones, most beautifully lingers; then withdraws and gives place to another theme, a songlike, simple one, now jesting, now grave, now popular, apparently brisk and robust by nature but as sly as you make them; and for someone with some subtle

---

3   Michael Puri, "The Agony and the Ecstasy," *19th Century Music* 25:2–3, 2002, 228.

cleverness in the art of thematic analysis and transformation it proves itself amazingly pregnant and capable of utter refinement. For a while this little song is managed and deployed, cleverly and charmingly it is taken apart, looked at in detail, varied, out of it a delightful figure in the middle register is led up into the most enchanting heights of fiddles and flutes, lulls itself there a little, and when it is at its most artful, then the mild brass has again the word with the previous choral hymn and comes into the fore-ground. The brass does not start from the beginning as it did the first time, but as though its melody had already been there for a while; and it continues, solemnly, to that climax from which it wisely refrained the first time, in order that the surging feeling, the Ah-h-effect, might be the greater: now it gloriously bestrides its theme, mounting unchecked, with weighty support from the passing notes on the tuba, and then, looking back, as it were, with dignified satisfaction on the finished achievement, sings itself decorously to the end. Dear friend, why do I have to laugh?[4]

But the fulminations of Jack Goody about the inflation of the word *narrative*[5] and, in particular and with respect to music, the influential demurral of the redoubtable Jean-Jacques Nattiez[6]—namely, that music cannot be considered in any way narrative, let alone a narrative as such—require a more elaborate theoretical response; and I hasten to add that much contemporary musicology has done just that, in particular the seminal work of James Hepokoski and Warren Darcy on what they call sonata theory, the appropriation of Northrop Frye by Bryan Almen and others, and the path-breaking work on Mahler by Seth Monahan.[7] That the specter of Adorno looms large behind all these efforts is perhaps merely inspirational, inasmuch as Adorno has little

---

4 Thomas Mann, *Doctor Faustus*, New York: Alfred A. Knopf, 1948, 133.

5 In Franco Moretti, ed., *The Novel, Volume 1: History, Geography, Culture*, Princeton: Princeton University Press, 2007, 4.

6 Jean-Jacques Nattiez, "Can One Speak of Narrativity in Music?" *Journal of the Royal Musical Association*, 115:2, 1990, 240–57.

7 James Hepokoski and Warren Darcy, *Elements of Sonata Theory: Norms, Types, and Deformations in the Late-Eighteenth-Century Sonata*, Oxford: Oxford University Press, 2011; Bryan Almén, *A Theory of Musical Narrative*, Bloomington: Indiana University Press, 2008; Seth Monahan, *Mahler's Symphonic Sonatas*, Oxford: Oxford University Press, 2015; Robert Samuels, *Mahler's Sixth Symphony: A Study in Musical Semiotics*, Cambridge: Cambridge University Press, 2004.

enough to offer of a practical or methodological nature on either narrative or ideology.

I cannot myself hope to contribute anything theoretically or methodologically useful to this already rich musicological research, particularly inasmuch as I here seek to exploit such musical analyses as mere examples in a more abstract discussion of allegory. But it is often revealing to observe from a distance and as an outsider the way the theoretical analysis of an unfamiliar art form produces an imaginary object for us: pure narrative form emerging from such purely abstract reading, which itself then insensibly becomes allegorical in its own right.

As for the limited context in which I wish to stage the problem of musical narrative, it must be grasped in two versions, external and internal, or, if you prefer, as the larger question of the symphony itself as a whole; and then the more technical and specialized problem of that sonata form taken by only one or two of its movements. The logic of the sequence of the four movements of the symphony raises quite different issues of continuity than does the internal sonata-form relationships of themes and "subjects" within a single movement, so that we confront an initial paradox here, in the subsumption of one complete formal development (the sonata) within a larger sequence of other, seemingly discontinuous but equally complete forms (such as the scherzo or the slow movement).

The paradox of this nested relationship of seemingly autonomous units can then be dramatized this way: if the first movement of a symphony is organized in sonata form (as generally seems to have been the case), then its completeness or resolution must somehow be left open, or in other words left incomplete on some other level of reception and unresolved in a larger perspective, which does not leave us utterly discontent on the level of that individual movement. The ending must in other words remain an unresolved resolution, an incomplete completion, an open closure: and this paradox, which we may even go so far as to consider a contradiction in the very form itself, is not to be wished away by some superficial evocation of the serial form in novels or narratives (the cliffhangers) or even the repetitions of a novelistic plot in which a problematic situation is laid in place, undergoes a host of variations and complications, and is then somehow ingeniously or at least convincingly resolved.

The discontinuity of the four movements of a symphony is too absolute to accommodate such traditional discontinuities of the novel, even in its serialized form, and this despite the conviction that the symphony, in its historical development, ought to be counted as a more distant relative within the generic or media family that includes the novel and its cousin, the feature film. Obviously, the innovations of the modern sometimes involve more absolute discontinuities, as in the semi-autonomous chapters of *Ulysses* or the episodic interweavings of more recent works such as Roberto Bolaño's *2666* (many of which, however, are inspired by the problems and forms of the musical tradition in the first place, rather than the other way round). To be sure, an experiment like the Symphony in D minor of César Franck, in which a single melodic protagonist is made to inhabit four very different formal environments, seems to confront and overcome the dilemma of symphonic discontinuity which its radicality in fact confirms: a one-time pyrrhic victory.

I want to draw two principles from this discussion before proceeding. The first is a preliminary rule: namely that whatever the hypothesis or theory to be entertained, it must not be psychological. The psychological presuppositions on which books like the classical work of Leonard Meyer are based[8]—namely, that we have here to do with feelings of anticipation which are somehow worked over and then "resolved" into this or that form of satisfaction—may seem to be adequate expressions of what this or that individual listener feels during the execution of a piece of music, but they are expressions drawn from a specific and systemic code, a humanistic and traditional language which articulates a specific and historical ideology. This ideology is not merely a system which is imposed on subjectivity but one which forms and constructs it in the first place. Its language is not simply a reflection (however imperfect) of human nature, not simply the attempt to do justice to what everyone more or less tacitly feels. It is not natural at all, but rather what Foucault might have called a disciplinary grid, which brings a certain conception of human nature into existence by way of our submission to it and our agreement that it does more or less name what everyone, from time immemorial, feels or has felt. The nomenclature of psychology is as nonnatural as language itself; and psychology is, as I have tried to show in earlier chapters, itself an allegorical system that cannot be taken at face value but which must always be historically identified, even where

---

8   Leonard Meyer, *Emotion and Meaning in Music,* Chicago: University of Chicago Press, 1954.

it is not ideologically denounced as a form of that humanism and that metaphysics contemporary theory has been concerned in so many different ways to overcome. This resolute opposition to everyday or "commonsense" psychology is however a political and theoretical commitment, which we must also faithfully keep when deploying the innovations of narratology, as prone to fall back on psychologism as any of the more traditional forms of aesthetic "appreciation." (There can be no doubt that the primacy of the concept of narrative today is also a historical and an ideological, an antipsychological, development in its own right.)

The other conclusion that can much more briefly be added to this one has to do with the inevitable and necessary role of philosophy in the discussion. Contemporary philosophy indeed offers an alternate and nonpsychological way of handling phenomena such as anticipation or thwarted resolution, and that task has mostly been assigned to the thematics of repetition, articulated in its modern form by Søren Kierkegaard and elaborately codified by Gilles Deleuze. Beyond that, what philosophy offers music in the way of a very different and antipsychological terminology is the interminable problem of time and temporality as such. Philosophy's business, its calling, surely lies in the demonstration of the impossibility of conceptualizing such experiences of the fundamentally and structurally contradictory nature of all the solutions we have historically imagined: Immanuel Kant is the name and symbol of this philosophical vocation. Unfortunately, contradictions are not to be dealt with by consigning them to a reservation where they can do no further damage; indeed, the experience of time is so fundamental that we cannot cease philosophizing about it even after agreeing that it cannot even be thought or formulated.

This ever-reenacted impossibility also holds for a problem that cuts across these problems of time and repetition; that is the question of beginnings and endings, about which we have been assured (again by Kant)[9] that it is unthinkable, even though it exists in the work of art. That there are beginnings and endings in life and time, in reality, even in history, is an assertion which is necessarily always ideological (even

---

9 Immanuel Kant, "Antinomies: The First Conflict," *Critique of Pure Reason*, Cambridge: Cambridge University Press, 1997, 470–75; and see also, famously, Jean-Paul Sartre, *Nausea*, New York: New Directions, 2013, 37–40.

when true). The privilege of aesthetic theory, however—maybe it's the only one!—lies in the fact that there, in art, beginnings and endings are demonstrable; and that art alone seems to offer a laboratory in which these otherwise imponderables can be observed if not regulated. This is perhaps the sense in which Deleuze might have suggested that music is also a way of thinking, and in particular a way of thinking about time,[10] but in its own specific form of thinking, which is musical and which uses time to think about itself. It cannot of course reach any definite or absolute conclusion: Wagnerian temporality is as different from that of Bach as Hegelian thinking is from that of Descartes or Augustine. Still, all these differences do converge somewhere, even if it is in a place in which inconclusiveness has become a kind of Absolute in its own right. The existentialists thought that place was human existence (or Dasein) itself; I think it is more likely to have been History, an opinion which can posit only action or praxis, radical change, as a "solution."

As for the symphony and its overall narrativity, however, the musicologists seem to have found their most convincing solutions in the work of Northrop Frye, whose seasonal and cyclical view of the genres has the advantage, not only of coming in fours, but also of suggesting a way in which a given four movements might be thought of as a kind of cosmic unity (a unity that Hayden White has completed by identifying Frye's four moments as tropes and thereby anchoring them as solidly in language as Frye does in nature).[11] Frye's cycle—Spring or Comedy, Summer or Romance, Autumn or Tragedy, and Winter or Irony and Satire—can no doubt be rotated as one likes; White's tropes—Metaphor, Synecdoche, Metonymy, and Irony—pointedly, and as it were theologically, conclude with that fourth trope he identifies with reflexivity or self-consciousness, (perhaps also allowing for a Viconian *ricorso*!). And certainly nothing is more tempting than to grasp the four movements of a given symphony as a tragic or heroic first movement, followed by a slow movement and a scherzo, which one might well identify in some way with romance and satire, so as to conclude, as does the "Eroica," with a comedy or at least a happy ending.

---

10 See also David B. Greene, *Mahler, Consciousness, and Temporality*, New York: Gordon and Breach, 1984.

11 Northrop Frye, *The Anatomy of Criticism*, Princeton: Princeton University Press, 2000, and Hayden White, *Metahistory: The Historical Imagination in Nineteenth-Century Europe*, Baltimore: Johns Hopkins University Press, 2014.

There is, to be sure, a good deal of Jungianism here (Frye explicitly uses Jung's language of myths and archetypes), a psychology itself explicitly based on the principles of narrative, with a kind of transcendent healing as a resolution. White's version absorbs all this into a much more contemporary rhetorical ideology of language. The two versions seem to share a foundational belief in the ethical binary of good and evil: optimism and pessimism, say, or the happy versus the tragic ending (of which perhaps the contemporary capitalist version would be more recent ideological notions of success or failure).

I suspect that such systems ultimately end up in psychology once again, and in normative conceptions of human nature. But what seems to be almost more significant is the numerology of the thing: numbers, and above all, numerical systems, are after all themselves profoundly philosophical. The philosophical stakes of the dualisms are well known; and at least since Christianity but certainly since Hegel, the virtues and vices of a trinitarian system have also become obvious. Why the number four should designate a kind of completeness is less evident, inasmuch as four can always in a pinch be folded back into a pair of dualisms. We may leave aside the power of the seven for mystics and that of the nine for composers. I believe that at least one philosophical solution to the lurking presence of a rather suspect numerology in these issues of aesthetic closure and autonomy is to be found in the logic of the semiotic square itself and its dialectical combination of identity and difference (see Appendix A); but for some this will be no less allegorical (if more abstract) than Jungianism or the tropes. To be sure, the Greimas level of abstraction will once again, if much less acutely than in the case of Frye's Jungianism and White's implicitly Viconian teleology, pose the problem of its own relation to narrative as such, which was the problem whose solution was to have been our starting point. At any rate, in all these schemes the problem of narrative coincides with that of allegory.

Let us assume that for our purposes here we have at least raised the issue of narrativity as far as the four movements of the symphony are concerned; and that these schemes can plausibly find some satisfying relevance to the symphony as practiced (or even reinvented) by Haydn or Beethoven. But when we reach the other end of its generic career, in the symphonies of Gustav Mahler, such fourfold schemes present new and more interesting problems, not so much because his symphonies rarely have the traditional four movements, but rather because all the terms of the succession of those movements have been here interiorized, and what characterizes the relative autonomy of Mahler's immense individual movements is that each one seems to include all the genres simultaneously, in a free-wheeling intermingling in which it is very difficult to characterize any one of them as being in and of itself tragic or comic, satiric or romance-oriented. The movement in question certainly goes somewhere, its individual moments press on toward something, and even his "indecisive" conclusions are decisive. In this ultimate moment of symphonic form, something has happened to genre as a defining formal value (and it will ultimately be this peculiar fate of genre which will lead us back to the problem of allegory).

In what follows I remain uncomfortably mindful of Roland Barthes's precautions in his book on fashion: what disappointed so many of us at the time was the warning that he meant to study, not the things themselves, the tangible, visible clothing and their properties and effects, their mutations, their very ideologies, but rather the local and contemporary reviews of those objects, in other words, the language and the codes of their description and classification. This was certainly a proper area of investigation which, opening onto contemporaneity and its multiple languages, was worthy of study; but it was far from confronting the material world of fashion itself, which continued to stand in relation to its mere description as the irrecuperable Real itself.

So here, too, the layman that I am must remain content with the various attempts to describe the form of the sonata—however technical and professionally specialized—rather than the Ding an sich of the music (itself sundered into our hearing and reception of its performance and the printed score which seems to encode the reality of the musical text, but which in effect merely translates it into yet another code or script in its own right).

My sense of what the varied theoretical and linguistic attempts to convey musical reality offer in the way of a narrative runs something like this: the sonata begins with some first, arbitrarily chosen subject. (Whether that subject constitutes a completed object in its own right—a melody or at least a theme—is a different question altogether, and one which justifies its postponement on account of the seeming neutrality of the term.) This first subject is dwelt on until it assumes a certain consistency, the relative stability and durability, recognizability, of an existent in the world, of an object as such. At some point, then, a second subject is introduced: whatever its relationship to the first subject, the formal requirement will be the acknowledgment of the difference of second from first and the former's relative independence and autonomy. The object of the game is then to stage a rivalry between these two subjects, which can be as *stürmisch* as an agon or as affectionate as a courtship or a seduction but which must come to some sort of definitive conclusion: triumph, compromise, an utter rout, an astonishing metamorphosis. I have already indicated one of the problems facing this construction of a sonata as the first movement of a symphony, namely the danger that such a conclusion be too definitive, that it be so overwhelmingly final as to shut down any momentum toward the following movements. And as for the form of some finale (also often in sonata form), we should note the interesting remark of Michael Steinberg on its historical fate after Beethoven:

> The symphonic finale presented a problem to several nineteenth-century composers, bent, as many of them were, upon imitating Beethoven at shifting the focal point of the symphony to a climactic, summing-up last movement. Schubert, for example, found himself stymied to the point of abandoning a symphony after two movements of extraordinary greatness. Brahms had no problems, but a whole run of excellent composers from Mendelssohn and Schumann to Franck, Dvořák, and Mahler show signs of strain in their finales. Tchaikovsky conquered the problem only when he dared the boldly original solution he put forward in his *Pathétique*. Nor was the challenge beyond Bruckner, who was exceptionally ambitious with respect both to grandeur and originality. In his Second, Fifth, and Eighth symphonies he confidently achieved finales commensurate with this ambition, symphonic summations that can stand with any in the repertory.[12]

Meanwhile, we have omitted a crucial dimension from our first account of the sonata, whose formal distinction from Propp's classic account of the folktale lies in the notion of a "restoration of order."

---

12 Michael Steinberg, *The Symphony: A Listener's Guide,* Oxford: Oxford University Press, 1998, 101.

The beginning of a symphony cannot be grasped as an order in this paradigmatic structuralist sense, unless we make the more metaphysical assumption that it is tonality itself which constitutes the initial "order." (We will come back to tonality in a moment.) What I find more seductive, as well as more critical, is Adorno's (allegorical) position on the very ideology of symphonic form as such, which he saw as the establishment of hegemonic order. The opening theme or subject, the fundamental key of the work, arrives as it were with all the arbitrariness of a new regime of some kind: what happens in the development of the sonata and with its final recapitulation is something like the ratification of that new order, its passage from the unfounded to the legitimacy of a nature and a norm, a sovereignty. Or to put it another way, the subject and the key that open the work are at first unfamiliar and unjustified: it will be the work of the form itself to press their claims home and to render them necessary and to confirm them in their hegemonic inevitability. It will be noted that this *Ideologiekritik* of the form by Adorno implicitly denounces the symphony as a specifically bourgeois form, which symbolically reenacts the right of this class (and its economic system) to power. This is then an allegorical reading of the form in political terms, a perspective we will shortly meet in a far more sweeping characterization of tonality itself by Arnold Schoenberg.

Before we proceed, however, two further observations need to be added to this as yet skeletal account of sonata form. The first and most obvious one is the matter of tonality as such, a system that academic musicology and psychology have taken to be grounded in nature itself. It is then in the very nature of this particular universe and its organic bodies that a sound is accompanied by specific overtones and undertones and that a key possesses a privileged relationship to its "dominant" and its "subdominant." Whether these phenomena, which are taken to be natural laws, are grounded in the specifically human anatomical system or somehow (like the tree falling in the empty forest) exist "in nature" as the very structure of vibration itself—these are indeed metaphysical and ontological questions, whose very existence, whatever the answers to them, is historical and ideological. Max Weber, indeed, has rigorously analyzed tonality as a specifically Western form of rationalization; the tonal system has its own history, which is closely linked to the development of European capitalism since the seventeenth and eighteenth centuries.¹³ Here is then Schoenberg's "political" analysis of the hierarchical spirit of Western tonality:

> It is important for us to recognize that in tonality there are regions that will remain neutral, so long as they are forced to do so, but that, as soon as the rule of the fundamental is even momentarily relaxed, are ready to submit to the enticements of a neighboring tonality. We may not wish to regard every chord that follows as an incipient departure from the tonality (even assuming reference back to it). We must acknowledge nevertheless that the strong will of the respective masters of the dominant and subdominant regions, together with the tendency of the neutral chords to conform to this will as well as eventually to the will of another, neighboring tonality, invites the danger of loosening the bonds. From this situation, and from the tendency of every degree either to become a fundamental or at least to gain a more significant position in another district, a competition emerges, which constitutes the excitement of the harmonic events within tonality. The appetite for independence shown by the two strongest subordinates in the district, the mutiny of the more loosely connected elements, the occasional small victories and gains of the competing parties, their final subjection to the sovereign will and their meeting together for a common function—this activity, a reflection of our own human enterprise, is what causes us to perceive as life what we create as art . . .
>
> Perhaps the rebellious ambitions of the subjects spring as much from the tyrant's urge to dominate as from their own tendencies. The tyrant's urge is not satisfied without the ambitions of the subjects. Thus, the departure from the fundamental tone is explained as a need of the fundamental itself, in which, in whose very overtones, the same conflict is contained as a model, so to speak, on another plane. Even the apparently complete departure from the tonality turns out to be a means for making the victory fundamental so much the more dazzling.¹⁴

---

13 Max Weber, *The Rational and Social Foundations of Music,* trans. and eds. Don Martindale, Johannes Riedel, and Gertrude Neuwirth, Carbondale: Southern Illinois University Press, 1958.

14 Arnold Schoenberg, *Style and Idea: Selected Writings of Arnold Schoenberg,* Berkeley: University of California Press, 1985, 151–52.

The rather Austro-Hungarian preoccupations of Schoenberg's analysis thus show all the complexity of the political analysis of a Machiavelli or Gramsci!

The other addition I wish to make to my description of the two "subjects" of the sonata has its specific reference to Mahler's Sixth Symphony, which will serve as our object of study here, and in particular to Seth Monahan's reading of it (who essentially follows the Hepokoski/Darcy "sonata theory"). In particular I want to dwell on what seems to me something of an anomaly in his reading of the symphony's first movement by positing a supplementary version of the official "second subject," an S_2 alongside the P of the primary or first subject and the S_1 of the second one (see Figure 4.1). Here already, it seems to me, we have a closer approximation to Propp than at first suggested. The latter was based on the notion of opposition and conflict, the appearance of any number of obstacles on the path of the protagonist-hero to the appropriate apotheosis. These obstacles most often took the anthropomorphic form of the villain, whose multiple ruses needed to be overcome (and indeed his very existence neutralized) before a triumphant conclusion could be assured.

We have deliberately avoided positing this kind of struggle as the only form in which the relationship of Primary Subject and Secondary Subject could be described in the sonata. Now, however, with the strengthening of resources made possible by the outright variations in the second subject that Monahan posits in his analysis, the likelihood of its relationship to the first subject being apprehended as one of a struggle between adversaries markedly increases. It is as though a first relatively independent appearance of this second theme had reworked itself into an additional character or "actant" capable of affronting the first theme more directly and efficiently; as though an innocuous passerby had suddenly unmasked himself as an unmistakable adversary.

There is no reason not to hear it this way: after all, the description turns on a more fundamental categorical distinction, namely the dialectic of identity and difference; and that lies to a certain degree in the attention of the listener. It is his perceptual choice whether to see S (the second subject) as two characters—S_1 and S_2—rather than one; whether to stage this opposition as a drama with three protagonists rather than two; or even—Monahan claims that ultimately we can identify the second subject as a derivation of elements of the first one—as a completely inner drama of mood and inner turmoil, as an identity inwardly stirred into distinct dispositions and humors.

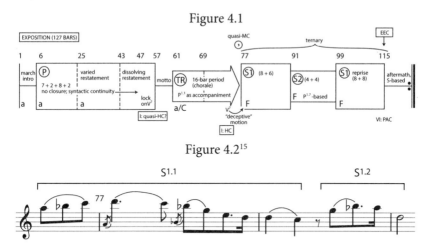

At this crucial level of attention, in which the listener's own formal shaping power comes into view, it even seems possible to glimpse additional actants at work and to grasp what seemed like fleeting variations as separate and distinct entities altogether. The initial agon or struggle—the two—would then suddenly become a multiplicity, a crowd of different characters vying for existence, if not indeed for that ultimate triumph promised by the very concept of closure and conclusion.

Meanwhile, one might mention at this point, the shadow cast by a later atonal music, that of Webern or Schoenberg, over these Mahlerian forms: for at that point, the very identity of this or that "subject"—which is to say the consistency and autonomy of each as a complete theme or melody—is problematized and even undermined (in the direction of the Schoenberg maximalism of the twelve-tone row—scarcely a melody you might hum in the shower—or of Webern's minimalism). In that case, the old-style subject finds itself broken into groups of two or three notes at a time, each group winning its own semi-autonomy and becoming a player in the larger form without having ever become a recognizable "character."

Indeed, in a grandiose vision of history, Carl Dahlhaus sees the

---

15 Figures reproduced with permission of Oxford University Press through PLSclear from Seth Monahan, *Mahler's Symphonic Sonatas* (Oxford: Oxford University Press, 2015), 103, 114.

development of nineteenth-century music as a bifurcation into two distinct lines, which might ultimately even lead in some evolutionary logic to two distinct species: it is the fateful moment in which alongside Beethoven, Rossini emerges, and the line that leads on to the absolutization of the anthropomorphic melody as an independent and autonomous aria can no longer affirm its kinship with a symphonic organization of absolute music whose logic leads toward a fragmentation and an atomization of the old thematic "subject" and then on into atonality and the end of the Western tradition.

It is a useful narrative or myth, insofar as it allows one to position Mahler in all his ambiguity as the ultimate parting of the ways of this distant kinship, the definitive splitting of the two genetic codes. I have elsewhere tried to stress the operatic nature of Mahler's work, the aspiration to rhetorical declamation and the kind of outsize and gesticulatory intensity and exaggeration the wide-ranging conductor found in the Italian works he was called upon to direct.[16] These great declamatory moments—and I want to argue in a moment that they are not just separate episodes in Mahler but govern the entire protean continuity of his music—are also those in which the later avant-garde composers found their inspiration, identifying the minute work of analytic differentiation present in the very intimate fabric of the score itself, page after page. For them, then, the task of reading the score does not consist in organizing notes into subjects, which then become so many characters or actants in a larger overall drama, but rather in finding their delectation in the way in which a virtually inaudible motif of three or four notes—one is tempted to call them subnotes on the order of atomic particles—can be observed to find inconspicuous places in the most incongruous moments of an orchestration or a transition from one thematic moment to a different one. Here, then, the dialectic of identity and difference takes the form of a dialectic between narrative and . . . what? Postnarrative? A narrative on some microscopic or even subatomic level, which may be nothing more than a repetition of post-Wagnerian clusters without any visible narrative logic altogether? This is indeed how Adorno characterized the logic of Schoenberg's twelve-tone rows: that at this point the musical text, which can by definition only consist in the repetition of

---

16 See "Transcendence and Movie Music in Mahler," in *The Ancients and the Postmoderns*, London: Verso, 2015.

these same rows over and over again, has to resort to the logic of pastiche in order to impose on that meaningless repetition the semblance of a traditional form in order to persuade the listener that something intelligible is in the process of happening (intelligibility being what I am here calling *narrative*).[17]

Derrideans and dialecticians alike will no doubt rejoice in the unparalleled undecidability between these two antithetical versions of the reading of (this prototypical Mahler work) the Sixth Symphony—melodramatic gesture versus micrological simultaneity. One is thereby fully justified as positioning at some absolute fault-line or watershed between the traditional and the new and as pronouncing it the last classical monument and the first achievement of modernism at one and the same time: eliciting an unforced admiration from both sides that does not exclude a certain malaise at its historical ambiguity (a feeling one detects everywhere in Adorno's book on Mahler, one long probing for contradictions which cannot but conclude, much against Adorno's critical habits, by saluting them).

However, I think it is still possible to seek that little lower level which is to be found in the historical situation to which these works respond, or indeed in the historical contradiction they seek, if not to solve, then at least to express and to articulate. We can, it seems to me, translate the dilemma of interpretation I have just outlined into a temporal language which clarifies the dilemma of a growing incommensurability between two schemes of temporality, two ways of talking and thinking about time itself. The first, the traditional option here, is the system of the past–present–future, the notion of some continuity of time beyond immediate existential experience, or perhaps—insofar as a totalizing concept of this kind always needs some experiential analogue from which to derive its plausibility and to ground its schematic structure—a projection of the experience of individual memory onto an ideological construction that transcends any possibility of personal experience. Clearly enough, in any case, forms like those of the sonata or even the novel, which seem at first glance to rely on our power of retention and memory as individuals both to identify repetitive motifs, to recognize their variations, and also to distinguish the interventions of the radically

---

17 Theodor W. Adorno, *Philosophy of New Music*, Minneapolis: University of Minnesota Press, 2006, 80–81.

new and as yet unfamiliar—such forms in fact depend very much on this cognitive category of the continuous in time for their deployment. One would however also want to add that this is not some ahistorical category but that, at least in "modern times," such attention to continuity changes and evolves with the complexity and also the dimensions of the historical situation as such. Indeed, when, as in modern history, that situation increasingly overloads the possibilities of individual experience, other features of time offer to displace the older organizational schemes of temporality and to propose new and more plausible substitutes, in particular our second temporal option—that living present which cancels the spurious continuities of the traditional model of past–present–future.

This is, I think, what explains the peculiarly disruptive and yet constitutive role of the living present in Mahler's work. Philosophically, the various existentialisms have been the privileged place for the expression of this new temporality, which is radically different from the old past–present–future continuum and indeed inconsistent with it, if not incommensurable. For we all live in both temporalities simultaneously, each one taking its significance or preponderance from the immediate situation; nor can one really affirm, as have existentialist thinkers since Kierkegaard, that the present is somehow real in the sense of a concrete experience, while the tripartite temporal continuity is at best a mere abstraction and can only affirm its claims to existential reality (as in Proustian memory) by allying itself with a living present of some kind. This would be so only if the "present" in question were a mere instant of the other kind of time, a moment or point on the continuum, a mere break in the flow: in which case the line is as real as the point. On the contrary it seems probable that there are many kinds of present and that the living present includes a good deal of temporal complexity to which we do not do justice when we (quite reasonably and understandably) reduce it to the simplicity of the Deleuzian schizophrenic, the confinement in the present of the amnesiac or the Alzheimer's patient, the fixation on the eternal of the mystic.

This absolute present is also what Adorno denounces as nominalism, that experience of being which excludes all negation or critical distance and which is the philosophical source of empiricism when the latter becomes an ideology and a worldview. I have elsewhere characterized this present, for good or for ill, as a reduction to the body, a formula that seems to be capable of doing justice to both sides of this historical phenomenon, seemingly unique in modern times, and which has its positive advantages and possibilities fully as much as those philosophical defects Adorno and so many others have deplored. For the new life structure is certainly materialistic in a new way and anchors our experience in being in such a way as to justify the (equally new) existentialist judgment of authenticity. I believe that it is also not merely the result but the acknowledgment and dawning awareness of the new globality of massive populations of living others—a scandal and a stumbling block for the former individual who can no longer encompass this multiplicity in older ethical notions of "the other" as such, and for whom the experience of temporality is displaced from recognizable ideas of the various cultural communities and drawn as by the irresistible magnet of sheer mass to the only synchronic experience we can imagine sharing, namely simultaneity or the living present itself. The global standardizations of capitalism and its new world market, which undermine community and region and whose production depends on a creative destruction even of its own past, cannot but reinforce this ontological dilemma, which even blots out death itself insofar as it can no longer encompass that future either.

Mahler's music, it seems to me, makes available to us something like this experience, in which a present of time at every moment challenges the official requirement of the form to integrate that moment in a formal continuum of past–present–future. Our charts and the musicologists can to be sure step away from the musical experience and demand that we reorganize our perceptions in such a way that consciousness of the whole always accompanies the part and that we agree to attend to and acknowledge the generic pretensions and retentions of this particular auditory moment in time, continuing to recognize its incommensurability with the absolute present of its "components."

That Mahler also wants us to do this is without question; he surely retains a passionate conviction in the existence of the great traditional forms and the demands they make on us. He believes, in other words, in the symphony: a belief that will be weakened and shattered for so many later twentieth-century composers. But at one and the same time he is as it were viscerally or even unconsciously committed to what Hegel called "the immense privilege of the present." He cannot admit what earlier practitioners of a far more transparent and legible symphony form could in all good conscience acquiesce in, namely that some moments of the musical development are necessary without being themselves interesting or eventful, like those parts of a sentence required for it to be grammatical, or those areas the traditional painter must fill in without any discernible intensity in the obligatory brushstroke.

This can be seen more dramatically in the orchestration than in the horizontal score: for here all kinds of unheard details affirm the absolute primacy of moment and detail. One remembers Proust's famous observation about Madame Swann's toilette:

> And I realised that it was for herself that she obeyed these canons in accordance with which she dressed, as though yielding to a superior wisdom of which she herself was the high priestess: for if it should happen that, feeling too warm, she threw open or even took off altogether and gave me to carry the jacket which she had intended to keep buttoned up, I would discover in the blouse beneath it a thousand details of execution which had had every chance of remaining unobserved, like those parts of an orchestral score to which the composer has devoted infinite labour although they may never reach the ears of the public: or, in the sleeves of the jacket that lay folded across my arm I would see, and would lengthily gaze at, for my own pleasure or from affection for its wearer, some exquisite detail, a deliciously tinted strap, a lining of mauve satinette which, ordinarily concealed from every eye, was yet just as delicately fashioned as the outer parts, like those Gothic carvings on a cathedral, hidden on the inside of a balustrade eighty feet from the ground, as perfect as the bas-reliefs over the main porch, and yet never seen by any living man until, happening to pass that way upon his travels, an artist obtains leave to climb up there among them, to stroll in the open air, overlooking the whole town, between the soaring towers.[18]

Maybe orchestration is too weak to express the well-nigh gravitational shift in attention propelled by the complexity of this scoring. It is a complexity marked first and foremost not by the number of notes or instruments involved, but rather by the articulation of their voices and

---

18 Marcel Proust, *Remembrance of Things Past: The Guermantes Way*, New York: Vintage 1982, 686–87.

the ideal requirement that we hear each one separately at one and the same time. It is this which can best convey the intensity of Mahler's compositional act and that led Leonard Bernstein, in a memorable remark to his players (the Vienna Philharmonic) to warn that in Mahler each and every note has to be played with "intensity"; "otherwise" he said, "you're just playing music and not even that." But this multicentered intensity clearly demands an attention from the listener which by locking us into the present threatens to weaken if not altogether to screen off any perception of the other temporal dimensions of the form, any sense of what went before and what is to come. That way, of course, a kind of temporal nominalism lies and will make its appearance and bring its resultant puzzlement and incomprehensibility to the audience in so-called modernism: to practice this present-oriented texture within the older traditional forms is as it were a fundamental strategy of Mahler, which is instinctive rather than planned or calculated.

The other feature of this increasing "attack of the present on the other temporalities" (Alexander Kluge) lies in what we may call the increasing materialism of our hearing. For this new articulation, this radical separation of the various instruments from one another within the unity of a swollen and overloaded present is not simply a matter of so-called orchestral coloration (although the latter also knows a unique practice in Mahler's composition); it forces the materiality of the musical instrument and its peculiar and distinct resonance on our attention by way of its unique sounds, whose specificity is only heightened by the simultaneity of the other different ones in a new kind of dissonance comparable only to Baudelairean synesthesia ("a green so intense it hurts"). Music, thereby, on its way to sublimation and (at least with Mahler) to some kind of transcendent spirituality, ends up immersing us ever more physically and inextricably in the sheer materiality of the world of sound, of this "most abstract of all the senses" (Adorno).

What then serves as a counterforce to this tendency to an absolute present (a historical tendency in contemporary experience as well as contemporary art) is of course precisely that narrative form (or "sonata form") that is at issue here and that attempts to enlist these masses of sound in an intelligible movement forward toward a conclusion that completes what gradually appears as a genuine historical past and can therefore be identified as an intelligible event. Just as a sentence can mesmerize in its own right but demands to be remastered and placed back under the control of its larger context and the web of successive sentences in which it has meaning and not merely style, odd words, rhythms, striking image content—so also this overwhelming Mahlerian present needs to be tamed somehow and marked with renewed force as a moment of an organized temporal progression in which time has again a formal unity and is not merely a succession of autonomous moments one after another. I have already specified a few of the institutional traditions that somehow enforce this shift of attention back to the absent whole: the isolation of distinct subjects from one another comparable to the individuality of separate characters in a dramatic action; the modulations which force us to attend to the keys of a given passage and thereby reactivate the whole tonal system of the keys—dominant, subdominant, and so on—that has been laid in place in a form determined by the tonal starting point of the work and which thereby also awakens our anticipation (but, as I warned about such psychological or psychologistic conceptions, can we not say it in some other way?) of this or that possible ending to come. The opposition between major and minor modes offers yet another, perhaps even central, structural possibility whereby an "optimistic" or positive expression—a comic worldview, as Frye or White might put it—can be ruthlessly modulated into a "tragic" one; and an apparent joy or even peacefulness can be undermined and become the contest for the overwhelming triumph of melancholy or despair or simply the spectacle of defeat. (That the latter is not at all inconsistent with aesthetic pleasure has been understood at least since Schopenhauer and perhaps epitomized by the title of Terry Eagleton's book on tragedy, *Sweet Violence*.[19])

Surely, however, the reduction of such conceptions of the action or "event" of the work to so many binary oppositions (tragedy–comedy, pessimistic–optimistic, success–failure) tends to work against the articulated notion of a drama with multiple characters; and indeed this very alternative is yet another version of the problem I propose to study here, namely the distinction between traditional allegory and contemporary allegoresis or interpretation. For the classical form of allegory—the play of personifications which interact on the order of a drama—is quite different from a text whose literal level is a style or a mood, let's say the

---

19   Terry Eagleton, *Sweet Violence: The Idea of the Tragic*, Malden, MA: Blackwell, 2003.

Walter Pater fin-de-siècle "elegance" of Joyce's early sentences. These are radical shifts I would be tempted to interpret in terms of the historical difference between an Aristotelian substantialism and more contemporary philosophies of process (and equally tempted to suggest that Mahler's practice subsumes and includes both modes, both forms of allegory).

Yet in this same first movement of the Sixth Symphony, Mahler himself explicitly marked and personified the more lyrical second subject as "Alma," his famous wife's famous name, thus endowing the movement with an allegorical spirit, which seems to demand a rewriting of the entire movement in terms of a kind of drama. What, then, does the first subject represent, with its ominous and threatening march and its oppressive promise of domination and catastrophe? Is it the world as such and its inexorable laws, its relentless and overwhelming power, as Adorno thought? Or would it make more sense to construe some more domestic situation in which the first theme conveys everything that threatens the lyric expressivity of the Alma subject, perhaps even including her obsessive and neurotic husband himself? Or can we generalize both these alternatives into some more abstract and yet more universal opposition between public and private as such, between professional and domestic, or state and individual? Or would it not be better to confine ourselves to the purely formal and generic connotations of a tragic versus comic antithesis, so that the development of the sonata registers the interferences and contaminations between these modes as well as the struggle of each to have the upper hand over the other?

Nor must the reading neglect the rhetorical aspect of these antitheses and forget to notice the relative vulgarity of the Alma theme (as easily caricatured as the personage herself) as well as the very limited expressive range of the march-and-drum motif, which can surely not offer a very comprehensive vehicle for conveying the pressure of the world itself, save for its impoverished inexorability. In this sense, the terms of the drama are also meant to convey the restrictive and limited, distorted way in which it is represented to us here; and the allegorical scan shifts from a reading of the content of the drama to an assessment of its mode of representation as such and a judgment on the adequacy of its form.

These readings also fail to register a dimension of music that falls under what Kant called the *categories of modality*, namely those of possibility, of existence, or of necessity. It may seem odd to evoke such levels of being in relationship to an art which does not involve propositions and in which the existence of its "statements" (the notes) can scarcely be in doubt (a note is played or it is not). It is worth remembering, however, that Adorno did just this when he judged the form itself in terms of an eventual confirmation of the necessity of a key or a theme; meanwhile, surely, in the tonal system there exist something like logical implications—the related keys that always accompany the twelve possible tonal centers of the scale. One key can negate another one, ruling it out or overruling it; another can summon a related key with it, as a kind of shadowy implication and tentative accompaniment (a minor character following in the entourage of a protagonist and perhaps becoming a new protagonist in its own right).[20] These "implications" arouse the awareness of multiple actantial possibilities (or impossibilities, as the case may be), which risk strengthening the feeling of that even more momentous event which constitutes the shift from minor to major and back, not to speak of radical changes of key. Such categorial potentialities make of the musical form something a little more multidimensional than an empirical set of notes; they can be compared to the perspectival in painting, where the absence of perspective or of the vanishing point, with its analogies to literary or filmic "point of view," suggests comparable modal and narrative freedoms.

We need, however, a terminology for all this, and it is just that with which Monahan has provided us, in his notion of *hypothetical music*:

> a concept which allows us to distinguish between what is merely wished for and what is conclusively attained. I submit that this would-be "recapitulation" [he is discussing the finale of Mahler's First Symphony] is exactly this kind of "hypothetical" music: the sonata dreams of a tonic homecoming for S [the second subject], but the resolution remains out of reach, and the dream darkens into nightmare. Worse still, the music awakens to find the "real" recapitulation tainted by the knowledge that S has *already* expended its one opportunity for a tonic key presentation. It has failed before it has even begun.[21]

---

20 Charles Rosen has, for example, read Haydn's sonata form in terms of eighteenth-century theater (*The Classical Style*, New York: Norton, 1998).

21 Monahan, *Mahler's Symphonic Sonatas*, 26–27.

This remarkable reading generates many new interpretive and analytic possibilities: for one thing, it allows for a kind of vertical reading of the score, in which both positive and negative statements are simultaneously possible: the positive outcome as a wish, the negative one as a reality. The idea bears some resemblance to the once popular literary notion of irony, by virtue of which an author could take two sides simultaneously in any given evaluation (for example, in *Wings of the Dove*, Merton Densher as both hero and villain simultaneously): it is a concept which historically has been an excuse for liberal ideological and political fence-sitting, and I believe that in current musicology it has most often been misused as a description of a kind of nonbinding and shamefaced citation or incorporation of other styles, as when Mahler "quotes" the kind of popular music Adorno tends to call vulgar or kitsch. To call this ironic suggests that Mahler himself agrees with our judgment and does not mean the quotations to endorse the quoted text in question as "serious" music in its own right but only to intend it as a deliberate allusion or indeed a wink (neither of which is at all consistent with Mahler's character).

Monahan's idea is, however, free from these ironic implications of the traditional concept of irony; and makes it possible, for example, to understand how a first movement could end with a certain finality and at the same time retain enough formal indecision to warrant the addition of further movements until we are finally able to reach a more conclusive and definitive ending in the finale.

It also allows us to reorganize the uses of Frye's seasonal generic categories in a new kind of vertical simultaneity, in which a moment of the development can be both tragic and comic at the same time and include each other according to the modes of virtuality or implication, or even negation, in that dialectical (or Freudian) sense in which to deny a thing is also to suggest it, if not to affirm it outright. "Hypothetical music" is thus a genuinely dialectical category, in which the irreconcilable demands history imposed on Mahler can be seen to have been genially coordinated, if not reconciled (it will be remembered that of all ideological stances, "reconciliation" [Versöhnung] was the one most detested by Adorno, a form of the common misreading of Hegelian "synthesis" and susceptible to construal as one of those positive or "affirmative" propositions he rightly judged ideological).

Hypothetical music then allows us to grasp how Mahler can have been able to navigate the gap already discussed between the contradictory logics of the living present and the temporal scheme of the past–present–future. Each step is as it were viewed stereoscopically, as though both perspectives were superimposed within a single image. The musical event will be grasped in all its implications for the past (which it revalues and indeed reinvents in a certain form) and the future it implies, fears, cannot hope to hope for, and so on. But at the same time another part of the musical imagination will become obsessed, stalled as in a trance on the possibilities of this particular now, which is for it musically inexhaustible; and so Mahler will not let go of the moment, will turn it in all directions and vary it according to all its structural possibilities, until at length he is willing to have had enough and to recall the direction this episode was to have progressed toward, a movement taken up with renewed determination, until the next moment of elaborative concentration and mesmerization arrives. I have elsewhere compared this momentum to that of the eddies in an ongoing current, an untheorized genre which it would be better not to associate with the "digression" as a form but rather with some of the elaborations taken by the new postwar episodic narratives of a Günther Grass or a Salman Rushdie.

EXCURSUS

But this is also the moment to compare the concept of "hypothetical narrative" with the seemingly antithetical notion of the "breakthrough," attributed to Adorno and yet endowed with the most remarkable variety of meanings by contemporary musicology. It has indeed two kinds of origin, if one may put it that way: the first is the coining of the expression as a technical term in Paul Becker's 1922 Mahler monograph. The second origin can be found in Thomas Mann's *Doctor Faustus*, for which Adorno was the "musical advisor" but in which the breakthrough has a very different kind of politico-psychological meaning, to which Adorno, even if he suggested the term to Mann, could not have been insensible. (We will shortly return to this issue, which turns on the military origins of Adorno's keyword.)

The musical meaning of the term *breakthrough* designates the eruption of extraneous or extrinsic material in the development, resulting in its interruption or deflection in a new direction. The most frequently adduced example of this phenomenon—almost always in the context of a Mahler–Adorno discussion—is the sudden arrival of a chorale in the finale of Mahler's First Symphony: the problem of its reduplication is a different one, and the example is limited in impact by the context of this most traditional of the composer's nine (or ten, or eleven) symphonies. But there are enough notable instances of such "breakthroughs" in the Sixth Symphony for the concept to have an immediate relevance here, as well as a more general theoretical interest.

The latter derives from its relevance to the question of the autonomy of the work of art: the essence of the sonata form, indeed, depends on its absolute unity and homogeneity, "which dictates that all significant motivic content of the development section be derived in some fashion from the material of the exposition."[22] *Breakthrough* can then technically be defined as the introduction of new content which did not figure earlier and which then of necessity unexpectedly interrupts, suspends, or deflects the ongoing development of the sonata's intrinsic material. Thus Mahler himself characterized the eruption of his chorale in precisely such terms: "My chord [the D-Major chorale] had to sound as though it had fallen from heaven, as though it had come from another world."[23] "Luft aus anderen Planeten" was the verse of Stefan George that Schoenberg famously quoted in another musical context, and certainly this version of the breakthrough suggests an apprehension of otherworldliness and can easily be read as approaching transcendence or the sublime. But in Bruckner (for example) the sublime is attained by remaining within the language of the initial material; here in Mahler, as for example in passages of the Sixth Symphony that Monahan characterizes as Utopian, otherworldliness is conveyed by the use of "instruments" not officially recognized as musical ones in either high or popular culture—namely the notorious cowbells and birch brushes and those already somewhat alien sounds that are made in full orchestra by harp or piano. But for Mahler himself these designated, not the afterlife of resurrection, as in the early symphonies, but simply the alien peace and calm of the mountain meadows and the snowy peaks: the *Naturlaut*, which marks the outside world beyond the city and its "civilization" and

---

22   James Buhler, "'Breakthrough' as a Critique of Form," *Nineteenth-Century Music*, 20: 2, 1996, 126–43.
23   Ibid., 127.

symphony concerts; and in that sense it simply designates the other of the social world of art rather than that of the earthly world as such.

The formal problem raised by such breakthroughs is indeed the philosophical one of immanence versus transcendence: have such passages really succeeded in breaking through the closure or the autonomy of the work of art, or have they not on the contrary subtly managed to draw the external into the work and to transform it into an intrinsic, albeit enlarged, artistic language? Is the sublime, in whatever form, a phenomenon that can be aestheticized and transformed into a properly artistic end and effect? For Adorno, for whom the autonomy of the work and of art in general was a fundamental concern, the problem lies here and it remains a source of uncertainty and even ambivalence, not to speak of ambiguity, in his thought. On the one hand, the work seeks, within the increasing dominance and multiple subsumptions of the commodity form, to free itself from commodity logic by commodifying itself; by turning the very form of the commodity against itself in the evolution of a strategy in which the work becomes a final enclave of noncommodification (what Kant refers to as the "disinterested interest" of the aesthetic). Clearly, Adorno became less and less sanguine about such possibilities as he saw the dawn of universal commodification and the repression of the negative everywhere in an empiricist society in which only the "positive" or the "affirmative" (and the empirically existing) is recognized.

On the other hand, was this not also that same Adorno who told us that we could not hear Beethoven properly unless we also heard, within the music itself, the unique fact and historical Novum of the French Revolution? Marxists have often, in their criticism, vulgarized such extra-artistic reverberations of history, class, revolution, and the concrete historical situation; nor have they often enough insisted that such reverberations are part of the very semantics of artistic languages and that the jubilation of Beethoven is the expression of a genuine class triumph which will not be heard again in Western music after the bourgeoisie becomes unable to conceal its hegemonic status or to evade the bad conscience of its domination (in 1848).

But that bad conscience will not only preclude the further elaboration of joy in Western music; it will also, even more fatally, call the very justification of the aesthetic itself into question and begin to undermine all those forms, like the symphony, which are institutionalized by the new ruling class. This is where Adorno develops a remarkable solution to his ambivalence about the breakthrough: for what the latter does is not to destroy art altogether—if anything, Mahler affirms the aesthetic in as affirmative a way as Joyce or Proust, Cézanne, or even Wagner before him. It is to challenge the form as such: breakthrough is the "Ideologiekritik" of the sonata form as such; it denounces the historical and ideological basis of its own now obsolete form. Its allegedly reflexive art is one which calls into question, not art in general (as the avant-gardes, which Adorno detested, would claim), but this particular form whose uses and achievements it designates and prolongs by way of continuing to practice it: something that accounts for Mahler's peculiarly unstable and Janus-faced position in the history of the symphony or perhaps of Western music in general.

This is then the moment to return to the relevance of Thomas Mann's deployment of the concept of the breakthrough in *Doctor Faustus*, his "biography" of an imaginary composer, Adrian Leverkühn, who feels and lives the crisis and the multiple contradictions of contemporary art in more lucid and historical ways than either Mahler or Schoenberg (naturally enough assisted in this new lucidity enough by Adorno himself). "Um ihn war Kälte": it is this proposition of Adrian's fundamental isolation, the icy force field around him that repels friendship, love, and any more general sociability—a return, no doubt, to Mann's own youthful aestheticism and to the pathos of the misunderstood genius. But here, the isolation of Adrian will be the isolation of Germany itself, stranded between the West (French "civilization") and Russia. ("The West has form, Russia depth, only we Germans have both," asserts a patriotic Wandervogel student in conversations that echo Mann's own ambiguities as they are much more elaborately expressed in that long World War I argument with his West-oriented brother Heinrich, in the mistitled *Reflexions of an Unpolitical Man*.)

At least since the Thirty' Years War, and perhaps even since Canossa, the Germans suffer their cultural isolation between their two great neighbors (with Italy as a dream wish fulfillment) as a turning inward in toxic ways on themselves. This is why in Mann's novel Hitler's armies constitute a desperate attempt at breakthrough: a military term easily confused with its cousin the *breakout* (*Kesselausbruch* or *Durchbruch*), where an army succeeds in breaking out of a seemingly fatal encirclement: the fate of the German army at Stalingrad. The more general

Durchbruch is associated with the famous Blitzkrieg; it is the breaking through of the enemy defense lines, the triumphant overrunning and appropriation of alien territory.

Doctor Faustus then identifies both forms of desperation, that of the musical contradictions that seem to spell the end of music itself and that of the national–cultural in which Germany as a new world power fails to produce its own hegemonic culture, and at length (in Adrian's Nietzschean syphilitic paralysis) attempts to escape its cultural–spiritual dilemma by way of the convulsions of Hitlerian "national revolution." But can fascism really be understood in this pseudopsychological, pseudoexistential way?

Mahler as an Austrian will scarcely have felt the same anguish Mann seeks here to express: the precarious Austro–Hungarian monarchy had other contradictions and other dilemmas (no doubt also reflected somehow in Mahler's music) but not exactly those of Central Europe and its successful or unsuccessful breakthroughs.

Yet the equivocations of this now omnipresent Adornian term raise another issue that is crucial for us in the present context, namely the distinction between metaphor and allegory, which it seems to revive and intensify. For is not the parallelism Mann dramatizes between music and war simply a homology whose allegorical force and consequences are strictly limited to some first point-to-point metaphorical parallel? Adorno's use of the military term to characterize an increasingly acute crisis in musical form implies the context of a whole narrative of musical history and not simply, as in Mann, a figural parallel between two situations that are presented in terms of psychological states (isolation, desperation, acting out, and so forth). The latter, indeed, would seem to present all the features of what, with all homage to the greatness of Mann's novel, we have already characterized as bad allegory.

But we have not yet come to terms with the tropes and in particular with that omnipresent and obsessive process (denounced by Roman Jakobson) whereby virtually every figure eventually finds itself subsumed under the metaphoric. Let me then briefly suggest that it was no accident that the key word I used to differentiate Adorno's use of *breakthrough* from Mann's was the word *narrative*. Metaphor is nonnarrative: indeed, it has seemed to me that we find our most productive approach to its operations by recognizing its fundamental effect as one of denarrativization, of breaking the horizontal line by way of a verticality or transcendence of the metaphorical comparison or identification. Metaphor lifts us into a world beyond movement or temporality, a world without figural change (inasmuch as it is itself a figure), a nonspace for which the word *eternal* is appropriate only if it is understood negatively, as the name of that something for which we have no name and which is probably language itself. I'm not sure whether this is always the element toward which lyric aspires (and out of which in its eventual failure it sinks back into narrative); but it disappears at once, when the identification is treated like legal evidence and examined part by part, the rose dissected into stamen and petals, stalk, color, odor, and so on. The metaphor has no parts; but their enumeration at once leads to allegory and beyond it to some protonarrative movement, and it is this kind of inspection that allows us to distinguish a metaphorical identification, such as Thomas Mann's military breakthroughs, from Adorno's historical allegory of the development of musical form.

I should add, in this instance, *breakthrough* is another example of the misuse of Adorno's thought (in which he was often himself complicit) to extract named and reified "concepts" like "late style" or "nonidentity": what made his work a model of dialectical thinking was precisely the dissolution of such commodified terms before they had a chance to harden into doctrine.

◆

Mahler's Sixth Symphony has always been considered the most difficult of his works, no doubt for players fully as much as for listeners. It was first performed in Essen in May 1906; and the setting has its own anecdotal interest, in that Essen, lying at the very heart of the industrial Ruhr, was even then home to the Krupp works and the family associated with them, in other words with the purveyors of the German war machines of both world wars. This premiere in the very "cradle of German heavy industry" has struck one of the composer's most astute commentators as symbolically significant:

> All those driving, relentless, militaristic rhythms, mechanistic percussion and harsh-edged contrasts that permeate so much of this work have always seemed, to me to share kinship with the place where the work was first heard. Here were the foundries and factories that put iron in the Iron Chancellor and built the guns that would spill the blood

of his "blood and iron" when fired in World War I, the cultural pre-echo of whose cataclysm eight years later the work seems partly to illustrate. So I believe this symphony is, first and foremost, a twentieth-century work, perhaps the first twentieth-century symphony. It breathes as much the same air of Krupp as it does Freud, and its concerns are those of our time because so much of our time was formed in the furnaces of Essen as in the consulting rooms of Vienna.[24]

The German component, then, is no more alien in this Austrian or Viennese work than the appearance of the great German businessman and intellectual Arnheim in Musil's *Mann ohne Eigenschaften*; and it leads Duggan to suggest that we

> strip Mahler bare of nineteenth-century sonorities and folk memories, contrast the sound of the Fifth Symphony, and project, as though on a bright stage, a bitter, unforgiving elegy that opens out the tragedy into something universal, held at one remove to reinforce the tragedy's universality and confirm its contemporary relevance.[25]

By this last, I believe that he means to correct the overly personal and autobiographical versions of the symphony that have proliferated since Alma Mahler's account, which generally turn on the problem of how so bleak a work should have emerged from what was to all accounts the happiest period of Mahler's life—marriage, children, the lake in summer, his little composing shed, the rowboat, and so on.

We must, I think, grasp these first two interpretations in a dialectical relationship to one another and conjecture that it was that very personal fulfillment which released the composer to far darker intimations of the modernizing world and its conflicts.

It remained, however, for a resolute and untraditional commentator to produce a far different and more realistic view of this "blissful" interlude in Mahler's life. Seth Monahan documents a view of this summer as the experience

---

24 Tony Duggan, "The Mahler Symphonies," May 2007, musicweb-international.com.

25 Ibid.

of a marriage in crisis—of a young wife beleaguered by unglamorous responsibilities, exasperated by her husband's aloofness [and, indeed, as he suggests later on, impotence], and deeply resentful of her social isolation and lack of a creative outlet ... Mahler was an imperious, workaholic killjoy and self-absorbed misogynist ["You ... have only one profession from now on," he wrote in 1901, "to make me happy"], while she was a vain, independent-minded hedonist, nearly twenty years his junior and well accustomed to being the center of attention.[26]

This revision is all the more significant, inasmuch as the identification of the second subject as "the Alma theme" inevitably forces interpreters to take some such domestic and autobiographical level of the symphony into account. I should add that Alma has been the predictable target of contempt and vilification by Mahlerians, thereby undergoing the fate of so many of the sometime companions or partners of "great men" from Flaubert's lover Louise Colet to the various evil empresses of Chinese dynastic rulers: namely the object of mockery as well as of the most scurrilous misrepresentation. She may have been a difficult character in later life, but she had her own musical and compositional gifts, which were officially silenced by commands of the type of the 1901 injunction of Mahler himself; who for his part seems to have shared the traditional image of the wife as "helpmeet" current everywhere in nineteenth-century bourgeois society and most visible in Ibsen (*Peer Gynt*) and Wagner (Senta, Cosima).

I dwell on these points not merely to underscore the inevitability of some such biographical reading of the symphony, however fleeting, but also to emphasize the tendency to frame such allegories around individual characters: if the Alma theme is to be a character in a symphonic drama, then, the march motif must also be susceptible to a complementary personification. The result can only be faintly ludicrous and archaic, inasmuch as modern allegory begins by eschewing personification altogether. We will return to this issue at the end of this chapter.

For the moment, I want to suggest that these two interpretations, the politico–historical one of a pre–World War I tension and the domestic one of a troubled marriage, in fact correspond to two levels of the classical fourfold scheme of allegorical analysis, namely the anagogic and moral levels.

---

26   Monahan, *Mahler's Symphonic Sonatas*, 133–34.

It is clear, then, that it remains to identify the initial levels at his set or scheme, namely the literal text and the allegorical interpretive code. I will assume here that something like Adorno's reading of a purely formal musical history (in the context of which this particular symphony includes the reflexive undermining and critique of the sonata form it is itself reproducing) will offer at least one of these missing narrative options: for its terms—an institutional narrative or generic structure which is "deconstructed" at the very moment of its replication—posit their historical origins (the emergent symphony in the moment of the French Revolution) and their historical outcome (the end of tonality after Mahler), and project yet another third narrative, this time a music-historical one, in its own right.

As for the literal level, which can surely only be the musical text itself, the philosophical question posed by its identification is one that has plagued musicology since the beginnings of its flirtation with narrative analysis.[27] It is as it were an ontological question: is the analysis, the narrative reading, really part of the musical structure or has it not merely been superadded onto the latter after the "parasitic" fashion of all interpretation? I won't try to take a position on all this, except to say that I believe the fundamental terminology of technical music analysis itself to be allegorical in some deeper sense: allegro, andante, and so on are after all easily unmasked as proto-allegorical pictures; major and minor are inevitably treated as comic and tragic alternatives; and even the visible score itself makes a language of rising and falling unavoidable. As for the number twelve, which presides over the tonal scale, I feel sure that numerologists have long since found meanings in its components which are distantly comparable to what Rimbaud found in the letters of his childhood ABC.

These findings may be summarized in the now familiar fourfold scheme of traditional allegory:

> ANAGOGICAL: conflict and modernity as war
> MORAL: the couple, the impossibility of marriage
> ALLEGORICAL: the end of sonata form and of tonality
> LITERAL: music as the tension between temporality and an eternal present

---

27 See note 6 above.

In conclusion, then, I return to the question of personification, which is so often the stumbling block and the source of all kinds of misunderstandings about the nature of allegory and in particular of allegory today. The dissolution of personification is part of what I have characterized as the dissolution of substantialism in modern thought and its replacement by relationality: it is a belief in things rather than processes, a personification-oriented allegory thereby giving way to a different kind of structure when that presupposition itself falls away.

Meanwhile, it would certainly seem historically perverse to continue to identify themes with anthropomorphic characters at a moment when the experience as well as the theories of individual subjectivity find themselves in crisis and are confronted with a variety of options: the "subject" as a space of multiple subject positions; the "subject" as itself an impersonal object for consciousness lacking in any of the traits we associate with the older individuality or personal identity; the Copernican decentering, if not the famous "death," of the subject; Nietzsche's position that nothing is achieved by acknowledgment of the death of God if it is not accompanied by the parallel displacement of the grammatical and psychological subject itself. These various theories, or better still, these ideological positions and programs are obviously reinforced by the widespread personal experience of fragmentation and disorientation in late capitalism, an accumulation of testimonies variously formulated as desperate "searches for personal identity" and the like, which would seem to render the traditional procedures of personification misplaced and futile if not unsatisfying. They then get transferred inside a multiple subjectivity and begin to name the various faculties of the mind, the multiplicity of subject positions which the dissolution of the traditional character leaves in its wake.

Still, there would also seem to be no doubt that a composition like the first movement of Mahler's Sixth stakes out a certain number of recognizable musical "subjects" that any narrative approach to music must confront. There can be no doubt that Mahler himself thought in terms of narrative, in a way wholly different from that tone-poem descriptive nomenclature officially attached to the earlier works (awakening, spring, and so on); indeed his own letters evoke this or that first subject as a "hero" to whom things happen. We do not have to follow him in this (the author's intentions not being particularly binding on the reader), and it is certainly permitted to think that this is simply a practical working terminology on the part of a composer handling complex masses of musical signs and developments.

But we have already shown that this first movement confronts us with an unmistakable pair of distinct musical identities (refraining from using the narrative terminology of character, actant, or the like). There is the initial driving, marchlike, relentless movement, with its own melodic banner as it were; and then there is the very different theme of yearning, romantic, florid expression.

Their interaction certainly constitutes the development of this rather skeletal and transparent movement. What transpires, however, is rather unexpected, for if it is a question of a struggle for mastery here, it is the "feminine" subject (Alma, the second subject), who triumphs in this first movement conclusion. That theme has effectively absorbed the first one into itself, so that it has appropriated all the driving and relentless force of the first "masculine" musical identity. To be sure, one could appeal to the psychological subtleties of dramatic confrontation to argue that on the contrary, this transfer is a defeat for the second subject, who has in effect been remolded into the spirit of the opponent and has been made to assume "his" traits and values.

At any rate, some such reading is useful at least to the degree that it solves a problem quite unique to this particular symphony, namely, the uncertainty about which movement is to follow this opening one. Mahler himself notoriously hesitated about the order of the second and third movements, one of them a scherzo that virtually replicates the marchlike intensity of the old first subject, and the other an andante far more romantic and subdued than the rather garish second subject we have been evoking. I would argue, in the light of the compromise formation with which the first movement ends, that it renders plausible some lingering dissatisfaction of its principal subject with this outcome; a frustration in which the imperious force of the first subject has not come to fulfillment and must then vent its energies in a new attempt in that scherzo, which in most performances is chosen to stand as a second movement but which feels very much like an embattled and stubborn, uncompromising return to the marchlike spirit of the previous one, the opening of the symphony.

Yet, as we have already observed, there are moments in this same first movement that somehow complicate the simplicity of the first movement's oppositions and suggest, for want of anything else, an enlargement of its rudimentary cast of characters. There is for example a wondrous moment of stillness that Monahan marks as "Utopian," in which both motifs are as it were taken up into heaven and played out in an ethereal transcendence in which struggle is suspended along with development as such, and in which the notorious aforementioned cowbells, along with the harp and a few cool notes on an otherwise inconspicuous piano, certify our removal to another world. Is this not—alongside equally distinctive perspectival moments in which the music takes place in a palpable distance, as though offstage (or under the strange prolonged ceiling of the pedal-point at the beginning of the First Symphony)—is this not also yet another form of what Monahan calls "hypothetical music," a qualitative transformation in the very space in which the musical event takes place? A shift in the very ontological modes that count as musical immediacy or reality?

How are such moments to be integrated into the narrative of the two named characters, whose drama is allegedly being told here? It is as though the characters were transferred to a series of different worlds to play out their eternal opposition in a bewildering variety of landscapes and their weathers, now in spring, now in deepest winter; and this not, as traditionally from movement to movement, but rather within the unity of a single musical elaboration.

I have in another place (perhaps prematurely) suggested that we reduce the Mahlerian drama to two alternating poles, the one I simply called *agitation*, the other facing the same linguistic problem as the state of calm or recovered serenity did in Aristotle's system of the emotions[28] (where the opposite of anger could find no ready-made name, let alone an adequate translation). Now, however, I wonder whether these states might not be enumerated in a more adequate variety and characterized in something like the following way: the driving or marchlike, the arialike and operatic, the Utopian-idyllic, the transcendental, the metamorphic (those moments in which a wholly different melodic and harmonic seethes within a given state and makes its way to the surface), and finally the chorale-haft or unison-affirmative in which a traditional solemnity seeks to bring the music to some stability if not some more definitive movement toward a more traditional and definitive conclusion.

---

28 See Chapter 2.

The point is that none of these states is successful in the fulfillment it seeks; none come to any real satisfaction, as we saw with the forward-driving first subject in the first movement. Mahlerian agitation ultimately infects all of them and undermines them to the point at which they make way for some new affective attempt. So even this new system of essentially allegorical names and allegorical identities gives way under the momentum of restless mood swings, repeated alternations and transitions: and indeed this which is modern and relational about what is still traditional in this musical language and its formal developments: as in all truly modern art, the inner essence of the thing is not a substance but a transition, many transitions, a perpetual modulation not only from one key to another but from one kind of identity, one kind of value or categorial perspective, to another. And in this sense I persist in thinking that my first diagnosis of the allegorical persistence of an inner principle of agitation, ever dissatisfied and pushing on to new kinds of developments, is the most comprehensive reading.

In an earlier text, I compared this principle to the Lacanian death wish, the drive: not in the well-worn assertions of this or that obsession with death everywhere in Mahler, but rather in that of a well-nigh immortal biological force that uses the individual organism for its own purposes before discarding its husk, like an old shoe, persisting irresistibly and impersonally within the merely mortal satisfactions that it imperiously traverses and reduces to nothingness in its path. Here, then, the formal law is absolute: there must be no ultimate satisfaction, no stopping point, there must be no fulfillment! (Such was indeed the very meaning of Faust's downfall, his ill-advised cry to the instant of time to stop: Verweile doch, du bist so schön!)

The finale of the Sixth Symphony acts out this ultimate law of the universe, that ultimate fulfillment is neither to be permitted nor attained. For indeed, at the climactic moments of its development, where something like fulfillment seems to draw near, a sound from another space altogether—not that other world of the cowbells and mountain meadows, but rather an inhuman world, neither malign nor benevolent, but icy, impersonal, as though from Montaigne's "épicycle de Mercure"—an explosive sound neither dissonant nor consonant, a sonority that does not figure in the human battery of sounds and their instruments gathered on the bourgeois stage, but rather a meaningless ear-splitting strident intervention breaking through the worldly developments of this still human and recognizable music: it is the notorious hammer blow, the voice of the Law, the blast of the Shofar, that warns us away from the tabooed satisfaction and sends us back to our sublunary worldly destinies.

Thus, although the conclusion of a work of art is always a happy ending regardless of its content—inasmuch as it certifies the successful transformation of suffering into sheer expression (as classically in Shakespearean tragedy: "And in Aleppo once . . .")—conclusions here in Mahler are truly "hypothetical" in the sense in which, naming fulfillment, they claim it at the same time that they demonstrate its impossibility: satisfying and unsatisfying all at once, desire thwarted and thereby realized by way of its very expression: such are the stakes in this work of Mahler and the well-nigh metaphysical outcome that can alone be the conclusion of the force he has awakened.

As for allegory, I will want to draw the conclusion that some new allegory of qualitative states and their transitions into one another here has replaced the older search for personifications and identities. It is with this historical development as with the great historical transition from named emotions to a gamut of nameless affect that I have sought to depict here and elsewhere: Mahler bestrides both, just as he unites for one last time the traditions of Beethoven and Rossini, tempting us with allegory and allegoresis alike and demonstrating that music is profoundly allegorical in its temporalities at the same time that, nonlinguistic, it eludes the analysis of a mode that arises from the alienating power of words and names, of language as such.

5A
Political: National Allegory

Third-World Literature in the Era of Multinational Capitalism

Judging from recent conversations among third-world intellectuals, there is now an obsessive return of the national situation itself, the name of the country that returns again and again like a gong, the collective attention to "us" and what we have to do and how we do it, to what we can't do and what we do better than this or that nationality, our unique characteristics, in short, to the level of the "people." This is not the way American intellectuals have been discussing "America," and indeed one might feel that the whole matter is nothing but that old thing called "nationalism," long since liquidated here and rightly so. Yet a certain nationalism is fundamental in the third world (and also in the most vital areas of the second world), thus making it legitimate to ask whether it is all that bad in the end.[1] Does in fact the message of some disabused and more experienced first-world wisdom (that of Europe even more than of the United States) consist in urging these nation-states to outgrow it as fast as possible? The predictable reminders of Kampuchea and of Iraq and Iran do not really seem to me to settle anything or suggest by what these nationalisms might be replaced except perhaps some global American postmodernist culture.

---

1 The whole matter of nationalism should perhaps be rethought, as Benedict Anderson's interesting essay *Imagined Communities*, London: Verso, 1983, and Tom Nairn's *The Breakup of Britain*, London: New Left Books, 1977, invite us to do.

Many arguments can be made for the importance and interest of noncanonical forms of literature such as that of the third world,[2] but one is peculiarly self-defeating because it borrows the weapons of the adversary: the strategy of trying to prove that these texts are as "great" as those of the canon itself. The object is then to show that, to take an example from another non-canonical form, Dashiell Hammett is really as great as Dostoyevsky, and therefore can be admitted. This is to attempt dutifully to wish away all traces of that "pulp" format which is constitutive of sub-genres, and it invites immediate failure insofar as any passionate reader of Dostoyevsky will know at once, after a few pages, that those kinds of satisfactions are not present. Nothing is to be gained by passing over in silence the radical difference of noncanonical texts. The third-world novel will not offer the satisfactions of Proust or Joyce; what is more damaging than that, perhaps, is its tendency to remind us of outmoded stages of our own first-world cultural development and to cause us to conclude that "they are still writing novels like Dreiser or Sherwood Anderson."

A case could be built on this kind of discouragement, with its deep existential commitment to a rhythm of modernist innovation if not fashion-changes; but it would not be a moralizing one—a historicist one, rather, which challenges our imprisonment in the present of postmodernism and calls for a reinvention of the radical difference of *our own* cultural past and its now seemingly old-fashioned situations and novelties.

But I would rather argue all this a different way, at least for now[3]: these reactions to third-world texts are at one and the same time perfectly natural, perfectly comprehensible, *and* terribly parochial. If the purpose of the canon is to restrict our aesthetic sympathies, to develop a range of rich and subtle perceptions which can be exercised only on the occasion of a small but choice body of texts, to discourage us from reading anything else or from reading those things in different ways, then it is humanly impoverishing. Indeed our want of sympathy for these often unmodern third-world texts is itself frequently but a disguise for some deeper fear of the affluent about the way people actually live in other parts of the

---

2 I have argued elsewhere for the importance of mass culture and science fiction. See "Reification and Utopia in Mass Culture," *Social Text*, no. 1 (1979).

3 The essay was written for an immediate occasion—the third memorial lecture in honor of my late colleague and friend Robert C. Elliot at the University of California, San Diego. It is essentially reprinted as given.

world—a way of life that still has little in common with daily life in the American suburb. There is nothing particularly disgraceful in having lived a sheltered life, in never having had to confront the difficulties, the complications and the frustrations of urban living, but it is nothing to be particularly proud of either. Moreover, a limited experience of life normally does not make for a wide range of sympathies with very different kinds of people (I'm thinking of differences that range from gender and race all the way to those of social class and culture).

The way in which all this affects the reading process seems to be as follows: as Western readers whose tastes (and much else) have been formed by our own modernisms, a popular or socially realistic third-world novel tends to come before us, not immediately, but as though already-read. We sense, between ourselves and this alien text, the presence of another reader, of the Other reader, for whom a narrative, which strikes us as conventional or naive, has a freshness of information and a social interest that we cannot share. The fear and the resistance I'm evoking has to do, then, with the sense of our own noncoincidence with that Other reader, so different from ourselves; our sense that to coincide in any adequate way with that Other "ideal reader"—that is to say, to read this text adequately—we would have to give up a great deal that is individually precious to us and acknowledge an existence and a situation unfamiliar and therefore frightening—one that we do not know and prefer *not* to know.

Why, returning to the question of the canon, *should* we only read certain kinds of books? No one is suggesting we should *not* read those, but why should we not also read other ones? We are not, after all, being shipped to that "desert island" beloved of the devisers of great books lists. And as a matter of fact—and this is to me the conclusive nail in the argument—we all do "read" many different kinds of texts in this life of ours, since, whether we are willing to admit it or not, we spend much of our existence in the force field of a mass culture that is radically different from our "great books" and live at least a double life in the various compartments of our unavoidably fragmented society. We need to be aware that we are even more fundamentally fragmented than that; rather than clinging to this particular mirage of the "centered subject" and the unified personal identity, we would do better to confront honestly the fact of fragmentation on a global scale; it is a confrontation with which we can here at least make a cultural beginning.

A final observation on my use of the term "third world." I take the point of criticisms of this expression, particularly those which stress the way in which it obliterates profound differences between a whole range of non-Western countries and situations (indeed, one such fundamental opposition—between the traditions of the great eastern empires and those of the postcolonial African nation-states—is central in what follows). I don't, however, see any comparable expression that articulates, as this one does, the fundamental breaks between the capitalist first world, the socialist bloc of the second world, and a range of other countries which have suffered the experience of colonialism and imperialism. One can only deplore the ideological implications of oppositions such as that between "developed" and "underdeveloped" or "developing" countries; while the more recent conception of northern and southern tiers, which has a very different ideological content and import than the rhetoric of development, and is used by very different people, nonetheless implies an unquestioning acceptance of "convergence theory"—namely the idea that the Soviet Union and the United States are from this perspective largely the same thing. I am using the term "third world" in an essentially descriptive sense, and objections to it do not strike me as especially relevant to the argument I am making.

In these last years of the century, the old question of a properly world literature reasserts itself. This is due as much or more to the disintegration of our own conceptions of cultural study as to any very lucid awareness of the great outside world around us. We may therefore—as "humanists"—acknowledge the pertinence of the critique of present-day humanities by our titular leader, William Bennett, without finding any great satisfaction in his embarrassing solution: yet another impoverished and ethnocentric Graeco-Judaic "great books list of the civilization of the West," "great texts, great minds, great ideas."[4] One is tempted to turn back on Bennett himself the question he approvingly quotes from Maynard Mack: "How long can a democratic nation afford to support a narcissistic minority so transfixed by its own image?" Nevertheless, the present moment does offer a remarkable opportunity to rethink our humanities curriculum in a new way—to reexamine the

---

4 William Bennett, "To Reclaim a Legacy," text of a report on the humanities, *Chronicle of Higher Education*, XXIX, 14, Nov. 28, 1984.

shambles and ruins of all our older "great books," "humanities," "freshman-introductory," and "core course" type traditions.

Today the reinvention of cultural studies in the United States demands the reinvention, in a new situation, of what Goethe long ago theorized as "world literature." In our more immediate context, then, any conception of world literature necessarily demands some specific engagement with the question of third-world literature, and it is this not necessarily narrower subject about which I have something to say today.

It would be presumptuous to offer some general theory of what is often called third-world literature, given the enormous variety both of national cultures in the third world and of specific historical trajectories in each of those areas. All of this, then, is provisional and intended both to suggest specific perspectives for research and to convey a sense of the interest and value of these clearly neglected literatures for people formed by the values and stereotypes of a first-world culture. One important distinction would seem to impose itself at the outset, namely that none of these cultures can be conceived as anthropologically independent or autonomous, rather, they are all in various distinct ways locked in a life-and-death struggle with first-world cultural imperialism—a cultural struggle that is itself a reflection of the economic situation of such areas in their penetration by various stages of capital, or as it is sometimes euphemistically termed, of modernization. This, then, is some first sense in which a study of third-world culture necessarily entails a new view of ourselves, from the outside, insofar as we ourselves are (perhaps without fully knowing it) constitutive forces powerfully at work on the remains of older cultures in our general world capitalist system.

But if this is the case, the initial distinction that imposes itself has to do with the nature and development of older cultures at the moment of capitalist penetration, something it seems to me most enlightening to examine in terms of the Marxian concept of modes of production.[5]

---

5 The classic texts are Friedrich Engels, *The Origin of the Family, Private Property and the State* (1884), London: Penguin, 1972, and the earlier, but only more recently published section of Karl Marx's *Grundrisse*, often called *Pre-Capitalist Economic Formations*, trans. Martin Nicolaus, London: NLB/Penguin, 1973, 471–514. See also Emmanuel Terray, *Marxism and "Primitive" Societies*, trans. Mary Klopper, New York: Monthly Review, 1972; Barry Hindess and Paul Hirst, *Pre-Capitalist Modes of Production*, London: Routledge and Kegan Paul, 1975; and Gilles Deleuze and Felix Guattari, "Savages, Barbarians, Civilized Men," *Anti-Oedipus*, trans. Robert Hurley, Mark Seem, and Helen R. Lane, Minneapolis: University of Minnesota Press, 1983, 139–271.

Contemporary historians seem to be in the process of reaching a consensus on the specificity of feudalism as, a form which, issuing from the break-up of the Roman Empire or the Japanese Shogunate, is able to develop directly into capitalism.⁶ This is not the case with the other modes of production, which in some sense must be disaggregated or destroyed by violence, before capitalism is able to implant its specific forms and displace the older ones. In the gradual expansion of capitalism across the globe, then, our economic system confronts two very distinct modes of production that pose two very different types of social and cultural resistance to its influence. These are so-called primitive, or tribal society on the one hand, and the Asiatic mode of production, or the great bureaucratic imperial systems, on the other. African societies and cultures, as they became the object of systematic colonization in the 1880s, provide the most striking examples of the symbiosis of capital and tribal societies; while China and India offer the principal examples of another and quite different sort of engagement of capitalism with the

---

Besides mode-of-production theory, whose validity is in any case widely debated, there have also appeared in recent years a number of important synthesizing works on third-world history as a unified field. Three works in particular deserve mention: L. S. Stavrianos, *Global Rift: The Third World Comes of Age*, New York: William Morrow, 1981; Eric R. Wolf, *Europe and the People without History*, Berkeley: University of California Press, 1982; and Peter Worsley, *The Three Worlds*, Chicago: University of Chicago Press, 1984. Such works suggest a more general methodological consequence implicit in the present essay but which should be stated explicitly here: first, that the kind of comparative work demanded by this concept of third-world literature involves comparison, not of the individual texts, which are formally and culturally very different from one another, but of the concrete situations from which such texts spring and to which they constitute distinct responses; and second, that such an approach suggests the possibility of a literary and cultural comparatism of a new type, distantly modeled on the new comparative history of Barrington Moore and exemplified in books like Theda Skocpol's *States and Social Revolutions: A Comparative Analysis of France, Russia, and China*, Cambridge: Cambridge University Press, 1979, or Eric Wolf's *Peasant Revolutions of the Twentieth Century*, Norman: University of Oklahoma Press, 1969. Such a new cultural comparatism would juxtapose the study of the differences and similarities of specific literary and cultural texts with a more typological analysis of the various socio-cultural situations from which they spring, an analysis whose variables would necessarily include such features as the inter-relationship of social classes, the role of intellectuals, the dynamics of language and writing, the configuration of traditional forms, the relationship to Western influences, the development of urban experience and money, and so forth. Such comparatism, however, need not be restricted to third-world literature.

6   See, for example, Perry Anderson, *Lineages of the Absolutist State*, London: New Left Books, 1974, 435–549.

great empires of the so-called Asiatic mode. My examples below, then, will be primarily African and Chinese; however, the special case of Latin America must be noted in passing. Latin America offers yet a third kind of development—one involving an even earlier destruction of imperial systems now projected by collective memory back into the archaic or tribal. Thus the earlier nominal conquests of independence open them at once to a kind of indirect economic penetration and control—something Africa and Asia will come to experience only more recently with decolonization in the 1950s and 60s.

Having made these initial distinctions, let me now, by way of a sweeping hypothesis, try to say what all third-world cultural productions seem to have in common and what distinguishes them radically from analogous cultural forms in the first world. All third-world texts are necessarily, I want to argue, allegorical, and in a very specific way: they are to be read as what I will call *national allegories*, even when, or perhaps I should say, particularly when their forms develop out of predominantly Western machineries of representation, such as the novel. Let me try to state this distinction in a grossly oversimplified way: one of the determinants of capitalist culture, that is, the culture of the western realist and modernist novel, is a radical split between the private and the public, between the poetic and the political, between what we have come to think of as the domain of sexuality and the unconscious and that of the public world of classes, of the economic, and of secular political power: in other words, Freud versus Marx. Our numerous theoretical attempts to overcome this great split only reconfirm its existence and its shaping power over our individual and collective lives. We have been trained in a deep cultural conviction that the lived experience of our private existences is somehow incommensurable with the abstractions of economic science and political dynamics. Politics in our novels therefore is, according to Stendhal's canonical formulation, a "pistol shot in the middle of a concert."

I will argue that, although we may retain for convenience and for analysis such categories as the subjective and the public or political, the relations between them are wholly different in third-world culture. Third-world texts, even those which are seemingly private and invested with a properly libidinal dynamic—necessarily project a political dimension in the form of national allegory: *the story of the private individual destiny is always an allegory of the embattled situation of the public third-world culture and society.* Need I add that it is precisely this very different ratio of the political to the personal which makes such texts alien to us at first approach, and consequently, resistant to our conventional Western habits of reading?

I will offer, as something like the supreme example of this process of allegorization, the first masterwork of China's greatest writer, Lu Xun, whose neglect in Western cultural studies is a matter of shame which no excuses based on ignorance can rectify. "Diary of a Madman" (1918) must at first be read by any Western reader as the protocol of what our essentially psychological language terms a "nervous breakdown." It offers the notes and perceptions of a subject in intensifying prey to a terrifying psychic delusion, the conviction that the people around him are concealing a dreadful secret, and that that secret can be none other than the increasingly obvious fact that they are cannibals. At the climax of the development of the delusion, which threatens his own physical safety and his very life itself as a potential victim, the narrator understands that his own brother is himself a cannibal and that the death of their little sister, a number of years earlier, far from being the result of childhood illness, as he had thought, was in reality a murder. As befits the protocol of a psychosis, these perceptions are objective ones, which can be rendered without any introspective machinery: the paranoid subject observes sinister glances around him in the real world, he overhears tell-tale conversations between his brother and an alleged physician (obviously in reality another cannibal) which carry all the conviction of the real, and can be objectively (or "realistically") represented. This is not the place to demonstrate in any detail the absolute pertinence, to Lu Xun's case history, of the preeminent Western or first-world reading of such phenomena, namely Freud's interpretation of the paranoid delusions of Senatspräsident Schreber: an emptying of the world, a radical withdrawal of libido (what Schreber describes as "world-catastrophe"), followed by the attempt to recathect by the obviously imperfect mechanisms of paranoia. "The delusion-formation," Freud explains, "which we take to be a pathological product, is in reality an attempt at recovery, a process of reconstruction."[7]

What is reconstructed, however, is a grisly and terrifying objective real world beneath the appearances of our own world: an unveiling or

---

7 Sigmund Freud, "Psychoanalytic Notes on an Autobiographical Account of a Case of Paranoia," trans. James Strachey, *The Standard Edition of the Complete Psychological Works of Sigmund Freud*, London: Hogarth, 1958, Volume XII, 457.

deconcealment of the nightmarish reality of things, a stripping away of our conventional illusions or rationalizations about daily life and existence. It is a process comparable, as a literary effect, only to some of the processes of Western modernism, and in particular of existentialism, in which narrative is employed as a powerful instrument for the experimental exploration of reality and illusion, an exploration which, however, unlike some of the older realisms, presupposes a certain prior "personal knowledge." The reader must, in other words, have had some analogous experience, whether in physical illness or psychic crisis, of a lived and balefully transformed real world from which we cannot even mentally escape, for the full horror of Lu Xun's nightmare to be appreciated. Terms like "depression" deform such experience by psychologizing it and projecting it back into the pathological Other; while the analogous Western literary approaches to this same experience—I'm thinking of the archetypal deathbed murmur of Kurtz, in Conrad's *Heart of Darkness*, "The horror! The horror!"—recontains precisely that horror by transforming it into a rigorously private and subjective "mood," which can only be designated by recourse to an aesthetic of *expression*— the unspeakable, unnameable inner feeling, whose external formulation can only designate it from without, like a symptom.

But this representational power of Lu Xun's text cannot be appreciated properly without some sense of what I have called its allegorical resonance. For it should be clear that the cannibalism literally apprehended by the sufferer in the attitudes and bearing of his family and neighbors is at one and the same time being attributed by Lu Xun himself to Chinese society as a whole: and if this attribution is to be called "figural," it is indeed a figure more powerful and "literal" than the "literal" level of the text. Lu Xun's proposition is that the people of this great maimed and retarded, disintegrating China of the late and postimperial period, his fellow citizens, are "literally" cannibals: in their desperation, disguised and indeed intensified by the most traditional forms and procedures of Chinese culture, they must devour one another ruthlessly to stay alive. This occurs at all levels of that exceedingly hierarchical society, from lumpens and peasants all the way to the most privileged elite positions in the mandarin bureaucracy. It is, I want to stress, a social and historical nightmare, a vision of the horror of life specifically grasped through History itself, whose consequences go far beyond the more local Western realistic or naturalistic representation of cut throat capitalist or market competition, and it exhibits a specifically political resonance absent from its natural or mythological Western equivalent in the nightmare of Darwinian natural selection.

Now I want to offer four additional remarks about this text, which will touch, respectively, on the libidinal dimension of the story, on the structure of its allegory, on the role of the third-world cultural producer himself, and on the perspective of futurity projected by the tale's double resolution. I will be concerned, in dealing with all four of these topics, to stress the radical structural difference between the dynamics of third-world culture and those of the first-world cultural tradition in which we have ourselves been formed.

I have suggested that in third-world texts such as this story by Lu Xun the relationship between the libidinal and the political components of individual and social experience is radically different from what obtains in the West and what shapes our own cultural forms. Let me try to characterize this difference, or if you like this radical reversal, by way of the following generalization: in the West, conventionally, political commitment is recontained and psychologized or subjectivized by way of the public–private split I have already evoked. Interpretations, for example, of political movements of the 60s in terms of Oedipal revolts are familiar to everyone and need no further comment. That such interpretations are episodes in a much longer tradition, whereby political commitment is repsychologized and accounted for in terms of the subjective dynamics of *ressentiment,* or the authoritarian personality, is perhaps less well understood, but can be demonstrated by a careful reading of antipolitical texts from Nietzsche and Conrad all the way to the latest cold-war propaganda.

What is relevant to our present context is not, however, the demonstration of that proposition, but rather of its inversion in third-world culture, where I want to suggest that psychology, or more specifically, libidinal investment, is to be read in primarily political and social terms. (It is, I hope, unnecessary to add that what follows is speculative and very much subject to correction by specialists: it is offered as a methodological example rather than a "theory" of Chinese culture.) We're told, for one thing, that the great ancient imperial cosmologies identify by analogy what we in the West analytically separate: thus, the classical sex manuals are at one with the texts that reveal the dynamics of political forces, the charts of the heavens at one with the logic of medical lore, and so forth.⁸ Here already then, in an ancient past, Western antinomies—and most particularly that between the subjective and the public or political—are refused in advance. The libidinal center of Lu Xun's text is, however, not sexuality, but rather the oral stage, the whole bodily question of eating, of ingestion, devoration, incorporation, from which such fundamental categories as the pure and the impure spring. We must now recall, not merely the extraordinary symbolic complexity of Chinese cuisine, but also the central role this art and practice occupies in Chinese culture as a whole. When we find that centrality confirmed by the observation that the very rich Chinese vocabulary for sexual matters is extraordinarily intertwined with the language of eating; and when we observe the multiple uses to which the verb "to eat" is put in ordinary Chinese language (one "eats" a fear or a fright, for example), we may feel in a somewhat better position to sense the enormous sensitivity of this libidinal region, and of Lu Xun's mobilization of it for the dramatization of an essentially social nightmare—something which in a Western writer would be consigned to the realm of the merely private obsession, the vertical dimension of the personal trauma.

A different alimentary transgression can be observed throughout Lu Xun's works, but nowhere quite so strikingly as in his terrible little story, "Medicine." The story portrays a dying child—the death of children is a constant in these works—whose parents have the good fortune to procure an "infallible" remedy. At this point we must recall both that traditional Chinese medicine is not "taken," as in the West, but "eaten," and that for Lu Xun traditional Chinese medicine was the supreme locus of the unspeakable and exploitative charlatanry of traditional Chinese culture in general. In his crucially important Preface to the first collection of his stories,⁹ he recounts the suffering and death of his own father from tuberculosis, while declining family reserves rapidly disappeared into the purchase of expensive and rare, exotic and ludicrous medicaments. We will not sense the symbolic significance of this indignation unless we

---

8   See for example Wolfram Eberhard, *A History of China*, trans. E. W. Dickes, Berkeley: University of California Press, 1977, 105: "When we hear of alchemy, or read books about it we should always keep in mind that many of these books can also be read as books of sex; in a similar way, books on the art of war, too, can be read as books on sexual relations."
9   Lu Xun, *Selected Stories of Lu Hsun*, trans. Gladys Yang and Yang Hsien-yi, Beijing: Foreign Languages Press, 1972, 1–6.

remember that for all these reasons Lu Xun decided to study western medicine in Japan—the epitome of some new Western science that promised collective regeneration—only later to decide that the production of culture—I am tempted to say, the elaboration of a political culture—was a more effective form of political medicine.[10] As a writer, then, Lu Xun remains a diagnostician and a physician. Hence this terrible story, in which the cure for the male child, the father's only hope for survival in future generations, turns out to be one of those large doughy-white Chinese steamed rolls, soaked in the blood of a criminal who has just been executed. The child dies anyway, of course, but it is important to note that the hapless victim of a more properly state violence (the supposed criminal) was a *political* militant, whose grave is mysteriously covered in flowers by absent sympathizers of whom one knows nothing. In the analysis of a story like this, we must rethink our conventional conception of the symbolic levels of a narrative (where sexuality and politics might be in homology to each other, for instance) as a set of loops or circuits which intersect and overdetermine each other—the enormity of therapeutic cannibalism finally intersecting in a pauper's cemetery, with the more overt violence of family betrayal and political repression.

This new mapping process brings me to the cautionary remark I wanted to make about allegory itself—a form long discredited in the West and the specific target of the Romantic revolution of Wordsworth and Coleridge, yet a linguistic structure which also seems to be experiencing a remarkable reawakening of interest in contemporary literary theory. If allegory has once again become somehow congenial for us today, as over against the massive and monumental unifications of an older modernist symbolism or even realism itself, it is because the allegorical spirit is profoundly discontinuous, a matter of breaks and heterogeneities, of the multiple polysemia of the dream rather than the homogeneous representation of the symbol. Our traditional conception of allegory—based, for instance, on stereotypes of Bunyan—is that of an elaborate set of figures and personifications to be read against some one-to-one table of equivalences: this is, so to speak, a one-dimensional view of this signifying process, which might only be set in motion and complexified were we willing to entertain the more alarming notion that such equivalences are themselves in constant change and transformation at each perpetual present of the text.

10 Ibid., 2–3.

Political: National Allegory   171

Here, too, Lu Xun has some lessons for us. This writer of short stories and sketches, which never evolved into the novel form as such, produced at least one approach to the longer form, in a much lengthier series of anecdotes about a hapless coolie named Ah Q, who comes to serve, as we might have suspected, as the allegory of a certain set of Chinese attitudes and modes of behavior. It is interesting to note that the enlargement of the form determines a shift in tone or generic discourse: now everything that had been stricken with the stillness and emptiness of death and suffering without hope—"the room was not only too silent, it was far too big as well, and the things in it were far too empty"[11]— becomes material for a more properly Chaplinesque comedy. Ah Q's resiliency springs from an unusual—but we are to understand culturally very normal and familiar—technique for overcoming humiliation. When set upon by his persecutors, Ah Q, serene in his superiority over them, reflects: "'It is as if I were beaten by my own son. What is the world coming to nowadays ...' Thereupon he too would walk away, satisfied at having won."[12] Admit that you are not even human, they insist, that you are nothing but an animal! On the contrary, he tells them, "I'm worse than an animal, I'm an insect! There, does that satisfy you?" In less than ten seconds, however, Ah Q would walk away also satisfied that he had won, thinking that he was after all "number one in self-belittlement," and that after removing the 'self-belittlement' what remained was still the glory of remaining 'number one.'"[13] When one recalls the remarkable self-esteem of the Manchu dynasty in its final throes, and the serene contempt for foreign devils who had nothing but modern science, gunboats, armies, technology, and power to their credit, one achieves a more precise sense of the historical and social topicality of Lu Xun's satire.

Ah Q is thus, allegorically, China itself. What I want to observe, however, what complicates the whole issue, is that his persecutors—the idlers and bullies who find their daily pleasures in getting a rise out of just such miserable victims as Ah Q—they, too, are China, in the allegorical sense. This very simple example, then, shows the capacity of allegory to generate a range of distinct meanings or messages, simultaneously,

---

11   Ibid., 40.
12   Ibid., 72.
13   Ibid. I am indebted to Peter Rushton for some of these observations.

as the allegorical tenor and vehicle change places: Ah Q is China humiliated by the foreigners, a China so well versed in the spiritual techniques of self-justification that such humiliations are not even registered, let alone recalled. But the persecutors are also China, in a different sense, the terrible self-cannibalistic China of the "Diary of a Madman," whose response to powerlessness is the senseless persecution of the weaker and more inferior members of the hierarchy.

All of which slowly brings us to the question of the writer himself in the third world, and to what must be called the function of the intellectual, it being understood that in the third-world situation the intellectual is always in one way or another a political intellectual. No third-world lesson is more timely or more urgent for us today, among whom the very term "intellectual" has withered away, as though it were the name for an extinct species. Nowhere has the strangeness of this vacant position been brought home to me more strongly than on a recent trip to Cuba, when I had occasion to visit a remarkable college-preparatory school on the outskirts of Havana. It is a matter of some shame for an American to witness the cultural curriculum in a socialist setting which also very much identifies itself with the third world. Over some three or four years, Cuban teenagers study poems of Homer, Dante's *Inferno*, the Spanish theatrical classics, the great realistic novels of the nineteenth-century European tradition, and finally contemporary Cuban revolutionary novels, of which, incidentally, we desperately need English translations. But the semester's work I found most challenging was one explicitly devoted to the study of the role of the intellectual as such: the cultural intellectual who is also a political militant, the intellectual who produces both poetry and praxis. The Cuban illustrations of this process—Ho Chi Minh and Augustino Nieto—are obviously enough culturally determined: our own equivalents would probably be the more familiar figures of Du Bois and C. L. R. James, of Sartre and Neruda or Brecht, of Kollontai or Louise Michel. But as this whole talk aims implicitly at suggesting a new conception of the humanities in American education today, it is appropriate to add that the study of the role of the intellectual as such ought to be a key component in any such proposals.

I've already said something about Lu Xun's own conception of his vocation, and its extrapolation from the practice of medicine. But there is a great deal more to be said specifically about the Preface. Not only is it one of the fundamental documents for understanding the situation of the third-world artist, it is also a dense text in its own right, fully as much a work of art as any of the greatest stories. And in Lu Xun's own work it is the supreme example of the very unusual ratio of subjective investment and a deliberately depersonalized objective narration. We have no time to do justice to those relationships, which would demand a line-by-line commentary. Yet I will quote the little fable by which Lu Xun, responding to requests for publication by his friends and future collaborators, dramatizes his dilemma:

> Imagine an iron house without windows, absolutely indestructible, with many people fast sleep inside who will shortly die of suffocation. But you know that since they will die in their sleep, they will not feel the pain of death. Now if you cry aloud to wake a few of the lighter sleepers, making those unfortunate few suffer the agony of irrevocable death, do you think you are doing them a good turn?[14]

The seemingly hopeless situation of the third-world intellectual in this historical period (shortly after the founding of the Chinese Communist Party, but also after the bankruptcy of the middle-class revolution had become apparent)—in which no solutions, no forms of praxis or change, seem conceivable—this situation will find its parallel, as we shall see shortly, in the situation of African intellectuals after the achievement of independence, when once again no political solutions seem present or visible on the historical horizon. The formal or literary manifestation of this political problem is the possibility of narrative closure, something we will return to more specifically.

In a more general theoretical context—and it is this theoretical form of the problem I should now like at least to thematize and set in place on the agenda—we must recover a sense of what "cultural revolution" means, in its strongest form, in the Marxist tradition. The reference is not to the immediate events of that violent and tumultuous interruption of the "eleven years" in recent Chinese history, although some reference to Maoism as a doctrine is necessarily implicit. The term, we are told, was Lenin's own, and in that form explicitly designated the literacy campaign and the new problems of universal scholarity and education: something of which Cuba, again, remains the most stunning and

14 Ibid., 5.

successful example in recent history. We must, however, enlarge the conception still further, to include a range of seemingly very different preoccupations, of which the names of Gramsci and Wilhelm Reich, Frantz Fanon, Herbert Marcuse, Rudolph Bahro, and Paolo Freire, may give an indication of their scope and focus. Overhastily, I will suggest that "cultural revolution" as it is projected in such works turns on the phenomenon of what Gramsci called "subalternity," namely the feelings of mental inferiority and habits of subservience and obedience which necessarily and structurally develop in situations of domination—most dramatically in the experience of colonized peoples. But here, as so often, the subjectivizing and psychologizing habits of first-world peoples such as ourselves can play us false and lead us into misunderstandings. Subalternity is not in that sense a psychological matter, although it governs psychologies; and I suppose that the strategic choice of the term "cultural" aims precisely at restructuring that view of the problem and projecting it outwards into the realm of objective or collective spirit in some non-psychological, but also non-reductionist or non-economistic, materialistic fashion. When a psychic structure is objectively determined by economic and political relationships, it cannot be dealt with by means of purely psychological therapies; yet it equally cannot be dealt with by means of purely objective transformations of the economic and political situation itself, since the habits remain and exercise a baleful and crippling residual effect.[15] This is a more dramatic form of that old mystery, the unity of theory and practice; and it is specifically in the context of this problem of cultural revolution (now so strange and alien to us) that the achievements and failures of third-world intellectuals, writers, and artists must be replaced if their concrete historical meaning is to be grasped. We have allowed ourselves, as first-world cultural intellectuals, to restrict our consciousness of our life's work to the narrowest professional or bureaucratic terms, thereby encouraging in ourselves a special sense of subalternity and guilt, which only reinforces the vicious circle. That a literary article could be a political act, with real consequences, is for most of us little more than a curiosity of the literary history of Czarist Russia or of modern China itself. But we perhaps

---

15 Socialism will become a reality, Lenin observes, "when the *necessity* of observing the simple, fundamental rules of human intercourse" has "become a *habit*" (*State and Revolution*, Beijing: Foreign Languages Press, 1973, 122).

should also consider the possibility that as intellectuals we ourselves are at present soundly sleeping in that indestractable iron room, of which Lu Xun spoke, on the point of suffocation.

The matter of narrative closure, then, and of the relationship of a narrative text to futurity and to some collective project yet to come, is not merely a formal or literary-critical issue. "Diary of a Madman" has in fact two distinct and incompatible endings, which prove instructive to examine in light of the writer's own hesitations and anxieties about his social role. One ending, that of the deluded subject himself, is very much a call to the future, in the impossible situation of a well-nigh universal cannibalism: the last desperate lines launched into the void are the words, "Save the children . . ." But the tale has a second ending as well, which is disclosed on the opening page, when the older (supposedly cannibalistic) brother greets the narrator with the following cheerful remark: "I appreciate your coming such a long way to see us, but my brother recovered some time ago and has gone elsewhere to take up an official post." So, in advance, the nightmare is annulled; the paranoid visionary, his brief and terrible glimpse of the grisly reality beneath the appearance now vouchsafed, gratefully returns to the realm of illusion and oblivion therein again to take up his place in the space of bureaucratic power and privilege. I want to suggest that it is only at this price, by way of a complex play of simultaneous and antithetical messages, that the narrative text is able to open up a concrete perspective on the real future.

I must interrupt myself here to interpolate several observations before proceeding. For one thing, it is clear to me that *any* articulation of radical difference—that of gender, incidentally, fully as much as that of culture—is susceptible to appropriation by that strategy of otherness which Edward Said, in the context of the Middle East, called "orientalism." It does not matter much that the radical otherness of the culture in question is praised or valorized positively, as in the preceding pages: the essential operation is that of differentiation, and once that has been accomplished, the mechanism Said denounces has been set in place. On the other hand, I don't see how a first-world intellectual can avoid this operation without falling back into some general liberal and humanistic universalism: it seems to me that one of our basic political tasks lies precisely in the ceaseless effort to remind the American public of the radical difference of other national situations.

But at this point one should insert a cautionary reminder about the dangers of the concept of "culture" itself: the very speculative remarks I have allowed myself to make about Chinese "culture" will not be complete unless I add that "culture" in this sense is by no means the final term at which one stops. One must imagine such cultural structures and attitudes as having been themselves, in the beginning, vital responses to infrastructural realities (economic and geographic, for example), as attempts to resolve more fundamental contradictions—attempts which then outlive the situations for which they were devised, and survive, in reified forms, as "cultural patterns." Those patterns themselves then become part of the objective situation confronted by later generations, and, as in the case of Confucianism, having once been part of the solution to a dilemma, then become part of the new problem.

Nor can I feel that the concept of cultural "identity" or even national "identity" is adequate. One cannot acknowledge the justice of the general poststructuralist assault on the so-called "centered subject," the old unified ego of bourgeois individualism, and then resuscitate this same ideological mirage of psychic unification on the collective level in the form of a doctrine of collective identity. Appeals to collective identity need to be evaluated from a historical perspective, rather than from the standpoint of some dogmatic and placeless "ideological analysis." When a third-world writer invokes this (to us) ideological value, we need to examine the concrete historical situation closely in order to determine the political consequences of the strategic use of this concept. Lu Xun's moment, for example, is very clearly one in which a critique of Chinese "culture" and "cultural identity" has powerful and revolutionary consequences—consequences which may not obtain in a later social configuration. This is then, perhaps, another and more complicated way of raising the issue of "nationalism" to which I referred earlier.

As far as national allegory is concerned, I think it may be appropriate to stress its presence in what is generally considered western literature in order to underscore certain structural differences. The example I have in mind is the work of Benito Perez Galdos—the last and among the richest achievements of nineteenth-century realism. Galdos' novels are more visibly allegorical (in the national sense) than most of their better-known European predecessors:[16]

---

16 See the interesting discussions in Stephen Gilman, *Galdós and the Art of the European Novel: 1867–1887*, Princeton: Princeton University Press, 1981.

something that might well be explained in terms of Immanuel Wallerstein's world-system terminology.¹⁷ Although nineteenth-century Spain is not strictly *peripheral* after the fashion of the countries we are here designating under the term third world, it is certainly *semi-peripheral* in his sense, when contrasted with England or France. It is therefore not terribly surprising to find the situation of the male protagonist of *Fortunata y Jacinta* (1887)—alternating between the two women of the title, between the wife and the mistress, between the woman of the upper-middle classes and the woman of the "people"—characterized in terms of the nation-state itself, hesitating between the republican revolution of 1868 and the Bourbon restoration of 1873.¹⁸ Here, too, the same "floating" or transferable structure of allegorical reference detected in Ah Q comes into play: for Fortunata is also married, and the alternation of "revolution" and "restoration" is likewise adapted to her situation, as she leaves her legal home to seek her lover and then returns to it in abandonment.

What it is important to stress is not merely the wit of the analogy as Galdos uses it, but also its optional nature: we can use it to convert the entire situation of the novel into an allegorical commentary on the destiny of Spain, but we are also free to reverse its priorities and to read the political analogy as metaphorical decoration for the individual drama, and as a mere figural intensification of this last. Here, far from dramatizing the identity of the political and the individual or psychic, the allegorical structure tends essentially to separate these levels in some absolute way. We cannot feel its force unless we are convinced of the radical difference between politics and the libidinal: so that its operation reconfirms (rather than annuls) that split between public and private which was attributed to Western civilization earlier in our discussion. In one of the more powerful contemporary denunciations of this split and this habit, Deleuze and Guattari argue for a conception of desire that is at once social and individual.

---

17 Immanuel Wallerstein, *The Modern World System*, New York: Academic Press, 1974.

18 For example: "El Delfin había entrado, desde los úiltimos dias del 74, en aquel periodo sedante que seguìa infaliblemente a sus desvarìos. En realidad, no era aquello virtud, sino casancio del pecado; no era el sentimiento puro y regular del orden, sino el hastìo de la revolutión. Verificábase en él lo que don Baldomero habìa dicho del pais: que padecìa fiebres alternativas de libertad y de paz" (*Fortunata y Jacinta*, Madrid: Editorial Hernando, 1968, 585, Part III, Ch. 2, section 2).

> How does a delirium begin? Perhaps the cinema is able to capture the movement of madness, precisely because it is not analytical or regressive, but explores a global field of coexistence. Witness a film by Nicholas Ray, supposedly representing the formation of a cortisone delirium: an overworked father, a high-school teacher who works overtime for a radio-taxi service and is being treated for heart trouble. He begins to rave about the educational system in general, the need to restore a pure race, the salvation of the social and moral order, then he passes to religion, the timeliness of a return to the Bible, Abraham. But what in fact did Abraham do? Well now, he killed or wanted to kill his son, and perhaps God's only error lies in having stayed his hand. But doesn't this man, the film's protagonist, have a son of his own? Hmmm ... What the film shows so well, to the shame of psychiatrists, is that every delirium is first of all the investment of a field that is social, economic, political cultural, racial and racist, pedagogical, and religious: the delirious person applies a delirium to his family and his son that overreaches them on all sides.[19]

I am not myself sure that the objective consequences of this essentially social and concrete gap, in first-world experience, between the public and the private can be abolished by intellectual diagnosis or by some more adequate theory of their deeper interrelationship. Rather, it seems to me that what Deleuze and Guattari are proposing here is a new and more adequate *allegorical* reading of this film. Such allegorical structures, then, are not so much absent from first-world cultural texts as they are *unconscious*, and therefore they must be deciphered by interpretive mechanisms that necessarily entail a whole social and historical critique of our current first-world situation. The point here is that, in distinction to the unconscious allegories of our own cultural texts, third-world national allegories are conscious and overt: they imply a radically different and objective relationship of politics to libidinal dynamics.

Now, before turning to the African texts, I remind you of the very special occasion of the present talk, which is concerned to honor the memory of Robert C. Elliott and to commemorate his life's work. I take it that the very center of his two most important books, *The Power of Satire* and

---

19 Deleuze and Guattari, *Anti-Oedipus*, 274.

The Shape of Utopia,[20] is to be found in his pathbreaking association of satire and the utopian impulse as two seemingly antithetical drives (and literary discourses), which in reality replicate each other such that each is always secretly active within the other's sphere of influence. All satire, he taught us, necessarily carries a utopian frame of reference within itself; all utopias, no matter how serene or disembodied, are driven secretly by the satirist's rage at a fallen reality. When I spoke of futurity a moment ago, I took pains to withhold the world "utopia," which in my language is another word for the socialist project.

But now I will be more explicit and take as my motto an astonishing passage from the novel *Xala*, by the great contemporary Senegalese novelist and filmmaker Ousmane Sembene. The title designates a ritual curse or affliction, of a very special kind, which has been visited on a prosperous and corrupt Senegalese businessman at the moment in which, at the height of his fortune, he takes to himself a beautiful young (third) wife. Shades of *The Power of Satire!* the curse is of course, as you may have guessed, sexual impotence. The Hadj, the unfortunate hero of this novel, desperately explores a number of remedies, both Western and tribal, to no avail, and is finally persuaded to undertake a laborious trip into the hinterland of Dakar to seek out a shaman of reputedly extraordinary powers. Here is the conclusion of his hot and dusty journey in a horse-drawn cart:

> As they emerged from a ravine, they saw conical thatched roofs, grey-black with weathering, standing out against the horizon in the middle of the empty plain. Free-ranging, skinny cattle with dangerous-looking horns fenced with one another to get at what little grass there was. No more than silhouettes in the distance, a few people were busy around the only well. The driver of the cart was in familiar territory and greeted people as they passed. Sereen Mada's house, apart from its imposing size, was identical in construction with all the others. It was situated in the center of the village whose huts were arranged in a semi-circle, which you entered by a single main entrance. The village had neither shop nor school nor dispensary; there was nothing at all attractive about it in fact [Ousmane concludes, then he adds, as if in afterthought, this searing line:] There was nothing at all attractive

---

20 Princeton: Princeton University Press, 1960; and Chicago: University of Chicago Press, 1970, respectively.

about it in fact. Its life was based on the principles of community interdependence.[21]

Here, then, more emblematically than virtually any other text I know, the space of a past and future utopia—a social world of collective cooperation—is dramatically inserted into the corrupt and Westernized money economy of the new postindependence national or comprador bourgeoisie. Indeed, Ousmane takes pains to show us that the Hadj is not an industrialist, that his business is in no sense productive, but functions as a middleman between European multinationals and local extraction industries. To this biographical sketch must be added a very significant fact: that in his youth, the Hadj was political, and spent some time in jail for his nationalist and pro-independence activities. The extraordinary satire of these corrupt classes (which Ousmane will extend to the person of Senghor himself in *The Last of the Empire*) is explicitly marked as the failure of the independence movement to develop into a general social revolution.

The fact of nominal national independence, in Latin America in the nineteenth century, in Africa in the mid-twentieth, puts an end to a movement for which genuine national autonomy was the only conceivable goal. Nor is this symbolic myopia the only problem: the African states also had to face the crippling effects of what Fanon prophetically warned them against—to receive independence is not the same as to take it, since it is in the revolutionary struggle itself that new social relationships and a new consciousness is developed. Here again the history of Cuba is instructive: Cuba was the last of the Latin American nations to win its freedom in the nineteenth century—a freedom which would immediately be taken in charge by another greater colonial power. We now know the incalculable role played in the Cuban Revolution of 1959 by the protracted guerrilla struggles of the late nineteenth century (of which the figure of José Martí is the emblem); contemporary Cuba would not be the same without that laborious and subterranean, one wants to say Thompsonian, experience of the mole of History burrowing through a lengthy past and creating its specific traditions in the process.

---

21 Sembene Ousmane, *Xala*, trans. Clive Wake, Westport, CT: Lawrence Hill, 1976, 69.

So it is that after the poisoned gift of independence, radical African writers like Ousmane, or like Ngugi in Kenya, find themselves back in the dilemma of Lu Xun, bearing a passion for change and social regeneration which has not yet found its agents. I hope it is clear that this is also very much an aesthetic dilemma, a crisis of representation: it was not difficult to identify an adversary who spoke another language and wore the visible trappings of colonial occupation. When those are replaced by your own people, the connections to external controlling forces are much more difficult to represent. The newer leaders may of course throw off their masks and reveal the person of the Dictator, whether in its older individual or newer military form: but this moment also determines problems of representation. The dictator novel has become a virtual genre of Latin American literature, and such works are marked above all by a profound and uneasy ambivalence, a deeper ultimate sympathy for the Dictator, which can perhaps only be properly accounted for by some enlarged social variant of the Freudian mechanism of transference.[22]

The form normally taken by a radical diagnosis of the failures of contemporary third-world societies is, however, what is conventionally designated as, "cultural imperialism," a faceless influence without representable agents, whose literary expression seems to demand the invention of new forms: Manuel Puig's *Betrayed by Rita Hayworth* may be cited as one of the most striking and innovative of those. One is led to conclude that under these circumstances traditional realism is less effective than the satiric fable: whence to my mind the greater power of certain of Ousmane's narratives (besides *Xala*, we should mention *The Money-Order*) as over against Ngugi's impressive but problematic *Petals of Blood*.

With the fable, however, we are clearly back into the whole question of allegory. *The Money-Order* mobilizes the traditional Catch-22 dilemma—its hapless protagonist cannot cash his Parisian check without identity papers, but since he was born long before independence there are no documents, and meanwhile the money-order, uncashed, begins to melt away before an accumulation of new credits and new debts. I am tempted to suggest, anachronistically, that this work,

---

22 I am indebted to Carlos Blanco Aguinaga for the suggestion that in the Latin American novel, this ambivalence may be accounted for by the fact that the archetypal Dictator, while oppressing his own people, is also perceived as *resisting* North American influence.

published in 1965, prophetically dramatizes the greatest misfortune that can happen to a third-world country in our time, namely the discovery of vast amounts of oil resources—something which as economists have shown us, far from representing salvation, at once sinks them incalculably into foreign debts they can never dream of liquidating.

On another level, however, this tale raises the issue of what must finally be one of the key problems in any analysis of Ousmane's work, namely the ambiguous role played in it by archaic or tribal elements. Viewers may perhaps remember the curious ending of his first film, *The Black Girl*, in which the European employer is inconclusively pursued by the little boy wearing an archaic mask; meanwhile such historical films as *Ceddo* or *Emitai* seem intent on evoking older moments of tribal resistance either to Islam or to the West, yet in a historical perspective which with few exceptions is that of failure and ultimate defeat. Ousmane cannot, however, be suspected of any archaizing or nostalgic cultural nationalism. Thus it becomes important to determine the significance of this appeal to older tribal values, particularly as they are more subtly active in modern works like *Xala* or *The Money-Order*.

I suspect that the deeper subject of this second novel is not so much the evident one of the denunciation of a modern national bureaucracy, but rather the historical transformation of the traditional Islamic value of alms-giving in a contemporary money economy. A Muslim has the duty to give alms—indeed, the work concludes with just such another unfulfilled request. Yet in a modern economy, this sacred duty to the poor is transformed into a frenzied assault by freeloaders from all the levels of society (at length, the cash is appropriated by a Westernized and affluent, influential cousin). The hero is literally picked clean by the vultures; better still, the unsought for, unexpected treasure fallen from heaven at once transforms the entire society around him into ferocious and insatiable petitioners, in something like a monetary version of Lu Xun's cannibalism.

The same double historical perspective—archaic customs radically transformed and denatured by the superposition of capitalist relations—seems to me demonstrable in *Xala* as well, in the often hilarious results of the more ancient Islamic and tribal institution of polygamy. This is what Ousmane has to say about that institution (it being understood that authorial intervention, no longer tolerable in realistic narrative, is still perfectly suitable to the allegorical fable as a form):

> It is worth knowing something about the life led by urban polygamists. It could be called geographical polygamy, as opposed to rural polygamy, where all the wives and children live together in the same compound. In the town, since the families are scattered, the children have little contact with their father. Because of his way of life the father must go from house to house, villa to villa, and is only there in the evenings, at bedtime. He is therefore primarily a source of finance, when he has work.[23]

Indeed, we are treated to the vivid spectacle of the Hadj's misery when, at the moment of his third marriage, which should secure his social status, he realizes he has no real home of his own and is condemned to shuttle from one wife's villa to the other, in a situation in which he suspects each of them in turn as being responsible for his ritual affliction. But the passage I have just read shows that—whatever one would wish to think about polygamy in and of itself as an institution—it functions here as a twin-valenced element designed to open up historical perspective. The more and more frenzied trips of the Hadj through the great city secure a juxtaposition between capitalism and the older collective tribal form of social life.

These are not as yet, however, the most remarkable feature of *Xala*, which can be described as a stunning and controlled, virtually textbook exercise in what I have elsewhere called "generic discontinuities."[24] The novel begins, in effect, in one generic convention, in terms of which the Hadj is read as a comic victim. Everything goes wrong all at once, and the news of his disability suddenly triggers a greater misfortune: his numerous debtors begin to descend on someone whose bad luck clearly marks him out as a loser. A comic pity and terror accompanies this process, though it does not imply any great sympathy for the personage. Indeed it conveys a greater revulsion against the privileged new westernized society in which this rapid overturning of the wheel of fortune can take place. Yet we have all been in error; as it turns out: the wives have not been the source of the ritual curse. In an abrupt generic reversal and enlargement (comparable to some of the mechanisms Freud

---

23 Ousmane, *Xala*, 66.
24 "Generic Discontinuities in Science Fiction: Brian Aldiss' Starship," *Science Fiction Studies*, no. 2 (1973), 57–68.

describes in "The Uncanny"), we suddenly learn something new and chilling about the Hadj's past:

> "Our story goes back a long way. It was shortly before your marriage to that woman there. Don't you remember? I was sure you would not. What I am now" (a beggar in rags is addressing him) "what I am now is your fault. Do you remember selling a large piece of land at Jeko belonging to our clan? After falsifying the clan names with the complicity of people in high places, you took our land from us. In spite of our protests, our proof of ownership, we lost our case in the courts. Not satisfied with taking our land you had me thrown into prison."[25]

Thus the primordial crime of capitalism is exposed: not so much wage labor as such, or the ravages of the money form, or the remorseless and impersonal rhythms of the market, but rather this primal displacement of the older forms of collective life from a land now seized and privatized. It is the oldest of modern tragedies, visited on the Native Americans yesterday, on the Palestinians today, and significantly reintroduced by Ousmane into his film version of *The Money-Order* (called *Mandabi*), in which the protagonist is now threatened with the imminent loss of his dwelling itself.

The point I want to make about this terrible "return of the repressed," is that it determines a remarkable generic transformation of the narrative: suddenly we are no longer in satire, but in ritual. The beggars and the lumpens, led by Sereen Mada himself, descend on the Hadj and require him to submit, for the removal of his *xala*, to an abominable ceremony of ritual humiliation and abasement. The representational space of the narrative is lifted to a new generic realm, which reaches back to touch the powers of the archaic even as it foretells the utopian destruction of the fallen present in the mode of prophecy. The word "Brechtian," which inevitably springs to mind, probably does inadequate justice to these new forms which have emerged from a properly third-world reality. Yet in light of this unexpected generic ending, the preceding satiric text is itself retroactively transformed. From a satire whose subject-matter or content was the ritual curse visited on a character within the narrative, it suddenly becomes revealed as a ritual curse in its own right—the entire imagined

---

25   *Xala*, 110–11.

chain of events becomes Ousmane's own curse upon his hero and people like him. No more stunning confirmation could be adduced for Robert C. Elliott's great insight into the anthropological origins of satiric discourse in real acts of shamanistic malediction.

I want to conclude with a few thoughts on why all this should be so and on the origins and status of what I have identified as the primacy of national allegory in third-world culture. We are, after all, familiar with the mechanisms of auto-referentiality in contemporary Western literature: is this not simply to be taken as another form of that, in a structurally distinct social and cultural context? Perhaps. But in that case our priorities must be reversed for proper understanding of this mechanism. Consider the disrepute of social allegory in our culture and the well-nigh inescapable operation of social allegory in the West's Other. These two contrasting realities are to be grasped, I think; in terms of *situational consciousness*, an expression I prefer to the more common term materialism. Hegel's old analysis of the Master–Slave relationship[26] may still be the most effective way of dramatizing this distinction between two cultural logics. Two equals struggle each for recognition by the other: the one is willing to sacrifice life for this supreme value. The other, a heroic coward in the Brechtian, Schweykian sense of loving the body and the material world too well, gives in, in order to continue life. The Master—now the fulfillment of a baleful and inhuman feudal-aristocratic disdain for life without honor—proceeds to enjoy the benefits of his recognition by the other, now become his humble serf or slave. But at this point two distinct and dialectically ironic reversals take place: only the Master is now genuinely human, so that "recognition" by this henceforth sub-human form of life which is the slave evaporates at the moment of its attainment and offers no genuine satisfaction. "The truth of the Master," Hegel

---

26   G. W. F. Hegel, *The Phenomenology of Mind*, trans. A. V. Miller, Oxford: Oxford University Press, 1977: Section B, Ch. IV, Part A-3; "Lordship and Bondage," 111–19. The other basic philosophical underpinning of this argument is Lukács' epistemology in *History and Class Consciousness* according to which "mapping" or the grasping of the social totality is structurally available to the dominated rather than the dominating classes. *Mapping* is a term I have used in "Postmodernism, or, the Cultural Logic of Late Capitalism," *New Left Review,* #146 (July–August, 1984), 53–92. What is here called "national allegory" is clearly a form of just such mapping of the totality, so that the present essay—which sketches a theory of the cognitive aesthetics of third-world literature—forms a pendant to the essay on postmodernism which describes the logic of the cultural imperialism of the first world and above all of the United States.

observes grimly, "is the Slave; while the truth of the Slave, on the other hand, is the Master." But a second reversal is in process as well: for the slave is called upon to labor for the master and to furnish him with all the material benefits befitting his supremacy. But this means that, in the end, only the slave knows what reality and the resistance of matter really are; only the slave can attain some true materialistic consciousness of his situation, since it is precisely to that that he is condemned. The Master, however, is condemned to idealism—to the luxury of a placeless freedom in which any consciousness of his own concrete situation flees like a dream, like a word unremembered on the tip of the tongue, a nagging doubt which the puzzled mind is unable to formulate.

It strikes me that we Americans, we masters of the world, are in something of that very same position. The view from the top is epistemologically crippling, and reduces its subjects to the illusions of a host of fragmented subjectivities, to the poverty of the individual experience of isolated monads, to dying individual bodies without collective pasts or futures bereft of any possibility of grasping the social totality. This placeless individuality, this structural idealism which affords us the luxury of the Sartrean blink, offers a welcome escape from the "nightmare of history," but at the same time it condemns our culture to psychologism and the "projections" of private subjectivity. All of this is denied to third-world culture, which must be situational and materialist despite itself. And it is this, finally, which must account for the allegorical nature of third-world culture, where the telling of the individual story and the individual experience cannot but ultimately involve the whole laborious telling of the experience of the collectivity itself.

I hope I have suggested the epistemological priority of this unfamiliar kind of allegorical vision; but I must admit that old habits die hard, and that for us such unaccustomed exposure to reality, or to the collective totality, is often intolerable, leaving us in Quentin's position at the end of *Absalom, Absalom!*, murmuring the great denial, "I don't hate the Third World! I don't! I don't! I don't!"

Even that resistance is instructive, however; and we may well feel, confronted with the daily reality of the other two-thirds of the globe, that "there was nothing at all attractive about it in fact." But we must not allow ourselves that feeling without also acknowledging its ultimate mocking completion: "Its life was based on the principles of community interdependence."

5B
Political: National Allegory

Commentary

The preceding essay was, on its appearance in 1986, the object of numerous and varied attacks, both from Marxists who deplored the absence of class politics from its framework and from the various adherents of race, ethnicity, and gender (identity) politics who found it a useful vehicle for attacking socialist and Marxist positions. Indeed, the radical Indian intellectual who set off the debate has since regretted the way his own intervention was consistently used as a vehicle for various anticommunist attacks and critiques.[1] It is still worthwhile disentangling the issues in this debate, despite transformations of the world political scene which will perhaps make it less recognizable for some readers.

My intent was to raise questions about what (since globalization became a concept) has come to be called world literature, by insisting on the radical differences of Third-World Literature from the insularity and parochialism of an Americanist literary study for which foreign and foreign-language literatures (even the European ones) scarcely exist. It may therefore seem paradoxical that such a discussion should be attacked from positions of identity and minority cultural politics; but for the most part these critics felt that the term "Third World" was a slur, despite the fact that this slogan was initiated by the 1955 Bandung conference, which

---

1   Aijaz Ahmad, *In Theory: Nations, Classes, Literatures,* London: Verso, 2008.

united many of the poorer countries in the world who did not officially belong to either the American or the Soviet satellite blocs.

This was also the point with which Aijaz Ahmad took issue, inquiring whether the great tradition of Urdu poetry was somehow to be ranged under this incongruous label. I felt at the time that his remarks reflected the discomfort of formerly powerful imperial formations, such as were to be found in India and China, with a rather disreputable association involving "underdeveloped" countries of distinctly different cultural backgrounds. In fact, all the Indian leftists I have known personally were very free with the offending term (although their Chinese counterparts were not). But obviously enough, the concept of a Third World can no longer have the same currency today in a world in which some of the countries in question have evolved into industrial and manufacturing centers, China has become the second-greatest world power, and the former Second or socialist World has disintegrated, most of it enjoying a dubious "transition to capitalism."

I.

Ahmad's more fundamental objection to my essay sprang from his (quite correct) sense that the text reflected a Maoist practice at odds theoretically and politically with classic Marxist or Bolshevik principles. The central quotation from Lin Biao[2]—that the international class situation of the period could be mapped as an insurrection of the international peasantry of Third World countries surrounding the international city bourgeoisie of the rich countries—seemed to displace the class struggle within the various nation-states onto a global and as it were foreign-policy level; and thereby to dismiss the concrete class relations which inevitably obtained within both Third and First World countries alike. This was not at all my intention, particularly inasmuch as I felt that class struggle existed on both levels but in different forms.

The simpler way of staging this historic conflict on the left can be put this way: that while classical Marxism theorized the revolutionary

---

2 "The contemporary world revolution presents a picture of the encirclement of the cities by the rural areas." Lin Biao, "Long Live the Victory of People's War (1965)," *The Selected Works of Lin Biao*, New York: Prism Key Press, 2011.

function of an urban working class, Maoism on the contrary appealed to an immense peasantry as its primary revolutionary force, with a resulting tension that ultimately realized itself in the Sino–Soviet break of 1960. Perhaps this oversimplified version of the conflict needs to be revised in two ways, so as to reflect not an ideological dispute but rather a representational dilemma.

First of all, it makes a difference if one considers the Soviet Revolution of 1917 as two simultaneous and distinct revolutions,[3] one of anti-Czarist and anti-war urban working classes and a different one in the countryside, carried out by peasants who demanded private ownership of the land (as traditionally in the French Revolution and many other peasant uprisings). In that case, Stalin's collectivization of 1928 constituted a second Soviet Revolution, or if you like, the fulfillment of the first one. This is a view that would seem to sharpen the ideological differences in question and to underscore the originality of Maoism with respect to Bolshevism.

The second point to be made is that today the peasantry has virtually disappeared, with the green revolution and the subsequent emergence of an agribusiness for which the former peasants have simply become (farm) workers, their private plots absorbed, not into collective forms, but into monopolies. At the same time, however, the distinction between Third and First World states, now reformulated as one between developing and developed countries, has lost its political significance in the light of the industrialization of some of the formerly Third World powers, such as Korea, Vietnam, and even China itself; and that of an industrial working class as such called into question by automation and the development of information technology and computerization. Under these circumstances the very conception of nonnational social groups (which could be allegorized according to my proposal) has either become wholly problematic or has been adapted to the situation of other kinds of groups altogether (those of race, ethnicity, and gender, themes which always played their part in the construction of a national idea but had hitherto necessarily remained subordinate to economic production).

These political dilemmas have their bearing on the problem of allegory, for the culture of such "identity" groups necessarily remains allegorical.

---

3 A thesis defended by Stalin's latest biographer, Stephen Kotkin, in *Stalin: The Paradoxes of Power*, New York: Penguin, 2015.

But what seems to me more productive for any discussion of my old essay today is rather the earlier form of the debate: for it raised the fundamentally allegorical nature of international politics as such. Its two dimensions—class struggle with a given national situation and the globalized forces at work outside it on a world scale—are at least for the moment incommensurable: which is to say that it is their very disparity and the difficulty of finding mediations between them that is the fundamental political problem for the Left today, in a transitional situation in which neither form of traditional politics—the internal political struggle and the very different dynamic of international politics—has reached any kind of stable or definitive, recognizable, and identifiable form. Is a self-proclaimed resistance to American hegemony and empire (in other words, to world capitalism) sufficient to qualify its adherents as occupying left, revolutionary, or socialist positions in their internal political situations? In any case, Ahmad's objection, which did not include any criticism of the idea of allegory, foregrounds the crucial allegorical question of the relationship of the levels to one another, and whether any proper allegorical reading exists in a situation in which there is, if not a contradiction, then at least a fundamental disjunction between the anagogical (or world-political) level and the literal or domestic-political levels. Allegory thereby serves as a diagnostic instrument to reveal this disjunction, which is itself the cause of political aimlessness and apathy. We are in a period of global class formation; we cannot expect a coherent class politics to emerge from the antagonism between the levels of internal and external class struggle that Ahmad's article, perhaps unwittingly, reveals.

Perhaps I can best illustrate the dynamics of this incommensurability and the nature of simultaneous but multiple dimensions that interact by way of difference and nonintersection with a few familiar illustrations. In the area of theory, this kind of multidimensional incommensurability has famously been conceptualized by Ernst Bloch in his memorable phrase *nonsynchronous synchronicity* (*ungleichzeitige Gleichzeitigkeit*),[4] a far more pungent and arresting formulation of the Marxist notion of uneven development and one Bloch first designed to characterize the Germany of the 1920s.

But I prefer to think of the process in terms of a strange and incomprehensible thought image, namely that of so-called multidimensional

---

4 See Chapter 1, page 44, note 22.

chess, in which a number of distinct chessboards coexist simultaneously with distinct configurations of forces on each, so that a move on any one of these boards has distinct but unforeseeable consequences for the configurations and the relative power-relations on the others. We exist in just such a world, just such a totality, in which for the moment the moves on these various boards and in these various dimensions fail to coincide: is it unimaginable that a moment should come in which, by virtue of the most cunning multidimensional strategies, these moves might in one extraordinary conjuncture all reinforce each other? But this science-fictional example can easily be converted into a more homely and realistic contemporary one, if we turn to that activity which is, in the United States, called soccer.

For football (the "beautiful game") is in fact a combination of chess and stamp collecting. Contemporary world football indeed exists on multiple, yet very real, dimensions, which are those of globalization itself, and which we can simplify into the local, the national, and the international dimensions. In the beginnings of football, players train as children in the streets and tend therefore to come from the poorer neighborhoods. This is why in the first great footballing cities, there often spring up two teams, one of popular origins and one which draws its public, and many of its players, more substantially from the so-called middle classes and their schools. Such class oppositions are obviously not detrimental to the sport, which even within a single locality requires the stimulus of opponents and can only be enhanced by mass followings of a competitive and antagonistic kind on both sides. But such antagonisms, required in order for the game to develop, are only the first and most obvious natural class symptoms of the undertow of capitalism as it develops simultaneously with football itself, the directionality of the first moving transversally across the internal evolution of the game itself and its strategies.

In a second moment, the more successful teams will want to test themselves against their opposite numbers in other cities and regions of the nation-state. But as the profitability of the game increases, the wealthier teams will begin to buy star players from their adversaries, marking a first break from the dimension of the local. Fans may well adopt these outsiders, and the latter may well wholeheartedly adapt to their new athletic homelands; but the inner distance is still there, and the possibility that they may well be seduced by other local teams and owners undermines the local character of the game, however vigorously fans retains its local patriotism and loyalties

Meanwhile, a further intervention of the commercial into the autonomy of the sport becomes visible, not only in the increasing prosperity of the really successful teams and their national adversaries, but also in the increasing attraction of outsiders and even foreigners for the acquisition and transplantation. This development, of course, reflects increasing trade and commercial interactions on an international scale (such as the emergence of the Russian oligarchs as a new source of investment); and it heralds the expansion of the game itself on yet a broader and now international scale, both in the growth of minor European and non-European teams and in the (as it were) primitive accumulation of football "capital" from the Third World, and in particular South America and Brazil, where a remarkable "reserve army" of extraordinary players becomes available to the formerly local and now formerly national teams as such.

The new transnational competitions and international cups, on the model of the modern Olympic games, clearly offer a whole new "dispositif" for the investment of the various nationalisms, ranging from nationalism to xenophobic and racist passion. Those accompany the next step up from the more open class antagonisms of the local and national rivalries; and that ambiguous thing, the nation, begins to serve as the medium for (or indeed the mediation between) both types of collective emotion inasmuch as the struggles within the nation reinforce the latter's central role in what may be called *international class struggle*.

The seemingly positive development of an international market in football, however, is accompanied by other kinds of more negative effects in the home markets (and this is the moment to insist that our telling of the story is structural rather than chronological): above all, by monopolization, whereby little by little all the best players are bought up by a few major teams, downgrading the rest of the local participants to provincial status and rendering purely domestic competitions less and less interesting. The nation, then, takes on a twofold function: it is on the one hand the group of first-class teams who represent national football; and on the other, the actual "national team" that become the official participants in international competitions like the World Cup.

In that international world, then, rivals from the national teams find themselves obliged to play side by side against the enemy, in a paradoxical, and I may even say dialectical, shift in subject position. But it is a dialectic far more dramatically visible for the foreign players who have been recruited to play on the various national or local teams. Here the two systems visibly begin to intersect: and the stars from other areas, such as the Balkans or Latin America, find themselves (however enriched in fame and fortune) obliged to return to their home countries to play on a national team often opposed to that of their temporarily former teammates, who have themselves dispersed, however unwillingly, in answer to the call of their own respective countries.

This is a dual identity far more significantly fraught than that adoption of local provincial players by the more powerful teams of other national entities; and it conjures up a bizarre double standard in which a given player exists in two distinct modes of being at once, defined by the subsystems of which he is simultaneously a member. In each he has a celebrity coach whose methods and worldview may be in the sharpest conflict with his opposite number and teammates who may have been his most detested adversaries in another life. Yet in one of those paradoxes that characterizes globalization, in a period in which the nation-state continues to exist and to function as a form (often hostile to its assimilation into a different kind of world system), the international player who returns to play in his national team recovers his own original language, the one he spoke in his earliest existence as a local footballer.

It is the circulation of these foreign nationals throughout an essentially three-tiered system of institutions that seems to me preeminently characteristic of the mapping problems of the world system today, for, as in multidimensional chess, they may well experience autonomy and subordination simultaneously. The soccer player, caught between his origins, his home team, and his national representation, is only the most dramatic figure for the multidimensionality of globalization evoked and presupposed in the essay on national allegory.

The philosophical background of this experiment in cognitive mapping may be identified by the two concepts of simultaneity and incommensurability. The first of these, richly glossed in Benedict Anderson's work on the emergence of nationality,[5] must be accompanied by a vigilant emphasis on negativity and contradiction. This kind of simultaneity is best

---

5 *Imagined Communities: Reflections on the Origin and Spread of Nationalism*, London: Verso, 2016; see especially page 24 on simultaneity.

observed when the two or three planes in question are dissonant, and which both can emerge in their autonomy. It is a dissonance we have then characterized with the term *incommensurability*, borrowed from Niels Bohr's account of the representational dilemmas of quantum physics, a term which has the advantage of a properly historical undecidability which can be mapped, schematized, or diagrammed (that is to say, represented), without lapsing into either of the tempting alternatives of the mystical ineffability or dogmatic decisionism. But it should be understood that this situation, which we have illustrated by way of our two examples, holds for world politics fully as much as for world literature; and it is in the light of this situation that allegory must today be understood as a solution that is a problem in its own right.

II

Does not the very proposal of a national allegory mark a reversion to the practice of personification to which I have so often objected? A collectivity is not a person and cannot be reified in the form of this or that personification. The problem is that collectivity cannot really be conceptualized either, and, as I've argued elsewhere, cannot even properly be named (*proper* being the appropriate Derridean word here): even the seemingly neutral term *collectivity* is misleading, insofar as the cognitive abstraction it flaunts suggests some kind of interpersonal homogeneity that does not exist. But the same can be said for all the names collectivity has borne throughout history, from *clan* or *polis* all the way to *nation* or *people*, or its political cover in terms like *democracy* or *republic*. Rousseau's General Will is the most daring of these experiments in nomination, inasmuch as it designates its own distance from any numerical collectivity of existing individuals: despite its critics, it is not the state, which is an empirical entity. Perhaps the General Will is rather the ideological "regulative idea" every collectivity requires for collective action.

At any rate, it is this radical lack in the conceptualization of the collective—Lacan's "pas-tout"—that signals the scandal of the much-maligned word *totality*. The latter has the advantage of being nonanthropomorphic and the disadvantage of bringing numerical and additive overtones with it, making it seem a cousin of Hegel's "bad infinite." For critics who have imbibed a little Foucauldianism, its evil lies in its claim to assign a place of total knowledge, a place ripe for so-called totalitarianism. But the unhappy Lukács, who pioneered the slogan, never claimed as much and indeed theorized the very opposite, in his crucial expression, "aspiration to totality" (*Intention zur Totalität*), an aspiration his critics clearly do not share.

Perhaps this is clearest in the area of nationalism, another reproach the critics of this article have felt able to make. Nationalism is, to be sure, a powerful collective force that one can admire aesthetically and from a distance in that specific sense; it is at one with language and geography, and this, too, raises unexplored issues. But I share with Deleuze the conviction that it is only positive when emergent and still powerless;[6] a triumphant nationalism, a nationalism in power, a national *state*, if it does not in the process of coming to power transcend itself qua nationalism, is never very admirable. And this, for the very good reason that the very concept of the nation (like all the other collective concepts I have listed above) is vacuous and can lead nowhere except into unhealthy collective narcissism and soccer hooliganism. We have as yet found nothing satisfactory in the way of a new concept to replace it: federalism has not often worked, but more significantly, it does not seem to work as a concept, as a value. Perhaps it still carries a little too much of the atmosphere of tolerance and altruism and too little of a vital narcissism to be viscerally attractive. Here, to be sure, we approach the domain of collective psychologizing, which is to be avoided at all costs (and into which Marx, unlike Freud, never fell).

This is then the sense in which we have so frequently insisted on the unrepresentability of the collective, an argument which must candidly also denounce the use of this last term as well, whose terminological innocence, secured by an appearance of scientific objectivity, is as ideological as all the others. I would only add that its predecessors—people, nation, tribe, race, clan, group, *ethnie*, masses, along with all those strange words with which tribal peoples have named themselves in unknown or extinct languages—all express, not some universal condition of unnameability, but rather the specific historical conjuncture in which each of them has seemed a useful second best: in much the same

---

6   Gilles Deleuze, "Un peuple à venir," *Cinema II: The Time-Image*, Paris: Les Editions de Minuit, 1985.

way the absence of an analogous term in our current state of dawning globalization is not a permanent one and will no doubt ultimately be challenged by new proposals and possibilities. (Indeed, Hardt and Negri's contribution of the word *multitude* is one of those, and not the least valuable.)

At this stage I wish to propose another term—a suitably exotic and thereby fresh and unfamiliar one—for Deleuze's "peuple à venir," the collectivity that has as yet no name: and that is the word *asabiyya* which the translators of Ibn Khaldun render as "group feeling."[7] Like any other, it carries the stain and traces of its origin, in the clan system and might technically etymologically be translated as kinship or blood relation. This reflects the thinking of the great Berber philosopher of history, in the *Muqaddimah*, that stable societies can only be formed around kinship groups or clans. Indeed, the apparently cyclical character of Ibn Khaldun's vision of history finds justification in his conviction that a state disintegrates to the degree to which it develops further and further away from its original unity as a clan. It is probably wrong to consider Ibn Khaldun a philosopher of history, to the degree to which he has no ultimate telos in mind, not even that of a universal Islamic commonwealth. Rather, like Machiavelli, his real interest lies in what keeps a given state together, what ensures its duration, and what finally brings about its decay and dispersal. (This shared preoccupation explains why Machiavelli is so often and traditionally considered to be immoral: for his concern with the duration of a state in time extends indifferently to dictatorships as well as republics, oligarchies, and the rest of the logical forms of government.) Indeed, it might be worth speculating whether every alleged "philosophy of history" does not secretly share a similar preoccupation with what is lasting in a political formation. The so-called "end of history" thus reduces itself to that: how to found a state that will last forever; and Utopia is no different in this respect.

Yet the concept of *asabiyya* is useful to the degree to which it posits a collective cohesion that is not based on an idea or on that far more limited concept named family: for the group precedes the family. It is not a psychological concept either despite attempts to render it in English; and any identification with group psychology must be

---

7   Ibn Khaldun, *The Muqaddimah: An Introduction to History*, Princeton: Princeton University Press, 2015.

strenuously resisted. The notion of blood ties is a figurative or imaginary link, a kind of fetish, inasmuch as no one really knows who their relatives are, but only the tribe in which they are raised. Nonetheless the concept itself insists on an indistinguishable relationship between body and spirit, between object and subject, between a collective materiality and a collective ideology or group spirit; and it posits the constitutive relationship of this first solidarity to the social coherence of the society as such, without passing through abstract political arrangements. But it also includes a quantitative element in the conception of the clan, itself distantly related to that earliest intuition of the first humans that their groups of hunters and gatherers could not survive beyond certain dimensions and a limit on population growth.

This first requirement is what secretly undermines the nation as an adequate social form, inasmuch as the national is an imaginary solidarity, largely overstepping any concrete forms of coexistence. The nation must therefore have recourse, for its cohesion, to two analoga or quasi-physical substitutes for those direct relationships, and those substitutes are language and geography, material entities which however function in purely symbolic ways.

Today, in an era of full globalization, the distance between the life of concrete social networks and population size is so great as to be virtually unconceptualizable. The only theorist to have today confronted the issue of global population in any serious way is Peter Sloterdijk, in a position he summarizes as follows: "People today are not prepared to coexist consciously with a billion other subjects."[8] Unfortunately, his own complex and stimulating investigations and speculations are limited by the familiar fallback stereotype of a global–local formula.

Meanwhile, any new solution to this dilemma must take into account Rousseau's counterposition, which is that of a General Will, or in other words a group spirit absolutely divorced in advance from any existent and quantitative group and corresponding to no specific population size. This logical alternative is so far the only coherent alternative in this dilemma, for which minds formed in smaller traditional social units are "unprepared," just as we have seen that rational or philosophical speculation is similarly limited: the limits of our conceptuality, meanwhile,

---

8   *Der Spiegel*, June 22, 2017, 120; and see his recent work *Spheres*, much of which turns on space and population.

are also not to be found in the size of the brain but rather in the sheer number of other people who coexist with us. *Asabiyya* is as useful an idea as any other for driving home this fundamental idea.

The problem of the collective needs to be thought of as an engineering problem as well; and it might begin with Carl Schmitt's great definition of the political as such—the choosing of friend and foe.[9] Sartre puts this another way, namely that the collective cannot be formed, that a collective cannot achieve the living cohesion of a group however large or small, without an external enemy, an external threat.[10] This is a baleful structural principle, if true; and even if you take the realities of class and class struggle to be the ultimate ones, beyond even the spurious promises of the various nationalisms, it foretells the difficulties of any imaginable future classless situation.[11] (Ecological wisdom might suggest that in that case we might still be united by our ultimate enemy, namely Nature itself, a prospect no more appealing than the alternative. Right now, "nature" is a political ally in a crisis situation in which only socialism can save us from its destruction. Yet, as human mortals, nature always was our enemy in the first place.)

III

In all these senses, then, the collective cannot be conceptualized, yet we cannot not give it a name or acknowledge its being. This is why personification necessarily persists, as an indispensable second best, and flourishes everywhere from what I will call *diplomatic allegories* to the worst racist, ethnic, and even gender slurs, and also the most affectionate ones. We do not need ethical judgments, or binary oppositions such as good and evil, to sort out good from bad uses of collective personification: both are implicit and dialectically united in reification itself. When I single out a collectivity for my libidinal investment, what counts is not the emotional content but rather the singling out, the naming of the group, which can only occur stereotypically: and every stereotype or

---

9 Carl Schmitt, *The Concept of the Political*, Chicago: University of Chicago Press, 2007.
10 Jean-Paul Sartre, *Critique of Dialectical Reason, Vol. 1*, London: Verso, 2004.
11 For further discussion of these dilemmas, see Appendix C.

personification is always a potential slur: philosemitism being but a stone's throw away from anti-Semitism.

Yet wherever mixed groups live together, the individual is obliged to navigate them by way of stereotypes. The word *nation* itself emerged from the mixed populations and languages of the students in medieval Paris. Here is the way in which in one of his letters Gramsci describes the characterological views of his fellow prisoners on their fellow Italians:

> There are four fundamental divisions: northerners, people from central Italy, southerners (including Sicily), and Sardinians. The Sardinians live totally apart from the rest. The northerners evince a certain solidarity among themselves, but no organization, it would seem; for them it is a point of honor that they are thieves, pickpockets, swindlers but have never spilled blood. Among the people from central Italy, the Romans are the best organized; they will not even denounce their spies to people from the other regions, and keep their distrust to themselves. The southerners are highly organized, so it is said, but among them there are subdivisions: the Neapolitan State, the Apulian State, and the Sicilian State. For the Sicilian, the point of honor consists not in having stolen but only in having spilled blood.[12]

---

12   Antonio Gramsci, *Lettere dal Carcere*, 19 December 1926, 14. I am grateful to Alberto Toscano for this reference. To which we might add Walter Benjamin's contribution, in his essay on Naples: "The well-known list of the seven deadly sins situated pride in Genoa, avarice in Florence (the old Germans were of a different opinion—their term for what is known as Greek love was *Florenzen*), voluptuousness in Venice, anger in Bologna, greed in Milan, envy in Rome, and indolence in Naples" (*Selected Writings, Volume I: 1913–1926*, Cambridge: Cambridge University Press, 1996, 418). Proust's profoundly French yet altogether pan-European aristocracy might also serve as a useful reference: "M. de Charlus went further than merely failing to desire ardently to see France victorious; without admitting it to himself, he wished, if not that Germany should triumph, at least that she should not be crushed, as everybody else was hoping would happen. The reason for this was that in these quarrels the great groupings of individuals called 'nations' behave to a certain degree like individuals themselves. The reasoning that guides them is entirely subjective and is being continually modified by their passions, as in the case of people at odds in a lovers' quarrel or a domestic dispute, such as a son's disagreement with his father, or that of a cook with her mistress or a wife with her husband. The nation that is in the wrong nevertheless believes that it is in the right—as was the case with Germany—and the nation that is in the right sometimes advances arguments in support of its claims which it considers unanswerable only because they are in accordance with its passions. In quarrels between individuals, in

It goes without saying that such judgments will be even more extreme when it comes to the coexistence of peoples not bound together by a common "nationality." The racisms and ethnicities act all this out on a different level of collectivity; and on a larger diplomatic scale, we may observe characterizations that are not immediately formed by the materials and systems examined in our chapter on emotions, but which reflect the kind of common knowledge or cultural literacy offered by the public sphere, where there are no longer any "distant countries of which we know nothing." It is as though an esoteric development of theories of "affect" now relegated the systems of the older named emotions to lower class usage, where they lead their own posttheoretical life in the form of the various racisms and national stereotypes, all organized around categories drawn from the older emotional systems.

These now themselves become bifurcated into a rather antiquated collection of stereotypes of the various national characters, and a storehouse of invective, insult, prejudice, and ethnic or racial stereotypes as such, it being understood that generalizations about collective groups will always necessarily be caricatures and stereotypes even where they are used positively. One may, for example, wish to express one's admiration and fascination with this or that national or ethnic group, but what results is always a combination of features (they're so productive, or they really know how to enjoy life, for example) on which the valences can immediately be reversed (workaholics, lazy spongers), making the characteristics available for the most violent outbursts and vilifications.

Indeed, it has already been observed that the term *nation* originated as a classification of the various foreign students who came to live and study in Paris during the later Middle Ages and who lived together in various quarters which were called *nations* perceived to be distinct in language, dress, and behavior by the local population and its disciplinary forces. In the Renaissance these qualifications became systems in their own right, and a literary genre emerged around national

---

order to be absolutely convinced that one or the other party is in the right, the surest way is to be that party himself; an onlooker will never uphold him as completely. Now, in a nation the individual, if he is really a part of the nation, is only one cell in the larger individual, the nation. Misleading people by propaganda is a meaningless phrase" (*The Past Recaptured*, Vol VII of *Remembrance of Things Past*, trans. F. A. Blossom, New York: Random House, 1932, 797–98).

"character" that served as a guide to travelers in the various parts of Europe, the rest of the world being vague enough to be dealt with in even more general cultural stereotypes, like the one most recently called *orientalism*.

These characterological distinctions are all based on the available systems of emotions (as, paradigmatically, in one of the oldest of these, the system of the four humors), which serves to transcode the predominance of the various emotions into characterology (phlegmatic, choleric, sanguine, melancholic). The resultant systems of stereotypes are still alive in areas in which linguistically and religiously distinctive populations coexist, such as the Balkans, the Caucasus, Scandinavia, Southeast Asia, and so forth (in comparison with which our own local racisms are intellectually rather impoverished). We here thus enter the domain of what I venture to call *diplomatic allegory*.

Does such a thing as a "national character" still exist? Travelers often think so; but the development of a world tourism industry (along with the omnipresent doxa of the withering of the nation-state under globalization) makes such conjecture trivial if not disreputable.

IV

That such stereotypes, however, are also real—in other words that they have the effectivity of that "reality of the appearance" which Hegel so often evoked—and that they are also necessarily narrative in nature, I want to illustrate by way of one of the great historiographic cruxes—the causes of World War I—which has come in for renewed interest today, probably owing to the similarity of our own current decentered diplomatic world situation. I follow here the version of Christopher Clark in his monumental work on the subject, *The Sleepwalkers* (2012), where it is clear that much of the narrative interest itself lies not so much in the rigid identification of the national personification as in its very fluidity.[13]

Friend or foe: it is obvious enough that in the French Imaginary, since the Franco-Prussian War and the annexation of Alsace-Lorraine, Germany preeminently occupied the place of the foe, the primal national

---

13   Christopher Clark, *The Sleepwalkers*, New York: HarperCollins, 2012.

enemy. Yet since the defeat of Napoleon, there was already just such a foe in place, namely *perfide Albion*: and indeed Clark emphasizes the degree to which the British Empire uniquely inspired anxiety among all the other European powers—in Germany less so indeed (Clark downplays the naval rivalry) than in Russia, whose Great Game in Afghanistan positioned Britain as the principal adversary (and vice versa). This is the result of a crucial organization of space: the great colonial or imperial powers, Clark explains, can make their moves on two distinct chessboards—Europe and the colonies, whether in Africa, Central Asia, or China, all three crucial sites of struggle. The chessboard of the colonies then provides an alternate space in which rivalries can be played out and assuaged:

> As the possessors of vast portions of the earth's inhabited surface with a military presence along extended imperial peripheries, Britain, France, and Russia controlled tokens that could be exchanged and bargained over at relatively little cost to the metropolis.[14]

But the Austro-Hungarian Empire was in a more ambiguous spatial position: in some sense the Balkans corresponded to that second, extra-European playing field; on the other hand, as the very border of that empire, moves in the Balkans could already be considered as European, and in any case, as far as Austria was concerned, there were no tokens to give and no one to bargain with—Serbia being not one of the great-power rivals but rather itself a kind of token in the game.

As for Germany, it was almost wholly restricted to Europe as such; and the only equivalent of African or Chinese tokens to be exchanged in this imperial competition was Alsace-Lorraine, whose abandonment, as with Bosnia-Herzegovina for the Austrians, did not come into question. These two powers, then, Germany and Austria, were reduced to a single playing field, namely Europe itself.

Returning now to our primary allegorical exhibit, we have seen that France faced a fundamental dilemma in its selection of a primary enemy or foe. Can one not have two different enemies at the same time? I suspect that for the Imaginary, or the political unconscious, the one will always be subordinated to the other and emotionally assimilated to it.

---

14   Ibid., 132.

Political: National Allegory

To be sure, the allegorical array into which otherness is multiplied and organized, like the constellations of the starry heavens, will inevitably be parceled out into a cast of different characters and a rank order running from the starring roles to the extras, as well as being divided into the two basic camps.

In this case, however, Clark isolates the moment in which France is able to reassign its antagonisms: it was the Moroccan crisis of 1900. Before that, "the shared suspicion of Britain that had helped to bring about the Franco-Russian Alliance also prevented it [the Alliance] . . . from acquiring an exclusively anti-German orientation."[15] The implication is that the issue of Alsace-Lorraine was only one of the components of French Germanophobia: this issue could be libidinally subordinated in situations in which the desire for cooperation with the Germans (particularly in a situation of rivalry with Britain) took center stage. What happened in the Moroccan crisis with Britain, however, was that the Germans refused a potential alliance with France against Britain: "from this moment, the French foreign minister abandoned any thought of Franco-German collaboration . . . the decision to appease rather than to oppose Britain facilitated a more forceful articulation of the anti-German potential in French foreign policy."[16]

This is to say, in allegorical terms, that the situation had realigned in such a way as to allow Germany to be substituted for Britain as the ally of choice, a rearrangement that, after the disappointment of Morocco, was not to be. To be sure, Clark goes on in his next chapter to warn against such allegorical readings. Citing a political cartoon from the eve of the Boxer Uprising in China (1898), he observes:

> personifying states as individuals was part of the shorthand of European political caricature, but it also reflects a deep habit of thought: the tendency to conceptualize states as composite individuals governed by compact executive agencies animated by an indivisible will.[17]

---

15   Ibid., 131.
16   Ibid., 133.
17   Ibid., 135.

He goes on to chart the personal rivalries and animosities within the various foreign offices and public opinion itself, replete with the most savory anecdotes; but this shift of emphasis to the distribution of the various allegorical "semes" (envy, hostility, theft of employment, contempt, and so on) among distinct individuals, where the bearers of various distinct kinds of antagonisms to Germany are realigned in new combinations, is itself an allegorical narrative that only shifts the levels of this material and the bearers of its meanings, rather than changing the structure of this multidimensional chess game.

Still, this is a moment in which we must dispel a basic misunderstanding of our topic, which Clark characterized rather unreflectively as "a deep habit of thought." Is not his own shift of attention from the national diplomacies to the individuals involved in the various national decisions in some way a shift from appearance to historical reality? Is Clark not suggesting, in the most complete agreement with common sense, that the idea of antagonisms (or friendships) between nations is a misleading fantasy, inasmuch as a "nation" is not a substantive entity, whereas individual acts of the decision-makers constitute a reality that the historian can document with some precision? So there would be a reality of history, particularly when the discipline identifies and restricts itself to something called diplomatic history; while the rest would belong to the nebulous realm of so-called public opinion, itself easily dismantled into the decisions of administrative newspaper publishers and the even more nebulous ideologies of the various classes and subgroups. We must emphasize that Clark is not interested in this essentially philosophical problem about reality and appearance in history (or in historiography, for that matter): since his argument, in this excellent work, lies elsewhere, namely in his conclusion that the cause of world war is to be located in the uncertainty of the various national players about each other's intentions in the first place.

An allegorical reading, within its multiple levels, would seems a more adequate solution; this is precisely the point at which our practical problems begin to arise. For Clark's argument would seem to suggest the advantages of a clear and relatively fixed narrative, a relatively fixed set of characters, over a confused narrative, in which a number of plots are superimposed and the value of the characters themselves in constant flux depending on which narrative position

Political: National Allegory

they find themselves. Which is the enemy? Britain or Germany? It depends on whether it is the British Empire that is the threat, or the occupation of Alsace-Lorraine, and those are two distinct narratives, which could themselves be multiplied by others—the value of Russia as a partner, the ambiguous status of the Ottoman Empire and the control of the Dardanelles, and so on. World War I emerged from the superposition and confusion of these narratives. But then our basic question arises: if instead of that confusion, the dominant narrative were clearly delineated, with friend and foe distinguished on a single level in some relatively stable and identifiable way, would the outcome then be more desirable? But here we are describing, not the onset of World War I, but rather the Cold War, long or short, which did not in fact eventuate in war (although its equivalent in the seventeenth century certainly did), but which has also been characterized as ending in a "victory" of one of the parties and a "defeat" of the other (even though from another perspective Hobsbawm feels able to characterize it as the "golden age" of capitalism).[18]

Does not the fundamental scenario of narrative as such—based on the distinction between friend and foe, or to use the more traditional terms, hero and villain—always necessarily tell the story of a struggle that is a zero-sum game and in which there is a winner and a loser (or perhaps, to use Marx's bleaker version, "which ends in the mutual destruction of both parties")?[19] In fact, the original structural or narrative theorists preferred to think of the process as a return to order. We begin with order, an equilibrium or homeostasis, into which an element of disorder is introduced; the narrative then works through this disorder, which is in the process gradually (or violently) resolved, so that the end of the narrative is able to restore order, albeit of a different kind than what we confronted at the outset. This has always seemed to me a very conservative way of interpreting narrative processes, but perhaps Marx's alternative way of putting it—"ends with the revolutionary reconstruction of society"—offers a more progressive take on the "order" that is reestablished at the end (which we then call *closure*).

---

18   Eric Hobsbawm, *The Age of Extremes: A History of the World 1914–1991*, New York: Vintage 1996.

19   *The Communist Manifesto*; I have deliberately omitted the conclusion of this quote, which reads in full: "a fight that each time ended either in a revolutionary reconstruction of society at large or in the common ruin of the contending classes."

Anarchists, however, might well see even this formulation of Marx as a capitulation to that oppression of society, of the state and its normative order which was always their primary target and nightmare. I believe that the—to me utterly ideological and unacceptable—formula of the open versus the closed was always an attempt to paper over this interpretation of narrative "closure": if closed is bad, and open is good, then it follows that we should always somehow call for an open ending rather than a closed one.

A final reading is thus possible in which the very notion and structure of narrative itself is denounced and repudiated: this is more or less what happens in a famous passage of Sartre's *Nausea*, in which he shows that "stories" (adventures, as they are called here) always involve a chronological reversal and illusion.[20] We start with the ending and reorganize the aimless facts into a telos, a sequence of events that is going somewhere and in which something happens: here the aleatory is turned into necessity. Yet this classic denunciation of narrative or storytelling only reconfirms our argument here: namely that narrative is a ghostly allegory into which a given set of events is reorganized, a shadowy second-degree structure imposed on what Henry Ford memorably called "one damned thing after another." What Sartre does not resolve here, in a novel itself organized as a day-by-day journal, is whether this structure, this second-degree ordering of the initial raw material, can be avoided, and if so, what takes its place. In the philosophical tradition, that more direct contact with events without narrative meaning would be available only to the Deleuzian ideal schizophrenic, in the perpetual present of the schizo's wandering and aimless existence. Yet it would seem that for most of us, Deleuze here enunciated not a phenomenological description, but rather an ethic, the way an ideal life ought to be lived—a Utopian vision not necessarily attractive to everyone. In the earlier Sartrean world, the ethic is decisionist; we ourselves choose to organize our lives into specific stories of whose arbitrary nature we are aware in advance. This is the ethical solution of *Nausea*'s other protagonist, Annie: with age, however, she tires of this narrative freedom. The whole problem is then recast when, as more recently, we decide to abandon the narratological language of

---

20 Jean-Paul Sartre, *Nausea*, New York: New Directions, 2013, 37–40.

analysis for the terminology of the Event, which thereby subsumes narrative as such. The problem here then becomes its opposite, whose noneventful structure has already been defined in advance as daily life, the quotidian, habit, and so forth. But was it not precisely the achievement of modernism—or to be more precise, *Ulysses*—to have shown us how the smallest and most contingent if not altogether meaningless details of everyday life could be drawn back into a new kind of narrative structure and thereby rescued and renarrativized? Do they not, those details, themselves then become in their own way events, albeit of less visibility and notoriety than the great ones, the capitalized Event as such (the quotidian now itself coming to constitute History)?

These are problems of a philosophical nature, which can fall under the purview of metaphysics, of politics, of linguistics, or phenomenology (it being understood that each of these classifications will inevitably determine its own solution), but which we do not have to resolve here. All I have wanted to argue is that the problem of narrative is an allegorical one and that it holds for history fully as much as for daily life; and, I suppose, that it is a permanent problem as such. Allegory is always with us, in politics, in narratology, in daily life, and in "common sense."

It is therefore worth showing that it is also a synchronic or systemic problem and not just a narrative or chronological one. Schmitt's formula already implied this, but I want to put it out in the open, where its consequences can be assessed. My proposition consists in grasping national identity in terms of a cast of characters—sometimes large, sometimes small, just like concrete groups, families, and so on—whose imaginary presence defines the situation of the individual, who identifies it with this imaginary situation of his country or nation-state. It is not only in diplomacy, I think, that whole countries are taken to be allies (friends) or adversaries (foes): I want to assert these structures as existential ones, and indeed, as proto-narratives. Let me take as a relatively distant example the China of the 1980s, which knew a sufficiently complex imaginary cast of characters to enrich Schmitt's scheme as well as to add interesting complications to Propp's classical format. (I hasten to add that it is an exercise that could be practiced on any country in the world.)

The principal question to be decided about China's twin enemies—the Soviet Union and the United States—is how each could function differently in this momentary constellation. China fought a war against the United States in Korea, and yet, with the famous Nixon visit, neutralized that antagonism without yet wholly opening itself to US business. Perhaps at this point we could add to the standard analyses of trade a narratological function: in these as it were diplomatic-level narratives, trade takes on the function of love and marriage on the level of personal stories ("la douceur du commerce"); and the objects of trade ("Made in Japan," "Made in Germany," "Made in China")—while not exactly the Lacanian objet petit a—nonetheless are greeted with something of the mixed familiarity, nostalgia, or repulsion of Baudelaire's old souvenirs and love tokens—unpleasant reminders of dependency or grateful tokens of mutual aid.

Meanwhile, the Sino-Soviet split involved no outright warfare (save for several now well-known border clashes) and yet left behind a bitterness that only temporal and spatial distance has gradually assuaged. The Soviet Union was a former friend, but the United States a former enemy with whom a warm friendship was in the process of developing, which was itself intensified by the world-historical dimension of meaning of a kind of second-level allegory: for the United States as the land of new technologies (particularly of information technology) and of universal entertainment commodities and consumption, as the land also of English as the new universal lingua franca, was also identified as a locus of Utopian desire—not so much of envy as of a new type of historical wealth the Chinese were intent on acquiring.

Japan, to be sure, figured as a former enemy that can never be forgiven and is talked and thought about as little as possible, but with which one has correct and distant dealings. Taiwan was something closer to an alienated cousin—tainted by Japanese culture and corrupted by the self-proclaimed and alleged friend, the United States—but whom one does not despair receiving back into the family, a blood relationship officially to be publicly proclaimed from time to time.

As for Vietnam, it was a very ungrateful neighbor, whose help in its hour of need was rewarded with independent views and a resistance that provoked a not very lovely little war.

I could go on, noting the peculiarities of Hong Kong, some of which were deflected onto the British; and also, much earlier, the gratifying

Political: National Allegory 209

reception of China into the great third-world or "non-aligned" alliance of Bandung—something like recovering the admiration of society at large, in a situation in which China had little libidinal identification with the majority of the third-world countries, in perhaps a ghostly survival of the pride of the Middle Kingdom. (India is another special case here, as another former empire whose mentalities survived on into modern times.) As for Europe, it will have become clear in our illustrative map (Figure 5.1) of Chinese judgments that it is today, as far as China is concerned, little more than a collection of oddities; while Africa has acquired a new (and old) value as a space of extractive colonization.

Figure 5.1
Source: Reprinted with permission from
Financial Policy Magazine, March 2, 2016

One could then very easily go on—I have only included a few hints—and turn this into a full-blown family novel, perhaps a dynasty during the transitional passage to modernity and the nuclear family, but still internally cohesive with neighbors and rivals and a more distant geography outside the family compound. I call this allegorical fantasy a *proto-narrative* to the degree to which each "character" in it is accompanied by its own history and by the fantasy of its own relationship to the protagonist in both past and future and also in the sense in which, given such an initial cast of characters, in any decisive encounter or dramatic crisis there will be an accounting, a lining up of various figures on multiple levels and their assessment in terms of alliances or unreliabilities: who can help us out here, who is deceitful and not to be trusted, and so forth. And I will add that, as in personal identity, the *partage d'alterité*—the way in which these varied others are taken to map out a combination of dependence and autonomy—will necessarily define or better still construct my own national identity.

I have not yet pointed out the obvious, that the main character has not been dealt with in this enumeration and that the center has been taken for granted, as "my" position, as what does not require characterization, as the inside of which all these friends and foes form the heterogeneous outside, the situation, the terrain, and thus define "selfhood" itself and as such.

V

We must, however, end this commentary on a metaphysical note. What has been affirmed here, what is presupposed by the specific text in question, is the status of the collectivity as the "ultimately determining instance." That is Marxist terminology for the primacy of the economic (speaking loosely), the infrastructure, the mode of production, over all superstructural forms: the legal, the cultural, the religious, the philosophical, and the like. It has most often been taken to mean capitalism, since that is what we are in and is the only mode of production Marx analyzed extensively; and one possible conclusion to be drawn from this primacy is the superstructural omnipresence of the commodity form, of commodity reification, a position I thoroughly endorse.

But in Marx's very rudimentary model of base and superstructure (it really only appears once, in the 1859 Preface to the contribution to a

Critique of Political Economy), we confront what is clearly an allegorical schema, complete with "levels":

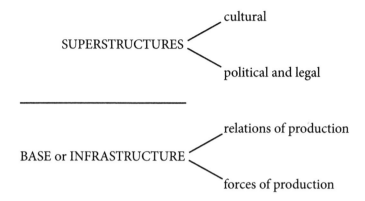

If we understand the forces of production to be the technology of a given mode, while the relations of production essentially names the collective structure of the labor process, then it would certainly seem as though this distinction is replicated on the more fundamental levels of the mode, namely in the distinction between base and superstructure itself. Typically, that distinction will be taken to be modeled after the incorrigibly human (or let's say anthropocentric) opposition between object and subject, or, to put it even more crudely, between body and soul. (And perhaps I have not insisted enough in this book on the irresistible temptation to read allegory and its interpretation according to the same conscious or unconscious paradigm, namely that of letter and spirit.) As humans, we do not ever really get out of this instinctive, unconscious, deeply rooted category mistake, which we certainly can't solve but whose illusions it would be disastrous to ignore. The human mind is idealistic in its very nature; at best we can attempt to discount this epistemological distortion in advance or reckon it into our experiments.

As for the allegory of the modes of production, however, we need to take it further: for the initial opposition of base and superstructure will then reduplicate itself and recur within the superstructure itself, where in general the materialist term will turn out to be one form or another of the state or the law, while the superstructures of the superstructure will be assigned to the relative sandboxes of culture, religion, philosophy, and the like. This sort of Foucauldian materialism of the superstructures is a widespread vice of our current thinking, in which it is so often politics and political power which are alone the truly materialistic levels, the more fundamental lower level of the economic being sublimated into those superstructures themselves: not capitalism but the idea of capitalism, not production but productivism, not production but consumption and so forth. If then, we try to correct the idealism of this political and judicial bias with some new emphasis on the base, what mostly comes out is a fetishization of the forces of production and the technologies of modern or contemporary capitalism, which are today, of course, informational and digital, communicational and cybernetic, that is to say, immaterial. But that is also a category mistake.

What must be understood is that Marx is not a mechanical materialist but a historical one. Not the chapter on the commodity form but rather the chapter on cooperation—*asabiyya*—is in Marx the crucial and "materialist" intervention. The fourfold scheme emerges here as the allegory of production itself: the literal level, the text itself, is the illusion that it is our machinery, our technology (the industrial revolution, the digital revolution), which is the driving force both of the bewildering metamorphoses of our daily lives and also the direction of our history as such.

Paradoxically, then, this means that what has generally been understood as the base or infrastructure in Marxist theory—the forces of production and the relations of production—is itself more complicated than its stereotypes allow: and is in fact divided internally into a kind of base-and-superstructure combination in its own right. What is not generally understood is that it is the social relations of production—the labor process itself—which is the truly material base of the process, while the so-called forces of production—technology and science—are somehow (in a material sense) "superstructural" to the relations and determined by them. The most consequent Marxian historians of science have insisted (generally in vain) on the priority of class relations and the labor process (including population) over scientific and technological "discoveries" and innovations whose story necessarily results in the various idealist theories of progress that still govern our textbooks and our unconscious or habitual pictures of historical change.[21] Philosophies based on technological progress are necessarily ideological; and their "materialism" must ultimately be identified as a

---

21 Basic correctives to this scientific idealism are to be found in classic essays by Boris Hessen and Henryk Grossman in Gideon Friedenthal and Peter McLaughlin, eds., *The Social and Economic Roots of the Scientific Revolution*, Berlin: Springer, 2009.

mechanical materialism of the static, deterministic type developed in the eighteenth century and denounced by Marx in his proposal for a more dynamic and more truly dialectical historical materialism.

This is no doubt the point at which metaphysics enters the argument, along with the various temptations to posit this or that human nature. Human individuals are biologically incomplete, and the intelligible unit of which they are a part is not even the reproductive unit of the two sexes but rather the larger group whose work in whatever way assures their existence, their survival, and indeed their reproduction.

It is important to avoid the temptation to classify the historical variety of such groups, whose dimensions and structure vary widely, in political terms such as the polis or the empire, or in cultural terms such as the clan or the kinship group, or the religious or linguistic community. The level on which these various collective structures are determinate is unrepresentable; and political science, along with cultural anthropology itself, are themselves mere allegories of its deeper structural determination.

But if we cannot account for the collectivity in positive terms, which are invariably tainted by their various self-generated ideologies, then at least we can try to discern them by way of the limits they impose on all the other levels. This is the sense in which the shape of the group limits our thinking, our representations (as for example in the various literary genres), and even, I would argue, our conceptual knowledge itself. For each age has the science (and political science) it deserves, and the dimensions of that specific historical collectivity is the ultimate instance that either permits the mind's invention of the calculus or of quantum mechanics, or prevents it. Perhaps it is this notion, that the forces of production, now grasped as the evolution of Western science, take the form of Enlightenment progress, which is the most pernicious pre-Marxist illusion, not to speak of the quantity of books produced by its pseudodiscipline, the so-called history of ideas.

A Marxian revision of the allegory of the capitalist mode of production would then look something like this:

ANAGOGICAL: culture (commodification)
MORAL: power and domination (politics, the state), the juridical system
ALLEGORICAL: the collective (relations of production)
LITERAL: technology (the forces of production)

I would add that it is also an ideological mistake to situate class struggle on the political level, whereas in reality its existence lies in the labor process itself, whose form the other levels cooperate to preserve and to legitimate, at the same time that the whole structure is swept forward by time and historical contradiction into those unintended consequences of our intended ones which Hegel called "the ruse of reason."

But we must also emphasize the positive by underscoring the productive effects of this unrepresentability of the collective: something very precisely to be found in the allegorical structures that complete and compensate our empirical experience of the defects, the insufficiencies, and the failures of our particular collective system with Utopian foreshadowings of a radically different system. This shadowy Utopian dimension of our represented realities is a kind of anagogical consciousness always present even if by negation in the most reactionary or dystopian images of our "current situation"; and it is also the unrepresentable transcendence which fulfills the most explicit progressive and political representations of that situation, whose practical thrust its conscious identification can only enhance.

VI

In conclusion, I return to the texts at issue in the essay on which this is a commentary. One of the most frequent misunderstandings of this essay lay in the assumption that it fetishized the national or state form and that it is meant to propagate the idea that all allegory is national.

This was an illusion essentially produced by my choice of texts, both of which arise from a specific historical period in which the nation is called upon to regenerate the collectivity, as in Lu Xun, or is literally in the process of emergence and state formation as in Ousmane, whose production was largely stimulated by decolonization (along with an accompanying disillusionment). But a later period of world literary development that one might still characterize as Third World began to allegorize other kinds of collective units, subgroups, and ethnicities, as in the Biafra rebellion and (from another side of the political spectrum) the resistance of the Zulus to South African liberation. Indeed, the whole period of the wars of national liberation produced a variety of group models that resist the old models of the nation and of so-called nation formation, as in the Palestinian resistance or the Cuban conception of the *foco*. At the same time, one finds elegiac celebrations of the nation in countries in decline (my example was the Galdos of the Spanish loss of empire at the end of the nineteenth century), as well as the promotion of seemingly private and individual relationships as forms of Utopian protest against a universal conformism or an omnipresent and puritanical traditionalism. The situation is here, as always, everything; and our slogan should be, not only that everything is allegorical, but even more, that all allegory is Utopian!

6
Poetic: Spenser and the Crisis of Personification

Medieval narrative is liquidated by two paradoxically antithetical writers: Cervantes and Spenser. The first does so by taking that narrative literally; the second by denarrativizing it by means of an allegorical complexity that reduces it to the temporality of the individual stanza. The two great traditions of medieval literature had both emerged in the twelfth century; on the one hand, in a mystico-erotic lyric that culminates in Dante's unique epic; the second, in the more properly narrative "romans" of the epoch's greatest "novelist," Chrétien de Troyes. Intricate legends are spun from this last, which are dutifully developed for centuries (and find true literary achievements in Italian "epic") until they sink under their own weight in Spenser's megallegory, thereafter only fitfully remembered by the Romantics in Novalis (*Heinrich von Ofterdingen*) and Wagner's *Parsifal* (to which I suppose we need to add Tolkien and the effervescence of contemporary commercial fantasy literature).

Spenser was notable for being one of those rare combinations of culture and politics—an elite poet of great distinction (today one might describe him as an avant-garde writer) and a repressive colonist and military governor who left a history of what we might today call human rights abuses behind him in a newly conquered Ireland. In short, only D'Annunzio springs to mind as a weird modern analogy for this career, until we remember that the poetry was also political, *The Faerie Queene* itself constituting one long tribute of flattery to a sovereign who showed no interest in it whatsoever (although she was herself an Italianist and an intellectual *à sa manière*).

At any rate, few works of the tradition combine such extraordinary literary gifts with an architectonic ambition that makes of this monumental unfinished epic one of the strangest and most impressive ruins upon which one may stumble in the jungle of the written archive. The apotheosis of allegory, it virtually destroys the whole allegorical arsenal in one great natural disaster, visible from miles in all directions; it thereby merits our attention, particularly for what it has to tell us about the framing of the allegorical process as well as the destiny of one of its most basic instruments, namely personification.

I

To understand the operation of the allegorical frames, we need to draw back a little from our central exhibit and examine a modern text which shows off the play of such interacting references in a simpler and more accessible form. Ursula Le Guin's great political novel *The Dispossessed* presupposes twin planets, one of which, Uras, is civilized, being geologically and metereologically well favored, while the other, Anarres, far more barren, has been uncolonized until its settlement as the result of a peaceful revolution in which the anarchist opposition, under their woman leader Odo, is allowed to secede with a fleet of aged spacecrafts and to build their Utopia on the unpromising twin planet. The resultant revolutionary society is an impoverished and regimented one; everyone must work (their tasks assigned by computers); bureaucratic conformism has set in, which is oppressive for misfits and oddballs, the characterological heretics and dissidents of this particular social order; finally, communications with Uras are reduced to a strict minimum, no capitalist propaganda, few exchanges, and a single spaceship landing once a month in a carefully patrolled and sealed off checkpoint. Leaving aside Le Guin's Jeffersonian rhetoric, it is surely very difficult not to read this 1974 novel as a thinly disguised fable about the opposition between the United States (or the capitalist West) and the Soviet Union (the protagonist Shevek being an ambivalent kind of defector or dissident who moves between the two).

So far so good; there would be nothing very surprising in such a fictional transposition (of which many others exist). But when we get to

Uras, a peculiar discovery awaits us: the richest part of Uras, where Shevek first lands, is to be sure a capitalist analogue of the United States. But alongside it, on the same planet, there exist other countries and continents: and they turn out to "represent" Maoist China, the Third World, and finally even the Soviet Union itself. So now suddenly we have a bewildering multiplicity of referents: it is not that Anarres includes several things at once (different social systems, different regimes, different places). It is rather that other "places" within this novel also simultaneously mean "the same thing" on different levels. The situation is then compounded and heightened into a genuine representational and interpretive dilemma when we learn that beyond Uras and Anarres, somewhere else in the galactic system at large, there also (or perhaps one should say, there still) exists a real Earth, that real planet on which the real United States and Soviet Union once stood, and which has now been reduced to poverty and bare subsistence by nuclear war and ecological disaster.

I believe that this peculiar and seemingly aberrant structure of multiple frames and references puts us on the track of a significant and essential feature of allegory itself. For one thing, this is precisely the kind of nonspace we have been looking for: surprisingly, however, it is not to be found in the representation itself, where each space remains "realistic" and homogeneous—there are the two planets, with real countries on one, and somewhere beyond them, but in the very same real world and "real" galactic space, even though incalculably far away, there is the real Earth. (Were we here pursuing the originality of the work of Le Guin itself, this would be the moment to bring up the central datum on which her plot turns, namely the "ansible," the hypothesis of a nonspatial simultaneous communication across just such enormous distances.)

What is discontinuous after the fashion of Western medieval paintings is not the represented space itself here, but rather the discontinuity of its allegorical references. What does the allegorical referent "Soviet Union," designated by Anarres, have to do with the allegorical referent "Soviet Union" designated by the country on Uras, let alone with that subsisting or destroyed on Earth itself? There is here an undecidability of narrative frames, the historical Cold War projecting various fictional versions of itself onto several science-fictional scales (that of Uras/Anarres, that of the cosmic planetary system of the Ecumen). But the difference between these frames is not confusing, inasmuch as their active presence is only detected by way of the allegorical references they suggest. They are, in other words, simply distinct "frames of reference" that remain largely homogeneous within a single historical situation, that of the Cold War itself. (I resist distinguishing between fictive or imaginary frames and real historical ones, insofar as all are narrative, and in any case the notion of a "Cold War" is itself an abstract, or "transcendental," totalizing concept whose function is to organize a series of disparate "historical" facts into a narrative unity that is no more binding than any other such narrative version.)

We may for the moment leave aside the semiotic debates about levels of reading or isotopies—linguistic or textual units supposed to ensure the homogeneity of a certain reading, a certain way of "following the story"—and observe that classical allegory, from the *Roman de la rose* (1230) to Bunyan's *Pilgrim's Progress* (1678), secures the unification of its reading by way of the framework of the dream, which serves to rationalize the variety of its episodes and to deproblematize the allegorical transversalities and inconsistencies of interest to us here. Meanwhile, upon the device of the dream a second form will customarily be superimposed, namely that of the spatial journey, which has the advantage of specifying a goal or terminus, in the *Roman* the rose itself:

> In spite of Wealth, that villainous creature who showed no pity but refused me entry to the path she guarded (she paid no heed to the path by which I came here in secret haste); in spite of my mortal enemies who caused me so many setbacks; in spite particularly of Jealousy, weighed down by her garland of marigolds, who protects the roses from lovers (much good her guard is doing now!), before I left that place in which, had I had my way, I would have remained to this day, I plucked with joy the flower from the fair and leafy rose-bush. And so I won my bright red rose. Then it was day I and I awoke.[1]

Compared to Bunyan's vision of the Gate of Gold and in the second part, of the Celestial City, the plucking of the rose is no doubt as peremptory and inexpressible as orgasm itself, while the final entry into the City in *Pilgrim's Progress* remains in the future of living readers and believers.

---

1 *The Romance of the Rose*, trans. Frances Horgan, Oxford: Oxford University Press, 2009, 335.

But the journey itself organizes space (and vice versa) and can surely be said to constitute some final form of that Babylonian star journey Bloomfield saw as the origin of the system of the seven deadly sins.[2] The journey motivates (in the sense of the Russian Formalists) the discontinuous "device" of the episodes, the stops on the way, the variety of encounters, in other words, the synchronic dimension of the allegorical apparatus; while the journey itself does not so much produce space as it generates narrative temporality and sequence from out of it.

But in both these initial examples, this structure would seem to offer little more than a map on the one hand and the allegorical label on the other, a two-level process appropriately ridiculed in conceits like the seventeenth-century "carte du tendre" of salon and court society. That the thirteenth-century *Rose* emerges from debates on sublimation no less philosophical than those in the as yet unrediscovered *Symposium* or later on in psychoanalysis restores a certain significance to this simple-minded allegory; while as far as Bunyan is concerned, no one can fail to appreciate the unique agony of guilt recorded in its opening pages, a momentous psychic experience of which Luther's own is henceforth for us the historical marker. But both these subjective experiences are uncharted, and find no place in the various historical systems of emotions or passions we have examined in an earlier chapter. I am tempted to say that both are in that sense allegorical passions, partly experiential or phenomenological and partly textual (in the special sense that word has come to have in poststructuralism). Both are in other words phenomena which are distinct from either lived experience or literary and linguistic expression, while sharing features of both; and it is as an approximation to just such unique structures that I stage the following readings of Spenser, Dante, and Goethe.

But *Pilgrim's Progress* possesses an additional interest for us, insofar as it would seem in certain respects to resemble what have been latterly characterized as a genre, the "postmodern novel." It will be important to avoid this anachronism, which has some justification, by showing that it is the restriction of Bunyan to a two-level scheme that encourages it. The so-called postmodern novel can in this spirit be characterized by the inclusion of textuality within the text itself, so that the narrative itself becomes "textualized" (as in Robbe-Grillet's descriptions), or else the

---

2   See Chapter 2, note 17.

"text" itself appears within the novel as a mysterious and missing document (as in *House of Leaves*, or in Dick's *Man in the High Castle*), or by the assimilation of life to writing, or the characters to authors, or events to media processes or mechanisms (as in *Infinite Jest* or *Cloud Atlas*), and so forth. But we must remember, when dealing with Bunyan (and especially with Protestant allegory) that the text of the Bible is a central object in such allegories: so that the visit of Christian to the Interpreter and the crucial place of the library or textual "room" is scarcely a postmodern thematics but rather a central issue in the political struggles of the period (and in its personal experiences of conversion). The contamination of the two levels of text and narrative activity therefore—however much it may recall such interferences for postmodern readers—is a fairly limited structure that will become far more complex in the three major allegorical texts to be examined here.

But there is another distinction to be noted, and one which goes some distance toward explaining not only how Bunyan can have been thus novelized but how his relatively simple dream tale might come to remind us of the Moebius strip of recent literatures. This is its prose redaction (and we may also recall here how many of the earlier medieval verse narratives such as the *Roman de la rose* were also "translated" into prose in the later Middle Ages).

It would seem unnecessary to review the unique versification of our three principal exhibits, yet in our "world of prose" (Hegel) verse narrative, and even Goethe's versified "reading play," constitutes an increasingly rare and rarified experience. Versification is in fact the control of the reader's lived time; it imposes a unique formal sequentiality on our own loose informal personal temporalities (not for nothing did Augustine choose a hymn to illustrate his own discussion of Time in Chapter 11 of the *Confessions*), in that bearing some resemblance to music or to film as temporal media which demand a certain kind of uninterrupted attention. It would be premature to speak of the construction of subjectivity in the context of such temporal discipline: its forms are already there, in the structure of the sentence, for example, or in that of the hours of the day, or of emergence and disappearance in the realm of emotions.

Yet verse sharpens a regulated sequence of instants, and it also submits us to temporary and ephemeral experiences of closure. Thus, Dante's extraordinary terza rima both completes its sequences and (by way of the overlap of its rhyme schemes) ensures their interlocking continuation as well; it enforces an interplay of "difference and repetition," which strikes a compromise between the synchronic and the diachronic and keeps us going at the same time that it arrests us, in this very much like Virgil's twin contradictory insistences on looking and on moving on. We will have occasion to examine the episodic in Dante later on, but even at this stage it is clear that terza rima must pay for it by inventing the concision of the one-liner, the epigrammatic characterization, that ephemeral yet definitive formula that T. S. Eliot compared to some of Dickens's great characterological effects ("I'll never leave Mr. Micawber!" "Barkus is willing!").[3]

Closure is then far stronger in the unique Spenserian stanza, which seems to complete itself at every move, its definitive last long line shutting down the verse paragraph and forcing the narrative to begin again as a new and yet renewed totality. Here the role of the episode is taken over by the verse form itself, which makes the episode itself over into a series of smaller episodes. This is an enforced temporality very different from that of Dante, one which changes the nature of the journey just as surely as it does that of its reading. What remains to be determined is its relationship to the allegorical structure as such.

Finally we must come to terms with that extraordinary variety of verse forms in Goethe's *Faust II*. In a historicist age, these cannot but stand as reminiscences of the past and of the verse forms of a nascent world culture (or "world literature," as he called it): a true anthology in the classical sense, a memorialization of all the prosodic forms invented in that Alexandrian world that stretched from Rome to Persia, from the Germanic forests to Alexandria and the world ocean. Here the *knittelvers* of German folksong meets the most august epic temporality of the hexameter. Even in English, in Whitman's underground rhythms, hexameter exerts its authority and breathes an epic monumentality on everything it touches: hexameter thereby constitutes a kind of allegorical amplification in its own right and contributes to the bewildering heterogeneity of Goethe's drama in a way that seems to open it up, rather than, as in Spenser and Dante, to close it down.

---

3 T. S. Eliot, *Selected Essays*, Boston: Harcourt, Brace and Company, 1932, 411: "Dickens' figures belong to poetry, like figures of Dante or Shakespeare, in that a single phrase, either by them or about them may be enough to set them wholly before us."

Yet prosody and meter, beat, even pulse and accent, all seem to play their role in the release of allegorical impulses, just as their absence condemns Bunyan's text to a half-life in the antechambers of the novel. Is it possible that the enforced temporality of verse serves to compensate the dispersal of allegorical structure as such? What might dissolve into a rhizome or hypertext of cross-references—as indeed it does in the attempt to theorize these texts—is here transferred to a sonorous and linguistic level where it must submit to a different kind of order—a horizontal continuity masking the vertical chaos of the levels and the break-up of the *isotopie*.

This is, however, the moment to return to the question of frames in the *Faerie Queen*, a work that does not rely on the framework of the dream, but rather with the classic invocation to the Muses sets forth resolutely after the fashion of the epic narrative as such:

> A gentle knight was pricking on the plaine,
> Y cladd in mightie armes and silver shielde
>
> (I/i/1/41)[4]

This is an epic framework, but a deceptive one, insofar as we do not enter a unified Event such as a war *in medias res* but confront instead what one is tempted to call the homogenous landscape of medieval romance. What is then doubly deceptive in this narrative strategy is the discontinuity of those landscapes themselves.

In the *Faerie Queene,* the action (if one can even call it that) takes place in two overall localities: England (to be sure, present only in flashbacks or interpolated chronicles) and Faeryland, in which the present of the poem finds both readers and characters, and whose problems we must not too hastily dismiss with Coleridge's notion of "mental space" (as though all artistic representations did not in one way or another take place in mental space). From one point of view, Faeryland is considered to be a kingdom somewhere east of the then Ottoman Empire; the various knights travel there to fulfill their vows and complete their quests. In that case, the whole varied topography of the poem is "set" in this

---

4 Edmund Spenser, *The Faerie Queene*, eds Thomas P. Roche Jr. and C. Patrick O'Donnell Jr., London: Penguin, 1979. All references in the text are to this edition and are made in this format: Book/Canto/Stanza/Page.

kingdom, one that has a monarch (Gloriana) and a location on the existing globe (albeit a fictional one). But leaving aside the quality of the spaces and narrative settings within Faeryland for the moment, this setting itself poses further problems. What of the presence within Faeryland of properly British rivers (the Thames and the Medway, for instance, and their "marriage")? Perhaps one could maintain that it is only the physical rivers that exist in Britain, while their allegorical spirits and personifications are housed in this other place. Are we then to suppose that, far from being another locality altogether, Faeryland is superimposed on the real Britain much as More's *Utopia* is superimposed (with all manner of inversions and structural recombinations) on the real England of his time?[5] In that case, is such superimposition still to be considered allegorical? And what do we do with the second superimposition of some supplementary theological space, as when Redcross's journey takes him to what are called "Eden lands"? Meanwhile, it is necessary to insist on the relevance of our previous account for the inner space within the poem, or, better still, for the nonexistence of any continuous space between those local places of the various episodes. Perhaps it would be better to say that the poem is constructed in such a way that between its episodes the reader is never inclined to ask embarrassing questions about their interconnections: their "space" and their travel times. (Nor are those pictorial in any modern sense of asking us to visualize a perspectival scene and to fill in its components.)

But l don't mean by all of this to reach the conclusions either that Spenser was sloppy or self-contradictory in this regard, or that all this spatial slippage is of no interest and significance at all (so that asking questions about it is rather like the naive reader's referential ones: who Lady Macbeth's father was, in a famous Thurber story or how many children she had, in another equally famous critical essay).

Better to turn now for a moment to the beings or characters who populate these spaces and in particular to the official inhabitants of Faeryland: the Elves. Were these last mere Tolkien-style figures of various secondary kinds, among whom properly human (or British) heroes move, no great problems would arise: but it so happens that one of the protagonists also happens to be an Elf. (Leave aside the fact that several

---

5 A. C. Hamilton, ed., *The Spenser Encyclopedia*, Toronto: University of Toronto Press, 1997, 293.

of the other human figures have been snatched away and raised in Faeryland.) This is Guyon, the hero of Book Two, and the allegorical personification, according to its title, of the virtue of Temperance. How are we to read this distinction? It surely cannot mean that Elves are by nature more temperate than humans (or Englishmen); yet the destiny of this particular Elf ought to help us distinguish the properties of his race from those of the race of Arthur himself (a central figure in this book).

I follow Harry Berger Jr.'s classic account at this point[6]: the Elfin race is like the human, but without original sin and the Fall. That ought to make them superior to human beings; but to think so is to forget the theological doctrine of the *happy fall* or in other words the way in which grace lifts the human being above any conceivable prelapsarian innocence, whether the innocence before the fall or that of the noble pagan. This is indeed Berger's argument, that the first part of the Book, in which Guyon is on his own, reflects a classical ideal (in style as well as in ethos). But Guyon's fainting spell at the very moment in which he has surmounted his greatest temptation so far—the offerings of Mammon's cave—is the allegorical signal that he can get no further with a purely Elfin (prelapsarian) nature and requires the theological supplement supplied by Arthur's arrival and assistance. At this point the Book becomes a Christian poem, and the reason for Arthur's centrality—even though he is the central protagonist of none of the books we have—becomes clear. But I also want to add that this is a purely local message: Guyon does not reappear in the existing poem we have (except as a misprint in the next book), but one can conjecture that he will not always have this specific allegorical value and that even the system of levels of perfection thus briefly epitomized in him will not be a permanent feature of the completed poem:

> The Soul and its Salvation
> ___
> The Individual Possessing Classical Virtues
> ___
> The Fashioning of the Courtier

In other words, his destiny is to rise from the lowest level, the worldly one to

---

6   Harry Berger Jr., *Revisionary Play: Studies in the Spenserian Dynamics*, Berkeley: University of California Press, 1990.

the highest, in this superposition of the gentleman, the hero, and the saint.

In that case, if one follows the commentators, perhaps we should posit the linguistic texture—puns, figures, the words that come to fill up each stanza as a self-contained unit—as something like a literal level on which the other levels episodically build. The medieval or knightly material is little more than a pretext for these figures, and they remain local. Thus, unlike Dante's cosmos or the general medieval system, Spenser must rearrange his components for every episode, every throw of the dice, and so the "meaning" of Faeryland is no more stable than the logic of its space.

But now we need to look at the most strategic example of this spatial slippage, which can be observed around the person of the monarch herself. But which one? For the "real" monarch is fully as present in the poem, by way of the various addresses and appeals as to her, as her poetic alter ego, Gloriana, the queen of Faeryland ("as fully": that is to say, no less but also no more—both are in fact charged absences). But there are subtle discrepancies, and nagging difficulties, about identifying these two figures in any stable way. Various episodes for example allude to events of Elizabeth's reign or at her court (proposed marriages, for example), which have no analogy in the Gloriana scheme. But in this last we find the service of Arthur, who not only has no stable equivalent in Elizabeth's life history (an identification with Leicester impossible, given the outcome, and that with Essex unlikely, although the latter has been associated with Calidore and Arthegall),[7] but whose possible courtship of an ultimate marriage with the eponymous figure is both suggested by the logic of the epic and refuted by the legendary history of the "real" King Arthur himself.

It is true that in that unfulfilled project he outlines in *The Letter to Raleigh*, Spenser ingeniously invents a well-nigh postmodern solution to his formal problems: he there imagines the final unwritten book as a virtual coronation festival for Gloriana in which selected "wights" present themselves to act out the various virtues at work in the legendary figure and career of King Arthur. Each book is then a reading of those exploits, like the bard's recitation of the story of Odysseus before the unrevealed hero himself, unless they are the narratives of more authentically medieval trials and missions, where the attendant knights are

---

7   Hamilton, *The Spenser Encyclopedia*, 254.

sent forth to prove themselves. The ultimate frame that would reconcile all this is then either a properly Arthurian cycle or rhizome of round-table adventures, or a play that reenacts those before the sovereign; but obviously enough, the text we have never reaches that moment of the fulfillment, the Viconian ricorso.

Then there are the various mythological references: is the sovereign not from time to time Venus, or perhaps on the other hand Diana? These would be dangerous associations if allowed to persist for long; rather, there is a constant movement of coupling and uncoupling as the royal reference comes and goes. Much more explicit—the Proem to Book III declares it outright—is the association of Elizabeth with Belphoebe, a prototype of cold or cruel chastity who is more uniformly allegorical of the identification than Britomart herself, sometimes also suggested as another Elizabeth figure. But it is the flat characters that can carry off such properties better than the round ones; we need to think of such momentary references as aspects of a being-for-others: now it is power and sovereignty, now chastity, now heroism and the like; and everyone can be shattered into such aspects that fail to add up organically, nor are they futures of subjective identity, either. And this is why that splendid expression, subject positions, although having some analogies, is not altogether right either, since these are somehow more objective. They exist as aspects for other people, they are somehow institutional virtues within monarchy; and perhaps this is the clue to the function of the allegorical operation itself, which seeks gropingly to correlate these "objective" entities (called *virtues* or *vices* or psychological phenomena that have been reified into names) with some inner placement, some blind correlation with what is not yet completely an existential and phenomenological inner space.

Belphoebe's twin Amoret seems a less likely equivalent for royal identification (given the otherwise scandalous account of a successful courtship), but the structural effect of the "reference by multiplication" aims not to promise certainty about any of the allegorical identifications, but rather constantly to allow the possibilities to rise and fall, as so many moments for the "endlesse worke," so many readerly hesitations, self-doubts, and conjectures by the *Grübler*, who turns the pages of such emblems. The confusions are then mimicked and textuality acted out in the well-known referential confusion of Spenser's pronouns—the unidentified "him" and "her" that can only be sorted out in the further course of reading and whose appositions are never clarified by syntax. The reader first assumes this to be his own weakness or failure; then Spenser's sloppiness as a writer; and finally concludes, à la Spitzer, that the linguistic peculiarity is a meaningful symptom in its own right and corresponds to deeper structural originalities in the work itself. The pronouns thus lie open to reference, they lie in wait like so many snares prepared for the "capture" of allegorizable elements (to use Teskey's admirable phrase).[8]

In the normal scheme of things in the allegorical world, that capture would take place in the form of personification (which will be examined later). But what is more significant for the development of allegory—not a chronological matter, as the placement of our chapter on Dante later on suggests—is the emergence of revealing slippages in such allegorical fabrics, of what, following Stephen Knapp, we will call *spatial anomalies*.[9] These are moments in which personification interrupts the allegorical narrative rather than ensuring its development and precipitates a kind of crisis in the form.

Knapp is dealing with the textbook crux or scandal of Milton's twin personifications of Sin and Death in *Paradise Lost*: two names or actors who seem very much out of place in their style and structure to the general "realism" of Milton's epic narrative, and which indeed seem to have become virtually unavoidable in any discussion of allegory and its discontents: are they not flaws or lapses in Milton's great poem? But the three wild animals that threaten Dante in the First Canto of *Inferno* might equally have served the purpose, as we shall see shortly.

At any rate, Knapp usefully leads us through a variety of peculiar yet constitutive features of such "characters": the interchangeability in them of passive and active, for example (83–84), or the way in which ultimately "personifications 'know' only the abstractions they designate" (102). But his major exhibit, Wordsworth's "allegorical figures," calls forth a host of spatial puzzles, in its diagnosis of what he oddly calls the "naturalization of the allegorical personifications" (106) (as though this movement from abstraction to naturalization did not centrally define personification in the first place):

---

8   Gordon Teskey, *Allegory and Violence,* Ithaca: Cornell University Press, 1996.
9   Steven Knapp, *Personification and the Sublime,* Cambridge: Cambridge University Press, 1985. Page numbers in the text refer to this edition.

> How and where, for instance, is the Old Man located in the landscape with which the descriptive similes might seem to identify him? The protagonist sees a Man before him, but at what distance and at what angle? If the Old Man resembles a huge stone on the top of an eminence, then presumably the speaker is looking uphill at a distant object. But a sea-beast can only crawl forth at sea level, which suggests that the Old Man is at, or more likely below, the speaker's own elevation. The sea-beast, moreover, has an obvious origin—namely, the sea—and an obvious means of arrival—namely, crawling forth. But the stone amazes all its viewers, who wonder "By what means it could thither come, and whence." This ambiguity about the Old Man's mode of arrival applies as well to the speaker's mode of discovery: should we assume that the speaker's perception took the form of sudden or of gradual recognition? "I saw a Man before me unawares"—is "unawares" an adverb modifying the speaker's action ("I saw him unexpectedly") or an adjective indicating the Old Man's obliviousness of—or indifference to—the speaker? (106)

At any rate this description confirms our feeling (already encouraged by the Le Guin example) that the peculiarities in question are to be defined first and foremost by spatial incommensurabilities, a kind of radical disjunction or disconnection between the familiar Gestalt terms of figure and background.

There are to be sure other descriptive alternatives, which contribute their own value to the problem. Paxson's classic *Poetics of Personification* cites Gérard Genette's rhetorical classification of the phenomenon as metalepsis to characterize his own interesting version of Knapp's "naturalization" process, namely the incompatibility between a personification figure and a "human" character (as the former grows in centrality, the latter "diminishes," at length even losing its "human" voice).[10] But the latter, after all, continues to be essentially constituted by the incompatibility of the two contexts; the insertion, for example, of Job, a biblical–historical figure, into Prudentius's battle of the conventional personified Virtues and Vices, nonetheless itself constitutes a superposition of two distinct levels or isotopies. Paxson prolongs his theorization into

---

10 James J. Paxson, *The Poetics of Personification*, Cambridge: Cambridge University Press, 2009, 78, 93.

the late deManian preoccupation with prosopeia and facing or defacing, but this seems to me to return us unproductively to the narrower and more specialized domain of the dynamics of personification as such, rather than widening the inquiry into the larger field of allegory.

For the "spatial anomalies" at question here constitute invaluable clues as to the structural effects of allegory in general, as it lives on after the putative extinction of the personification device in modern times. The latter was already visible in Knapp's allusion to Wordsworth's "naturalization" of his figures (which assumes, incorrectly I think, that they began as abstractions) but is also implicit in the very ambivalent nature of the actant or character in the first place.

Such figures are at one and the same time potentially static essences and mobile players in a narrative: it is the very duality of the category of the "character" that is at stake here; and the movement of an abstract idea toward personification—already inherent in the very naming of an emotion—is at one with its transformation into a character. The reference back and forth between these two "contexts"—the system of abstract ideas such as emotions or cosmological elements; on the other hand a narrative movement on its way to the closure of a full-fledged story—is a subset of that allegorical heterogeneity, that confusion of reference we have in mind here. The more all-encompassing presentation of this "form problem" will then prove to be better served by returning to the fourfold system we have been exploring and by substituting the conceptuality of the level for that of a context (which has itself no context) or a ground, both of which presuppose a naturalistic psychology. The phenomenon we seek will therefore be best defined in terms of an interference, if not a perpetual cross-referencing or even transversality, between the four levels.

Thus, to return to the rather blatant example we have cited in Dante, the three ravenous beasts that frighten the poet at the base of the mountain on whose summit is situated the earthly paradise (or in other words, the former Garden of Eden), remain unnamed but have traditionally been identified in allegorical terms as cupidity, pride, and greed, respectively, on the basis of literary allusion and traditional bestiaries. They are here, in fact, only a leopard, a lion, and a she-wolf, each described with extraordinarily sculptural economy: the "lonza leggiera et presta molto" (32)[11] with a spotted hide (movement); the lion "con la test alta e con

---

11 Page numbers refer to Charles Singleton's edition of *The Divine Comedy, Vol. I:*

rabbiosa fame" (47) (bearing), and the she-wolf "che di tutte brame / sembiava carva ne la sua magrezza" (49–50) (skin and bones). It is significant that in his copious notes, Singleton does not deign to mention even the traditional allegorical identifications of these creatures, which, long before Luther was even thought of, forbid Dante's personal achievement of salvation (still conceived idyllically, as pastoral happiness; "il dilettoso monte"; 77), thereby confirming the later Lutheran critique of salvation by works.

Yet the meaning of the beasts is so far somehow inherent in their movements, which takes us a step beyond the physical attributes (the deceptive loveliness of the leopard's coat, the port of the lion's head, the skeletal emaciation of the wolf): for the leopard is not given any visible movement other than its lithe suppleness, the lion is meanwhile bearing down on Dante alarmingly, while the she-wolf ominously shadows Dante, moving back and forth alongside. Meanwhile, each one vanishes from the text after the appearance of the next, and by the time Dante pleads for help from Virgil there seems to be left only the last ("vedi la bestia per cu'io mi volsi"; 88). Does this not suggest first, that they are all forms of the same drive, even though each can be individualized in the form of specific temptations: that of beautiful false appearance (the pelt), that of aggression, and that of a generalized hunger in which the physical and the moral or spiritual are indistinguishable? Those temptations might then themselves be further allegorized as that of art, politics or warfare, and commerce or moneymaking. The allegorical impulse is then a kind of contagion that restlessly infects a wider and wider interpretive circle.

The most convincing allegorical interpretations of the beasts are those, appropriately enough, drawn from the scheme of sins embodied in *Inferno* (malice, force, incontinence).[12] However, this very reading illustrates the spatial incoherencies we have identified with allegory here, for not only do the sins and these initial perils occupy two distinct places in Dante's narrative (*Inferno* and *Purgatorio*), they embody two distinct aesthetics, that of the allegorical beast and that of the realistic or "naturalized" sinners. This very identification of the one set of phenomena with the other (a

---

The Inferno, Princeton: Princeton University Press, 1990.
   12   Richard Lansing, ed., *Dante Encyclopedia*, London: Taylor & Francis, 2000.

more recent effort)[13] shows something of the appearance of a quasi-mathematical reconciliation, in which the embarrassing inconsistencies of the two sets of data are minimized in ways that bring them into a harmony that can surely satisfy no one. The incompatibilities we are here dealing with need on the contrary to be brought out as sharply as possible in order to emphasize the peculiarity of the structure in which they are all housed.

The provisional impression one takes away from these problems is a useful rebuke to the traditional association of allegory with didacticism or the pedagogy of abstraction: for one sees here some first demonstration that an allegorical structure might well be grasped as the response to some doctrinal contradiction rather than as straightforward teaching and indoctrination. Yet it is only by way of underlining the problem of the representability of the doctrines in question that one can avoid the properly Crocean objection that we are here dangerously close to abandoning the poetic and the figural or the purely conceptual.

But there is another path to the domestication of allegory that is even more dangerous, inasmuch as it is far more accessible for modern readers: what one may call the novelization of the allegorical work, or in other words its rewriting in purely subjective (and in most cases, autobiographical) terms. Here the beasts are rewritten as dangers or temptations which concern some biographical Dante himself, an "implied narrator" or point of view, whose salvation, the poem allegedly shows us, is here at stake. From this perspective, then, one might hazard the guess that the mesmerizing visuality of the leopard's coat obscurely reflects the perils of art itself, and the temptation to transform the "dolce stil nuovo" into an end in itself, into a pure aestheticism; the lion's fury might then be the fear of losing oneself altogether, not only in politics, but in political anger, and being wholly absorbed by righteous indignation and obsession; while the she-wolf, in its sinuous movements, might well illustrate the distractions of exile and the desires that result from its hither-and-thithering, if not, perhaps, those of transient attractions and

---

13 Ibid., by Casella, 1865. (Lansing's summary of the four types of traditional interpretive options oddly resembles the fourfold system itself: first, the theological system of sins; second, the political vices; third, Florence and its intolerable realities for Dante himself; and finally—what looks closest to Casella's "justification"—an assimilation to the systems of *Inferno* and *Purgatorio*: allegorical, anagogical, moral, and textual.)

erotic hungers. The assignment of these biographical interpretations to the third, or moral, level then demands a certain restraint or discipline on the part of subjectivized and biographically habituated modern reader.

That such a novelization is always a temptation latent in allegorical structure, that such subjective and narrative translation is always a temptation for its readers, can also be demonstrated by the two great narratives I have already touched on, namely the *Roman de la rose* (1230) and *Pilgrim's Progress* (1678). The dates alone make an important point, namely that the history of this form, or formal structure, is not a continuous one; and that allegory seems to arise in unique and unrelated national situations, out of the failure of more traditional genres to express a given historical and psychic content. Meanwhile, the immense discrepancy in that content between these two works—the one secular and emerging from the theoretical and experiential situation of courtly love, the other religious and expressing the deepest anguish of the Protestant revolt—shows that religion is not a very adequate characterization of that content either, whose subjectivities take another form than those which will later on produce the unique new modern form of the novel and people its narratives.

This is the point at which to conclude that the spatial anomaly is not an aberration in the practice of allegory but rather constitutes the moment in which the heterogeneity of the allegorical levels breaks through and makes its presence felt. The levels are not a collection of complete narratives superimposed upon one another. Rather they come at reality in an utterly different way, by a jarring and sometimes dissonant differentiation of their various dimensions. And this heterogeneity holds, not only for the narrative unities we inevitably seek to form out of the elements and raw materials of the allegory, but also for the most tempting form of reunification for modern readers, which is that of the psychic level, the unity of the moral or psychological message or development, which I here propose to replace with the concept of a construction of subjectivity (subjectivity not constituting a unity at all, neither a homogeneity nor an identity or personal self). Yet in these intricacies one must not lose sight of the other levels of the allegory: if the allegorical or mystical key is to be found in the identification with Elizabeth, and the moral level in the constructions of subjectivity I have just outlined, we must not neglect the anagogical level, or vision of history

Poetic: Spenser and the Crisis of Personification

which the identification of the previous two levels (court intrigue, the system of the virtues) produces. It will therefore not be inappropriate to cite the following delightful reenactment of the *Faerie Queene* as a vision of History:

> Why not allow Book I to be an allegory of modern Russian Communism? The Red Cross Knight stands for the working class armed with the Marxist faith: naturally his colour is red, and his cross refers to the *crossed* hammer and sickle. Una is clearly the spirit of Communism. The opening battle against Error refers to the Revolution. That monster's books and papers which she spews at the knight refer to the flood of Trotskyite writings, and her death marks the first triumph of the oppressed peasant class (the knight is *Georgos*, one brought up in ploughman's state). The scattered brood who feed upon Error's body represents the landed kulaks who used the time of distress to get rich; and the account of their swollen bellies "with fulnesse burst,/ And bowels gushing forth" shows what rightly happened to them. But the knight is then separated from Una by the wiles of Archimago who stands for the hypocrisy of the *bourgeoisie*. Though he able to defeat Sansfoy, who is lack of faith in Marxism, he becomes the willing tool of Duessa, the Church of Rome, which is in league with the Western imperialists—her father is an emperor who "the wide *West* vnder his rule has, / And high hath set his throne, where *Tiberis* doth pas." She leads the knight to the house of Pride which is the modern capitalist world—hence the old on the roof, the weak foundations, the general corruption, and the masses chained in the dungeon. Here the knight is attacked by Sansjoy, obviously referring to the misery of the working class under capitalism, and betrayed into the hands of Orgoglio who is the U.S.A. After he is rescued by Arthur, the agent of the Comintern, he enters the house of Penance, where he repents his deviationism, is trained in the Marxist dialectic, and sees a vision of the future classless society—note the mingling of angels (probably a pun on Engels) and men. Finally he overthrows the dragon of Capitalism in order to free mankind from its chains.[14]

---

14 A. C. Hamilton, *The Structure of Allegory in the Faerie Queene*, Oxford: Clarendon Press, 1961, 24, 9–10.

Everything the Anglo-Saxon reader may find comical in this (not unrealistic) political narrative holds, not only for most other kinds of political stories one might want to imagine but also for the ethical or moral ones, as the author himself indeed goes on to show. But in those, as the chapter on emotions has already suggested, one necessarily deals, not with history as some ideally unified teleology, but rather with individual emotions, virtues or vices, properties, individual strengths and weaknesses, which it is the drawback of personification to isolate from their specific historical systems; the strength of the technique lying rather in its capacity to furnish characters suitable for an edifying tale. The isolated representation then reconfirms the reification of the feeling in question and makes its relationship to the original system of emotions more difficult to discern. Indeed, Spenser's *Letter to Raleigh* (which, like the *Letter to Can Grande* or some of Goethe's comments to Eckermann, can then function as an often misleading gloss on the enigmas of the work in question) suggests that each of the twelve projected books of the poem are meant to illustrate "the twelve private moral virtues, as Aristotle hath devised" (in the *Nichomachean Ethics*), a plan which, even unfulfilled, will make for difficulties, as we will see shortly.

At any rate, the books clearly dramatize a personification of Arthur's multiple virtues. It is worth dwelling on the technique, inasmuch as it was personification, more than any other feature, that gave allegory a bad name in the Romantic period; it was with personification that allegory has most often been identified, while its defenders have equally often sought to distance themselves from this awkward and old-fashioned medieval form, which even in Bunyan's time, encourages a one-to-one reading of the older Alexandrian variety. This is why Tuve argued vigorously against Christological interpretation (in Spenser and elsewhere),[15] and why Milton's Sin and Death in *Paradise Lost* have seemed to be blots on an otherwise still complex yet coherent narrative surface (or isotopie).

But personification will not go away as easily as that, and therefore we need to learn how to use or to interpret its manifold presences. Angus Fletcher gives a clear directive when he evokes the concentration of the daimon and the demonic, the way in which the various personifications

---

15 Rosemond Tuve, *Allegorical Imagery: Some Medieval Books and Their Imagery*, Princeton: Princeton University Press, 1977.

of feeling or emotion seem to be obsessive intensifications or crystallizations of normal emotive activity.¹⁶ This puts us on the track of reification, at the same time that it suggests a new way to consider personification not as a thing or entity, but rather as an event. But these two consequences are one and the same. Personification clearly does give itself out as a thing or an entity: that event turns out to be the very process of reification itself, when something that was not thinglike suddenly became crystallized into the appearance of thingness, if not an outright thing itself. Once again, this means that the personifications will be ephemeral and context specific; they will come and go like reference itself, never forming any stable system (although Spenser includes systematicity as we shall see later on), but forming and dissolving according to a logic that is neither narrative nor thematic.

In fact, Spenser has inserted an account of this very process into his text, which as far as personification is concerned here becomes sharply self-referential. This is the famous episode of Malbecco, at which all the commentators I have consulted pause briefly or at length, so striking is it (the most comprehensive reading being that of Alpers).¹⁷ The whole comic cuckolding episode—Malbecco is the unhappy husband and victim of a Paris–Helen rerun—develops into a nightmarish sequence in the course of which, in a genuinely Ovidian metamorphosis, this still human character and figure of fun turns into a strangely disembodied monster, who lives in a cave,

> where he through priuy griefe, and horrour vaine,
> Is woxen so deform'd, that he has quight
> Forgot he was a man, and *Gealosie* is hight.
>
> (III/x/60/535)

No better exemplification of Fletcher's notion of demonic possession could be imagined: the concentration of the mind on a single emotion has wasted the rest of the human substance. The intent to kill himself (leaping from a cliff) is taken metaphorically and realized in that spirit, for he has already done so, and there is nothing left to die or to be killed:

---

16   Angus Fletcher, *Allegory: The Theory of a Symbolic Mode*, Princeton: Princeton University Press, 1970.

17   Paul J. Alpers, *The Poetry of "The Faerie Queene,"* Princeton: Princeton University Press, 2015.

> But through long anguish, and selfe-murdering thought
> He was so wasted and forpined quight,
> That all his substance was consum'd to nought,
> And nothing left, but like an aery Spright,
> That on the rockes he fell so flit and light,
> That he thereby receiv'd no hurt at all,
> But chaunced on a craggy cliff to light;
> Whence he with crooked clawes so long did crall,
> That at the last he found a cave with entrance small.
>
> (III/x/57/534)

This is no doubt reification with a vengeance; and it should be noted that its final form—the state of thingness or false objechood in this poetic surface—is the act of naming itself: "Gealosie is hight." It has in any case often been remarked how Spenser withholds the name, whether of narrative characters such as Redcrosse, or Arthur, or, as here, of personifications. One can say this differently by observing (as Alpers does) that Spenser always does eventually give us the name, thus avoiding the hermeticism of standard Renaissance allegory: but the structure whereby the name comes as the climax of the process of reification is not merely to be understood as a form of identification for the general public. It is first and foremost an activity of construction; it is in fact the very construction of subjectivity itself.

One must be careful to avoid the language of psychology, which assumes that the conventional individual, who comes complete with a constructed subjectivity in the first place, already exists in advance of whatever he/she is or does. What is called self-fashioning is only the external form of the possibility of reconstructing this subjectivity, that is to say, as the Renaissance conceived it, of constructing something like a genuine subjectivity for the first time.

(Antiquity went about the process in a different way, with the help of its pantheon. Thus, in a similar situation, that of Erysichthon, Ovid does not need to call on personifications: the god Hunger is there at hand to meld with the victim:

> Her skeletal embrace goes around him.
> Her shrunk mouth clamps over his mouth
> And she breathes

>   Into every channel of his body
>   A hurricane of starvation.[18]

The sufferer then disposes of the remnants of this reification by devouring himself. Flaubert, in his account of the triumph of Christianity over paganism in *La Tentation de Saint Antoine*, gives us, contemporaneously with Marx, a virtual catalogue of such divine or diabolical commodifications.)

And this does not so much amount to inventing new emotions for the new individuals of this new age, but rather groping about in either nameless or conventional already existing inward realities and attempting to reorder them in ways that can only be thought of in terms of the act of naming. Lacan already taught us that the name is some first primal alienation, a violence done to the infant subject of desire by the familial and parental Others: indeed, language in general shares in this violence, which is that of a repression that is at one and the same time an ordering. The name of these inner processes is the reifying nail that holds each one in place (or, coming loose or wobbling, lets the alleged subjectivity drift out into psychosis).

What must be named, therefore, are the negative things, the sins, the taboos and stigmatized impulses: they come first, because they must be mastered, and the positive ones follow (or so the organizers and the moralizers hope). Harry Berger has brilliantly offered the fable for this process as a whole. In a commentary on Fidelia's

>   cup of gold,
>   With wine and water fild up to the hight,
>   In which a Serpent did himselfe enfold,
>   That horrour made to all, that did behold. (I/x/13/163)

he reminds us of the allusion to Apocalypse:

> On Ephesus the poison given to John by the Emperor Domitian miraculously condensed into a serpent and left the cup. The serpent in Fidelia's cup suggests the need for faith by showing forth the enemy found in the very cup of faith; it also suggests how faith can reveal the poison in its true and primal nature. In the gradual development of a

---

18 Ted Hughes, *Tales from Ovid*, New York: Farrar, Straus and Giroux, 1997, 84.

single soul through and toward faith, the scattered evil is gathered together until it is trapped and displayed.[19]

The word *condensation* (Berger also uses it for phenomena such as Malbecco)[20] is significant and retains its Freudian connotations. Subject formation as we are describing it here reifies its inner raw material precisely by way of such condensation, which it seals with a name or noun or a system of nouns and substantives. As Berger suggests, it must first do this with the negative energies and feelings, those to be cast out and expelled, or at least to be quarantined and placed under surveillance. "Psychology" will eventually become precisely this surveillance system, in which nameless inner movements, stirrings, barely perceptible reactions and tropisms, are matched up against an accredited and evaluative nomenclature.

But all such attempts—which are much more closely related to toilet training (Freud), penmanship (Foucault), and table manners (Elias) than they are to Renaissance manuals of courtly behavior, let alone handbooks of virtue Aristotelian as well as theological—are also fraught with permanent contradictions, which do not result from the "sinful nature of man," but rather from the coexistence of the various feelings and names simultaneously: in other words from a multiplicity and difference within the alleged psyche itself which can never fully be overcome or unified. Let Malbecco also stand as the fable for this reality: when we first meet him, as a stock comic character, he is identified not only as the jealous husband, who locks his wife up and is very reluctant to allow her to meet guests, but also as a miser. But these are two distinct personifiable "vices," which can only be unified by some strong interpretive and metaphorical act—in other words, jealousy as the miserliness of the husband possessing a wife or miserliness as the jealous husbandry of the treasure considered as a kind of spouse. That these metaphorical efforts, while implied, are ultimately not fully successful, is illustrated by the narrative itself: Hellenore escapes by setting the treasure on fire, Malbecco is thus torn between his miserliness and his jealousy. Later on the theft of his treasure comes as a supplement to the definitive loss of the wife (who now prefers to live among the satyrs): yet being the last

---

19 Berger, *Revisionary Play*, 51–52.
20 Ibid., 166–67.

straw, it cannot quite be "the same thing." Ultimately, of course, personification and the reification of the ruling passion come about when Malbecco has neither object, so that the passions must somehow feed on themselves: no longer concentrated on a specific object, they somehow "produce" a Self in order to take that as an object—"And he himselfe himselfe loath'd so forlorne" (533)—a verse preceded by the even stranger "And ran away, ran with himselfe away." Berger's snake then reappears:

> So shamefully forlorne of womankind;
> That as a Snake, still lurked in his wounded mind.

And in this state of "narcissistic melancholy," without an object of desire in the outside world, turning into a figure, Malbecco astonishingly becomes immortal:

> Yet can he never die, but dying lives,
> And doth himself with sorrow new sustaine,
> That death and life attonce unto him gives.
> And painefulle pleasure turnes to pleasing paine. (III/x/60/535)

Paul de Man would have read such a passage as irrefutable proof of the triumph of the tropes over anthropomorphism. At any rate, Malbecco is truly one who has followed to the letter Žižek's admonition, "Enjoy your symptom!" Or in other words, as the existentialists used to put it, he has chosen his fundamental passion, and his immortality—which is to say his inhumanity—lies in this freedom.

But even here the emotion is not unmixed. For in a curious final description Spenser shows us the batlike, clawed, hermit cowering forever in his cave, the perpetual prey of a rather different emotion, namely fear:

> continual feare
> Of that rockes fall, which ever and anon
> Threates with huge ruine him to fall upon. (III/x/58/534)

No doubt, as Alpers suggests, jealousy is also a kind of fear; but these distinct reified psychic objects are not really to be dissolved again and reunited in a new one. There remains something ungovernably heterogeneous about Malbecco's passions, even in this supreme moment in which we are given to witness their ultimate textual and tropological, linguistic triumph.

It is a triumph dearly paid for in style: Ben Jonson famously remarked that Spenser "writ no language," a judgment echoed down through Dr. Johnson to the New Critics and Eliot. Despite the unique music and the form of the stanzas, this is not good writing, fine style, poeticity heightened, and concentrated language. How could it be?

> At length they came into a forrest wyde,
> Whose hideous horror and sad trembling sound
> Full griesly seemed . . . (III/i/14/388)

> so choosing solitarie to abide
> Far from all neighbours,
> that her develish deeds
> and hellish arts from people she might hide. (III/vii/6/477)

Spenser needs these "horrendous" adjectives, the very instruments of penny dreadfuls and the Gothic, of H. P. Lovecraft and melodrama in general: and this, not particularly because he is a full participant in the melodramatic imagination—the villainies are too obvious, the move to armed conflict too swift, the intrigue doesn't really interest him, all the monsters look alike. No, it is his allegory that needs them, and not his sensibility: for the reading of this allegory—of all allegory perhaps?—is absolutely dependent on the ethical binary, the distinction between good and evil. It lies so profoundly at the heart of allegorical reading and decipherment that it scarcely seems to have anything to do with lofty abstract philosophical ethics any longer, seeming closer to the friend-foe, inside-outside, self-other distinguishing mechanisms of the organism in evolutionary biology: the ethical "judgments" if we can dignify them as that, being inseparable from movements of sheerly physical disgust and loathing. And no doubt all this is deeply inscribed in the Protestant rhetoric of the period, such visceral disgust richly mobilized by the wars of religion and informing the hatred of idolatry, priests, Rome, the Whore of Babylon, and everything physically (I'm tempted to say racially) related to them. But this is merely the primal and primordial form of the dialectic of Otherness itself: ethics is at one with it and constitutes the Manichaean identification of the Other as evil. Perhaps Sartre was right after all, and Nazism and anti-Semitism can never produce great literature but only just such caricatures and just such stereotypical expressions of visceral loathing and hatred. And yet the literary and cultural fortunes of the ethical binary have been great indeed and very durable. I think it becomes productive only when it is tapped for something else, harnessed for a different kind of task than that of sheer expression: melodrama at its greatest, for example, has a secret epistemological function—it lifts the corner of the curtain on such passions, and gives a brief glimpse into the most ignominious fears at the heart of being itself, in the light of which one suddenly understands that good is as evil as evil itself and that ultimately the opposing terms of all binaries turn into one another.

In Spenser all these trappings, which made him as unserviceable a poetic model for the modernists as Milton was (for other reasons), serve a very different function. They are the maps and the geography of that construction of subjectivity we have evoked above. The latter was characterized as a blind groping about the *informe,* the inchoate, the primal and unorganized, with a view toward separating its masses of heterogeneous materials, collecting them, designating them with a name and an identification. The ethical binary is primordial and biological because it is the original instrument of separation; only by identifying the bad and evil— through concentration and reification as we have seen—can the psychic movements be sorted out and something permissible, exemplary, good, be identified by contrast and assigned its place. This is the new fruit of Protestant introspection: you have to do it by yourself and inside yourself; the older classification schemes are still there (as we shall see shortly), but the external and objective signposts by which they organized behavior are unreliable and suspect; only language and names remain and they come after the fact. They are the result of discovery and decision. Self-examination thus becomes a confusion and a pathless agony; nothing answers from inside as it is supposed to. The adjectives of good and evil are thus the only signs and clues, and they can sometimes be adroitly wielded:

> She seemd a woman of great bountihed,
> And of rare beautie, saving that askaunce
> Her wanton eyes, ill signes of womanhed,
> Did roll too lightly, and too often glaunce. (III/i/41/395)

Perhaps "wanton" jumps the gun a bit, as though Spenser were apprehensive that we might not get the point soon enough: the overzealous placement stands out in a poetic narrative that most often—and deliberately—exaggerates in quite the other direction and makes us wait unconscionably for the crucial denominations. But those are generally the names for "good," for the virtues; the signals for evil precede them. In the emergence of the Christian system, as we have seen, the sins come first, the taboos, after which the virtues are fashioned as so many symmetrical afterthoughts and complements: a transcendental system cannot allow itself any very convincing belief in this-worldly perfection (nor do the pagan ones succeed in fashioning anything much more satisfactory than this "handbook for courtiers," of which Spenser's poem is also the most grandiose version).

But the structural problem does not lie in the possibilities of the afterlife or in the commitment to a belief in some ineradicable human corruption. It is rather to be found in the coordination and superposition of these "virtues" with one another, and for that matter, in that of the sins as well. In Spenser (but in medieval allegory as well) this is supremely evident in the discrepancies between the various lists and tables of the virtues: are they to be classical, pre-Christian ones, mostly derived from Aristotle, but as selectively as you like? Are we then to add the theological virtues to them? But are there not theological powers and categories that cannot fit into the older systems? Do they not also demand new systems of their own? Indeed, the same problem arises for the virtues as for the vices: if it is a problem how jealousy and miserliness (not to speak, later on, of sheer fear and timorousness) somehow "combine" in Malbecco, it is equally a problem to know how the virtues themselves combine. What are we to take of that initial, quickly annulled, conflict between Guyon (Temperance) and Britomart (Chastity)? Can there really be a conflict between virtues? At the very least the operation would seem to demand rank and hierarchy: one virtue agreeing to be somehow inferior in rank and power and thereby subordinate to this other one. When in doubt, the theological can be called upon to out-trump the secular and classical virtues: whence the raison d'être of Arthur himself, as both Christian knight and king-to-be. We have already seen how his unique powers—grace itself—are needful if the more secular and classical virtues of Guyon are to win through. But anyone searching for some definitive classification scheme will be sorely disappointed, while anyone attempting on account of this confusion to do without all classification schemes will be stalemated from the outset.

Here, as in our discussion of the stylistic reflexes of good and bad, we have to observe that the evil comes first and that the system of the virtues cannot come into being without some preexisting system of vices or sins on which to organize itself. Rosemond Tuve has shown how the principal medieval organization of the theological virtues, in the "gifts of the holy spirit," is called into being by way of the seven deadly sins they must combat.[21] In Dante, the circles of *Paradise* are organized around the virtues in name only; in fact each circle necessarily turns on the sin it cancels, so that the latter still stands as the deeper organizing principle. In *Purgatory* it is granted that several sins can coexist (the soul lightening successively as it is freed from each one in turn and flying up to another level); in *Inferno* the sins provide ruling passions; in *Paradise*, however, it is difficult to see how this or that virtue takes priority over the others.

Indeed, what argues against any such synthesis is the movement of the text itself, the temporal structure of its allegorical operations, which remain bound to a specific thematization of the reading process. Take for example Britomart's wound in Book III. At its very opening, and the beginning of her quest, a semi-comic episode is inserted in which her embodiment of Chastity proves to be a relatively undeserving virtue indeed, since it is a woman (Malecasta) who attempts to seduce her. The episode commences with her overcoming of the chatelaine's six knight-servants (with the help of Redcrosse), each of whom bears an allegorical name, presumably designating the six stages of seduction: Looking, Speaking, Joking, Kissing, Revelry, Late Nights. Later on, when Malecasta fails in her attempt and sounds the alarm, the six knights again attack Britomart, one of them grazing her slightly:

> yet was the wound not deepe,
> But lightly rased her soft silken skin,
> That drops of purple bloud thereout did weepe,
> Which did her lily smock with staines of vermeil steepe.
>
> (III/i/65/401)

---

21 Tuve, *Allegorical Imagery*.

This lone successful attacker is the first of the former list, Gardante (Looking). We should add that later on, when Britomart rescues the imprisoned Amoret from the sadistic Busyrane's castle, the latter also manages to wound her slightly:

> From her [Britomart], to whom his fury first he ment,
> The sicked weapon rashly did he wrest,
> And turning to her selfe his fell intent,
> Unawares it strooke into her snowie chest,
> That little drops empurpled her faire brest.
> (III/xii/33/558)

Such events, the very possibility of wounding so otherwise scarcely assailable an allegorical figure as Britomart, necessarily carry a charge of meaning: the wounds designate the figure in question, along with her virtue, as somehow vulnerable, at least in the one specific particular. In the case of Gardante, the implication is clear: Britomart is at least minimally assailable by way of the sense of sight itself (see also scoptophilia in general, in *Castle Joyous* (III/i)).[22] Chastity can be tempted by the act of looking, even if no further. And this is exactly what will be dramatized for us in this Canto, when, in the present of our reading, we witness the fatal *coup de foudre* in Britomart's past that decides her destiny.

Nothing is stranger than this episode: nothing so closely approaches science fiction in Spenser (save for the robot Talus in Book V) than the magic globe in which Britomart catches first sight ("one day it fortuned") of her future groom. It is a well-nigh televisual experience, one that presents all the trappings of the postcontemporary simulacrum (the very central mechanism of our "society of the spectacle"). It will be agreed that this is a very special "penetration" by the eyes in which the traditional image of Cupid's arrow is maintained:

> the false Archer, which that arrow shot
> So slyly, that she did not feele the wound.
> (III/ii/26/408)

---

22 See Thomas P. Roche, *The Kindly Flame: A Study of the Third and Fourth Books of Spenser's Faerie Queene,* Princeton: Princeton University Press, 2015, 68–69.

but with the interesting effect of a time lapse, so that Britomart, imagining simply that she has done no more than "view his personage and liked well," wakes up suddenly in the throes of nascent passions:

> Tho gan she to renew her former smart,
> And thinke of that faire visage, written in her hart.
> (III/ii/29/409)

When readers come to know Arthegall himself, they may have some additional questions to raise about this sudden infatuation: for the moment, however, it is the predominance of sight that concerns us. I will argue that the temporal loop (first, Malecasta, then the flashback to the magic glass) is necessary in order to establish the priority of sight for Britomart and thereby to justify (retroactively) her deeper but more metaphorical wound by the image of Arthegall. But how are we to position this in the construction of subjectivity: are we to understand that sight is the one sense channel that is permissible for the chaste subject? Or on the contrary, that sight is the most fundamental danger that menaces such a subject? But we do not have to choose, nor to decide this question: subjectivity is in this sense not formed by imposing a system on these components, let alone a normative or evaluative system. (In this I disagree with Roche's moralizing.[23]) It is formed on the contrary by sensitization and identification: sight must be separated off as a sense with a very special kind of power, and it is thus isolated by the giving of a name. After that, it does not matter much whether the subject resists or falls, sins or remains virtuous: the constituents will have been established and can participate in either of these events and outcomes. Nonetheless, as has been suggested above, the sin comes first in the process of separation and crystallization. Sight is first a wound and then a power or a property. And this yields a second crucial observation: for "first" here designates the text and not the chronological events: this is very precisely the argument for a textual–contextual specificity of the allegorical operation. The episode does not argue for some eternal status of sight in love (although it is a status conventional in a Petrarchan tradition that survives all the way up to Stendhal and Proust). Rather it yields a punctual event and a purely local allegorical meaning: the proof

---

23   Ibid., 70.

lies in the next episode of wounding, which comes at the very end of the Book and means something quite different.

In his excellent discussion of Busyrane, Roche does not venture to interpret this second wound; yet his own reading gives us the means to do so, suggesting that reading the mask and the sadistic spectacle concealed behind it (Busyrane has extracted Amoret's heart) project a fear of the violence of male sexuality and marriage onto the female figure.[24] She is in fact a prisoner of her own terror; it lends her an enforced and fearful chastity, which like that of the fleeing Florimel is inconsistent with Britomart's own meaning, and rather analogous (in the male) to Marinell's peculiar self-defenses. But if this is so, then the wound means that Britomart is also mildly accessible or vulnerable to this view of sexuality as well, although she combats and defeats it. Note that this episode immediately precedes the meeting with Arthegall (Book IV) in which her love is acted out in violent combat. In a sense, then, the new wound may be said to modify the meaning of the old one: sight remains as a constant (she finally meets the object of her gaze, after all) but is now completely intermingled with the threat of the violence of male sexuality, along with the threat of the fantasy of it, yielding a completely different "combination" of these elements.

But all of this is cast in a very different light by a curious episode from Book IV, Canto VIII, in which Arthur, having rescued two damsels, Aemyilia and once again Amoret (and perhaps this second and more definitive rescue by a male reinforces the interpretation given above), is obliged to take shelter with them in the hovel of a Hag identified as Sclaunder (Slander). That she should malign them and shout lies after them as they leave the unpleasant shelter is normal enough: a male knight travelling unaccompanied with two gentlewomen who are not "his" (in the sense of service or engagement or other such official relationships)—what could more easily give rise to the worst suspicions and the most impure thoughts? What is astonishing, however, is that these thoughts are at once attributed by Spenser to the reader himself:

> Here well l weene, when as these rimes be red
> With misregard, that some rash witted wight,
> Whose looser thought will lightly be misled,

---

24   Ibid., 72–84.

> These gentle Ladies will misdeeme too light,
> For thus conversing with this noble Knight
> (IV/viii/29/663)

Now it is the reader who is in danger of being overpowered by Slander: she is not operating directly on us since she remains inside the text where she can vilify only her guests. But it is as though her powers—we know from the ultimate picture of the Blatant Beaste, as well as from his biography, how supremely sensitive Spenser was himself to this "vice" and its effects—seeped out of the text and into its reading, giving us the same bad thoughts she allegorically encourages in her fellow characters. Now the reader becomes the allegorical level and is woven into a new and unique episode whose function is to show and prove the dangers of malicious gossip. To be sure, the reader necessarily assumes the burden and the responsibility of interpretation far more self-consciously in allegory than in other, more homogeneous kinds of texts. But he or she cannot break out of the reifications of personification and is driven fatefully in the direction of the ethical binary and its subforms (as in the gender-oriented reading I have proposed above).

That Spenser's text—if not Spenser himself—is ultimately aware of this structural restriction is perhaps best demonstrated by its final form. For the poet, facing an early death at the age of forty-nine, unrewarded for his services either poetic or political, and confronting the immense and unfinished plan he has unwisely set himself, at that point leaps into a new space in the two final "Mutabilitie" cantos, in order, as it were, to place himself at once on the missing anagogical level and to reach the dimension of History itself, where, in that age-old pessimism that runs from Heraclitus to the Benjaminian baroque, he identifies the movement of human events with the meaningless cycles of natural history, as personified by the demi-goddess or Titanesse whose name he has inscribed above this final allegory.

There thus reappears here a familiar dialectic of the maximal and the minimal: the infinite time of history revealing itself as somehow inseparable from the perpetual present, the miniature and obsessive gaze, of the closed Spenserian stanza, which faithfully immobilizes movement forward in time, in history, in narrative, into a harmonious and decorative stasis.

7
Epic: Dante and Space

The most formidable opponent any theorist of Dante's allegorical structure has to face is Erich Auerbach, whose doctrine of *figura* marked an explicit attempt to replace traditional medieval allegorical schemes with what he characterized as "a realism of the created" (*kreatürliche Realismus*): the term was meant, not only to affirm a certain solidarity with the Thomist tradition, but also to emphasize everything physical and "earthly" (another useful term for Auerbach)—everything nonotherworldly, nonspiritualistic—about Dante's characters.[1] This attack on allegorical meaning was not meant to be a modern or postmodern attack on meaning as such: the wisdom of the implicit or explicit spiritual judgments, the truthfulness of the syntheses of the Thomist system, remain intact here; but rather, the three-dimensionality of these spiritual realities was to be affirmed, as it was indeed articulated in the original meaning of his key term—*figura*—as a three-dimensional or sculptural shape, and not some mere two-dimensional or schematic image. Meanwhile, it is to the canonical *Letter* of Dante to his patron Can Grande della Scala—a letter whose authenticity has often been put in doubt—that Auerbach attributed the wilder misreadings of Dante that he stigmatized as "allegorical," a word not inappropriate for this particular text, which sets out the traditional fourfold scheme of the levels as unabashedly as any of the Church Fathers.

---

1 The 1938 essay "Figura" has been reprinted in Erich Auerbach, *Time, History, and Literature,* Princeton: Princeton University Press, 2014.

I doubt if a materialistic age is as susceptible to such now academic glosses and to the quarrels among specialists that they once inspired. Not only are our contemporary medievalists a good deal more "modern" and theoretical than Auerbach's colleagues, but in a postliterate age the approach to an author like Dante will as likely make its way through fantasy literature as through the canon, while the latter will tend to be anthologized in the form of the most readable and exciting, the most "realist" excerpts, with the ample footnotes of the more scholarly editions replacing the absent content.

At any rate, what I want to argue in the following pages is that Auerbach's *figura* is a mediatory concept rather than a structural one; and that his authority is not to be invoked against the revivals of allegory such as this one unless it is restaged in a contemporary semiotic arena in which questions of meaning and reference are measured against the philosophical problems of immanence and of representation in general. Thomism is certainly a Christian version of immanence, in which God's creation is suffused with meaning, even in its imperfections; but its aesthetics do not extend much further than classical notions of beauty and harmony.

In fact, however, Christian typology has solved this philosophical problem for us in advance: for in its Biblical form it is a kind of prophecy. The fulfillment of the "type" is the foretelling of the future, Moses being fulfilled by Jesus. History therefore here becomes the mediation, and Dante will ingeniously preserve this temporal function of his "method" by way of the future of the poet–narrator himself, whose textual revelation precedes his biographical exile. The historical mediation is thereby constructed within the text, and its formal problem is transformed into a solution in the very content.

Not all previous cultures have known this eschatological relationship to the future, but it is only in the twenty-first century that the future has actually arrived: for the right, who own more than 80 percent of the planet's value and confront the ultimate contradictions of the world market; for the center, which now enjoys "freedom and democracy" in a henceforth unexportable system; for the left, which now tries to find its way within those enormous collective monopolies Marx saw developing within capitalism's "integument"; along with an unparalleled mass mobilization of a politically awakened but cynical and passive population. Prophecy no longer has any place in this kind of situation; or rather, it becomes the process of attempting to detect that real present–future within the appearance of a commodified present of infinitely proliferating simulacra—which is to say, that prophecy in our time has become interpretation, and interpretation the reading of hidden figures and undiagnosable symptoms.

My working premise (here and elsewhere) has always been to search for the internal divisions of a work—its gaps, its multiple tensions, its contradictions—rather than for the rather obvious unity it seeks, in the name of whatever genre, to display. Obviously the allegorical genre—when allegory has taken a generic form, as in the three canonical works considered in these chapters—will display its external unity in the form of separation, juxtaposition, a well-nigh spatial division; and it is therefore for the internal conflicts and contradictions of those divisions that we must search today. Laying my cards on the table first, I will propose to find that deeper and more ultimate rift in the political philosophy the poet outlines in *De Monarchia*, namely that between pope and emperor, but it remains to be seen how that particular opposition could have poetic or formal consequences.

Nor will I take sides, except implicitly, on the debate Auerbach famously initiated, between critics who took the *Letter to Can Grande* literally and scanned the poem for its fourfold structures, and Auerbach's promotion, in the name of "figura," of that "earthly" realism he found everywhere in the work and rightly took as the grounds for its extraordinary value. But Auerbach could not have overlooked the stylistic and formal inconsistency between what we may call the *Commedia*'s allegorical flourishes and decorations—I have already discussed the three allegorical beasts of Canto I in some detail in the previous chapter—and the persistently vivid realism with which its multiple human characters are conveyed. But for support in his argument he might well have pointed, as I suggest, to the bodily and well-nigh muscular evocation of the individual beasts in question as living material creatures.

Realism is, as I have said elsewhere, a slippery concept, whose meaning depends very much on the aesthetic term with which it stands in opposition. I prefer to begin with narrative as such and with its dual structure in Dante: reminiscent of the modern detective story, we here confront two superimposed narratives quite distinct from one another: the story of the detective and his investigation on the one hand is the present journey on which Virgil leads the protagonist, and on the other the narrative material, the encounters that make up the journey; these constitute the crime to be solved, the victims or perpetrators to be identified. So from the outset we may observe a form invented to reconcile or better still to combine these two very different types of raw material, one experiential and in the first person, the other anecdotal and taking the form of what might later on be called objective historical fact. This, double structure prefigures a later differentiation within the novel itself between what its practitioners, under various terminological forms, called the *roman* and the *récit* dimensions of their production.

But we have not yet chronologically reached the moment of the novel, that is to say, the moment in which the contradictions and form problems of the traditional genres proved so extreme as to motivate the invention of that wholly new and as it were postgeneric form. This is, indeed, the formal history Georg Lukács sets out to tell in his *Theory of the Novel*, and so it will be instructive to see where he positions Dante in that influential chronology.[2] Indeed, there is something blasphemous and also quite unsurprising in his juxtaposition of the *Commedia* with Dante's younger biographer and exegete Boccaccio: for Dante's poem is indeed, like the latter's *Decameron*, a collection of tales and from that perspective quite discontinuous.

To get a sense of his kinship with Boccaccio, or with comic storytelling in general, readers have only to witness the spectacle of the devils in Malebolge (*Inferno* XXI–XXIII), who are divinely assigned to punish the fraudulent but of whose reliability Virgil and Dante have some reasonable doubts. That these devils relish their duties is obvious enough (pushing the sinners back down into their lake of burning pitch "come i dalfini, quando fanno segno / a marinar come l' arco de la schiena"; "like dolphins when with their arching backs they give sign to mariners that they should prepare to save their ship"; XXII, 19–20, 224); but whether they can be trusted to comply with the divine instructions for the pair of travellers, indeed whether they will even take the time to understand them, is another story.[3] The devils are certainly not infallible: witness the glorious scene in which a malefactor has been allowed to tell Dante his

---

2 Georg Lukács, *Theory of the Novel*, Cambridge, MA: MIT Press, 1971.
3 All references in the text are to Charles Singleton's edition of the *Commedia*, Princeton: Princeton University Press, 1982, and are expressed in the following format: (Canto/verse/page) where the context identifies the canticle.

story and then takes the opportunity to dive back into the pitch in order to escape further individual torture. It is precisely this triumph of the sinner over his jailors that causes the alarmed pilgrims to escape, fearing the wrath of the devils on themselves; and indeed, they glimpse a flying group of angry infernals searching for them as they flee down into another *bolge*. It is a cinematographic masterpiece and miniature, at the same time that it richly illustrates in two ways what I call *transversality*: the sin for which these victims are being punished is not anger but rather "barratry" ("groundless litigation," which we might more quaintly render as *pettifogging*); and yet little in the mode of punishment, save for the lawyerly cunning of the escapee, conveys this particular "sin" symbolically. Meanwhile, if rage and fury are the central ground-tone of this canto, it is notable that the guards and executioners feel it even more strongly than its victims and also that Virgil is himself contaminated by it—so suprapersonal is this "named emotion" and so allegorically susceptible to expression in either active or passive forms. The farce of the devils then comes as a kind of supplement to the fungibility and free-floating detachment of the allegorical emotion.

Dante's is however a far more numerous compendium, and not many of these single-verse destinies take on an even anecdotal, let alone a narrative, form. Is the fate of Francesca, for example, even as diegetically organized or narratively fashioned as in Browning's "Last Duchess," which is evidently based on it? Yet in this last, we started out with a courteous host who is in Dante dispatched with a summary judgment "Caina attende" ("Cain awaits"), so that Browning's monologue offers the kind of unexpected reversal we have become accustomed to expect in the short story or récit, or even in the *fait divers*, which must always, as Barthes and others have shown, contain some element of paradox. Still, it would be possible to take an inventory of these destinies that followed a different taxonomy than Dante's religious or doctrinal one: victims and criminal agents, to be sure, but also life choices (poor Ciacco's gluttony), unhappy accidents (the defeated Manfred), legendary betrayals, the passive and the active, the anonymous and the world-historical. The multiplicity of these potential "subjects" (as Henry James might have called them) then slowly wheels our attention back in the direction of the journey, the other narrative level.

Still, Lukács pays homage to that totality the Christian cosmos still preserves (and perpetuates in the form of Dante's geography) even as he seems to rank these multiple tales, this collection of stories, among those smaller "epic" forms or unities that survive the break-up of the larger epic form or narrative as such. Here one may draw theoretical profit from the otherwise obfuscatory ambiguity of the German term, which as an adjective—"episch"—simply means narrative, while it continues a nominal life [Epos] as the "epic" of epic poem: Lukács suggests that the smaller forms—short story, joke—are still "episch" in the sense in which their narrativity retains its formal unity—as with Georg Simmel's enclave "forms" but on an even smaller scale.[4] They represent, in other words (and very much in Simmel's spirit), little unities of life experience that have been spared from the universal fragmentation of modernity but that have not yet passed over into the epiphanic and lyric instant. In that sense, perhaps Dante's micrological destinies are the smallest surviving units of a traditional narrativity, the atomic temporalities of whole lives lived under the Medusa's gaze of God's eternal judgment. In that sense, even the other narrative level—that of the poet–protagonist's journey—is also subject to this violent miniaturization, this seemingly irrevocable and absolute reduction to a single fate and single-sentence confession. This would then greatly reduce the poem's multiplicities and efface its fault lines, and one might well discover a unity of the microcosm in place of its macroscopic distances and varieties. (An inspection of *Purgatorio* will, however, discover that this is not exactly the case, and that a "destiny" is always in some sense compound.)

Let us now, however, shift perspectives and examine the poem from that of the operations required by its line-by-line reading. I have already mentioned geography in passing: it is a place to start from, inasmuch as the reader is here necessarily called on to perform a mental spatialization no less complex than what one has to summon up in reading Balzacian descriptions. Everyone presumably already knows the shape of Hell from the diagrams included in the various editions, as well as the extraordinary invention that allows the mountain of Purgatory to be extracted from the funnel-pit of Inferno, just as the moon was extracted from the earth billions of years ago, or more recently South America from Africa. But, some forensic or prosecutorial critic might ask us, where does Dante actually say this? Quote me

---

4   The minor epic forms are, for Lukács, what survive the breakup of the traditional genres in modernity: see *Theory of the Novel*, 50–55.

the verses in which this geography is laid out for some more abstract understanding. We must ourselves deduce it, we must mentally construct it along with the various bolge. (How many of them? and which one are we on right now?) The mental faculty appealed to here surely remains the traditional one of the Imagination, the faculty of forming images; yet it is put to the test of then exploring its own images and internally constructing something whose outlines it does not know until it begins to deduce them on the basis of its own internal limits. Meanwhile, as some second unexpected consequence, any intelligible reading will have to take into account an up and a down, or in other words, reckon, inside the language somewhere, with a force of gravity that is not normally a component of our daily speech, nor is it necessarily present in the poem's narrative sentences. But the pilgrim protagonist Dante will have to climb downward, painfully, awkwardly, and with some trepidation (and not without the occasional help of his divinely sponsored *adjudant*): and he will just as laboriously, but far more ponderously, have to climb the sometimes even steeper inclines of the mountain of Purgatory. (I note in passing that its base is one of those loci of the inconsistencies of allegorical isotopies—in the beginning an impenetrable wood, peopled with dangerous predators, later on in the next canticle a shore of the sea, marshalled by the illustrious Cato himself.)

But this contingency of weight and gravity, of a peculiarly unique property of our material existence (still unexplained by the scientists), will here also acquire a narrative, indeed an allegorical meaning; the human body will itself be endowed with a kind of spiritual sense. For with Minos's judgment, the individual souls will fall to their appropriate level in *Inferno* as if on their own, and by their own weight. (Even more mysteriously beforehand, we witnessed the way in which the recently deceased souls on their own are driven by an irresistible force and desire to crowd upon Chiron's boat and to hasten toward Minos's terrible and definitive judgment: how to get them on board otherwise?) Meanwhile, in *Purgatory*, the opposite effect: the soul that has purged its sin is suddenly lightened and flies upward toward its place in the Empyrean (just as Dante himself, on the inspection of the respective sin and a consciousness of his own complicity with it, finds himself lightened, his climb upward becoming ever less strenuous, ever more effortless and light-headed, as though flying in a dream).

This theme of the body's spiritual weight accompanies the reader throughout the poem, therefore, like an overtone or an undertone in music, always ready to precipitate an overt effect, as when, at the very beginning of his journey, Dante confronts the outcome of his metaphysical sublimation of love in the very concrete fate of Paolo and Francesca (joined together like dogs in heat throughout eternity): "E caddi come corpo morto cade" ("and fell as a dead body falls"; V/142/56–57). The toll of falling bodies in the *Commedia* is considerable, and even though its dead souls are not yet really physical (they will only take on their physical dead bodies again at the Last Judgment), it is not only the living Dante who feels the effects of this imaginary geography. In the next Canto, for example, the bodies of the dead sinners are pressed face down into what must only euphemistically be called mud, compounded by a "piova / eterna, maladetta, fredda e greve" ("rain / eternal, accursed, cold and heavy rain"; V/7-8/58-59). As it is with this physical mud that Virgil stuffs into the mouth of Cerberus, the gatekeeper, one assumes that the punishment appropriate to these particular sinners (they are the gluttons) is to eat it.

The subliminal gravity we have identified as the poem's ground-bass does not yet seem associated with any of the conventional senses, but rather with something like spatial orientation, vertigo, dizziness, and the like, yet it fleshes out our reading experience just as surely as any sensory memory and thus functions as an analogon. Here, however, the reader confronts the subliminal presence of a specific bodily "sense," that of taste, and it will be useful to practice a kind of phenomenological analysis of the immediate reading process in order to detect the variety of other subliminal features it is called upon to combine.

The sinner who exemplifies this punishment—Ciacco—blames his self-indulgence on the rich luxury of Florence; and inasmuch as he is called upon to pronounce himself on its politics, we may imagine his life as that of a privileged and obese observer in a cafe, grousing about the political situation (a veritable Florentine civil war) without doing anything about it and only too willing to furnish a list of the illustrious party leaders responsible. He blames three great sins for this civil discord: "Pride, Envy, and Avarice" (VI/74/62). The reader may conjecture that they refer back to the three beasts of Dante's first approach—thereby activating our textural memory—just as the sufferer asks Dante to "recall him to men's memories" when the poet returns to the world of life. So remembering is a process touched on here, the memory of remembering is as it were initially yet still very faintly activated but has not yet become what we might call an outright "theme" (nor is remembering a sense exactly, even though it can cause pain—"nessun maggior dolore"). Yet it contributes its note to the phenomenological thickness of this reading (whose temporal organization and unification by terza rima must also be noted, along with the purely musical effect of the word sounds and rhymes themselves).

Tactility is obviously omnipresent in the cold rain and mud, but there comes a moment when the contact is broken off: Ciacco falls silent with a pronouncement "più non ti respondo" ("nor do I answer you more"), of which it is indeterminable whether it results from his own decision or simply foretells and confirms the effect of some external force, like a jailor breaking up a conversation in the visitors' room. And then something extraordinary fulfills this warning:

> Li diritti occhi torse allora in biechi;
> Guardommi un poco e poi chino Ia testa:
> Cadde con essa a par de li altri ciechi.
>
> Thereon he twisted his straight eyes asquint,
> looked at me for a moment, then bent his head
> and fell down with the other blind ones.
> (VI/91–93/64–65)

This is the very center of the Canto, a return to an extraordinarily vivid and grotesque corporeal *gestus*: Ciacco's eyestrings break, a cross-eyed grimace still seems to focus the Pilgrim for a moment, and then all sense is lost (the sinners being for the first time characterized as "blind": a punishment, if it is not simply a figure of speech, that seems superfluous under the circumstances). Singleton glosses this abrupt symptom by way of the medieval association of gluttony and hebetude; and it is certain that Ciocho's final stare might express the latter as something like an event, yet one quickly cancelled and replaced by the sightless glare of the unconscious. The allusion would be very much in keeping with Dante's practice of associating each sin with a specific corporeal symptom. Finally at the end, with Virgil's explanation, sound enters this picture with the Angel's trumpet on Judgment Day (which is described unexpectedly as resounding "for all eternity," as though another feature of the end of time were this unending assault on hearing).

It is tempting to associate the quite unexpected visual grimace that meets us at the moment when the senses of its victim are broken off with the whole de Manian (and Paxsonian) rhetoric of the "face" of personification (*prosopopeia*) and its "defacing" in the silencing of the speaking "face" or mask.[5] At any rate it marks yet another abrupt turn in the reading process from dialogue to description and also from explanation to sense experience; and thereby intensifies the temptation of "allegoresis" or in other words a sudden reactivation of the interpretive operation itself. We begin to ask ourselves about the possible (and meaningful) relationship or connections between this particular sin and what breaks off contact with Ciacco (for other episodes are terminated in quite different ways—Farinata returns to the grave in which he has been lying, Brunetto Latini takes up the eternity of his jogging once again, and so on). Does gluttony somehow collect the pleasures of the other senses (including conversation) and concentrate them in a single "blind" obsession? Or is the intelligibility too faint to read here, so that we must ourselves break off the interpretive exploration, swept forward irreversibly by the overlapping rhythm of a prosody that only knows a relative pause at the end of each canto?

In any case, the preconditions for both structure and interpretation (allegory versus allegoresis in Teskey's argument)[6] are these: a differentiation of the various senses and other phenomenological levels of "experience" and a mobile seemingly random yet properly transversal play of attention back and forth, which seems to dwell in turn and without any particular order on point-to-point relations between individual strands.

It is a peculiar process that can now be examined more closely in one of the most famous and abundantly commented episodes of *Inferno*, namely that of the hero Farinata, who alone stands out in Hell with something of the glamor of Milton's Satan: "com' avesse l'inferno a gran dispitto" ("as if he had great scorn of Hell"; X/36/100–101). He is the heroic leader of Dante's political enemies: a positioning that lends even

---

5   See, for example, Paul de Man, "Autobiography as De-facement," *The Rhetoric of Romanticism*, New York: Columbia University Press, 1984.

6   Gordon Teskey, *Allegory and Violence*, Ithaca: Cornell University Press, 1996.

greater vividness to Dante's apparent admiration and even more strikingly dramatizes the paradox of this apotheosis of the rebel in a poem dominated by ideal images of order, harmony, and submission. But this is not the question that interests us here.

Rather, it is the intersection of this confrontation with another one—Dante's questioning by the dead father of his friend Cavalcanti: a crux that occasioned a famous commentary of Gramsci on Croce's aesthetics[7]—and an interruption that raises even more dramatically the problem of the thematic cross-references or transversalities that lie at the very center of allegorical structure as such. The contingency of interruption is everywhere in the *Commedia* underscored, precisely in order to awaken or exacerbate our interpretive questions about the thematic relations which bridge such gaps.

In this instance, a political discussion, a rather reflective one, not yet sharpened into argument or mutual insult, is arrested by the elder Cavalcanti's question about his son, and his misunderstanding of Dante's use of the past tense of the verb, which he takes to mean that the younger Cavalcanti is no longer alive: "non fiere li occhi suoi lo dolce lume?" ("does the sweet light not strike his eyes?"; X/69/102–103).

The two discussions then merge in an account of the peculiar temporality of the damned, who can see future and past but not the present; and certainly it was be possible for readers like Croce himself to conclude that this—one of the most powerful episodes of the poem—is little more than a pretext for another one of those boring doctrinal expositions (here, on posthumous temporality) that it is normally the task of Virgil to administer but which here Farinata himself undertakes. (Virgil limits himself to the rather odd injunction to Dante that he not forget this encounter: it is true that it contains a prophecy by Farinata about Dante's own unhappy fate, so that we are free to read it internally as well.) But I prefer to underscore the recurrence in yet a fourth voice (Virgil's) of the theme of memory ("la mente tua conservi quel qu'udito"; "let your memory preserve what you have heard against yourself"; X/127/106–107), which can now serve as the random thematic connector between any number of representational details. Art even enters the picture in the form of political strategy, the "arte" of the two sides of the civil

---

7 Antonio Gramsci, *Lettere dal Carcere*, September 20, 1931 (Rome: Einaudi, 1947), 170–74.

conflict, a veritable premonition of Machiavelli's epistemological invention several centuries later. So it is that a thematic homophony (the "seme" of art reappearing in different contexts under different lexical auspices) randomly lights up spatial coincidences between various levels: but these vertical "stylistic events" are not to be confused with the thematics that emerged in post–New Critical theory, where a Wilson Knight, for example, discovers thematic clusters in Shakespeare, often unique to individual plays, metallic imagery emerging everywhere in *Coriolanus*, while that of nausea and corruption seeps through the verbal texture of *Hamlet*. (Later, in the absence of any adequate instruments for dealing with the novel—inasmuch as the New Critics had concentrated their attention on poetic language—this emphasis on recurrent themes and thematic clusters became a staple of narrative criticism in general and of the novel in particular.)

But thematics still foreground the content of their material and essentially work with recurrence or repetition, with what will later be called *redundance*: the method is horizontal and tends to substitute the construction of this or that "phenomenological world" for the form and shape of the novel's events. It looks for homologies between different kinds of content: thus, in the episode that concerns us here, we may be tempted to see in the allusion to Dante's best friend, the poet Guido Cavalcanti, a kind of rivalry, in which Dante opposes his own transformation of lyric into narrative or epic ("episch") to Guido's sublimation of it into the philosophical and the theory of love (something which long interested Ezra Pound). The supposition is, however, gratuitous until we remember that in the political realm too, rivalry has become a crucial form; the old ideological struggle between Guelph and Ghibelline (the priority of pope or emperor, their struggle for sovereignty in the Italian city states) has in Dante's Florence been transformed into a rivalry between two currents within the triumphant Guelph party ("the one going into two"). Farinata therefore is identified no longer as the absolute ideological enemy, but rather as the leader of a rival clan among the enemies, so that this whole structure can be taken as homologous with the poetic rivalry of the two friends, Dante and Cavalcanti, within a properly poetic politics, the dissensions within what used to be the unified avant-garde of the "dolce stil nuovo." This approach then turns "rivalry" into a doubly political theme and presumably inspires us to hunt for its presence elsewhere in the *Commedia*.

An allegorical method, however, would read this parallelism as an event, as the punctual intersection of two fundamental levels of the poem: the political and the poetic. For one brief moment, something new happens in this crossing of the lines, which is neither a metaphorical transfer nor an addition to a thematic inventory; but rather a conjuncture, a striking of sparks and the ephemeral activation of a specific occurrence in the reading process, a narrative event on the level of form (rather than, as in conventional narrative, in the content). Such purely formal "events" then characterize allegory better than the parallel occurrences in this or that purely representational storytelling: they are short circuits within the structural system of levels, whose interactions—seemingly random either from a thematic or a narrative logic—constitute a reading experience utterly unique and quite distinct from that of either conventional narrative or pure lyric.

Meanwhile we must return to the critical comments of Antonio Gramsci on this same Canto of *Inferno*, Canto X, which here become something of a crux or touchstone. In his letter of September 20, 1931, to Tatiana he raises the issue—it is directed against Croce—of the discursive heterogeneity between the affecting scene of Cavalcanti's (erroneous) mourning for his son and Farinata's scholastic lesson on the temporality of the *Inferno*. For Croce—master of a properly modernist differentiation and as keen on distinguishing poetic "expression" from other kinds of language as were the New Critics in their own search for the essence of poetic language—it was the exercise of his trademark judgment on "what is living" and "what is dead" (in Hegel, Marx, Dante, and others) that the offending canto called into action: clearly motivating the radical separation of Cavalcanti's poetic pathos from the rhymed prose of Farinata's disquisition.[8]

My point is simply that in quite properly defending Dante and demonstrating the functional role of Farinata's explanation in that larger

---

8 Benedetto Croce, *Aesthetics*, Boston: David R. Godine, 1984; and see for Croce's oblique and rather plaintive allusion long after the fact, "De Sanctis/Gramsci?" *Lo spettatore italiano*, V, 1952, 294–96. See also Croce's comments on the "explanations" of the temporality of Farinata's circle of hell: "L'autore doveva pagare un debito ai lettori del romanzo teologico-etico, et lo paga alla prima occasione, tutto in una volta, per non averci piú a pensare." *La Poesia de Dante* (Bari: 1943), 78; ironically for us, Croce reserves the epithet "allegorical" for just such nonpoetic, nonexpressive, prosaic, expository segments of the *Commedia*.

effect of pathos, Gramsci has retained an unspoken literary value—that of unity or of the isotopie—that he shares with his master and which we need not retain today, in an age of fragmentation, heterogeneity, and indeed of allegory itself. No dramatist would indeed object to Farinata's variations in tone—from the haughty to the politically intent, from regret to avuncular instruction—but this is merely to reinstate a unity of multiple tones from a different and now more theatrical perspective. What I want to suggest is not only that heterogeneity of raw material— the political struggle, paternal grief, the geographical situation—on which Gramsci's Althusserian critics always insisted (as over against his "humanism"); but also the differentiation of mental operations called into play by these distinct elements, which it is the function of terza rima not only to reunify but also to designate as an act of reunification in the process.

All this is today easier enough to grasp thematically: and it is enough to suggest that the whole canto, with its personal prophecies (Dante will shortly be exiled from Florence) and its political perspectives (the fate of the factions), along with the trumpet of doom that seals these graves forever, is staged under the overarching thematics of temporality and memory. But I think we lose something of the rugosity of the thing in this complacent flattening out into mere themes (themselves at best those very "bad allegories" we have been intent on denouncing in "humanist" readings).

Better to insist on, and hold fast to, a disruptive movement of attention back and forth between these varied "intentional objects," in the process making ephemeral connections between them. Thus, the Florentine civil war has its poetic counterparts. Nor is it itself any unified event: for to the struggle between the Ghibellines and the Guelphs, which concludes (at least in Dante's lifetime) with the triumph of the latter, there succeeds (as I have already noted) another struggle within the Guelph party itself, to which Dante will, a few years after this encounter in the afterlife, himself fall victim. It is to this last, far more fraternal conflict (the One into the Two) that his sectarian opposition to Farinata is referred. Meanwhile, in a kind of alternation of voices and operatic duets, their conversation is interrupted by the reminder of Dante's friendship with his great fellow-poet Cavalcanti, whose father wonders why the latter is not eminent enough to accompany him on this extraordinary journey. This is the point at which a determined yet subtly malicious

Dante observes, indicating Virgil, that his friend and poetic comrade perhaps chose the wrong path, that of philosophy rather than of Virgilian epic. This is an argument no less politically fraught than the overtly political one, which it parallels, designating a similar rift in the poetic avant-garde of the Dolce stil novo. At which point old Cavalcanti collapses and the exchange with Farinata continues as though without a break.

I would like to suggest that two allegorical levels are here activated and intersect with one another in the fashion of a musical composition in which two distinct instruments—flute and oboe, say—project a single note in unison. The political level is itself allegorical of the grandest of the fourfold levels, namely the anagogical one, the future of the human race as it progresses, slowly or swiftly, but with historical inevitability, toward the Last Judgment. Dante is of the Emperor's party (see below) but has been raised among its opponents, until a splinter group of the latter turns again to oppose the pope (the ideological complexities of modern Trotskyism might well convey something of this political ambivalence).

Meanwhile, although the internal dramas of any avant-garde are in and of themselves political, I will assign these debates on poetics and on individual style and creation to the "moral" level, or in other words, the fate of the soul (the construction of subjectivity). For this is a poetic production that formally inquires into the very nature of sublimation and seeks to transform desire into a new kind of drive (the classical description of the process being Plato's *Symposium*). Something of this process was apparent in Spenser: it is a lateral operation and cannot be conducted by way of the direct taboos (in the ten commandments, for example, although Lacan's analysis of them is instructive),[9] nor is it representational, in the sense in which the model of the subjectivity to be produced is the very soul whose purification is described in the content of the poem itself. Rather, it must consist of the aftereffects and *habitus* of those effects and that reading, something far more difficult to register. Here, Dante's smug satisfaction at having chosen "the right path" suggests that Cavalcanti's method, a rather psychoanalytic and introspective exploration (well known to Poundians), will not be satisfactory; and it implies that narrative has constructional powers that

---

9 See Jacques Lacan, *The Ethics of Psychoanalysis, 1959–1960* (Seminar VII), ed. Jacques-Alain Miller, trans. Dennis Porter, New York: Norton, 1997.

introspection and philosophy necessarily lack. Still, inasmuch as a psychoanalytic framework is the only satisfactory one we currently have for representing psychic change, we may identify the well-nigh telepathic Virgil as a kind of analyst, whose function is there to warn and to prompt and in this canto to insist on memory.

So in what way does this canto, laterally, form our sense of temporality? A formative pressure is to be found in the way we are asked to imagine the future. The inhabitants of this circle have and do not have a future: blind to the present, they can see our future as long as they themselves have one, all the while knowing that they are without a future, that the lids of the coffins, like those of the eyes, will be nailed down definitively upon them, that they will then only exist in an empty present, a darkness without content. This is a training in a duality of time which simpler groups only knew, at best, in the form of the family and ancestor worship, immortality being its most satisfactory replacement in a spatially expanded age. (There must have been much celebration in ancient Egypt on that memorable day on which immortality was extended to the dead of the common people!)

Dante offers us a particularly challenging model in which the eternal present is not one of action, while a future that transcends our individual biological life is itself potentially blocked and finite. The two types of temporality here express a dawning historicity, as Christianity first began to develop it, a universal history of which Farinata sees consequences that Dante himself can only hear from him in prophetic form, locked as he is in his own present of time, even on this day of Jubilee and its dream vision.

What transcends individual biographical existence is then twofold: it is the universal time established by scripture and chronicle, and the world space of the Roman (and Christian) empire and of Dante's wanderings in exile. Both dimensions are to be interiorized so as to assign the individual "subject of desire" its modestly restricted position. In our own time, no doubt, they correspond to the absent omnipresence of globalization on the one hand and on an inconceivably scientific projection about the duration of the galaxies on the other: transcendencies we have probably not yet assimilated into our more traditional phenomenological psychic structures.

This particular axis—between phenomenological time and history as such—is, however, only one set of the coordinates that construct subjectivity in Dante's work (and presumably in one way or another in his cultural moment as well). The other weighs on the very structure of the *Commedia* itself as well as on Dante's politics: it is the dual power outlined in *De Monarchia*, which opposes the spiritual authority of the pope to the temporal order of the imperial monarchy (Rome constituting the ideal image and historical embodiment of their unity): soul and body, private and public, the two levels of the moral and the anagogical.

What I have hitherto examined is the way in which the moral level (or psychoanalytic one, if you prefer) projects its divided structure onto the anagogical one (that of the collectivity) in the form of an impossible consciousness of history. Now we must proceed in the other direction and try to grasp the way in which the collective or political level intersects with the moral or psychological one and leaves its traces in private or personal destiny.

It is natural enough for modern people to find the problems of Dante's political theory and commitments rather antiquated in the light of a history from which the Empire and its emperors have long since vanished, and in which the pope is scarcely the claimant for that universal authority for which he once fought in a parochial Western middle ages (before Protestantism). But systems like those of the Islamic Republic of Iran, with its supreme spiritual leader on the one hand and its political apparatus (complete with a president) on the other, suggest that the problem is not altogether obsolete in modern times. Meanwhile the stewardship of the communist parties in a now older socialism (as they operated in a kind of duality or parallelism with the bureaucratic mechanisms of the state and the economy) can also be read in this fashion: at least in principle, in both systems, the "spiritual" center was to serve as a guide or check, a kind of moral guidance, for the secular operations of administration and production. It is only the army, treason, warfare, or civil unrest that disturbs this seemingly reasonable scheme, this dual sovereignty, about which it remains uncertain where the "monopoly of violence" is to be housed. In Dante's Italy, indeed, the popes have armies and rule territories, while the Emperor is far away, often weak, and at best a kind of "regulative idea."

But if the dualistic scheme is to be complicated by other questions, such as those of freedom and elections (both pope and emperor are actually elected in some sense of the word), then it must be interpreted in a different way. No mode of production willingly disappears; social structure has its Spinozan conatus, just like living organisms; the freedoms a given socioeconomic system specifies, or even encourages or forbids on the order of incorporating their specific infringencies into state law, never extend to the freedom to change the system as a whole. Revolt can be tolerated not only because it can be put down but also because it changes nothing: dynastic successions, the coup, and the seizure of power are tolerable to the degree to which "power" as such remains "the same" under the new regime. But revolution as a wholesale transformation of the system as such can have no place, either in monarchies or dictatorships, oligarchies or democracies: the anti-systemic (as Wallerstein termed it) must be rooted out, whether it takes the form of Spartacus, the Confederacy, or the Paris Commune.

So now the concrete function of the "supreme" or spiritual leader becomes much clearer: it is to prevent the transformation, modification, or even suppression of the system, a fragile system, surrounded by powerful systemic alternatives (to which it is perhaps better to say that it is itself the alternative, isolated and in permanent danger from without and from within as well). In the socialist countries it was only too clear that the function of the party was first and foremost that, to secure the permanence of the revolution, to prevent its dissolution and its reabsorption into world capitalism—a mission that overrides all more immediately "socialist" concerns or "communist" ideals, any possibility of achieving which will obviously be extinguished by the disappearance of the system itself.

The contemporary parallels are therefore still available in various embodiments; but if they no longer take this starkly classical form—primitive Christianity versus the Roman road, the imperial networks—then it is perhaps for another reason that also plagued Dante himself. For there is a third center, alongside the pope and the emperor, and that is Florence itself: commerce, nascent capitalism, finance, money, and greed—phenomena that make their presence felt on every page of the *Commedia*. To be sure, individual popes also fall into this third category and take their punishment for corruption, simony, treachery, and gluttony like all the rest: but the papacy as such is not in question here, and Dante's theorizing turns on the preservation of this duality of the cross and the eagle and on how it is to be imagined to function properly. What was not to have been part of the vision was what Florence so preeminently stands for, not just a sinkhole of sins, but a wholly different system, a commercial one, for which there is as yet no place within the older world order, nor any proper conceptual or theological category, either. Dante's fury at Florence seethes through the *Commedia* and is given vent eloquently on every available occasion; but neither pope nor emperor is really capable of dealing with the historical dilemma it constitutes, namely the emergence out of feudalism of a wholly new social dynamic, a wholly new and untheorized mode of production. Indeed, one is tempted to suggest that it is precisely this form dilemma that is the driving force behind the *Commedia* itself and its well-nigh infinite inventiveness.

As for the framework, then, it is already laid in place by a dualism that is itself a juxtaposition of two incommensurate dimensions rather than some easy parallelism. The proof is to be found in the genealogy of the virtues and the vices themselves, which are not symmetrical: the virtues are not simply cancellations of the system of sins, the latter not merely the infringements of the former. As we have shown in an earlier chapter, the theological virtues have little to do with the cardinal sins, nor the venial ones, either (we remember that even Aristotle had trouble with his own attempts at mediation): each system comes from a different world, a different set of preoccupations.

And this is how the *Commedia* is able to construct its fundamental architecture: the sins will be individual, they will house the individual narratives, the anecdotes, the concrete acts. They are, so to speak, the domain of the papacy; and what the pope stands for, in his authority, is the empirical judgment on individual characters; theology provides the categories according to which their stories can be collected and the distinctions that govern their classifications and their punishments. As for the empire, it is the very space of the afterworld itself, particularly as it culminates in the astronomical system, as but one form of a palpably centered and hierarchical space. That space is not geographic in the sense in which the individual sinners in this afterworld are at one with their landscapes and their dialects: imperial space is a kind of absent totality, as witness its dual forms in Paradiso—in the constellations and various spheres and their attendant virtues and the great unity of the rose into which they all dissolve, as so many appearances, with the approach of the beatific vision. Sovereignty is nonphysical and nonmaterial, even though it exists in a concentration somehow beyond representation: it is indeed, as Schmitt explained, very much a state of exception. I am both situated somewhere within its hierarchy and dissolved with it into an indistinguishable collective consciousness. Such is then Dante's unique representational solution to the problem—both political and aesthetic—of the incommensurability between the individual and the group, between phenomenological experience and the totality as such. Yet like all such solutions, *Paradiso* is an imaginary one, a triumph of picture-thinking over the inconceivable contradiction.

It is therefore time to take an inventory of such levels within the reading present insofar as we can abstract them from this, the most elaborate allegorical structure ever devised. We might well begin with that subliminal level we have already touched on, namely the establishment of a kind of phenomenological verticality embodied in the effects of gravity, in the sensations of weight and of lightness. That conceptuality is present in this virtually unconscious (and seemingly natural) phenomenon can be demonstrated, not only in its motivation of the geographical system—descending, climbing, and then rising—but also in the relationship between verticality and the sublime, which can for the moment be considered a kind of *amplificatio* or sublimation of that verticality. Clearly, however, this virtuality of gravity, this permanent possibility of its punctual registration as an event, will depend on its intersection with any one of the other levels virtual within the poem's historical aesthetic.

The sensory levels are then clearly no longer unconscious but rather the media for specific perception: the stench of the *bolgi*, the effects of light (as in the blinding illumination that causes Dante to swoon, much like the effects of light-bombs in modern military technology), the shadow and ominous blood-darkened color of a watery landscape, sounds of wailing, and the like. All of these make an immediate appeal, if not directly to our sense experience, then at least to our memory of it (which often brings with it subliminal experiences of its physical effects); but (in the spirit of Lukács's great essay on description versus narration) we need to be aware of the degree to which this level of static sensation is transformed into perception by what I will call the level of the kinetic and of narrative.

Mere sensations, taken by themselves, are simply invitations to the decipherment of a purely symbolic meaning; an older kind of bad allegory deploys them as so many signs, of which a symbolic table might be laid out. The kinetic, on the other hand, transforms them into events in their own right: thus the "lonza" of the beginning is not merely particolored, like an exotic and decorative rug or skin, it is also "leggiera"—which could by itself remain a static attribute—but with the adjective "presta molto" the beast becomes visualizable in the supple play of its muscles as it arouses alarm, it becomes something like the essence of a mobility that fascinates and also awakens danger signals ("a leopard light-footed and very fleet, covered with a spotted hide"; I/32–33/4–5).

Meanwhile it can be asserted that these moments—in which the poem breaks into narrative, as it were, and returns to the "isotopie" of sequentiality, of following the segments of an action, a reaction, a continuation—are essentially kinetic ones, driven on by Virgil's constant admonitions and interrupted by "pauses" that are no less kinetic for bringing a momentary stillness or rest to the bodies they follow. Dante's geography thereby reveals its formal "motivation": it necessitates and ensures the reactivation of the kinetic at every moment. This is the difference between this journey and the traditional allegorical ones of the *Roman de la rose* or of Bunyan: this cosmos not only, like theirs, has a meaning, it also determines a corporeal content, a complex of physical reactions that not only transcends static perception but also provides material for that sublimation into the various "spiritual" or allegorical senses I have been touching on here (in what is misleadingly called *interpretation*).

But geography then determines new levels in its own right: and they can be distinguished from one another as explanation and exploration, respectively. Explanation activates that mental function sometimes loosely identified as *Imagination* or *picture-thinking*, in which we are called on mentally to construct spaces of various kinds and to combine them with one another in ways that draw on that land surveying which Husserl considered to be the basis and foundation of mathematics itself and of which the most mysterious and contingent is that of left and right. (Who has not laboriously attempted to follow Balzac's interminable accounts of a building or Parisian apartment, only to find, at its end, that we have put all the left-hand rooms of an enfilade on the right and thus completely misconstrued what will turn out to be the scene of a drama to come?) The cosmological explanations of Virgil are then something like a ground zero of theology, on which all the later elaborate lessons in the economy of sins and virtues, for example, or the levels of paradise, build. Pedagogy here takes the form of geography, and this lends the otherwise sterile abstraction of Dante's scholasticism its materiality; indeed, it could be argued that it is precisely this spatial structure of Dante's theology that saves it from didacticism and turns its seeming lessons into maps, its abstract argumentation into travel guides for the soul.

Exploration then repeats these formal imperatives on the more seemingly physical level of emulation, when we attempt to reproduce in our reading minds what the difficulties of Dante's narrated body might approximate as it navigates asperities of the journey downward (often assimilated, with an exile's eye, to distinctive places in the Italian landscape) or struggles upward, distinguishing the steep and the gradual inclines, the chasms and the relief of a path.

We often distinguish explanation and exploration as appealing to the mind on the one hand and the body on the other, forgetting that it is the task of the poem to overcome such distinctions: sometimes even by insisting on them, as when Virgil's nonmaterial shape eludes the material obstacles that Dante's living body has to face. But it is precisely in such moments—which exemplify one of those intersections between the levels we have in mind here—that materiality itself and corporeality are most strongly affirmed and intensified for the reading mind. I have conjectured that it was this bias toward the physical that Auerbach meant to emphasize when he repeatedly used words like *earthly* or *kreatürlich* and attacked "allegory" in the process, reinventing a new and for him more Christian or Thomist version of "figural" realism of the type stressed by André Bazin and Kracauer in their postwar film theories. This "knight's move" from literature to cinema, from language to a mobile visuality, can perhaps be explained by the increasing skepticism about representation in literary modernism, and the moment in which film seemed to offer the more appropriate opening onto a visual sense for the moment still capable of saying everything that henceforth abstract literary realism used to say.

But in all this we have not yet reached that other level which is speech itself: for the geographical explanations as well as the physical evocations are all necessarily conveyed in language, and by way of another fundamental opposition, that between the speeches and dialogues and the first-person narrative—the two then reunited in the flow and discipline of terza rima as a form.

There is an argument to be made about allegory and syntax that would seem in direct contradiction to Auerbach's strenuous efforts to disable traditional allegorical readings of Dante (particularly as they are based on the *Letter to Can Grande*). I want to show a way through this stark opposition between "allegory" and what Auerbach called *figura*; but it must start by correcting the conventional reading of *Mimesis*, which reads the opening juxtaposition of Homer and the Bible as one between hypotaxis and parataxis, associating the latter, as illustrated by the biblical texts, with the *sermo humilis*, that is to say the vernacular language, as opposed to the high-flown and artificial rhetorical one in which our hypotactic traditions flourished, nourished on classics that were for the most part, from the Greeks and Cicero on down, oratorical. In fact, the opening chapters of *Mimesis* play with a fourfold set of coordinates, simple versus rhetorical along with parataxis versus hypotaxis: the winning combination is that of a hypotactic *sermo humilis*, which amounts to a conquest of complex syntax in the vernacular language, and which obviously, for Auerbach, reaches its climax in Dante.

Sonorities to be sure have their own autonomous level, what Lacan called *llalangue* (ingeniously translated as *language*), the babbling sound of the various tongues into which human language is divided and which can then revert back into meaningless sound in the noises of an idiosyncratic patois or a reversal to sheer wailing and outcry. This level is then a return to the more purely sensory, leaving behind it the empty frameworks of meter and rhyme to be deployed in the service of a kinetic forward-driving verse itself and used to buttress and reinforce narrative movement and temporality.

Sentence structure is however something else, something which has its own peculiar autonomy; and it was the unique contribution of Auerbach to have singled out syntax as the central exhibit of his theory of "realism" in *Mimesis* and above all in his studies of Dante. The philosophical background of this linguistic and stylistic position needs some initial clarification. It should, for example, be added that Auerbach's frequent denunciations of allegory as artificial and decorative were in fact so many attacks on Neoplatonism and what he considered an idealistic transcendence of matter toward the Idea: this is the sense in which Auerbach's closet Thomism can be considered a kind of transcendent materialism, an attention to "worldly" or "earthly" detail that glorifies even the most imperfect created phenomena in the name of an immanent transcendence, a perspective in which the imperfect thing or character can be seen against the background of its own implicit perfection. This is, of course, precisely the perspective of the *Commedia*, and according to Auerbach it is this inner movement of the phenomenon toward its entelechy which secures the movement of its evocation and as it were the "event" of its unfolding ("as a bud opens").[10] Such an inner movement governs the form of the three canticles as a whole, developing toward the beatific vision; but it also governs the microcosmic narratives of the episodes, as the souls move toward their ultimate fates: we have already witnessed static fates of the condemned, for example, dramatized not only by the coffin lids that will close forever on Judgment Day, but also by the temporality of their knowledge of earth, which still allows them to see the future even though the present is now no longer visible, but which will obviously lose even that prophetic power when, after Judgment Day, the future no longer exists. They are therefore (in a very Sartrean fashion) nothing but their own pasts, their own life histories, which can no longer change: they have become in other words (those of Mallarmé) their own destinies.

Auerbach's position is that it was Dante's conquest of the periodic sentence that put him in a position to model or represent this complex and "realist" combination of Aristotelian ontology and Christian temporality. Only Auerbach could have dared to publish the following remark (on one of Dante's earlier lyrics): "no sentence of that kind was written in the Middle Ages before Dante"[11]; and although the poet had no relationship with the as yet unrecovered Greek classics, his commentator sees his stylistic achievement as a reinvention of Greek rather than Latin linguistic power, a rediscovery of the "language that created *men* and *de*."[12]

Dante's own classification of sentences is to be found in *De vulgari eloquentia* (II, 6); but Auerbach's is most powerfully articulated in the very structure of his *Mimesis*, which opposes the paratactic sentence—the "and," the accumulation of simple sentences and static or descriptive details—to the "hypotaxis" that gradually overcomes it and makes of the

---

10   Erich Auerbach, *Dante: Poet of the Secular World*, New York: New York Review of Books Classics, 2007, 42.
11   Ibid., 55.
12   Ibid., 48 (the quote is from Willamowitz).

sentence a complex instrument of clauses and subclauses, along with a rising and falling inner movement (from the *men* to the *de*), a structure capable of capturing the multiple perspectives of the reality we have just described. *Mimesis* tells the story of a laborious ascent of the vernacular to a first climax in Dante's style; and then another slow recovery through Western literary practice to the stylistic achievement of Zola (the book's second "climax"): what may seem a mysterious or even paradoxical analogy between Thomism and naturalism is explained by the centrality for both of the body as such (and the syntax able to do it justice).

But there are intermediary steps here as well: for example, the kind of periodic sentence Auerbach has in mind, in which a statement or proposition is filled in by all kinds of appositions, qualifying and dependent clauses, and logical connectives of all kinds in a linguistic construction which becomes capable of touching a range of aspects of the topic including the temporal perspectives and its rhetorical relationships to speaker and listener. But Auerbach necessarily conveys this extraordinary structure (Proust might have been a better reference for him than Zola) by comparison, first with the respective syntax of Dante's other poetic comrades in the *dolce stil nuovo*, and, then, in *Mimesis*, with earlier and later literary generations. This gives us a feeling for Dante's linguistic innovation, which we cannot take from a direct reading, against the background of all those variant possibilities (or the absence of them, the failure to follow up on the new syntactic possibilities of the vernacular). We can get a sense of his style as a uniquely signed idiom, but not of the syntactical history on which it is embedded.

The argument is not that the periodic sentence is all by itself an instrument of realism: for the mere periodic sentence as such, as an oratorical structure, simply becomes an instrument in an elaborate rhetorical arsenal, as in the bombast of the later Roman Empire. The argument here is that its medieval recovery from the parataxis of the vernacular then allows a true "verse paragraph" to come into being— that is, a multiplicity of individual sentences, which, in their syntactic variety, put to use the hypotaxis elaborated by the period and its subordinations, dependencies, modalties, modifications, and repetitions. These now fan out into a larger text and sequence of which the sentences are so many intricate articulations.[13]

---

13   Ibid., 13.

This is why the mediation of verse is required: to serve as an analogon, in the present of reading, to this synchronous system of relationships, which the prosody echoes as a dialectic of identity and difference (in a Jakobsonian projection of the syntaxical axis onto the temporal one, each reflecting a shared yet distinct form of closure in time).

What then dialectically parallels this strenuous touching of all the walls in the microcosm of syntax is what we will call *thick narrative* in the macrocosm of the events: namely the presence of the levels and the multiplicity of their intersections. Narrative goes transversally from one to the other, unexpectedly setting them in unpredictable contact with each other—by juxtaposition, by metaphoric identification, by repetition of dialectically ambiguous words—in a touching of all the bases, which replicates the operation on the dimensions of the individual sentence. Indeed, it seems to me that this conception of thick narration as a value—that it is somehow more interesting and admirable than the simplified dual levels of traditional allegory, or the one-dimensional sentence of a merely contingent or private story—holds the key to the deeper function of the levels as a literary phenomenon. I've said elsewhere that it seemed to me the advantage of a Marxist criticism, far from being "reductive," lay in the fact that it includes more, it expands the phenomenon of the text to greater and more multiple dimensions of both reference and signification, making of the literary work an act in history and time as well as an inert and static objective structure. I would now say that those possibilities of expansion are internally predicated on the existence within the text of the four levels themselves, which allow and develop just such a complex of multidimensional relationships. Thus, in an allegory like this one (but there really are no other allegories like this one of Dante), the articulations of the periodic sentence have as their correlative the practice and pulsation of the four allegorical levels.

In a more modern realism, to be sure, all this will have been reabsorbed into narrative in a very different way and according to a historically distinct aesthetic. The theological institutions of interpretation are gone, and it is meanwhile a more subjectivized and individualized narrative itself which will have to assume the twin processes of articulation that we found in the allegorical levels and their sentences, reducing them to a universal isotopie. But literary history is itself a sequence of just such distinct paradigms, the story of each demanding interpretation in its own right.

One may perhaps rewrite this priority of the periodic sentence and of syntax as such in terms of verse by insisting on the function of rhyme here: the rhymes not only ensure that progression forward in time imposed by terza rima, they also stand in tension and opposition to the meter of the verses they interrupt, intersect, or bring to closure. The opposition is itself symbolic, or better still allegorical: it dramatizes, on the level of art or poetry itself, the way in which a present of time punctuates a moving temporality. The return of the rhyme demonstrates that the absolute present can be reconciled with the radically different temporal system of past–present–future, even though that reconciliation cannot be conceptualized in philosophy or abstract thought: showing how the static object of description can be set in motion by the kinetics of narration. But for the demonstration to work, the sentence, in all its complexity, must retain the natural movement of ordinary speech, which it must not interrupt with artificial or rhetorical flourishes or decorations. Its regular punctuation by rhyme is enough to secure its status as something more than ordinary speech; and this is why the impact of Dante on his still emergent vernacular can be matched only by a Baudelaire in French or a Yeats or a Rilke in English or German: a speaking voice that is miraculously formed into verse as it follows the logic of its own sometimes tortuous syntax.

Were one, however, to adopt as a stylistic guide not Auerbach but rather Leo Spitzer, the weight of the analysis would certainly fall elsewhere: perhaps on that peculiar construction of effacement—the verb and its unmaking in un- or dis- "Siena mi fé, disfecemi Maremma" ("Siena made me, Maremma unmade me" (*Purgatorio* V/134/52)—which we may take as a final or micrological version of epic paraphrase. Spitzer might well have taken this stylistic tic as an entry point into his famous "hermeneutic circle" as it winds itself through all the levels of the work's meaning. His debate with Auerbach (who declared, "my purpose is always to write history") turned on the specificity of the detail (which Auerbach is alleged to have submerged in his larger historical story); but from our perspective here—that of the intersection of contradictions, or of "the identity of identity and non-identity" (Hegel)—there is no need to sacrifice either the detail or the historical narrative, and indeed the reinforcement of each can only bring the central tension and contradiction out more sharply. In the case of the example or detail I have selected—effacement by the prefix—this peculiar stylistic mannerism would be best understood as the linguistic reinforcement of an organic view of phenomena, which avoids death or negation by folding it back into the temporal and evolutionary process as the latter's simple undoing.

The dualities themselves (caricatured in the twin bodies of *Inferno* XXV) remind us of the invisible omnipresence of Ovid in Dante's imagination, for which the temporality of language and the sentence has elective affinities with change and metamorphosis, rather than with static description. In thought and conceptuality, however, alternation seems at first limited to that between active and passive: the "turbulence" in question varying from a literal passion to an action and a source of contagion. In *Inferno*, the "sins" must be distinguished from one another in order to furnish the stops on the journey, the episodic structure of a story collection like Boccaccio's. But we have seen how this impossible pressure determines a kind of laterality, in which the qualities of the individual sinner (and of his Canto) tend to slip away from their official classification and to gain a kind of autonomy, a contagion of the abstract. It is this initial discordance that triggers the allegorical reading (as at the very beginning of the history of allegoresis in Alexandrian times) and makes for an interrogation for which the intersection of multiple levels becomes visible.

In *Purgatorio*, however, as Tambling has shown with great detail and acuity,[14] the very conception of a possible purgation and purification, the prospect of a cleansing away of that specific sin which has hitherto defined a character's identity, makes for a much more fluid interaction between the sins themselves, which he identifies as that protean and ambiguous category, the chiasmus. "The divisions, between Dante and the souls he addresses, may be crossable: at moments, a chiasmic reversal seems near."[15] But this kind of transfer also takes place between the various sins themselves (and their shelves or places), in a far more open display of what we have called transversality than anything in *Inferno*. For in a sense (the seven P's incised on his forehead), Dante must himself symbolically purge the whole scale of sins on his way to the Garden and its rivers (and in particular, the river of Lethe, which in a far more beneficent way than in *Faust* determines a healing forgetfulness of all the sins

---

14   Jeremy Tambling, *Dante in Purgatorio*, Turnhout, Belgium: Brepols, 2010.
15   Ibid., 221.

hitherto accrued: as it were itself a jubilee, a wiping clean of the slate, a forgiveness of debts). The doctrinal question is then whether all the souls passing through Purgatory do not need in the same way to purge the gamut of sinfulness of which Adam's children are guilty, or whether their own specific offense is serious enough to take all the others with it in its final release. If so, then in a sense all the sins are somehow related and combined into a single comprehensive flaw or category, so that, as realized in *Paradiso*, we already have avant la lettre a kind of virtual duality in which the degrees of Difference are at one and the same time folded back into one stupendous Identity.

Meanwhile, as Tambling significantly notes, the whole canticle is the site of an enormous release of affect, as opposed to the named emotions, a relief which is the sign of the latter's dissolution and a place of a kind of Christian apatheia or ataraxia, and at the same time a place of heightened spiritual concentration: thus, for example, he demonstrates that the various figures of the poem receive their perceptions with heightened intensity and heightened attention and curiosity, as an index of their progress.[16] He himself insists, quite rightly I think, on the crucial role here of that ambiguous emotion named anger, about which we have already seen Aristotle's perplexity, his hesitation to posit its opposite number. Here, however, Christian peace will come to fill that empty semiotic space. In contrast to the omnipresence of anger in *Inferno*, where even its witnesses (Virgil, in the example I have cited, Dante himself on the lake of blood) are contaminated by the power of this central named emotion, the figures of anger in *Purgatorio* are purely aesthetic representations (in this case, visions) and therefore at some second remove from the thing itself: they constitute its spectacle, rather, or at best its simulacrum. When we reckon into this observation the omnipresence of poets in this canticle, as well as the striking role of the multisensory frieze and other artistic representations (owed, no doubt, to God himself as the artist or at least to his explicit intentions), we will not be far from making a fundamental link between aesthetic sublimation and the nature of the purification that *Purgatorio* offers. The sins are transformed into their own images. They cannot be literally expunged, inasmuch as they are either part of some original nature or inherent in our original sin; there is no room, in a paradise thickly peopled with

---

16   Ibid., 210.

concrete virtues of various kinds and types (which to be sure are also capable of folding back into the unison of the celestial rose), for the kind of ataraxia or apatheia envisioned by the ancients. Meanwhile, the calm through which Dante sees these images of a now neutralized wrath is not a void either, but in its aesthetization of the named emotions, something closer to an affect, and one that has its own kind of psychic influence on Dante's ascension, which is thereby that much more "lightened." We do not, therefore, need to appeal to the biographical, and Dante's legendary irascibility and intolerance, his documented fits of rage, to appreciate anger's centrality in this scheme of things.

It is proper to conclude these observations about Dante's allegory with some final remarks about the new terms we have found useful in characterizing it. The word *thick* is chosen, not merely for its anthropological overtones (Geertz), but also, more literally metaphorical (if I may put it that way), in view of the levels that thicken the narrative material. That Dante also grasps it in this way may be argued on the basis of one of the most controversial verses in *Purgatorio*, where he explicitly addresses the reader and foregrounds the matter of interpretation:

> Aguzza qui, lettor, ben li occhi al vero,
> Che'l velo è ora ben tanto sottile,
> Certo che 'l trapaasar dentro è leggero.
>
> Reader, here sharpen well your eyes to the truth,
> for the veil is now indeed so thin,
> that certainly to pass within is easy.
> (*Purgatorio* VIII/19–21/76)

The episode that follows, and to which our interpretative sense is so strongly directed, is a regression into the older form of a purely symbolic allegory, with the serpent—"Vedi là 'l nostro avversaro" ("See there our adversary!"; VIII/95/82)—attempting its entrance into the Valley of the Princes and being put to flight by guardian angels. The recurrent (nightly) onslaught of the enemy is generally taken to be the temptations of pride and power that routinely assail such great and virtuous (if failed) leaders; but the very fact that the image is a personification that can be assigned a meaning as such (whichever one is chosen) thereby marks it as a different type of discourse from the narrative in which it is embedded. This is symbolism of the type of the three beasts (or of the later triumphal progression in the earthly paradise), and Dante's interpolation confirms our distinction and warns us that it is easier to deal with ("sottile") than the complexity of the "thick" and fourfold narrative.

This characterization then sets a certain distance between Dante's practice and what it has been traditional to call *allegory*; but this distance is misleading, I think, inasmuch as we have associated the traditional view with a threefold system of one-to-one parallels (on the order of personification), rather than the fourfold scheme advocated here. It is in order to reinforce the structural differences at stake that I have proposed the term *transversal* or lateral for the relations of the levels of the fourfold scheme to one another—a term which seems to me to allow more randomness and freedom (in the sense of the clinamen) than our static image of levels: fitful connections and intersections suggestive of a flitting of consciousness from one form of attention to another, a slippage in *niveau*, a perception by distraction analogous to what Benjamin ascribed to our awareness of architecture as we move through it on our way elsewhere, or of those unhappy souls who have too many ideas at once and try vainly to marshal them like sheep the shepherd risks "now losing in one direction and another in another" (as Manzoni puts it).[17] For, as Dürer showed, if we want a full pictorial representation of allegory, it can only be as random or broken objects (and lifelike figures) scattered about, some in intelligible clusters, others simply abandoned in the midst of some unknown activity or failed construction project. Yet in Dürer's *Melencolia*, there is still the continuity of space against which this junkyard is registered: and the greatness of Dante, as opposed to the more openly allegorical allegoricists, is that he keeps the thread, whether temporal or geographical; and secures a homogeneity—perhaps one could call it some properly allegorical isotopie?—against which such extreme divagations can safely be indulged.

Yet laterality has some first far more concrete meaning here: it is the deliberate gap between intention and act, or meaning and exemplification, which first keeps the invitation to such mind-wandering attention

---

17 Alessandro Manzoni, *The Betrothed*, New York: Alfred A. Knopf, 1956, 158: "We have to play the same game with our characters."

open. Thus, the sinners in Hell are not punished for the sins we are directed to see in them: the poem avoids these simple-minded correspondences and rather fixes our poetic attention on the distraction itself.

This is the sense in which Farinata's juridical or divine judgment has little or nothing to do with what he is presented to us as embodying: his invulnerable pride and refusal to bend either to argument or to divine punishment, his factionalism as a leader who has led his followers into disastrous triumphs ("another victory like that and we're done for," said Pyrrhus), and who continues to foment civil war and bloody discord after his death. Those would surely, particularly when they characterize the enemy, be material for moral and even theological condemnation—and indeed, we are happier when our narrator (who is otherwise intermittently fearful, obsequious in his pleas to Virgil either for enlightenment or help, or finally unpleasantly righteous and full of a dislikable rigor in his denunciation of the fallen sinners) is at least sufficiently mature to respond to both characters in this Canto with a becomingly polite and yet unyielding opposition ("maybe that art your side forgot"), which is the only truly appropriate one for the protagonist of the lofty poem.

Yet Farinata is not punished for any of that, what our legal system would describe as "incitement to violence" or perhaps "hate crimes" or more quaintly, "sedition"—but rather for a purely theological heresy, namely the Epicurean conviction that there is no life beyond the grave. Now the geography of this level certainly defines the sin for us, by assigning them permanent graves for all eternity in a mirror image of their belief. But the figures themselves ignore this destiny—indeed, it seems possible that it is this very willful disregard of their eternal fate, which constitutes the heresy in the first place (in which case my observation is not exactly disproven but only intensified to a second degree, in a laterality of the very laterality itself). In any case, it is this discrepancy between the ostensible topic of the pedagogical journey and the characters chosen to act it out which institutes some initial allegorical gap, that initial separation between the levels that makes their allegorical reconnection by way of interpretation necessary.

But lateral transversality, and the fate of the fourfold system, also allows us to gain some more concrete sense of the movement from one canticle to the next, and their profound differences, which are not merely stylistic, but which one would also not wish to characterize in any evolutionary one (and not even some biographical heightening of self-consciousness or developing spirituality of the author–protagonist).

What happens, I think, as I have already hinted here and there, is a shifting of the literal level of *Inferno* from that bodily and "kreatürlich" level insisted on by Auerbach to the "moral" or psychic one in *Purgatorio*: this does not mean the abandonment of the other levels but rather their reorganization and rearrangement around a new allegorical center, a new isotopie that solicits commentary and interpretation at the same time that it brings with it its own characteristic system of overtones and undertones, which are distinct from the preceding set. The result, as has been noted by Tambling, is a release of affect (in its new sense as the unnamed and free-floating protean opposite number of the named emotions and the codified sins).

Affect, then, at least in this historical instance, provides a propitious new laboratory for a significant transformation in the content, one that has multiple consequences for the form itself and in particular for the allegorical system. This is the simultaneous grasping of spiritual purgation as what we would call *sublimation*, and the latter's effectuation by way of what would now be identified as aesthetization, aesthetic distance, "derealisation" (Sartre), the transformation into the image, and so on. Sublimation in any case implies that the initial drives (which here inevitably result in sin) are not eliminated but rather transformed and spiritualized: this is not even a changing of the valences, from negative to positive, even though the Christian theological tradition (including Dante himself) is suffused with the idea that all human action is an attraction to the divine (love), which can be deviated and deformed by unworthy terrestrial objects. Rather, here the act has become the image of the act, and an artistic image at that (whether, as in *Purgatorio*'s elaborate decorations, God himself is the artist or simply a human poet or artist—albeit a genius, as Dante likes to insist in his persistent yet not intrusive self-esteem). The mountain of purgatory is a mountain of poets, and if laterality still persists (so it is that Arnaut undergoes purgation for sodomy, but not for his essential poetic talent), it would seem that somehow the process of making is capable of displacing the inevitable (and fatal) pride of the great political leaders onto a fashioning of objects, which thereby frees their makers from it. The same process can be observed for the other sins, in which the very displacements of laterality themselves offer the hope and promise of some eventual "purification": so it is, for example, that Statius, the great example of a soul redeemed virtually before our very eyes, has been in fact expiating the sin of avarice, something astonishingly alien to the character we have just met. But it is that very oddness and pettiness of the official "sin" which allows it to be figuratively purged from our attention and thereby from the reading of the poem itself.

What then of *Paradiso*? I have maintained that theology is essentially a picture thinking which, like Lévi-Strauss's *pensée sauvage*, elaborates its complexities without the aid of abstraction and is able to develop into the most complex forms of intellection (and of quasi-philosophical debate) according to its own autonomy. It touches on the play of categories that are the raw material of philosophical abstraction and no doubt deploys many of them, but in wholly different and sometimes unrecognizable forms and with quite different yet still essentially narrative outcomes.[18] Or at least that is how one is tempted to characterize theological elaboration from the standpoint of a henceforth irretrievably abstract and secular, "philosophical" conceptuality, it being understood that "visual" cannot mean exactly what it does after the differentiation and scientific and aesthetic establishment in modernity of an autonomous (or semi-autonomous) "visual field."

Paradiso is then the locus of such an extraordinary play of figuralities: it remains allegorical in our expanded sense of the word, but its "literal level" has now once again shifted position and has come to redefine itself as what one might today call a self-consciousness of representational language and its dilemmas and antinomies, which stand for the meanings of the other levels as well, the Job-like incomprehensibilities of soul and judgment, of texts, of some ultimate "end of history."

But were one to undertake some fuller exploration of this ultimate canticle (which will not happen here), it would also be crucial to introduce an aesthetic concept I have not yet had occasion to invoke in the present work, namely the idea and the experience of the Sublime, which has its relevance in the upward movement of the poem, as well as in the Kantian premise of an incomprehensible mass and force ("mathematical" and "dynamic" at one and the same time), which one can

---

18 As in the Talmudic distinction between doctrine and illustrative tale, Halakhah and Haggadah (see Preface, note 9).

nonetheless represent by way of its nonrepresentation, and thereby at least poetically "master." The sublime transforms the entire *Commedia* into a single instant, after which it vanishes.

So it is that by a remarkable formal leap over the centuries, Dante's three canticles speak with and against one another by way of modal variations beyond mere style. The very complexity of their transversalities—allegorical entanglings that separate the levels at the same time they fuse their meanings—yields what one may call *modal colorations*—fiery, blued, and blindingly luminous—whose qualitative successions themselves yield the allegorical message.

8
Dramatic: *Faust* and the Messages of Historicism

Faust II has the reputation both of being unperformable and also of being the privileged vehicle for some fundamentally humanist message of the Master, as famously in the verses:

> Wer immer strebend sich bewegt
> Den können wir erlösen.
>
> The striver, the endeavourer, him
> We are able to redeem[1] (249)

Neither of these accomplishments is very attractive for the contemporary reader: the first, precisely because it would seem to impose reading at the same time that it places insuperable visual and performative demands on the reading process; the second, because it turns Goethe into a nineteenth-century Victorian moralist and metaphysician in an age beyond metaphysics and moralizing and follows a practice of (nationalist) interpretation long since itself fallen into disrepute.

Both of these crippling reactions have been dispelled at one stroke by Peter Stein's prodigious staging of both parts of *Faust* in 2000, which must henceforth be included in any reading of the original inasmuch as

---

1   All references to act and page of Insel edition (Köthen, 1956); English translations by David Constantine, *Faust: The Second Part of the Tragedy* (London, 2005).

for most of us it is difficult enough to "stage" a script imaginatively in the mind without dramatic training.[2] Still, this means taking as the literal level of our allegorical analysis a multidimensional phenomenon offering us even more perspectives than the words-and-music of an opera, perspectives which would seem to interrupt the possibilities of allegorical analysis as disruptively as history does sociology or the event does structure (the great inner conflict in a Marxism which alone tried prophetically to do justice to both simultaneously). The absorption in the time of the spectacle crowds out the unwanted and obsessive search for multiple meanings; the medium becomes its own meaning and very much in the spirit of Goethe's satire of academics (of whom Faust was once one) replaces interpretation with performance. But perhaps such a replacement is itself historical and deserves some second-level interpretation in its own right, as we shall see at the conclusion of this chapter. In any case, the two parts of *Faust* seem inconsistent with one another in any number of ways, which are not reconciled by Mephistopheles's initial statement of the program:

> Wir sehn die kleine, dann die grosse Welt.
>
> First the little world, then the great one we'll see.
> (*Faust I*, "Studierzimmer," 187)

The little world or village, and then the great one, the imperial court: a homogeneous milieu and then all the complexities of an already modernizing traditional world and its administration (Vienna and the Holy Roman Empire). *Faust II* will then raise innumerable topics and problems unsuspected in the "little world" of Part I, of the no-longer-aging scholar's love for the country girl: that of paper money in Act I, which, for example, will set in place the great theme of the assignats in the French Revolution, and a pose crucial representational problem for all modern narrative literature, in which money is too impersonal and collective an institution to be

---

2 Thus, Pound used to say that performance is a more powerful vehicle for interpretation than mere literary criticism; and Stein's "interpretation" is recorded on ZDF, 2005, as well as memorialized in a volume of essays and notes: Peter Stein, *Inszeniert Faust*, Koln: Dumont, 2000. I must also thank Franco Moretti for introducing me to the essential critical text, Heinz Schlaffer's *Faust Zweiter Teil*, Stuttgart: Metzler, 1981.

dealt with in its fundamental structure; the theme of science, medicine, and humanism in the episode of the homunculus, where, as in *Frankenstein* or current information technology research, life is notionally invented by human beings; that of political structure in the survival, beyond the Revolution and the Napoleonic era, of the degraded imperial forms of the past (in our day, this problem takes the form of the superstate); finally, that of land tenure and of the commodification of the soil, of individual versus collective ownership, in the final drama of eminent domain and the wresting of land from the sea.

Faust I was to have been a simple, tragic story; *Faust II* is immediately, and in advance, episodic. Thomas Mann thought it marked a return to the schemes and swindles of the historical charlatan and magician, the Faust of the chapbooks (despite Goethe's effort to place their onus on the diabolical partner who brings them into being). The effect was strikingly foretold in a remark by the author himself (in a letter to Schiller dated July 1, 1797): "If only I had a month of peace and quiet to work on it, *Faust* would suddenly, to the admiration and horror of mankind, grow into an enormous family of sponges."[3] And so it did by the last weeks of Goethe's life. There are many reasons for respecting the autonomy of *Faust I*, rather than considering it a mere sponge among the sponges, an opening episode among the many others of what then becomes the central work itself: we will here do so only in the sense in which it embodies a unique historical style—that of what German literary history calls the Sturm und Drang, the youthful revolt of what is also called the "preromantic" generation, as epitomized by the private and fatal alienation of *Werther* and the public and historical uprising of Goethe's *Götz* play. This hopeless rebellion of the last youthful subjects of an "enlightened" Absolutism soon to be shaken and delegitimized in real life by the revolutions in America and in France marks out the historical situation in which, according to the present essay, *Faust* and Goethe himself are to be read. Generational Sturm und Drang is however also the first of a series of distinct historical styles whose allegorical interplay gives the text its unique meaning, in a transition or historical interregnum unparalleled elsewhere.

At the same time, however, *Faust I* can be shown itself to be an allegory, albeit of a wholly different type. In fact, it is a version of the classical

---

3   *Briefe Goethe-Schiller*, Zürich: Artemis, 1949, 371.

eighteenth-century "Gothic" paradigm in which a young woman is threatened, by seduction or outright rape, by a man of higher station or power. The bourgeois reader will scarcely expect this to be anything other than an allegory—political in the largest sense—of class fear and of the threat of another more powerful class, the reigning aristocracy in the period of bourgeois revolution, or of Roman Catholicism and the Spaniards in the English situation: villainy in the form of a Lovelace or a Don Giovanni. Gender is here mobilized politically, against the background of a universal subordination of women, by the deliberate assignment of the victim to a different class from her oppressor; and presumably the fear in question can be a pleasurable one aesthetically, insofar as it emphasizes and makes visible a more general power struggle that has in it the possibility of a happy ending, an overcoming of the oppression, a rescue of the threatened protagonist (as in Beethoven's *Fidelio*): in other words, the frightening threat can also encourage the possibility of a political wish fulfillment, of Hope à la Bloch.

But all of this becomes more ambiguous when the bourgeoisie itself becomes a "rising class" and comes to consciousness of itself as a new subject of history. To be sure, Don Juan (Don Giovanni) can threaten all classes at once, noblewomen as well as peasant girls. But is it conceivable that a young bourgeois could assume the position of the licentious nobleman (the "libertine," in the somewhat archaic language of the day)? In that case, the class allegory tends to turn against itself and to become an exercise in guilt and bad conscience; and this is what happens in the tragic situation of *Faust I*, where the memory of the aristocratic villain is invested in the evil counselor, Mephistopheles, and it is the oppressed bourgeoisie itself that becomes the oppressor of the popular classes, the peasants and the villagers.

In short, this revision of the original cautionary tale is calculated to fascinate a young bourgeois poet tempted by the anticipation of an upward class assimilation, an eventual ennoblement and the conversion to a court culture. For this is exactly what Mephistopheles's travelogue offers him: not so much personal and physical youth as the historical youthfulness of an older social system, with its transparent power structure and its hitherto unimaginable security, its unambiguous roles and satisfactions. Was not Werther precisely the victim of a situation in which, as with the more energetic Wilhelm Meister, only court bureaucracy or bourgeois commerce were available options?

But in that case, *Faust I* and the dalliance with Gretchen are mere trial runs for the more ambitious tour d'horizon of Part II: the playful exercise of a class power and privilege that will have to be more dearly won, more explicitly strategized, than as some simple magical transformation. And when, in the new situation, Faust against all expectations confronts erotic temptation (along with the aesthetic vocation) once again in the person of Helena, he is traumatized, seized by a fit of rage and jealousy and then struck to the ground by the power of an unresolvable contradiction.

This is the sense in which we will read Goethe as the poet of a contradictory absolutism, as the subject of a uniquely transitional historical moment which, like the sun striking the statue of Memnon, releases him into an incomparable literary engagement with all the then imaginable genres.

But *Faust I* will have one more claim on our attention before we confront its enormous, sprawling successor: it stages what has most often been considered a psychological and biographical peculiarity of its author, a characterological flaw, generally downplayed in the celebration of his "genius," namely the propensity to shun engagements, particularly on the affective level; to abandon the love affairs in mid-course when they become too serious, to flee the lovers who grow too attached to him (a propensity easily covered later on—in old age—by that ethical value called "renunciation").

I am not alone in feeling that we would do better to insist on the dilemmas of this guilty practice, particularly inasmuch as it is abundantly underscored by Faust's abandonment of the condemned Gretchen, who will be executed for a pregnancy out of wedlock. It will not do to blame Mephistopheles for this unattractive behavior: we do not find in Faust himself much convincing evidence for expressions of any great guilt or searing remorse. The play (and its sequel) is not interested in the thematics of guilt as such, but rather, in a somewhat different perspective on the matter, in how to escape it. This is Goethe's Nietzschean side, the discovery of the life-giving powers of strong forgetting as a way of consigning guilt, the past, one's own crimes and failures, to oblivion, in that endless resurrection and renewal of primal innocence which is the true ethical message and doctrine of the Faust story. If there is a moral to the tale, it is not exactly the stereotype of that boundless "striving" which constitutes Faust's perpetual renewal and the precondition of that famous dynamism of an alleged modernity which has made this figure into the last of the modern myths. The true moral does not lie in the angelic Gretchen's forgiveness at the end of *Faust II*; it is to be found in that reawakening to the world anew in the play's idyllic beginning: a rebirth from sleep, which has the virtue of the river Lethe in Dante's earthly paradise, namely to wipe away all traces of sin. *Faust* is the story of a genuine ethical and psychological discovery, which we would today no doubt express in terms of trauma and healing, but which is much more simply the power to forget, the energy to be drawn from the consignment of the past to oblivion. This is indeed the very meaning of the fateful wager, not so much a stake and a gamble, but a secret piece of advice: if you hold onto the present, you will never be able to get rid of the past. (I must not hesitate to add that this dynamism, this "magical" power of forgetting the past and thinking only of future projects, is proper not to "modernity" but above all to capitalism itself!)

Nor should we be unmindful of the play of aesthetization here, the (very postmodern) possibilities of derealization offered by the transformation of an event into a spectacle. That jumble of the isotopies that is *Faust II* is admirably described by Richard Alewyn,[4] who warns us to distinguish between the imaginary Helen of Act I conjured by Faust in his role as court magician (and casting a baleful spell of obsession and infatuation on the magician himself) and the "real" Helen in her native habitat of Act III whom some equally "real" Faust, now in knightly guise at the head of a crusader army, advances to conquer. When we add in the past of the *Iliad* in which this same Helena was the stakes and the prize, along with the Greek War of Independence in which Lord Byron (Euphorion) died of fever, we confront a superposition of several time periods that comment on one another.

This is the temporal version of Spenser's spatial overlaps: the Trojan war and its outcomes, the Crusades, the absolutist Imperial world to which Faust lends his services, and finally the altogether contemporary war for Greek independence, all stage a confrontation between East and West, or (if you prefer) Germany and the ancient world, which ends badly. Alewyn usefully points out that nineteenth-century research into archaic Greece, from which the grotesque simulacra of the Classical Walpurgisnacht of Act II derive, push the modern conception of Greek culture further and further in an Asiatic direction; and that the Greece of

---

4 Richard Alewyn, *Probleme und Gestalten: Essays,* Frankfurt: Suhrkamp, 1983.

Byron is still literally part of the Ottoman Empire. We may add that Homer is himself the source of a fateful Western orientalism, insofar as the Trojan War anticipates the struggle between the Greek city-states and the Persian Empire, and the single combat between Menelaus and Paris (in Book Three) mobilizes all the Orientalist stereotypes: Menelaus already ruthless and as brawny as any wrestler; Paris effeminate, cultured, cowardly, and sophisticated (Macauley's stereotypes of Bengal).

So the archetypal centerpiece of *Faust II*, the "marriage of Faust and Helen," is not only the allegory of the rediscovery by European intellectuals of Greece and the East (Goethe's translations of Persian poetry as opposed to Winkelmann's ignorance of anything but Roman copies): it is also associated with an imperialistic venture of Europe into the vast "house of Islam." (France's first incursions into Algeria date from 1827, in the very years in which Goethe was composing *Faust II*.) The death of Euphorion/Byron then signals the failure of this attempted synthesis of West and East and thereby marks yet another withdrawal of Goethe himself from an earlier avatar.

Faust, I have claimed, is the epic of strong forgetfulness, which cleanses Faust of guilt and frees him for further ventures, new selves, new projects, very much in the new capitalist spirit in which the past (and history) is supposed to play no part and the history of accumulation is blotted out in favor, not merely of accumulation of wealth in the present—for that must always be reinvested and increased ceaselessly under pain of stagnation, regression, and loss—but also of perpetual increase. The "make it new" of modernism applies fully as much to capital itself, and the Faustian dynamic, sublimated and glorified in the final scene, governs both, at the same time that it seems mildly chastened by the memory of Gretchen and the ambiguous spirit of an "eternal feminine" that can just as surely mean desire and the Lacanian death wish as it does eventual pardon.

This ambivalence—characteristic of the dialectic in general (as witness Marx's praise of capitalism's dynamism in the *Communist Manifesto* at the same time he is denouncing it)—clearly enough reflects Goethe's ambiguous position between the old world of the absolutist court, with its enlightened despots, and the new world of capitalist production and expansion, even in the domain of letters, where Goethe's attempted conceptualization of "world literature" is at one and the same time imperialistic and commercial (Sanskrit texts alongside literary periodicals and their mass public)—the conquest of Algeria alongside the worldwide fame and publicity of Lord Byron (and of Goethe himself). Nor should it be forgotten that Faust's magic show, from which this whole adventure derived, was but one episode in the conversion of the Imperial Court to the world of simulacra, one organized around the novelty of paper money.

It is a dialectic that is dramatized in the very opening moments of *Faust II*, as Faust awakens to the rising sun of a wholly new existence, after the oblivion of sleep has healed him of the guilt of his previous sin in *Faust I*, the abandonment of the condemned Gretchen. Yet as the elfin chorus promises him the glories and renewed strength of this resurrectional awakening, the rising sun announces itself in a monstrous cacophony of deafening noises: "Welch Getöse bringt das Licht!" (I, 268). How could it be otherwise when the world's alarm clock shatters this peaceful night of healing: Faust will himself reexperience the duality of life in the blinding light of the sun, to which he must turn his back, observing the waterfall and its rainbow dissolving into an appearance in which material reality and mesmerizing image are indistinguishable. The famous line is then ominous at best—"Am farbigen Abglanz haben wir das Leben" ("We have life only in its flung-off colours"; I/270/6)—a conjuring of the simulacrum which will derealize all the events of this play or pageant, from the assignats to the illusions of Greece, from the feints of warfare to the misprisions of the blind billionaire, who takes the agitation of the lemurs for the noises of his construction workers. Already in the first act of *Faust II*, the message is not the medium but rather the form, and as it were the fixed forms and outmoded genres of a rapidly obsolescent traditional world, beginning with the empire itself, whose vacuous ruler cannot even pay the bills accumulated by his own entertainment. Faust, then, remains the magician, as it were, the alchemist, on the brink of a new science (and Mephistopheles its jester): but as magician he remains an artist, the old art of the festival and the great baroque processions, masque, carnival, mummery and dumb shows, *triunfi*, Benjamin's "funereal pageants," all the way back to the mysteries and images of the great Pan. For these are all images, *Schein*, empty show, as their dispersal in fire testifies; and with them Goethe bids farewell to the spectacles of the past, and above all to their forms, which he manipulates with sovereign poetic power—the rhymes and adornments of a spectacle-oriented baroque culture still distantly resonant in Milton's

Comus and the Spanish *Autos sacramentales*; but wearisome for the new bourgeois publics and on the point of disappearing. The bourgeoisie craves history and authenticity, it wants to see the authentic ancient past, awakened to life by a taste for history and the new realism, as in the paintings of David. This is, however, a new and unexpected task for the Faust magician; Mephistopheles tries to explain to him that the dead realities of the heathen pre-Christian world of the Greeks are beyond his powers. History demands some new visionary energies, some new poetic power, for which Faust must descend to the "Mothers" (Act I, 311). Why does this word ("die Mütter") "klingt so wunderlich?" ("sound so strange?"; 54). Why does it induce that "Schauer" (shudder) which is "mankind's best part" (a line that has been unsurprisingly pasted into the "cultural literacy" of popular sayings)? I think it has something to do with the plural, which we so rarely use in any of the modern idioms, each of us having but one of these "mothers," whose generic name or term is virtually a proper name.

We are, then, at one of the crucial paradigm shifts of history or modernity, which only the radical change in styles allows us to identify—a little more than a symptom, and less than a representation, the word *culture* offering little enough of either detail or conceptuality to grasp what was for Goethe both a lived experience and an observed one. To call this a shift from the baroque to romanticism scarcely helps us, either, insofar as Goethe's freeing himself from the absolutist past was achieved at the very moment in which he was personally and professionally becoming ever more deeply integrated into that superannuated past and Weimar's court culture. The critics and historians, the biographers and hagiographs, periodize Goethe's life into several distinct symbolic styles: Sturm und Drang acts out a revolt against late-feudal society (even though it is really a refusal of commerce and bureaucracy): a kind of romantic realism, if you will; a classicism then emerges as yet another repudiation of baroque decoration but whose austerity recalls the styles of the great theater of French absolutism (an affirmation of the promises of enlightened despotism, perhaps). The trip to Italy is staged as a fundamental break with the provincial late-feudal life of this little principality; but it is bridged by unfinished projects in both styles (*Faust, Tasso*). From this perspective, the second *Faust*, with its Renaissance pageants, could strike one as a regression to the older Baroque culture itself, as it seems to Alewyn, who characterizes it as a retreat from the clean separation of the arts from one another and in particular the limitation of theater to the spoken word, with a minimum of mimetic play, along with a withdrawal of art from the social realm[5]

or in other words from the emergence of aesthetic "autonomy."
This cumbersome chronological schematism is useful only insofar as it helps us realize that all these styles are symbolically repudiated here: the *Faust* of the later panoramic work—vaguely analogous to the immense biographical epic of Ibsen's *Peer Gynt*—is very far from the heroism of the Sturm and Drang figures (or even from Werther's desperate gesture); but classicism is also foregrounded as a distinct language within the great reading play by assigning it a separate stylistic enclave— first as a representation of a representation, a play within the play, and then the experimental spectacle of the historic "Marriage" in its own right, its claims to universality reduced to those of some merely cultural option. And for all the excess of baroque decoration and generic mongrelization, the baroque has itself become an object of representation rather than a stylistic practice in its own right: this is already a historicist perspective on the baroque as such, and it is noteworthy that both these foregrounded styles end in catastrophe. In the pageants of Act I, each sequence of the festival so carefully planned by its master of ceremonies ends badly, its allegories disintegrate, its characters begin to infiltrate the neighboring processions, most notably with Plutus, the allegory of gold and greed; the final evocation of the great god Pan ends in conflagration. But the classical drama of the marriage of Faust and Helen also ends badly, with the death of their son, the return of Helena to the underworld, and the withdrawal from the whole experiment of Faust himself (characteristic of Goethe's own frequent and repeated withdrawals and "renunciations") in another therapeutic coma.

This episode is presumably meant to put definitive end to Germany's fascination with Greece, the famous nostalgic "tyranny" of the cult of antiquity: in fact, it is a chapter in the development of the historical novel, the approach to realism through historicity. As in the conclusion of the "Querelle des anciens and des modernes," which is revived here, the abandonment of the classical is not the end but merely the beginning of historicity, analogous to that of Balzac's development of the

---

5   Alewyn, *Probleme und Gestalten*, 278.

Walter Scott historical romance into a new novelistic realism in which social and historical reality itself changes, not from period to period, but from year to year and decade to decade.

Whatever the transcendental conclusion the drama owes itself to stage, the raw exploitation and the land grab of the final act, the blind man's delight at the commotion of the lemurs waiting for his death, which he joyously takes like any slumlord to be the sound of the erection of new buildings and the creation of new value—all this grimly marks the close approach of the centenarian to the unvarnished realities of his own postrevolutionary era. Even the great democratic salute to freedom ("a free people on a free land") "Solch ein Gewimmel mocht ich sehn, Auf freiem Grund mit freiem Volke stehn!" (V, 468) faithfully reproduces its liberal bourgeois illusions.

To be sure, much of *Part II* derives from the tradition of the pageant as it developed in the Italian Renaissance and became a symbolic staple of absolutist court culture (along with opera, which developed alongside it). But there is also another genre, relatively unnamed and unrecognized, which plays its invisible part here, and that is what I call the *reading play*. I'm not referring to the bad or unwieldly imitations of Elizabethan drama that flourished among the Romantic poets, sometimes among the very greatest. Rather, I have here in mind a specific hybrid that attempted to make its way among a literate bourgeois public, in rivalry with the descriptive freedom of the novel (an equally new form), yet longing desperately to retain the immediacy of drama, as though it could magically transform its readership of one into that living audience which the Germans at least, from Lessing to Goethe himself, took as an analogon of the nation as such, "le peuple à venir" (the nation-to-be). Such dramas are not to be characterized as epic either, for they do not really stage heroes as such (and Brecht's much later use of this term in "epic theater" simply means storytelling or narrative drama). More anachronistically and prophetically, the reading play may be said to relate to the development of "special effects" in cinema, which for this older period are wholly beyond the resources of the theater to stage: later on, even Wagner would turn a stubborn denial of these practical impossibilities into a will as it were to summon forth future resources, to influence future stage machinery and technology in this visionary direction (something his heirs will have by now been successful in doing, theatrically drawing on just such "special effects" as modern technology has conjured up for film). Still, there remain the imaginary theaters of the individual writer, in which such fantasy projects continue to be pursued. In the East, the epics of Madan or Mickiewicz emerge, no doubt nourished by an intensifying nationalism, for which the analogy of the theater public with the nation has a more intense resonance than elsewhere; and no doubt the influence of the novel also plays its part in the emergence of a biographical spectacle as grandiose as Ibsen's *Peer Gynt*.

But I am more inclined to think of the follies of Flaubert's early project of a *Saint Anthony*, rewritten three times before his success as a popular novelist gives him the courage and the discipline to distill its final, extraordinary version. And then there is the Nighttown section of *Ulysses*, which no longer seems so exceptional an experiment in the light of what has been developing in the earlier chapters (and what is by now happening all around the lonely author in the heyday of symbolist and expressionist theater).

Still, these remain reading plays, and in them a peculiar thing happens to the visual. The normal transpositions of description are here subverted by the pretext of some hallucinatory immediacy; and even the written emergences and disappearances—for it is always in a strange space of unheard of visual spectacles that figures suddenly arise against their blank background and just as unexpectedly vanish—come laterally across the field of vision of the inner and imaginary eye like hallucinatory images which have their own momentum: the eye does not turn in their direction to observe them, as is the case with more mimetic written description, but submits to their passage from outside the immobilized gaze and across it into another nothingness. This inner eye posited by the reading play does not look (let alone read). It is passed through, and the reading of such works at its most intense approximates a drugged state, a pharmacological trance.

Goethe was of course himself a man of the theater; and in any case *Faust* began life as a dramatic spectacle, however much it already (in the Walpurgisnacht scene above all) strained the limits of its stagecraft. It may well be that *Faust II* set the scene for all those later purely written visionary productions I have mentioned above; but it was also certainly informed by all the practical experience of a craftsman who had staged court pageants fully as much as realistic or poetic stage plays and who no longer cared whether this one could or would be staged in its own

Dramatic: *Faust* and the Messages of Historicism

right. (Nor must we forget the parallel evolution of operatic staging, which had at the same time to rely on a good deal of imaginative indulgence on the part of its audience, repaid by the riches of a different sense organ.) Yet the older Goethe, in his renunciation of classicism, was willing to drift back into the aesthetic abundance of the *Gesamtkunstwerk* of the baroque—without any of its later Wagnerian overtones, to be sure: no delirium here or real intoxication; if sublime there is, it is the chaste sublime of the ascent into heaven, without Wagnerian love-death nor even the transcendence of *Vierzehnheiligen*. On the contrary this "baroque" is the satiric baroque, which may be called the devil's share.

What the pageants show us, in any case, is the persistence of the allegorical in the person of the hermeneut, the interpreter, and tour guide: it is said that in the early days of film, in peasant countries, remote from spectacle and often indeed from literacy itself, the film crew (now projectors and the like, rather than cameras) was accompanied in their tours by an explainer, who stood next to the screen on which the image was projected in order to identify the characters for the peasant audience and separate heroes from villains, so as to keep the public abreast of the moral of the tale itself. Virgil plays this role in Dante, but we sorely miss such a figure in Spenser (its place taken by the poet himself); and perhaps this is why the episodic temporality of the individual, finely wrought stanzas is there to bring us up short against the interpretive problem: each unity more like an emblem, heraldry, a coat of arms, than an unrolling landscape in the spirit of the classical Chinese scroll. In Spenser what remains medieval is the impenetrable forest, a Brocéliande where the hero has no map and wanders lost, sometimes for years, until he makes his fatal encounter. Dante, however, who already had a poetic guide to help him translate his new style into epic narrative, endows his Master with the additional task of explaining the geography, which remains somehow the original, the literal text to be deciphered and holds all the clues to the mysteries, even in heaven.

But in *Faust II* we glimpse the original allegorist: it is the master of ceremonies himself, who explains what he has planned and organized to the court as though it were a natural event and sometimes intervenes and sometimes takes the consequences, remaining as he does an actor within his own pageant: writer, director, and actor, like Goethe himself (or Shakespeare). What is prepared, however, in that lengthy parade calculated to fatigue the reader but not the spectator (when Peter Stein has designed it for him) is the role itself: and that will be taken by Mephistopheles in the second act, the Classical Walpurgisnacht.

Critics have complained that this interesting figure, more fascinating in many ways than Faust himself and beloved of the great actors, retreats significantly in Part II in proportion to Faust's own advance. In Part I, Mephistopheles was an active party to the intrigue and the seduction; here, however, and with abundant complaints, he has had to be charged with the staging and the set design, the behind-the-scenes material arrangements, the tedium of the stagehand. (He has made it clear to Faust that bringing the past back to life is no small thing, even for the devil, and involves a good deal more than a few magic tricks and a flying carpet.)

Yet he has a whole act to himself during Faust's paralysis; and I want to suggest that this long intermediate transition—itself a kind of pageant, drawn from the antique—is also a moment of linguistic transformation as well. Faust was not the only remnant of the Sturm und Drang style and culture: so was Mephistopheles himself. The "two souls that dwelt in one breast" were for Goethe as a wordsmith the language of "passion" (the individual self, love and flight, the anxiety of this transitional period in which the young bourgeois without a role or status finds a place to be invented in the now antiquated court principality); and the language of satire (distaste for late-feudal bureaucracies but also for petty and provincial Bürgertum, a taste for glamorous, sweeping nihilism and the proud youthful stance of refusal and denial). This last is the function of Mephistopheles ("Ich bin der Geist, der stets verneint," I am the spirit that always negates), and it affords a glimpse into creative destruction "der stets das Böse will und stets das Gute schafft" (that always wills evil and always brings forth the good; Part I, 168). Goethe was right: what was distinctive about him was the union of these two impulses, which, taken individually, risk the commonplace of a vacuous poetry of sheer feeling or a tedious whining and complaining about everything. The grand epigrams (which like those of Dante in Italian remain sedimented in the German language like natural formations) are born of the inseparable and unresolvable quarrels and carping at one another of these two functions.

Yet to this style—it has already been bleached and chastened by a Racinian classicism—there now must be added a practice reminiscent of the Greek epigram: the so-called Xenien, the potshots at your critics, little satiric couplets and stanzas that rival the venom and malicious humor of the best of Pope or Swift. But even more than from their classical letter, these verses spring from a less familiar sonorous richness of the German language in their multiple rhyme schemes and their decorative lightness: a dazzling exercise in specifically German wit quite different from the sarcasms of a Nietzsche or a Brecht, even though they sometimes tend proleptically in that direction. Unexpectedly, these begin to pour out of the hitherto lyric poet's language production in a well-nigh terrifying and interminable richness. They make up the more authentically classical dimension of Goethe, but like all those Roman copies Winckelmann took for the experience of their Greek originals, they are so to speak retranslated from the Renaissance and equally mark a kind of historical, if not personal, regression.

Someone must then become the bearer of this new form of stylistic production, and unsurprisingly it is Mephistopheles who proves to be the appropriate choice. He must himself be translated from Sturm und Drang negation to witty Baroque court-commentator and fop, and it is through the long darkness of the Classical Walpurgisnacht that the transformation will be effectuated, as the Northern devil confronts the peculiarities of a Southern archaic mythology that is anything but "edler Einfalt and stille Grösse" (noble simplicity and tranquil grandeur) in Winckelmann's influential phrase. This language will also carry with it the "scientific" commentaries (Vulcanist controversies and the like) to which we will return in a moment: but on the face of it such commentaries belong to the form itself. It is the inner formal destiny of the satire to opine on just such idle scholarly disputes and rancorous self-serving debates. (The appearance of Thales and Anaximander make it clear that if not eternal then they go back at least to the very origins of philosophy in the mists of time.) The animosity of Goethe and Schiller for their critics is nothing if not anti-intellectual and anti-academic. An ancient Greek style and form—the epigrammatic quatrain—is thereby adapted for polemical use in an essentially contemporary transitional state in intellectual life (the Enlightenment transformation of feudal and religious culture, within the sheltering integumen of absolutist court culture): the classical becoming satirical.

The purest form of this recourse to classicism is, however, French classical tragedy, with its Alexandrines and its unities: it, too, serves an essentially therapeutic purpose, in purging the remnants of the Sturm und Drang (which used to be called, in standard intellectual history, "pre-romanticism"). It is with the final full-blown exercise of this third style (after the baroque, and Sturm und Drang) that we arrive in the very heart of *Faust II*, with its most famous episode, the marriage of Faust and Helen, or, according to the standard allegory, of Germany and Greece, unless it is the central figure of the monstrous Phorkyas that is the more probable spawn of the marriage of Northern and Southern dark mythologies, the Christian devil and the classical teratologies.

This encounter puts into question the very concept of a play within a play: its first moment, indeed, is a kind of magical dumb show, in which, for the entertainment of the emperor, Helen of Troy and her lover Paris are called up in a phantasmagoric spectacle, which arouses in its master of ceremonies, the Faust now become a magician, an inexplicable and irrepressible jealousy and rage, a veritable fit (in the Elizabethan sense), in which, mesmerized by the prototype of classical Beauty, he intervenes between the pair and the spectacle disappears in an explosion, leaving Faust paralyzed in a coma. (He will have to be transported in that state to the real historical Greece in which he can alone be cured and awakened.)

But the "real historical Greece" is no longer a play within a play but has become the play itself (even though at its end, the courtly spectators reappear as though it had been one). Biographically, we are told, this final intensely concentrated classical effort, which ends, like so much in Faust, in disaster, may well represent Goethe's judgments on his own earlier classical efforts, above all in *Iphigenia*, and his judgment on them, or better still his renunciation of them. For Helen faces the same fate as Iphigenia, Menelaus having ordered her, on arrival back in Greece after the Trojan War, to prepare the sacrificial knife, which will presumably serve as punishment for the dishonor she has brought on the kingdom and the multitudes of the dead already sacrificed to avenge it. In the austerity of this episode we find all the trappings of the earliest Greek tragedies: a chorus, the two interlocutors, the unity of scene and action, which will culminate in her escape to Faust's "barbarian" camp and her rescue: followed by the onset of some properly Renaissance atmosphere in the Arcadia in which her marriage to Faust consists. But the child, Euphorion, proves too unearthly or unworldly to survive, bounding in the upper air, in partial flights, of which the final one culminates in his death and Helena's return to Hades with the body. Euphorion (already a classical figure, the son of Helen and of Achilles rather than of Faust) represents—for in this episode he is clearly called upon to mean something—grace and beauty, Poetry, ambition, celebrity, and finally (in an intensification of the momentum of these terms and the rising movement aroused by all of them) War, the very source for the ancients of Glory. This is why on another level, according to Goethe himself, here he takes Lord Byron as his contemporary reference, whose apotheosis was reached by his attempt to intervene in the Greek War of Independence and resulted in his death (1824)—perhaps for Goethe the last gasp of the Napoleonic paradigm that dominated the turn of that century and was to be replaced only a year or two later by the return of revolution in 1830.

Apparently then, we have here a fable in which a relatively intelligible moral is drawn and offered to the public: poetry and celebrity (Goethe was after all himself the protype of those, well before Byron), substituting for the praxis of statecraft along with the exercise of military prowess. (War will in fact be the centerpiece of the next act.) And then there is the ephemerality of Arcadia itself and of love and beauty, along with the interesting formal problem: why the devil does not choose this moment—which Faust explicitly beseeches to persist and to arrest the flow of time ("Verweile doch, du bist so schön"; "Bide here, you are so fair!"; Part I, 238)—the very stakes of the initial wager—to seize the pawned soul and drag it down into his own realm: no doubt because the moment destroys itself under its own inner logic and momentum.

But I must follow Adorno here and insist that the "meanings" vehiculated by the work itself are in fact its raw material rather than its artistic significance; and we must claim that if you wish to call this episode an allegory, then one must call *Faust II* itself the allegory of an allegory, for it stages for its viewers, not the failure of ideas and ethical motivations, but that of style itself as a historical symptom. The play diagnoses this style—classicism—as carrying within itself a dialectic of essentially moral or ethical questions, which it cannot immanently resolve, just as the analogous problems Hegel found immanent to Greek tragedy (in the Antigone chapter in the *Phenomenology of Spirit*) could not be resolved either, but only replaced by new problems and new contradictions as History abandoned the moment of the city-state and moved toward the new universal horizon of Rome, of empire and its universal religion.

The outcome here is not that historical one of Hegel; yet the transversal movement of the episode from one war (Homer's Troy) to another potential one (the resurrection and revolt of Greece) demonstrates the intervening Utopian interlude to have been a sham and a delusion, and this return of Faust to antiquity as having revealed only the omnipresence of Persephone, that is to say, of historical oblivion.

The wonderful seven-league boots of the next act are then, as in Hegel, the ineluctable succession of the historical periods, in this case, the medieval—legend and feudal reality all at once. Otherwise, there is something anticlimactic about this fourth act—the civil war in which the ageing emperor, confronted with an "anti-emperor," is saved by Faust (or rather by Mephistopheles) and agrees to grant him (in the general deterioration of his kingdom and his authority) the one last desire he has, a barren strip of beach, an offshore domain, in order, in some grandiose ultimate project, to convert the polders into a fruitful new province, in effect to "magically" create a new world out of the sterile remnants of an already existing Nature.

The fourth Act of *Faust II* is, nonetheless, a necessary link in the "plot" of *Faust II*, Valéry once memorably having observed that what is "necessary" in art is always bad; and here the long bombastic declamatory speeches have their own style, no doubt, that of the rhetorical style of a late absolutist court bureaucracy, so that at best their hollowness can signal the passage of this social formation into historical oblivion. Kenneth Burke used to speak of artistic debates in the 1930s as to whether novels could represent boring people by being boring: here it is the degeneration of language that is perhaps meant to stand for the degeneration of a social formation and the end of that long transitional phase which was Goethe's own life between two worlds. (This was indeed Auerbach's judgement on the Latin of Imperial Rome.)

Nor is the logic of content absent from this formal dilemma, for the act deals with the phenomenon of war, something Goethe himself experienced personally during the revolutionary and Napoleonic periods. But war is not so easy to stage (or to represent generally), and here it must come through offstage descriptions in the classical manner, reports that are not enlivened by our discovery that most of the complexities of the battle scene have been invented as a kind of ruse and illusion by Mephistopheles for his own (and Faust's) purposes. At best what rises to the fore here is that Kantian distinction between phenomenon and noumenon to which Goethe remained attached: the tangible and visible phenomenon through which we can alone sense the presence of that unpresentable Real or Ding an sich. This idealist Kantian dichotomy will paradoxically inspire the "realism" of the play's last act, among the best things Goethe ever wrote, which constitutes some final approach to what one may characterize as a kind of historical realism (without becoming involved in scholastic disputes about the meaning of this term).

Still, the inconsistency of these last two styles—bombast versus the language of political economy—continues to foreground style as such, overleaping much of the nineteenth century's anguished search for a single satisfactory stylistic medium ("le mot juste" being only one of the formulas devised in that long period in which a bourgeois culture seeks to find itself, without realizing that the search is itself a contradiction in terms). We do not need to summarize the events of this final act, in which Faust is unmasked as an unscrupulous land developer, endowed with a veritable mafia prepared brutally to evict all human obstacles to his projects; in which the great bet with the devil—no dwelling on the instant!—is revealed to be the imperative of strong forgetfulness demanded by capitalist accumulation, and Faust's famous "Western" dynamism simply the dynamic of Western capitalism as such, demanding constitutive blindness to self and others. The transcendental irreality of the final assumption into heaven and the rebirth of this unwitting hero of his times amid the souls of the children who were never able to be born, constitutes in its very spirituality, in that strange and simple nature imagery (or *Naturlaut*) commented on by Adorno and others,[6] something like a hypothetical sublime, the formal closure demanded by the bourgeois mind as it vainly seeks a way out of its own condition. It is this very irreality and impossible sublimation that is the Utopian message of the memorable ethereal conclusion—Utopian on account of its very irreality, yet realistic by virtue of the very fact that it exists and perseveres beyond the boundaries of what can be thought.

Goethe's flight from guilt, Faust's insistence on becoming the very symbol of *Tätigkeit* and productivity (that of what will shortly prove to be Western imperial expansion in business and in land), Mephistophelean

---

6 See Theodor W. Adorno, "Zur Schlussszene des Faust," *Noten zu Literatur*, vol. 2, Frankfurt, 1997.

"creative destruction," the bankruptcy of historicism and the aesthetic—all these powerful drives express the courtier's desire to break out of his unresolvable transition and the character's vocation to become that impossible thing, a "myth." They demonstrate that only allegory can accommodate these multiple levels into a single coherent work and image.

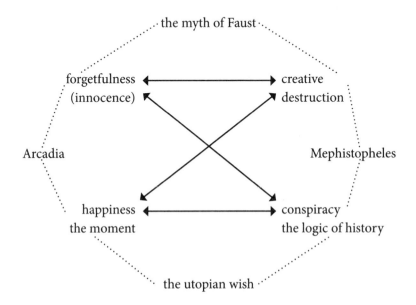

The director does not have to import any Brechtian spirit into these final scenes of *Faust*: it is all there already, sea shanties next to angelic tones, grotesque choruses and like-minded metaphysical outpourings, Mephistopheles as overseer and supreme master alike, and raging legal plaintiff, suddenly in prey to the unaccustomed human sexuality of concupiscence for angelic youth ("Selbst der alte Satansmeister / War von spitzen Pein durchdrungen"; Even the old Satan-Master's heart / Suffered a cruel transfixation; V, 479), the melodramatic ashes of the little hut that contain both the old couple and the nostalgic traveler returning to thank them for their hospitality and cut down with them by Mephistopheles's thugs, the *The Threepenny Opera* mingled with the solemnity of that Heideggerian *Sorge* alone able to penetrate the dwellings of the rich and powerful, and finally the transcendent tones of the unborn children to whom the Pater Seraphicus lends his sense organs so that they may feel the glories of the natural world. One would not say that Goethe was embarrassed, exactly, when he had to explain to Eckermann his choice of a Christian or religious language to convey the inexpressible, but his words do insist that the multiple and incommensurable codes of the traditions must nonetheless be used in order to convey the unrepresentable by way of our inevitable failure to represent.[7] We can therefore privately name this final "ewig-weibliche" (eternal feminine) in whatever language we like, from vitalism to the inextinguishable Lacanian death drive, from sexuality to the life force, from the Spinozan conatus to whatever animal instinct of self-preservation: all are as ideologically and metaphysically tainted as they are indispensable. Even Victorian notions of eternal "striving" are allowed provided they are relativized by an absolute historicism, and their origin in Goethean and Hegelian "Tätigkeit" and Marxian productivism included, as long as we supplement them with the very spirit of capitalism itself. Faust can be reborn and even reincarnated, no doubt, but not as this "mythic" identity, which has been burnt away in a new kind of purgatorial redemption.

Allegory allows all such codes and yet reworks them by way of their juxtaposition and the acknowledgment of their multiplicity. The nature images of the finale, whose very simplicity and undecorative abstraction caused Adorno wonderment, are redeemed by a cunning inversion: for the *Altitudo* of the ecstatic tradition, which we humans traditionally associate with height, with a gazing upward, with the empyrean itself, literally means depth: and we here in these verses gaze down at valleys and rifts, at the downward plunging momentum of the great ancient forests, and the gorges and shafts, the ravines and gulleys of the earthly, as though seen from a great height, the celestial bird's-eye view, the long look from Montaigne's Épicycle of Mercury (the mountains, we remember from Act IV, having been consigned to the upward volcanic momentum of the diabolic at the heart of the earth's core). All of which incites us to add Goethe's scientific (and thought) experiments to our multiplicity of styles and codes: a Spinozan pantheism that we too often rashly pass over as mere literary description (clouds, stars, landscapes). We may include it—along with its debates, volcanic versus Neptunian, and so on—in the moral level, that of subjectivity and its awarenesses and

---

[7] Johann Peter Eckermann, *Gespräche mit Goethe*, Basel: Birkhaüsen, 1945, 475–76, June 6, 1831.

lapses; or, alternately, in the anagogical, in which it can figure the Germanic lands themselves, nestled between the primitive Völkerwanderungen and the modernity of the West and its revolutions—the unspoken unity of Being which is that of a momentous historical transformation, of the suspension of a transitional moment between two ages.

So it is that we may also schematize the levels of *Faust* in more vertical fashion, as the allegory of those changing styles of culture that are the fundamental symptom:

>ANAGOGICAL: Germany, capitalism, Nature
>MORAL: strong forgetting, guilt and innocence
>ALLEGORICAL: style as such, historicism
>LITERAL: the search for bourgeois Myth, the transition from absolutism to the nineteenth century

9

Literary: Allegoresis in Postmodernity

Any work that seeks to restore the claims on us of a long dead genre will at once confront demands for a review of contemporaneity and what it includes (or needs). To be sure, if allegoresis simply stands for the conflict of interpretations, its relevance as a problem today will be a good deal more obvious: but the claim here, that allegoresis can itself be grasped structurally in a way that puts the various interpretations and ideologies in their places, is also insufficient. It should be clear that this is not a program and that I am not calling for a wholesale revival of allegory to solve our representational problems today. Rather, this is a historical claim, one that suggests that meaningful narratives today, in late capitalist globalization, tend to find their fulfillment in structures that call for allegorical interpretation. The newer allegorical structures, however, are not genres and could never evolve into a form of that kind, one comparable to Dante or Spenser, let alone *Le roman de la rose*. Postmodern allegory is comparable, rather, to a one-time event, which even the writers themselves cannot reproduce: a conjunction of factors, a favorable alignment of the stars and the planets not likely to occur again. The genres often play their part in these combinations, but as reminiscence and pastiche of their former selves rather than as living models and paradigms.

As for the secrets of these ephemeral conjunctions, and the causes or preconditions of the obsolescence of the classical allegorical genre (itself never a major or hegemonic form), those all cluster within that complex of developments so often known as modernity and are best studied individually. (I have isolated a few in the preceding chapters.) The disappearance of central or foundational texts that reflect this or that organizational authority is perhaps more symptom than cause; and it is perhaps better explored in terms of the very weakening of centrality itself as a concept and a social fact. As globalization (or the world market, to use Marxist terminology) becomes an existential as well as a systemic reality, one might well wish to approach allegoresis in terms of the three fundamental characteristics that define it: population, reification, and the problem of universals (or that of nominalism, which amounts to the same thing).

But clearly many other extrinsic factors bear on the possibilities of literary form in this period: the construction of subjectivity, in which affect begins to transform named emotions into feelings that challenge language itself; the form of the contradiction as such, whose protean affects disperse the old recognizable ideologies into a host of separate ideational expressions; the deterioration of the literary institution itself under the impact of the media and a culture of informational technology; the dissolution of the so-called central subject into a plurality of subject positions or neo-ethnicities or *tribes*, as they are now sometimes called; and the standardization of that "second nature" of the commodified object world into what are now so often called *simulacra* and the proliferation of images.

In what follows it seems best to follow the consequences of all these developments for the fourfold heuristic scheme of allegorical analysis I have been proposing here. It will then be clearer why this scheme and its four levels do not simply vanish under the impact of modernity, but rather persist in more varied forms and hidden combinations. I have explained above why Felix Guattari's concept of transversality seems useful in naming the dynamics of this transformation, in which the old levels enter on a variety of new and impermanent relationships and complex structural readjustments. These can range from the substitution of this or that level with one another, as when a thematic level momentarily takes the place of a textual one; to the relations of identity and difference among the levels, as when the traditional interpretive identification of moral and anagogical levels gives way to a play between the allegorical key and individual or collective motifs, rather than the classic combination of text and allegorical or mystical sense. These displacements are meanwhile unstable and in contemporary texts in perpetual dissolution and recombination in such a way that durable structures cannot be formed.

All of this is now thematically complicated, insofar as the very concept of a "history," of a central story or narrative line has been culturally dispersed. (The recognizable narrative lines then become quasi-genres, like the bildungsroman, subject themselves to perpetual rewriting, undermining, and replacement.) Analysis by way of content then becomes exceedingly unreliable; and it is rather the form of certain levels that often offers the unexpected clue. Here, too, however, a given form, taken individually and in isolation, is at once open to forces of social or cultural reification, which work to turn it into an object, to retranslate it back into content. This is why binary oppositions are precious dialectical resources and allow us to identify tendencies otherwise imperceptible in the individual texts. The proposition suggested here, for example, is that literature moves toward the nullification of content, something which used to be characterized as reference to the world (or "the referent") but which can now be grasped more precisely in a different way. The great anticipatory aesthetic statement was appropriately enough flung out passionately by Flaubert in one of his most famous letters:

> What I would like to write, what seems to me the most beautiful, is a book about nothing, a book without exterior attachments, which would be held together by the inner force of its style, as the earth without support is held in the air—a book that would have almost no subject, or at least in which the subject would be almost invisible.[1]

This has so often been taken as an expression of the very ideology of art for art's sake that it seems only appropriate to revise its meaning radically by shifting its focus to the function of that ideology, which we may now grasp as an attempt to range artistic production among into the innumerable specializations into which capitalist production itself becomes refined. This is not to deny the Romantic crisis of art, the

---

1 Gustave Flaubert, *Correspondence*, Letter to Louise Colet, January 16, 1852, vol. I, Paris: Pléiade, 1980, 31.

disappearance of feudal (and "cultic") patronage and the panic occasioned by its abandonment to the marketplace, the moment of the emergence of romantic and artistic individuality, if not the very faint dawn of modernism and modernity itself in the realm of art.

To be sure, like all such alibis for existence, art for art's sake can also be taken as a market slogan: the launching, as it were, of a new brand of commodity or the rebranding of something only now beginning to grasp its own existence as a commodity. For in the feudal period, art was a social relation to the patron, or to God, and a gift whose countergift was not yet understood as payment. But of course it is all of those things at once—Utopian and ideological alike, material and spiritual, public and private, exchange value and use value, and so forth. Flaubert, at the very fountainhead of this dilemma for prose and for the novel (Balzac did not understand it quite this way), is here attempting to separate his pure craft—that of the jeweler, according to Barthes—from the industrial producer of a saleable object. (Sainte-Beuve's pronouncement of "industrial literature" is just around the corner.) And so we can also see this in Bourdieusian terms as the production of a certain kind of "distinction," the attempt to create an activity—the contemplation of this not yet nonworldly yet already celestial form of consumption, distinct from the everyday kind—in order to secure, or rather to regain, for its producer a heightened social status, that of the Poet (rather than, say, that of the journalist, the purveyor of feuilletons for the newspaper, which emerges at this very same moment, or later on, the writer of best-sellers), who can now also obtain that different status in the form of the celebrity or the millionaire.

What I want to underscore here is rather the way in which this ideological effort moves us in the direction of a volatilization of content, a moving of the represented material away from its worldly reference. It is a purification process (here still a tendency) that can also be grasped in terms of contingency and necessity. Barthes's famous essay on the reality effect is another appropriate reference,[2] insofar as he identifies the surplus of contingency, the adding in of meaningless details simply because they exist (somewhere else, in reality), in order to certify the "realism" of the literary document. But in fact, "realism" is an

---

2 Roland Barthes, "L'Effet du reel," *Communications,* no. 11, Paris: Seuil, 1968, 84–89.

evanescent effect, which vanishes with each new generation; and each realism which succeeds, competes with, and overcomes the preceding one, now unmasked as mere literature and "fiction." Nominalism is a better category through which to view the matter; for it is the multiplicity of specializations that withdraws their justification—their "necessity"—from each of the social activities in turn. Meanwhile, as the content of "literature" becomes relativized and loses its self-evident significance, its essential reason for being, its status as "die Sache selbst," the desperate search for an adequate replacement proceeds in three distinct directions: new and as yet uncodified or unformulated content (as in naturalism or in new psychic or marginal realms); pure form (as in the symbolisms or the nascent experimental modernisms); or an ideal of purity that is at one with the nothingness evoked by Flaubert's prophetic letter. I suggest that faced with an increasingly stereotypical reality, the serious writer's options become reduced to two antithetical techniques for defamiliarization (the "making strange" of the Russian formalists) which are finally one and the same: minimalism and maximalism. With the gradual exhaustion of the three strategies outlined above, it is at the watershed of World War II that minimalism and maximalism come into their own, not as styles or techniques exactly, but rather as signs and signals, as allegorical messages in their own right.

But this binary opposition should not be understood in any simplistic two-dimensional way: in fact, it should be grasped as an incommensurability, as a tension between two distinct ontologies: the first, the minimalist one, needs to include all the polemics that raged around minimalism in sculpture, as well as in subatomic physics. It is not here a question of the smallest component of the work, such as the sentence or the narrative event; but rather the components of those components, the notes and overtones of a musical phrase, the parts of speech and even their phonemics, the particles and their mysteries and dynamics, which take place below the level of human perception. As for maximalism, its pedigree includes the sublime; witness the stammering enthusiasm of the inventor of the skyscraper (Louis Sullivan):

> what is the chief characteristic of a tall office building? And at once we answer: it is lofty. This loftiness is to the artistic nature its thrilling

aspect . . . It must be tall . . . it must be every inch a proud and soaring thing, rising in sheer exultation . . .³

The binary opposition of the minimal and the maximal can only be productive if it thus unites in a contradictory tension two such radically different realities—subatomic particle and altitudo—in an effort to subsume being as a whole.

The question nonetheless remains, why this particular opposition should offer any privileged key to postmodern aesthetic production, and more specifically why it should be considered in allegorical terms. The second question reopens the matter of allegoresis in an unexpected way: it dramatizes the lack of autonomy of any individual work in a social field now saturated by the aesthetic in general in all its forms. What is allegorical is now that opposition into which the former work necessarily inserts itself as an index of the autonomy of culture as a whole and not the rebellious autonomy of the individual work it enjoyed in the incomplete subsumptions of a nineteenth-century capitalism.

As for minimalism and maximalism as such, they demonstrate the absence at the heart of modern late-capitalist social reality, a hollowness that cannot be the object any longer of mimesis but must now be sought either by the micrological search for the ultimate elements and atomic building blocks of being itself or by the Hegelian bad infinity of a piling on of parts that reaches to the cosmos itself. Both searches are vain, and they mark a profoundly historical opposition that must be read alongside the parallel declarations of simulation and the derealization of the image as yet another variant on our current "peu de realité."

Camus's *L'Étranger*, presumably some kind of minimalist landmark, was written a few years before the war; and monstrosities like *Gravity's Rainbow* and *The Tin Drum* a good deal later (although oddly enough they both hearken back to that same cataclysmic event). In film, the two have seemed to have been combined, interminable movies like those of Bela Tarr or Lav Diaz moving through time with a truly minimalist deliberation in which you can virtually count the ticking of the clock as the moments pass. But if maximalism, or the mega-novel, is to count as

---

3 Quoted in Leonardo Benevolo, *History of Modern Architecture*, Cambridge, MA: MIT Press, 1992, 238.

a mode, length cannot be its constitutive feature. Nineteenth-century serial novels, like those of Dickens or Victor Hugo; twentieth-century French *romans fleuves*, often centering on a family or dynasty but not always (as in Jules Romains's *Hommes de bonne volonté*, which might then send us back to Dos Passos and *USA*); complex scenarios made up of intricate and interwoven plots, as in Doderer's postwar *Dämonen*—all are certainly long enough to qualify but would seem to have little enough in common otherwise will genuine maximalism.

The length of these otherwise heterogeneous products is probably best explored materialistically, by way of the institutions of publishing as such: it is clear enough in the case of serialization that the newspapers play a central role here, while the vogue of the three-decker novel, with its historical origins in class habits and taste, must also be evoked. Today, in the era of airport literature, one can note a decided shift from the two-hundred-page entertainment novel to the more substantial four-hundred-page requirements, a generic reminder that so-called entertainment sells time as such, the time of distraction (the Kindle machines, indeed, tell you how many reading hours you have left in a given text); and this social demand certainly needs to be noted in any assessment of the determinants of mass culture. As for art novels, we may assume that their public consists largely of university students, whose seminars exercise their own subtle shaping power on the aspirations of their authors and publishers: here the sheer length of experimental novels like *House of Leaves* becomes an aggressive challenge and a badge of nonconformism ("because it is there!"), if that urge has not already migrated into video games and invested its residual avant-garde energies in new media.

That there is a properly American genre of the long novel is, however, demonstrable. I believe that it finds its roots and ancestry in the confessional rhetoric of Thomas Wolfe and the more ostentatious "boundless sentences" of Faulkner, a veritable "Nile of language, which here overflows and fructifies the plains of truth."[4] This is not to say that it is from the content of Wolfe or Faulkner that the modern American "long novel" derives. ("All I ever learned from Faulkner," the East German writer Uwe Johnson once told me, "is that you could put pages and pages of a novel into italics.")

---

4 Walter Benjamin on Proust, in *Selected Writings, Volume II*, 237.

Rather, it is the interminable stream of "style indirect libre" which here replaces any classical stream of consciousness as such and allows you to put pages and pages of your main character's "thoughts" into narrative prose. If I credit Joyce Carol Oates with the prize for this sort of production, it does not mean that most of modern American fiction does not indulge in one way or another in this kind of linguistic and narrative "productivity."

I suppose that, in order to achieve some plausible definition of the mega-novel capable of including Wallace and Pynchon but excluding most of these other characteristically American effusions, one would have to be able to insert it into a new generic system, in the sense in which the classical genres of epic, dramatic, and lyric defined each other by a relationship in which the novel, forlorn in its lonely formal isolation, never quite achieved theoretical status.

But with the mega-novel, the system is already given in its name, where maximalism struggles productively with minimalism, each one celebrating its triumphs in relationship to the other. This is to say that you do not have a mega-novel unless it somehow explicitly defines itself against and in dialectical and allegorical relationship with minimalism. It must already have made the contingent fact of its length into a meaningful theme and a constituent part of its content; and it seems to me that this happens primarily in those specific historical moments in which the exemplarity—indeed, the very typicality or normalcy—of the narrator or central protagonist is discredited and in one way or another tainted and rendered suspect. Such is, for example, the case of *The Tin Drum* (1959), where no ordinary German, compromised in advance by the Hitlerian regime, can any longer be accepted as a reliable witness (or even an unreliable one, as far as that goes, in the sense in which the unreliable narrator is designed to be exposed as such and to return us to the conventional value standards of "reliability"). The witness must therefore be a freak, by definition outside of history, where he is relegated by virtue of his arrested growth, his vocal capacity, and indeed his geographical origins (in an anomalous Danzig at the forgotten "Kashubian" margins of the European nation-system).

As for *Midnight's Children* (1981), Kashmir is certainly just such another place of origin as well; along with the problematic status of the New Indian (the first born into an independent nation-state), confronted by the stark alternatives of Hinduism and Islam (and by virtue of uncertain paternity and family affiliation including both), Rushdie's protagonist, saddled with any number of other physical abnormalities, is sufficiently overdetermined to constitute a reliably unreliable witness, in a social and historical situation in which not objectivity but rather the most absolute marginality is required from the outset. Indeed, one may say in general about the increasingly corporatized and institutionalized postwar situation, from which the older forms of individuality, including eccentricities, deviations, and exclusions have disappeared, that only some exceptional and supremely unclassifiable characteristic (even this word is unsatisfactory) can serve as a satisfactory qualification, an unassailably Archimedean point of observation, for narrative registration.

The American situation is to be sure rather different from these traditionally national ones, insofar as the superstate already includes a hodgepodge of state categories and group affiliations: our mega-novels therefore seem to require a greater excess in the matter of either physical or moral norms: Slothrop's abnormality is sufficiently complex as to require an experimental prehistory, which removes it from "nature" altogether, while Hal's talented ordinariness—high school plus tennis genius—both historicizes him as a Holden Caulfield avatar and lifts him altogether out of the seamless drug-and-conspiracy world of his surroundings by way of Wallace's untimely moralism and puritanism. Hal is a historical freak of nature rather than a physical or experimental one. But only by virtue of such virtuoso nonrepresentativity can *Gravity's Rainbow* (1973) and *Infinite Jest* (1996) lift themselves by their own bootstraps out of the conventional category of the merely long (or excessively long) novel and stand as maximalist monuments and challenges to a minimalism they dare to come into being—a challenge mostly acknowledged only by the tired pathos of the short story of the loser, already, unfortunately, a familiar and fully institutionalized American category.

Whatever the fate of such categories, however, it is instructive to examine their origins, and in particular the seemingly privileged position of World War II in the generic changes we have been examining (and not only in those). It is thus instructive to return to that moment in Gilles Deleuze's film books in which the philosopher finds himself obliged to deal with the contingencies of empirical history in order to ground his narrative of the great transitional event, the shift from the movement-image (filmic realism) to the time-image (a new freedom to experiment and play with the older forms in which realistic narrative consisted). Scanning the Platonic Idea of this shift in the real world, he locates the strategic interaction of these two dimensions in Italian neorealism and offers five factors in the transition, factors as historical as they are formal: the dispersion of what had been felt as a unified situation; the weakening of the sensory–motor links or in other words, of the unity of the body as actor or agent; the emergence of the *balade* or the wandering through space as an alternative to action; the increasing sense of the clichés and media images that interpose themselves between us and the world; and finally, the sense that everything has become narrative, that what we took to be a static reality was in fact a conspiracy.[5]

Clearly, these changes, these new features, presuppose a narrative of which they are the consequences (even if Deleuze does not want to call it History). It should be noted, for example, that following a characteristic French version of modern literary history, Deleuze does not distinguish between a modernist and a realist moment, but rather seems to locate the interruption of both with some more decisive break in World War II. Clearly in France, where Proust was a passionate reader of Balzac, and Barthes (no novelist, to be sure) of Zola, the realist and modernist sequences separated in other national cultures were fused together in the moment of Baudelaire and Flaubert; the more global break with that continuity which he posits can therefore not be designated by the term *postmodern* (a break which in other cultures in any case takes place much later, around 1980). Still, even his story could be told differently (in the spirit of his own identification of an increasingly omnipresent narrative consciousness, a consciousness, indeed, of the relativity of narratives). Thus, where he sees a movement from the perceptual to the temporal, it might also be possible to frame the same movement as one from a temporal conception of action and reality to a spatial one. But these are merely different codings, or aspectualities, of the same fundamental break, in a situation where discontinuity has become more fundamental than continuity.

And inasmuch as we are here directed to the postwar period in general, a period Hobsbawm characterizes as involving the most radical

---

5 Gilles Deleuze, *Cinema I*, Minneapolis: University of Minnesota Press, 1983, 279–84.

changes of experience in human history,⁶ it would obviously be possible to narrate that change in a variety of other ways—technological, informational, interactional, and so forth—any one of which, incidentally, could be expected to make an impact on the way we tell the more purely formal or literary–historical narrative that is our focus here. (Nor do we feel it particularly necessary to follow Deleuze's theorization of the results of such changes in terms of what he calls the *time image*.)

Deleuze, however, stages his version under the sign of an organic unity—that of an action—which is in the process of dispersal. This is at one and the same time a unity of the situation and a unity of the agent of action in that situation. (The rather Greek identification of that action with movement as such seems to me to have been forced upon him by the nature of the medium in question, namely film.) Thus, he proposes on the one hand a dispersal of agency, a body gradually fragmenting into its various senses, and thereby enabling sight to emerge as a dominant; the agent losing the sense of a unified action, which weakens into an aimless displacement in space (the *balade*) and becoming a *flâneur*, whose former purpose is gradually undermined by the awareness of the mediation of clichés and stereotypes and the relativity of narrative. Meanwhile, the situation itself, in which agent, action, and setting have hitherto formed a kind of symbiotic unity, disintegrates into an anonymous spatial background, an anyplace,⁷ in a loss of any of the intentions or projects that would have entitled it to have been grasped as a scene or articulated field for actions, let alone a move in that larger intelligible totality we call *history*, or even in the personal strategies of a biographical unity, a career, a life, a romance, an adventure, or whatever other "minor epic forms" (Lukács) are still available in postmodern life.

For Deleuze, it is through the dispersal of all these features that one suddenly glimpses that unnamable and incomprehensible existential reality we call time. But one can imagine other ways of trying to put this collection of features back together, either on the level of the body, in what a Benjamin or a Williams chose to call *experience*, or on the level of space or of a "crisis" situation. These reunifications or "totalizations" are all in some sense choices, but they are no doubt "forced choices,"

---

6 Eric Hobsbawm, *The Age of Extremes: A History of the World, 1919–1991*, New York: Vintage, 1996, 287.
7 A concept he draws from Marc Augé.

based on the availability of whatever raw materials this or that reunification requires.

I suggest that it is the concept of the episode that governs the solutions we have in mind here, offering the possibility of transforming what might otherwise simply be called fragments, parts, the illusions of a lost unity, and so forth, into forms at least aesthetically intelligible. The emergence of the episode constitutes one such possibility, as a dialectical unity of fragment and infinite extension. Still, what one notices above all is that the terms of the form-problem have been modified: quantity now takes precedence over quality, so that even a writer like Günther Grass, as he piles episode upon episode with no clear sense of innate proportions, can still count as a miniaturist, albeit a maximalist one. Meanwhile, *The Tin Drum* is actually radically foreshortened in its post–World War II coverage, as though the contingent date of the writing of the thing governs its breaking off—Salman Rushdie at least gave us a date, the protagonist's age, to work with. As for Oskar, the fact that he reappears in a later book as an aged pornographer only demonstrates that quantity has its own advantages, which are distinct from those of quality.

Quality itself, however, can scarcely be said to disappear altogether; rather, it undergoes the sea change of reification. From being the stylistic spirit of a work as a whole, it becomes a kind of tangible thing in its own right, like a theme or a feature, thereby refashioned in such a way as to serve as an allegorical sign: so that the sequence of qualities or styles, as their variety governs each separate episode, becomes in itself a kind of narrative structure opened up to some properly allegorical investment. Just as a name outfits a reality for reification, so also this reification of styles makes pastiche into a vehicle for meaning. I stress this insofar as some readers have taken my account of the role of pastiche in postmodernism to be a purely negative judgment, something best refuted by an extended digression.

At this point it becomes desirable to furnish the reader with a transitional example, in which what looks like an older plot is subtly refashioned into a montage of qualities, into a series of pastiches that are themselves, unsurprisingly, an allegory of the metamorphosis of named emotions into affects. It is a metamorphosis of events into their own images or simulacra, which can most dramatically be grasped as a superposition of music upon words (recalling the predictions of Nietzsche and Benjamin alike, that tragedy or *Trauerspiel* would find their futures, their sublimations and dissolutions alike, in melos, the very language of affect).

The Threepenny Opera (1928), saluted by Adorno himself of all people as the greatest musical event since Berg's *Wozzek*, is a splendid example of the self-multiplication of the pastiche as such, the pastiche as palimpsest, in which Brecht's text is superimposed on John Gay's eighteenth-century original, while Weill's score is superimposed on Brecht in turn, each layer preserving a distance from the earlier one by way of its relationship to it. The structure is then itself something like a parody of a series of Hegelian *Aufhebungen,* in which the truth of the earlier layer is both canceled and preserved.

Weill's music does more than express the spirit of Brecht's verse; it separates the songs into distinct genres and at the same time reunifies the episodic form of the Brechtian epic drama (avant la lettre) into a quintessentially Weimar "jazz" style. So it is that each musical episode knots drama and melody together in an indissociability of Identity and Difference, which makes for a unique montage of attractions and lifts this work beyond the humdrum generic categories of satire or musical, or of didactic or thesis drama either (the appropriate "lessons" being delivered by Peachum in the form of yet another distinct genre, namely the sermon, reminiscent of James Joyce or Herman Melville or indeed of Abraham a Sancta Clara).

The Threepenny Opera, technically an earlier stage in Brecht's evolution than the full-blown theorizing of so-called epic theater, nonetheless most surely yields its secrets in the domain of acting. For while the named actor's body and recognizable features lend a continuity to his movement through the play, his professional versatility as a performer and player demands that—now in his capacity as "character actor"—he takes on a multiplicity not only of expressions but even of personalities and character types. (It is at these that his stage presence from scene to scene—larvatus prodeo—will point in epic theater, ostentatiously designating them as acting and as *gestus.*)

This is why one always feels a certain malaise in the performance of this music drama, and in particular with the inconsistencies of the character of the protagonist: a malaise swiftly dispatched and swept on beyond itself by the irrepressible and irreversible music. The Gay original constructed a now only too familiar romantic criminal and made a hero out of an antisocial marginal. It is too simple to say that Brecht makes a bourgeois out of this romantic hero without including in this representational reappropriation the whole critique of the bourgeoisie's criminality as well: clearly the motto and ultimate morale of the piece is the grand riddle: What kind of crime is the robbing of a bank compared to the founding of a bank?

But MacHeath is a far more intricate figure when it comes to scene-by-scene performativity. The famous opening ballad offers him as a serial killer, the bogeyman of domestic nightmare, a highwayman no longer of the open road and long-distance coach travel but rather of the lower depths of the big city, indeed the quintessentially imperial metropolis. But this is not the MacHeath we see on stage. He first comes before us as the house-proud groom of an improvised bourgeois wedding and a chief among the band of henchmen, furnishing the borrowed theater of his festivities with all the best in stolen bourgeois luxuries. But with the arrival of his old army comrade the Chief of Police, he acquires a past, revealed as the imperial warrior and colonial occupier, mercilessly mowing down all the "new races" he meets in his path: shades of Brecht's great model Kipling! But now the plot shifts: he has made the mistake of stealing his new bride from a great family—an aristocracy of organized crime, that is, namely the Peachums, bosses of an elaborate mafia of beggars (or of a kind of corrupt labor union, if you prefer)—he, MacHeath, little more than a petty crook with a few insignificant robberies to his name! So our protagonist is now precipitated into the altogether different plot of the young commoner daring to elope with an heiress. But each of these distinct generic paradigms is conveyed by way of a parody of itself: the aura it leaves behind is not the emotion itself but rather the latter's memory.

We should be in our right to expect a drama of flight and persecution: but no, it is yet another and different MacHeath, a bourgeois rentier secure in his habits, who, despite the peril, repairs, as is his wont every Thursday, to the whorehouse where he is a valued and familiar patron and lovingly catered to, the routine and domestic comfort being strangely doubled and overshadowed by the persona of the sex addict ominously evoked by Mrs. Peachum's immortal "Ballad of Sexual Dependency."

Now, however, a new layer of the past is revealed, to demonstrate how useful this character is for bearing different kinds of unrelated content in turn (a veritable "montage of attractions" as it were): for at this point Mac and his favorite doxy indulge in nostalgia and reminisce lyrically over that idyllic past in which the great MacHeath was little more than her pimp and lived together in a rather different kind of domestic comfort, where "I was the bodyguard and she the breadwinner": those were the days, now sadly long gone. Yet in the spirit of this aesthetic of radical discontinuity and the episodic, suddenly another note breaks through, the sublimest music of true love, which for an instant lifts these two sorry figures and their asinine words into eternity:

> Die Liebe dauert, oder dauert nicht,
> In dem oder jenem Ort.

(The words foreshadow the great romantic "song of the cranes" from *Mahagonny*.)

We may pause for a moment to reflect formally on this sequence, which must in no case be psychologized. If allegory there be here, it is not that of the postmodern multiplicity of subject positions, nor even the thematics of multiple identities, as when Peter Stein uses two different actors to embody two different aspects of Goethe's Mephistopheles, the one wallowing in Faust's own desires and projects, the other coldly manipulating them with a view toward the downfall.

Nor does it really act out the profound and constructivist message of Brecht's preceding play, *Mann ist Mann*, which demonstrated on stage the experimental possibility of taking any human being apart and reconstructing him, in this case turning the mild native fish-peddler Galy Gay into a bloodthirsty vehicle of British imperialism. *Mann ist Mann* argued the postmodern case against personal identity avant la lettre; here, however, I think the lesson serves as the precondition for a different kind of demonstration, the experimental deconstruction of the representations of action and experience as such, and the reduction of the reality of "real feeling" and its genres into the sheer images that are their simulacra and their affects. A row of distinct MacHeaths here conjures up an agent's handbook of great character-actors.

And so on to the predictable ideological climaxes of this bourgeois entertainment. On the one hand, existentialism: the ultimate Mac will then be the sweaty inhabitant of the death cell, whose anguish is so vividly expressed in Villon's terrible ballad, altered only by the characteristic Brechtian exception, the omission from this plea for mercy of the police, whose faces he earnestly prays to have battered in by iron hammers.

But the homo duplex of capitalist civilization is able to think two distinct and antithetical prognoses simultaneously; and at the same time as the individual fear and trembling of the death anxiety, there springs eternal the joyous and life-enhancing energies of the happy end: MacHeath is spared by the "messenger on horseback" bearing the King's pardon, and everyone lives happily ever after, the characters of this particular plot subsequently reunited in the vaster and more profitable conspiracies of *The Threepenny Novel*.

So it is that Brecht succeeds in his contradictory venture. His great watchword was "Erst kommt das Fressen, dann kommt die Moral!" Hold the sermons until we have enough to eat! Only his own sermon (this moral itself!) is smuggled into the autonomous work by way of Peachum and his own hypocrisy, which is less a psychological trait than a structural feature of bourgeois capitalism, the sermon delivered by way of the parody of a sermon.

Formally at any rate, we may here salute the emergence (the reemergence from ancient literary practice, perhaps one should say) of the episode, as the synthesis between maximalism and minimalism: the smallest analytical unit, which can nonetheless be multiplied indefinitely in a kind of aesthetic version of Hegel's bad infinity, pointing toward an imaginary totality in the same way that the minimal solution designated an imaginary nothingness as its end term.

The philosophical problem that poses seemingly intractable problems for an interpretation of this kind is the triangular relationship between episodism, allegory, and affect. Each of these poles works against the others and speaks against any coherent theoretical and historical combination of the three. The tendency toward episodic fragmentation, in either minimal or maximal mode, would seem to undercut any reading that seeks an intelligible sequence or series in the work in question: allegory is to be sure a unique and second-degree kind of sequence, in which the unity of the work's moments is secured by a seemingly external structure, a narrative form like that of the journey, or some more abstract notion like that of redemption. On the side of the episode, then, it is always a question to what degree it can be ranged under such a more unified organizational structure without forfeiting its autonomy.

But from the perspective of affect, it is the identification of the episodes as components of any kind of identifiable whole that is called into question. The historical emergence of affect, as well as its conceptualization as a phenomenon in its own right, had as its driving force the resistance to and negation of those very abstractions and their names, designations in which the named emotions were perceived as substances and which allowed them to be organized into systems of various kinds. Affect then acts as a kind of nominalism in opposition to the universals of the named emotions, and any attempt, however vague and general, to distinguish the various affects with a view toward arranging them in a sequence (positive–negative, tragic–triumphant, calm–agitated, bored–manic) compromises the existential uniqueness of the unnameable experience and stands in contradiction with the very spirit of the new feeling, itself the motor force in the reduction of a general action into so many unique and incomparable moments. In this sense, the presence of affect can only be identified as such by way of the opposition to the traditional named emotion it undermines; and is thus itself intelligible only as an allegorical phenomenon, a pole of a merely symbolic opposition.

These philosophical dilemmas (or contradictions) explain why there can never be a truly coherent and satisfying structural account of the new affective allegory, but only unique realizations that are unclassifiable and come into being as the result of a contingent conjunction of features, unrepeatable and incapable of generic classification. The works that thus come into being can at best derive momentum from the memory of genre, from pastiche, and not from any preexisting form. Their content becomes the simulacrum of content rather than any objective social reality. Here, for example, it is the association of class and history—a raw and undeveloped bourgeoisie, a unique political conjuncture—which meet in the cultural stereotype of "Weimar" and lend *The Threepenny Opera* its ephemeral unity as a picture-book of stereotypical scenes and situations from the "life" of this period, guaranteed by the allusive of this eighteenth-century prototype (just as *Ulysses* is legitimized by its *Odyssey* parallel), which supplies all the working unity the play requires.

♦

Thus, minimalism and maximalism can be seen to work two sides of the same street, dutifully knocking on the doors of formal and material possibility: it is probably on the poetic level of words and syntax that they become more starkly irreconcilable, the isolated syllables of a Celan or an Ungaretti contrasting sharply with the deeply held breaths of the pseudosentences of an Ashbery or a Prynne, with their delight in syntax for its own sake, producing innumerable montages of incoherent messages and pastiches of speech. Silence has been something of a fetish in contemporary discussions (the equivalent of "death" in humanist criticism?), but the idea of silence is most often a pretentious theme and as it were a mere Barthesian sign of the theoretical and the literary-critical; the reification of language would seem to offer a more productive clue for further exploration.

At any rate this particular dialectical opposition between the minute and the interminable offers at least one possibility for allegorical analysis in the postmodern age, where the belief in the literal level, or indeed any form of literality, truth, reality, empirical existence, and the like is subject to the variety of corrosive doubts expressed in Deleuze's factors, which at once set in to undermine and "disperse" its certainties, rendering the term *fictional*, among other things, derisive and inoperative.

In that spirit, let me examine a novelistic contradiction that has less often been taken as seriously as it deserves: I mean the incommensurability of the individual sentence and the overall plot. The former is supposed to be the execution of the latter, as the shooting of an episode might realize the indications of the storyboard, or the performance of a play its text or scenario; but I think that this particular opposition has deeper philosophical consequences and implications. One might restage it as the gap between the perceptually empirical and the ideal totality, if it is a question of hermeneutics; and I think that this is also the case, and that the antinomies of reading are only one example of the disintegration of simple traditional realism today and probably of the opposition between materialism and idealism as well—none of them any longer offering any clear-cut ideological alternative in a historical situation in which they have come to be understood as the linked dialectical opposites of a single ideological dilemma in its own right. Indeed, we might return this omnipresent duality to its place in the political as such, and recode or re-identify it as the incommensurability of daily life—the existential experience of the individual subject—and the immense invisible totalities of the capitalist world system, the network of finances or of informational mechanisms, of military alliances or even warring partners that depend on one another to keep military investment going, to perpetuate the competitions which are themselves the very logic of a unified system (which is to say, a contradiction in terms). The political form such incommensurabilities have taken is always the attempt to coordinate a local social issue, with its own recognizable cast of characters, of heroes, allies, villains, and the like, and the ideological stakes of some global anti-capitalist or pro-American strategy as it gets fought out on other levels, sometimes with an altogether different and incompatible set of personnel.

At any rate it is something more than a matter of mere attention or concentration when one reads the individual sentences each one for its own sake, or on the other hand, uses them as stepping stones, as rapidly as possible, to come to the narrative payoff, like Eliza crossing the ice. I have often used the example of Flaubert and how reading speed determines the very nature of the object to which his name is attached: at one rhythm offering the very prototype of a modern realism, at another the appreciation of a multiply savorous nascent modernism, and at its slowest pace that postmodernity Sartre discerned when he spoke of the immense gaps between each sentence (those fateful silences again!).

But Kafka will be an even more relevant example here, in a context in which it is time to assess the ideological import of the minimalist–maximalist tension. For what a standard realist reading of *The Trial* or *The Castle* identifies as this or that form of the suffocating or existential nightmare, a far slower attention to the sentences themselves reveals, not only to be Kafka's Chaplinesque humor (something only Thomas Mann was willing publicly to acknowledge), but also a line of hyperlogical ratiocination in which alternative narrative possibilities are weighed and tried out in succession (a stylistic peculiarity I have analyzed elsewhere)[8]: a hyperrationality utterly at odds with the oneiric progression of events at the narrative-realist level.

On this choice the profoundly allegorical nature of Kafka's novels depends. Everyone knows the conventional "conflict of interpretations" in which Kafka commentary has been immobilized virtually from the first discovery of his works. This conflict opposes interpretations of a

---

8 See *The Modernist Papers*, London: Verso, 2016.

religious bent—the rulers of *The Castle*, the supreme instance of the tribunal in *The Trial*, as figures of the unknowable divine—to politico-historical fans who see these fables, the one urban, the other rural, as a commentary on the bureaucracy of the Austro-Hungarian Empire. Or, if you should wish to amalgamate both of these views to some more generalized sense of oppression and faceless domination, there remains the individual or existential reading, in which they express the angst of the human condition or even the neuroses of the individual Kafka himself (tubercular like Albert Camus), living his life out as a bureaucrat (he worked for the state insurance company) under a death sentence.

All of these "interpretations"—and I hasten to add that they are not arbitrary but rather that the text solicits all of them and that we cannot not interpret it globally and figuratively in any single interpretive code—are to be ranged on the final levels of our allegorical system: clearly enough the traditional ones fall into the categories of the "moral" or individual, or else the "anagogical" or collective, levels. They are in other words secondary projections of the first two levels, which designate the text and its allegorical key, respectively.

No doubt there is some sense that these works of Kafka, along with any number of the canonized texts of modern literature, are for us in some sense "sacred texts." Their literary evaluations (as "great works" or masterpieces) is only the crudest symptom of our deeper feeling that they somehow remain privileged expressions of a modern reality that would be radically impoverished if we lost them as formal testimonies, as precious fever charts, of a disease as yet unidentifiable (let alone curable).

But what is the textual level of such sacred texts? And what can be the allegorical key of texts produced in a secular society, which can know only the most arbitrarily imposed ideological consensus? I suggest that it is precisely the opposition between the minimal and the maximal that can provide a way of disambiguating these seeming undecidables. The literal level will vary depending on whether you assign to it the individual sentences themselves (the minimalist dimension) or the narrative as such (the maximalist version). At that point the other alternative will become the allegorical key to the literal choice; and the edifice of your system will evolve either into the politico–existential duality I have sketched out above, or into the literary history of the form problems posed to modernism by a secular raw material as such and the problems of the contradictions of capitalism. I would like, therefore, to suggest that the first of these alternatives—the seemingly more historical and biographical one—is in reality a humanist construction of an idealist type, not terribly different from the interpretive structure demanded by Camus's *The Plague*: a secretly tripartite one, owing to the subsumption of both moral and anagogical levels into this or that version of the so-called human condition. That it is the second, seemingly formalist and formalizing alternative that is the truly "materialist" or "scientific" or at least concretely political one I obviously enough believe; but it will be enough if their differences have been convincingly articulated.

This has so far been as it were a vertical analysis of the present-day practice of interpretation, whose allegorical structure is meant to confront secular relativism only in the sense in which it allows us to dismiss sham ideological conflicts as so many dialectically related oppositions and to replace interpretive decisions in the concrete space of genuine political choice. In this sense, the analysis need not be limited to literary objects but holds for a wide range of issues and realities in the social sphere in general.

But I have not yet dealt with the more specific and contemporary issue of postmodern interpretation, where the seemingly postideological mood of cynical reason and radical depoliticization encourages the conclusion that interpretation is no longer possible, or that it is no longer desirable, or, finally, that it is so democratically widespread as to be utterly devalued and in the long run politically worthless. Let the text be its own interpretation, runs this conclusion in areas where texts still exist and are read; and this is precisely my position here, namely that we do not impose allegorical interpretations on texts but that they rather today tend to allegorize themselves.

How to form a narrative out of a sequence of qualities or affects? I have already alluded to the golden idea of Schoenberg's *Klangfarbenmelodie*. But other musical analogies are available if we want to use them. There is Sibelius's enigmatic Seventh Symphony, for example, with which he deliberately terminated his career and spent the last thirty years of his life in a (perhaps none too symbolic) compositional silence. Its single movement assembles whole blocks of separate thematic developments, any one of which might have been unfolded into a whole sonata-type "development," but which are here foreshortened, tantalizingly incomplete and unsatisfying, following each other like waves of the sea, each one of them leaving luminous debris and gleaming froth behind them to be projected into future riptides to which they are alien, an incomprehensible momentum promising climaxes and returns on which it never delivers, arising to some fever pitch of an undiagnosed restless malaise only to be broken off by an inconclusive ending, a mere stopping point, as if, like Nielsen's analogous *Inextinguishable* (his Fourth Symphony), it were a mere drought of the sea, drawn up at random and then poured back again.

But it may be better to come at all this more analytically, by way of number and its seemingly rational properties. Indeed, I have often been asked whether it is not some numerological obsession that drives me to frequent use of two distinct fourfold systems that seem to have no relationship with one another: the Greimas square and the present fourfold system of levels. There is an answer to this, and it has to do with two shifts in postmodernity that seem to me both interesting and fundamental: difference and spatiality.

The latter has to do with visual schemata and what Deleuze calls "diagrammatism," something abundantly visible in structuralist (or French) thinkers and a good deal less common in dialectical (or German) ones. I see this tendency as part and parcel of the replacement of a preoccupation with and experience of temporality in modernism proper by a wholesale spatialization of which "writing" is only one version. It has to do with a supersession of synchrony over diachrony, a development Fernand Braudel explained by the enormous proliferation of specialized theories and disciplines, which turn the search for a simple linear cause, a simple linear narrative of causality, into a conjuncture or meeting place of multiple "factors" (including the temporal ones) in an atemporal present of thinking[9]: at that point, then, the relationship of the factors to each other needs to be visualized and not surcharged in time, where, as in Chinese "black letter" characters, they become illegible. Space then becomes a kind of multitude of synonymies, ambiguously translatable or substitutable, which one has to articulate and which form the hinges of the Greimassian rectangle, the mediators that enable passages from one logical context or relationship to a different one and

---

9 Fernand Braudel, *On History*, trans. Sarah Matthews, Chicago: University of Chicago Press, 1982.

thereby bring a whole system into emergence and legibility. Much more could clearly be said about this kind of diagrammatic practice that prospers in theory, but to which an old-fashioned philosophy prefers the logical argument or reasoning, the propositional steps in time.

This does not yet, however, account for the emergent primacy of difference over identity in the postwar years; for that we need to go back to Hegel and that crucial moment in the dialectic in which identity gives way to difference and difference turns out to be identity scarcely disguised (identity defining itself by what it is not, differences requiring a certain identity to be more than mere distinctions, oppositions and contradictions being the next steps, and finally the return to ground).[10] The problem with the fourfold levels lies just there: they are correlations of difference, which seem to offer thinking only the most mechanical and arbitrary mediations from level to level: visual parallelisms which scarcely speak for themselves or make their own case.

Returning to the polemics that still swirl around the difference between the symbol and allegory—but which return strengthened by the prestige of metaphor as the inner logic of the symbol—one notes that it rests on purely psychological arguments (arguments, in other words, which somehow presuppose a human nature as their basis), and that their persuasiveness is dependent on a logic of similarity: metaphor is, indeed, a temporal act of identification where difference turns out to be similarity.

Allegory, however, turns initially on difference; and the Greimas square, as a bundle of distinct negations, is an apt vehicle for its analysis. For it is the garish differences between the very modes of the levels—subjectivity or collectivity, narrative and ideology—which then turns into an exploration of their more secret identities and affiliations. Allegory is a scan, mobilized by a search for differences and negations; while metaphor is a flash grenade that blinds you for an instant out of time. In metaphor you go no further; whereas an allegorical bent follows each identification on to the next level of its difference, and, as in the Greimas square, the difference of its difference; its narrative is that of differential consequences, and transversality scrambles the levels of those, leaving us in unexpected places, and in particular in that missing

---

10   See in particular the chapter on "the determinations of reflection" in *The Greater Logic*.

fourth place, the negation of the negation, of which I have spoken elsewhere (see Appendix A).

But the square, and allegory in general, depend on another principle altogether different from the rather visual one of similarity—that of undisambiguated synonymity, a place in which the multiple words throng like so many shadows or souls of the dead, their differences elbowing each other and seeking possession of the central signifier (which does not have to be a word, but of which words are the easiest versions). Movement then, like ritual possession, takes place within the multiple personalities of the signifier itself and articulates its capacity to annex radically different contexts. Far from the empty signifier of Laclau and Mouffe, this is a vessel of excess, its associations pouring out in all directions, which allegorical structure is there to organize and to channel. This is what Benjamin called "the violence of the dialectical movement within the allegorical depths"; it is the logic of multiple publics, in which each group, from preteens to genders, takes something away for itself. I would use the word *universality* if it did not simultaneously carry with it the twin overtones of stuffiness and stigma: but surely universality is allegorical and not just some univocal pronouncement. Yet the final word of allegory is political in any case, with the reassertion of the demands of collectivity in its ultimate, anagogical, instance.

Still, these two diagrams seem to have little in common and to have been constructed for utterly different purposes, which a visual combination will hardly suffice to reconcile. I think we must here adjust the Greimas square to a different kind of negation, which I will call *aesthetic* or *generic*. What one term denies of the other—whether absolutely or in some very specifically antagonistic and antithetical way—is not its logical meaning, but rather its generic consonance. We may evoke that fine and strong word *incommensurability* here, for it is rather the unrelatability of wholly different dimensions to one another that is affirmed. But this very unrelatability itself creates a new kind of coherence, one that I have tried to express with the slogan, "Difference relates!" It is this teasing out of the radical inconsistency which creates a new relationship, as when we affirm the incommensurability of a biblical chronicle of events having to do with the Hebrew people with the biographical and hagiographic genre of the life of Jesus. One must avoid drawing artificial similarities here to that of Moses, the revolutionary protagonist of the first narrative; that would be another kind of fulfillment allegory. Here what is essential is that collective history and an individual life, even one of supernatural properties, have nothing formally in common with one another and that it is this very radical difference that makes their intersection here so piquant.

Negation thus here designates what distinguishes the levels from one another qualitatively rather than logically, what causes a shift in the reading process and foregrounds an attention to the multiply generic rather than to the content and its coherence. Thus, the historical chronicle of the destiny of the Hebrews is quite different in its allure and categorical reception than the hagiographic biography of a local faith healer and his disciples; but at the same time the chronicle has little enough to do with inner life and the states of the soul. Yet the life of Jesus also has a generic opposite: it is the fate of mankind as a whole, the last judgment as a concealed fourth place. This is then the sense in which the four levels are sharply enough distinguished from one another in quality for their interpretive and allegorical reunion and superposition to form a complex stamp or surcharge, a world-historical statement:

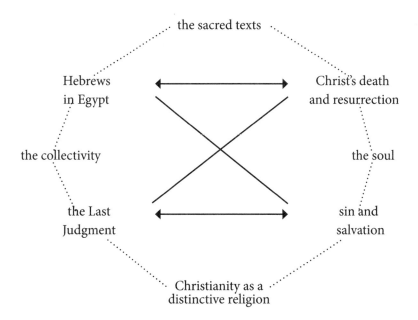

A longevity (owed as much to late capitalist pharmacology as to Shavian will power and the life force?), which ought to have made me a more receptive registering apparatus for the historical than those with less exposure, has on the contrary begun increasingly to convince me of the phenomenological, the experiential relevance of Althusser's famous sentence, "The lonely moment of the last instance never comes." It is traditionally read as the evocation of a kind of raw epiphany in which production and the base would suddenly open up before us as before an abyss. I now think it means that we never have any direct or immediate experience of History, and that the moments in which it seems nearest or most dramatic—that moment in a Viennese hotel in 1956 when a child, peeking around a column timidly asked me, "Magyar?"; or when in June 1959 I passed among bearded men in the Havana airport and failed to find the Revolution in the crowds of its downtown streets and shops—reduce themselves to empirical detail, their objectivity quickly swallowed up in the subjective and assimilated to autobiographical anecdote. Memory doesn't exist. Later on, of course, society at large will know this confiscation of the real by means of an overdeveloping media, only too ready and willing to turn even that glimpse of History into an image and drawing us all with it into what we learned was the simulacrum (or the society of the spectacle). Change—what Baudelaire famously regretted in Haussmann's (truly historical) rebuilding of Paris—slowly turns into the memory of nostalgia films about the 1950s and the detestable Eisenhower era, now as alien to us as the habits and customs of the ancient Greeks, or of Weimar, themselves also, however, safely out of reach in the sheltering arms of cliché and stereotype. The youthful Marx, so touchingly portrayed in Raoul Peck's admirable film, turns out to be a genre portrait from the old-fashioned storytelling of historicist novels and Hollywood biopics: you are there! A shout in the street! Panicky crowds fleeing the police in the distance, across a deserted avenue!

It is a situation in which no scrutiny of the famous "trace"—of the potsherds or of those surviving buildings Edward Yang searched for in his film of a still Japanese Taipei, the "monuments" so many people wanted to build (and then theorize!) to commemorate a past they could no longer find anywhere—none of these desperate measures and searches ended up detecting the carbon dating or the faint atomic signature of historical radiation anywhere.

This is, I will claim, a crisis of symptomatology: and I conclude, at least for myself, that the only adequate symptoms are to be found in the surviving works of art the past has left behind it. But not in their content: in the forms themselves and their slow mutation, emergence, or decay, a process in which their approach to the Real or retreat from it requires us to come to terms with representation as reality and to adjust such unwieldy apparatuses as the one I proposed here to detect the significance of its inevitable failures.

I conclude with two novels that exemplify the internal process of allegorization within postmodernity and which do so on the alternate yet complementary modes of maximalism and minimalism by way of generic signals and pastiche. I wish to avoid calling them postmodern novels, as this adjective has currently taken on a more specific and generic meaning today (just as "postmodern" philosophy has come to designate a distinctive new cynical and relativistic philosophy in its own right, quite different from theories which address and respond in their various ways to the historical situation of postmodernity). I understand the *postmodern novel* as naming a specific type of avant-garde or experimental book that designates itself and its own process of production and has as its content a play of narrativities not terribly distinct from the "relativisms" allegedly affirmed in so-called post-modern philosophy, and stemming, according to the latter's critics, from the omission of categories of truth, or in the case of the novel, of the fictional. These specific genres (of novelistic or philosophical discourse) themselves claim the ideological positions associated with the modifications of reality associated with a new universe of global media: they are aesthetic manifestos or philosophical ethics or ethical programs in their own right and can therefore be considered as ideologies.

The novels I have in mind, however, are not merely symptoms of postmodernity, they are also instruments designed to explore this unparalleled new universe of late capitalism; and as such they constitute one-time experiments, uniquely constructed laboratory situations, which cannot be replicated in their author's work, nor can they serve as paradigms for the formation of new genres.

I have characterized the revival of extinct traditional forms in the postmodern as a practice of pastiche; and have tried to show how that practice echoes and in many ways replicates the preoccupation with a relativity of multiple narratives in so-called postmodern philosophy. But in my first illustration, the novel *Cloud Atlas* by David Mitchell,[11] this transformation of older narrative forms into a pastiche of their former selves, this practice of a kind of foregrounding of style in such a way that it is itself an object of representation, becomes itself a content and a formal reflexivity: the six episodes that make up this work are indeed imitations of six distinct styles, six distinct historical genres, thereby transforming the novel of which they are constituent parts into a new kind of metanovel whose narrative is the sequence of the genres and styles themselves, rather than a playful and nonbinding work within any one of them (as when, for example, a contemporary film imitates classical film noir canons, or a novel pretends to offer the satisfactions of a latter-day bildungsroman).

It may seem paradoxical to classify what nowadays seems a relatively short book of some three or four hundred pages as an exercise in maximalism, when the foundational works in that tendency offer a dialectical shift from quality to quantity and confront us with the well-nigh indecent demands made on our attention by thousand-page-long "baggy monsters" (as Henry James rather unreasonably described the Russian masterpieces of his era).

But *Cloud Atlas* offers us, after all, a journey that begins on sailing ships virtually redolent of the era of Captain Cook and takes us forward to an unimaginably distant future populated by dystopias and postapocalyptic tribal villages in a time span which it might have taken a James Michener thousands of pages to navigate, and compared to which the relatively restricted chronologies of *Infinite Jest* or even the biographical dimensions of *The Tin Drum* or *Midnight's Children* pale in comparison. Meanwhile, it will be noted that all of these last and more properly maximalist works are unified (if that is the right word) by genealogy and can still claim to be mutant reversions to the older family novel. This is, to be sure, precluded by the deployment in *Cloud Atlas* of breaks rather than continuities as the narrative medium of historical time and change; and its eschewal of the invention of a single bombastic

---

11 *Cloud Atlas*, New York: Random House, 2004. I have discussed this work as a historical novel in *The Antinomies of Realism*, London: Verso, 2015. I should add that one of the peculiarities of the text lies in the differences between the US and the UK editions, the former, on which I have relied here, being an earlier version than the latter.

style production in favor of a curatorial juxtaposition of various period styles and forms in succession.

These may now be enumerated, passing from the initial travel diary or log to the fin-de-siècle epistolatory narrative of the first two chapters, which represent our past. It is to be sure a relatively recent past (the voyage from New Zealand to San Francisco, as ancient as it seems and suggestive of the eighteenth century, is in fact a nineteenth-century event; while the young composer's letters from Bruges also evoke a *symboliste* era long since over and done with, even though rather recent as the crow flies): this effect of distance, however, very much corroborates Hobsbawm's sense of the changes wrought in world history by World War II, which are so radical as to consign everything that preceded them, even in the twentieth century, to a distant, increasingly alien and incomprehensible past. It should also be noted that the two genres imitated in these first two chapters are relatively marginal ones and stage their historical moment not in the way it liked to see itself—the realist novel, the symphony—but rather from its own not yet mass-cultural minor forms. Kant loved to read travel books, a taste consistent with a life lived entirely within one city; but this very taste confirms the as-yet-undeveloped spaces of the life of earlier periods, without airplanes or automobiles, with poor roads and cumbersome vehicles, where even an eventful sea voyage à la Melville is the epitome of extreme spatial restriction. As for the music of Delius and the master–apprentice situation evoked in the second episode, the unique atmosphere of Bruges, the rather Balzacian drama of the undiscovered young genius and his Werther-like suicide—all this also seems to concentrate and distill a variety of Romantic and post-Romantic or symbolist aesthetics with picturesque places and situations far enough from contemporary life and culture and only unified by the theme of cruelty and exploitation that runs, virtually unnoticed, throughout the harried chapters of this seemingly episodic work ("the strong do eat/ the weak as meat").[12] One

---

12   To be sure, and all morality aside, it is true that this motto holds for current evolutionary theory as well (which, having abandoned the old-fashioned telos of vitalism or idealism, has now invented the allegedly materialist goal of "complexity"), where life still feeds on life: "The earliest organisms may have extracted their energy from chemicals below the earth's surface. They 'ate' chemicals. If the earliest organisms were archaebacteria, they probably extracted the energy they needed from chemical vents deep within the seas. But quite early some organisms learned to acquire energy by eating

may also be reminded of that Faulknerian work in which the author combined two unrelated and unsalable novellas into what we might call an "assemblage" that the publishers, duly impressed, at once brought out in book form. Is it possible, then, that David Mitchell has here simply pasted together a batch of unsuccessful juvenilia, arranged together and stitched up in some more or less acceptable consecutive order? If so, they were certainly very talented efforts indeed; but the emergence of such formations as installation art in present-day curatorial practice testifies to a historical development in which the quality of the part has little enough to do with the value of the assemblage as a whole and of that one-time unique ideal form that arises from the idea of such juxtapositions. In any case, Faulkner did not write a pastiche (save perhaps of his own style in later years), while Proust's extraordinary collection of such performances (in *Pastiches et Melanges*) consisted in the virtuoso imitation of famous and identifiable masters, such as Balzac or Madame de Sévigné.

The marginality of these first two "historical" chapters then gives way to the outright acknowledgment of the dominance of mass culture in the second pair, in which a lurid American tale of corporate malfeasance and conspiracy is followed by a scurrilous plot to sequester and institutionalize an aged and failing, embittered English publisher for his money. The two backgrounds are distinguished by the characteristic paranoia of the first and the class acrimony and nationalist passions of the second; and they represent the discourses of investigative journalism and popular thrillers, respectively, in their accounts of the two modes of domination of our period, big business and wealthy dynastic families. They can be said to find their realism in the depiction, not so much of our realistic social situations (although they are not, in that sense, unrealistic) as rather in our fantasies about those situations, in which the faceless corporate enemy and the fears of the powerlessness of

---

other organisms. In this way, there emerged a clear distinction between primary producers, which extract their energy from the nonliving environment, and organisms higher up the food chain that feed on other living organisms, including the primary producers. If these had been the only ways of extracting energy, then the history of life on Earth would have been limited by the energy supplied from the earth's molten core and available to organisms living deep within the sea. But by at least 3.5 billion years ago, some organisms were living near the surface of the seas, where they learned to feed on sunlight." David Christian, *Maps of Time,* Berkeley: University of California Press, 2004, 109–10.

old age—the anagogical and moral levels so to speak—paradigmatically evoke our deepest and most widespread anxieties.

But this is the moment to underscore another less visible system of continuities in this ingenious novel: for by definition a pastiche necessarily evokes period fantasy and activates the kinds of fears and anxieties proper to the age it expresses as a cultural dominant. But such associations and subjective experiences also necessarily demand transmission and a material vehicle of communication; and so it is that *Cloud Atlas* is also a novel about media as such. Its deeper continuities lie in the relatively unobtrusive way in which each episode is linked to the next by way of a well-nigh material vehicle of communication. Thus, the young composer of the second chapter avidly reads the bound volume in which the travel narrative of the first has been printed. The heroine of the third or conspiracy chapter has inherited the packet of letters in which the drama of the second is conveyed. Her story, meanwhile, is given us in the form of a manuscript submitted for publication to the elderly publisher victimized in the sequel, while his own sad tale is filmed in a lively Guy Ritchie fashion, boisterous with UK accents of all kinds and surviving in a film-bank passed on down to the North Korean–type inhabitants of a far-future dystopia of obviously science fictional character (but having more in common with *Soylent Green* than with *1984*) and transmitted by way of a judicial interrogation reminiscent of that most ancient of all dramatic genres, the trial.

Here we approach the tipping point at which a great historical turnover sends us chapter by chapter back in time to finish each of these stories in what can only be called happy endings (despite the deaths of some of their protagonists). For the dystopian future tale of the unhappy Sonmi—conveyed by way of the archaic genre of the trial and the interrogation—is unexpectedly transmitted through a three-dimensional holographic capsule (à la *Star Wars*), which becomes the basis for a new religion of suffering and redemption.

It is this religion that is transmitted to the postapocalyptic reversion to primitivism and barbarism of the "final" episode, told in a dialect reminiscent of *Huckleberry Finn* and describing the rescue of a peaceful tribe of human survivors, threatened by a warlike neighboring tribe, by advanced scientists who have also survived in some secret pocket of the remaining earth and who contemplate the fate of their fellow humans with the sympathy of an alien race from another planet. History ends here, in this final oral tale (where it will have to begin again, if at all), abandoning us to make our way back down, through history, overshooting our own present and landing as it were in a San Francisco halfway between Melville and Norris (and in American rather than British or world literature, as befits an expatriate author who has spent his life in Japan and Ireland).

We can now map out the allegorical levels navigated by this unique work where the very notion of history itself is at stake. The moral and anagogical levels are clearly enough articulated by the ambiguity of the theme of persecution and domination, which can be read either as a representation of collective agency—imperialism, the great corporations, bloodthirsty tribes, and the like—or as an inventory of all the personal and individual forms of suffering such domination can take, from fear to filial resentment, from physical danger to virtual confinement, and so forth. The articulation of the common situation into its subjective and objective forms then offers an alternative focus in which the work can be read. But it is in the initial choice of the allegorical and literal levels that the most interesting and decisive choices must be read. For the work gives itself alternately as a history of styles and a history of media, which might well be read as a subjective or idealistic and an objective or materialistic version of the same history. Indeed, history will emerge as the raw material and also the very subject of this work in any case, but which version of that history emerges is dependent on our determination of the literal level: which is the more real, subject or object? And it is the very transversality of this choice, which one constantly reverse in reading, that certifies the allegorical principle of this "historical novel."

The levels in *Cloud Atlas* might then provisionally be schematized as follows:

ANAGOGICAL: the cruelty of the various historical regimes
MORAL: the crushing of the weak or the rescue (tragic or happy endings)
ALLEGORICAL: the development of the media
LITERAL OR HISTORICAL: the sequence of styles (pastiche)

One may then use this scheme to demonstrate the operations and effects of that discovered transversality. For everything depends on the relative positioning of the allegorical and literal levels. If I take the literal level as the historicist sequence of styles or pastiche with which *Cloud Atlas* furnishes, then the interpretive level—the allegorical one—becomes a materialist reminder of the formative role of the media in just such an ideal sequence. If, on the other hand, it is the development of the media that is taken as the essential story this novel has to convey, then style becomes the cultural correction of a mechanical materialism that proves itself to have been an intellectual, that is to say, an idealist construction in its own right. (Sartre once powerfully reminded us of the not-so-secret idealism of vulgar or mechanical materialist interpretations.)[13] Meanwhile, the humanist or moralizing interpretation with which the book tempts us is also put in its place as itself a kind of reflex or overtone of a wholly different kind of structure; while the vision of history—itself deriving from a subgenre of Science Fiction—is reabsorbed into the series of pastiches of a lower level of the text.

Given such displacements, it is nonetheless important to point out that nowhere here do we touch History as such, or the Real. Pastiche is not historical, it is historicist; it projects the relativism of the historical periods and not their inexorable and infrastructural logic. This is why artistic work with pastiche needs to be confronted with a very different type of production more closely approximating what Barthes long ago prophetically termed "writing degree zero." This will be, as the reader already guesses, the place for some narrative minimalism, of a rather different type than that displayed in the evolution of lyric poetry.

I will suggest that one place to look is Tom McCarthy's novel *Remainder*.[14] It is not an "experimental" work (let alone an avant-garde or "postmodern" one), but rather the sober description of an experiment and of the process of constructivism insofar as that can be represented by way of a series of events. For in a sense, the maximalist passively receives the flood of simulacra and records it in the release of unconquerable linguistic debris; the minimalist, however, proceeds from the other direction and patiently seeks to reconstruct these empty events, these unpeopled stage sets that claim to be the real, all the while discrediting themselves as what philosophy calls semblance or sheer

---

13   Jean-Paul Sartre, "Matérialisme et révolution," *Situations III*, Paris: Gallimard, 1947.
14   Tom McCarthy, *Remainder*, New York: Vintage, 2007.

appearance (*Schein*). But it remains a question whether they once existed or whether they were always simply the phantom member of imaginary bodies: that *peu de réalité* of which the Surrealists were once willing to speak.

In other words, one is entitled to wonder whether amnesia is a satisfactory narrative excuse. McCarthy's hero begins with that, indeed—not merely an accident that wipes out his previous life, but also that insurance claim which mysteriously endows him with the money to outfit and launch his great Experiment, which is something like the artificial creation of Life itself. This thereby with one mighty Gordian stroke solves two fundamental form problems, namely (a) how to begin when there are no beginnings (a problem literature shares with philosophy) and (b) how to elude the historical form-and-ideology critique which searches for its clues and symptoms in the raw material, in the contingency of the situation which makes this particular narrative possible. How, in other words, in the context of bourgeois literature does the hero or heroine get enough money to live whatever interesting drama the novel thinks worth showing us? In art, however, artfulness consists in arranging matters in such a way that these damaging questions do not arise in the first place. Here, McCarthy confronts them in the crudest, boldest, most admirable way, and simply cuts the famous knot. There was a settlement: I don't remember when, where, how, and what.

The narrator then, like any good theater manager, will begin to shop around for the raw materials his author no longer needs to supply in advance. He will reconstruct a scene, a particular event, which he supposes to have happened on the strength of a crack in the wall that seems to stimulate his nonexistent memory. That crack is the famous "silence" I denounced a few pages ago: it is the hole in the world, the secret emptiness, the geological fissure that is the legendary path to the underworld (maybe that at least is real!). Locate the right building with the right southern exposure, the right windows, the right courtyard; hire actors who are also somehow and unaccountably the right ones and in the right number. Assess the weather at the right time of day. Have an eye to the most minute gestures (construction is also an analytic method, breaking the larger unities up into their most insignificant parts). When everything is right . . . At that point the demands of everyday realism set in again: what do we do with our new event (for this society, at its technological level, the instinctive answer might be, record it for all time!), and better still, what do we do after it, and finally, how do we break this off and this constitutes the antithesis to our first form problem or better still, its return as its own opposite—the problem of endings (sometimes pompously baptized closure).

The novel is not the story of the solutions to those problems (which might have taken the more truly postmodern form of a filming that preserves and reifies the constructed simulacrum for all eternity), it is the story of the problems themselves; and the rented plane in which we circle interminably over Heathrow, waiting for the gas to run out—this plane is the novel itself; in a later novel, McCarthy will cunningly suggest that it does intervene in the real, at least by interrupting the flight plan of all of Europe and putting any number of scheduled takeoffs on hold—perhaps in itself a worthy enough achievement, for did not Benjamin himself claim that revolution was not acceleration but rather pulling the emergency brake? So it is that constructivism leads to nihilism, and we would prefer to believe in natural processes, however imperceptible. It is the human age, the world of commodities, the eclipse of nature by this second nature of construction, that is meaningless; we would prefer to think that what it ended up universally displacing, concealing, repressing, occulting, maybe even stifling and destroying—namely nature, or the world of needs—used to be the real one. But that is no longer believable, that is to say, the prehistory to which it nostalgically appeals is available only in the past–present–future dimension of temporality, which has been abolished. The phenomenological present is the problem: it is an empty mailbox, a dead phone, an agenda without appointments.

I suppose, however, that even nothingness might mean something, might have its own inner allegorical structure; and so, without too much conviction, I offer this representation (it is nothing but a reconstruction):

> ANAGOGICAL: the simulacrum
> MORAL: amnesia
> ALLEGORICAL: producing and directing
> LITERAL: the empty present

At least one feature is clear: if nihilism there is (or minimalist silence, if you prefer), at least it incites to activity. This is not pessimism, or melancholy, or depression: it is what Faust saw at the beginning of biblical creation: the act, *die Tat*. This is a joyous novel, full of people doing things, however incomprehensible; it is far from the modernist gloom, the modernist dejection of unemployment and inaction or even of the ecstatic high of drugs and rock-n-roll. But perhaps, as some contemporary philosophers affirm, it is aesthetic rather than epistemological or ontological; and maybe praxis is still poesis. But ontological aestheticization does not exactly seem the right treatment for an already overly aestheticized age. Still, perhaps existentialism was aesthetic after all, in its insistence on the choice and the deed? And is not a making a form of production?

To be sure, the formal tendencies I have been calling *maximal* and *minimal* are themselves from one thematic perspective simply those of the dual temporality on which we have come to insist in these books, namely the increasingly abstract idea of a past–present–future temporal continuity (the totality of world time) and that of the living instant which each individual subjectivity is given to live as best it can. These temporalities—abstract and concrete, if you like, or philosophical and phenomenological—are to be sure inseparable; but it is only by their distinct and separate formal developments and expressions in the two artistic traditions that one can begin to perceive a difference that turns out to be an identity.

It would be tempting to invoke the long-standing figure of matter and antimatter and to suggest that these two representations simply cancel one another out. But for one thing, that would be to ignore the double sense of negation as such, which suggests that alongside antimatter there also exists a logical space for nonmatter. But it would also ignore the dialectical position according to which these two negatives—the maximalist and the minimalist—are in fact simply one and the same: two antithetical perspectives, so to speak, on the single unrepresentable reality which is reality today.

But perhaps, in this era of globalization, the question of national allegory ought to kick in here, for our juxtaposition would have lacked all legitimacy without the shared nationality—the commonality of a national situation—that authorized my choice of these two emblematic works. That both are in one way or another British—so that the maximalist and minimalist visions might somehow reflect the unique coexistence of Imperial and isolated or insular self-identifications—merely reflects the unique content of the multiple nationalisms and national traditions today, for which collectivity is always a lost object if not simply an affair of mobs and conspiracies. I suspect that the maximal and the minimal are to be found, conjoined, in different forms, in all the national literatures of the world market, inflected, in equally different ways (as these two novels are), in an uncanny science-fictional cast, by the half-light cast by some unknown future. Utopian allegory is presumably one of the jumbled mutterings emanating from that future, but we still have much work to do on our speech recognition technologies to identify, let alone to represent it.

This book began life as a methodological proposal that gradually developed into a formal history. It may not come as any great surprise to find that its story also developed into an allegory in its own right, whose political consequences it is not inappropriate to draw as a provisional conclusion.

Modernity—setting aside all the problems loosed by this suspicious word—began with differentiation, or so Luhmann teaches us; this emergence of Difference characterizes the great historical transitions from what Weber called *traditional societies* into those powered by the emergence of all kinds of new specializations; new mental faculties; new zones of reality; and new projects, ambitions, productive activities, subjectivities, and varieties of human flora and fauna.

Allegory turns out to be one way of sorting through these multiplicities and finding analogies between the differentiations, identities among the differences: the "levels" relate fully as much as they separate. The Greeks, in their small and ferocious communities, discovered abstraction and the universals as a way of organizing their language and ordering the chaos of an older "pensée sauvage": this was a philosophical path and a logical one, and indeed ended up in the establishment of both philosophy and logic—born not out of the spirit of music but rather of mathematics, itself a supreme exercise in the dialectic of identity and difference.

But it turns out that another force is at work in the emergence of Greek philosophy, even from its pre-Socratic origins: and that is the category of substance, one that derives from the visual practice and experience of separating one object from another. Today we have a philosophical word for this force: it is reification, and perhaps it is time to pay a brief tribute to this much maligned phenomenon, whose spirit is after all that of the production of objects as such, or, put another way, of that supreme activity that makes us human and that defines activity itself. (Recent theory has had a field day demonstrating how much of human life is taken up with the production of what can now be seen as new objects: new desires, new kinds of thinking, new forms of social relations, new feelings, new sins and virtues, and so on down the line to new gadgets and new technologies: these demonstrations indeed ground that new philosophy or ideology we call *constructivism*.) It was all very well for Marx to insist on a fundamental distinction between two kinds of production or reification, that between externalization and alienation. This fundamental political reminder (how an object can become private property; how the very category of objecthood encouraged another and less admirable human potentiality) did not, except for Nietzsche, sufficiently underscore the seeming entanglement and inseparability between the notion of the object and the philosophical category of the substance (a commonsense Aristotelianism against which the modern notion of process will struggle interminably!).

This is the point at which to reintroduce one of the key players in the present book, namely personification. For personification is itself the allegorical figure of reification; I have posited it at work in its virtual form in the name itself and the act of nomination, but the name itself is surely the form reification takes in language, and personification unites both name and objecthood. Names are the very heartland of dogma, and their baleful power extends from the sacred exaltation of the tyrant all the way to medicalization, the -isms, and the brand names of both commodification and the pathologies of the self and its mirror images.

In a sense, then, we have staged our story of the allegorical impulse as a struggle against personification, struggle between personification and a certain modernity (or process), a desperate attempt to de-reify what differentiation has brought about in the way of "fixed ideas" and named concepts. To be sure, this struggle has been successful to the degree to which it has destroyed traditional allegory itself, replacing it (when necessary) with symbols on the one hand and empirical realism on the other. I have tried to chart this movement in a discussion of the shift from what I called *named emotions* to what is now widely termed *affect*: a shift that fully as much constitutes a new construction of subjectivity as it marks a date in the history of ideas.

So to put in a good word for personification at this stage would seem to involve a reversal and a defense of reification from a new and hopefully political perspective. Here and there throughout these chapters, we have hinted at the way in which the interrelationship between the various levels of allegory invents connections between dimensions or reality otherwise imperceptible in the complexities of modern social life. Never have such complexities become so impenetrable in the global class society now emerging across so many different kinds of barriers. To mention only the most obvious of the interrelationships everywhere lacking today, we may affirm that political action and effectiveness is only possible when great collective projects find their allegorical resonance—their identity as well as their differences—with the existential experience of individuals in an atomized society. Meanwhile, our fourfold scheme has shown that such resonance, as complex as musical overtones, always includes transformed subjectivities, narratives and their interpretations, the Event, vertical crises and transversal horizontalities, and a sudden opening onto the perception of the totality as well as of the radical differences whose identities make it into a conjuncture.

The flash of a social map of this kind, however, demands the legible points of a constellation, a new kind of reification, which must replace the sense of drift and tendency with the identifiable space of a cast of characters, a personification of friend and foe, a movement of social classes in conflict and in alliance: classes in formation, perhaps, where everything static about traditional personification is replaced with the process of personifying and of identifying agencies to come. This is to set the allegorical machinery in motion and to grasp it as an instrument of political perception, if not, indeed, a precondition of great prophecy, whose current absence leaves only a desolate landscape of dystopian simulacra on the frozen screen of history. The far future, however, the ending of Wells's *Time Machine*, life extinct, the sun burning out—these are certainties the remedy for which can only be found in Mallarmé's magnificent consolation—*que c'est d'un astre en fête allumé le génie*. But they are imaginary certainties, which Freud posited as concealing the more real worries of the present. The human animal is an essentially incompetent species, finding its heroes in specimens who, like Napoléon, exceed the norm only by a degree or two. The glory of the Anthropocene, however, has been to show us that we can really change the world. Now it would be intelligent to terraform it. But symptoms of the future are far less reliable than symptoms of the present.

Appendix A:
The Greimas Square[1]

The relevance of these proposals for Greimas's work turns on the whole matter of the so-called elementary structure of signification, or, in other words, the famous "semiotic square," for many of us the supreme achievement of Greimassian semiotics. Here finally we find opened up the "black box" through which narrative is somehow "converted" into cognition and vice versa: finally we have the equations, we can witness the processes of transfer, which need no longer be posited mystically since it is "visible" before us. How this can be so, however, obviously demands yet another simplified exercise in the explanatory capacities of the "square," whose canonical form is herewith reproduced (Figure A1):

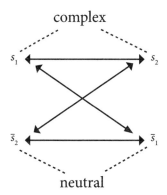

---

1 From the author's foreword to Algirdas Julien Greimas's *On Meaning* (Minneapolis: University of Minnesota Press, 1970).

The enumeration of the advantages of the square can begin at once with the observation that it is a decisive enlargement on the older structural notion of the binary opposition: S_1 versus S_2 is clearly just such a binary opposition, or in the language of philosophical logic a "contrary," that is, a strong opposition (white versus black, male versus female), but one that the square now reveals to encompass far more than two available positions. It immediately implies, for example, the two supplementary slots of what logic calls a "contradictory," where $\bar{S}_1$ and $\bar{S}_2$ are the simple negatives of the two dominant terms but include far more than either: thus "nonwhite" includes more than "black," "nonmale" more than "female." Meanwhile, the two compound or "synthetic" positions of complex and neutral offer still greater conceptual enlargements, the complex or utopian term, in which the opposition of "white" and "black" might be transcended (mestizo, for example), whereas the neutral term stands as the space in which all of the privations and negations are assembled ("colorless," for example). Finally, the transversal axes map the place of tensions distinct from the principal or binary one, while the synthesis hypothetically proposed by uniting the two sides of the square ("white" plus "nonblack") designates alternative conceptual combinations. The entire mechanism then is capable of generating at least ten conceivable positions out of a rudimentary binary opposition (which may originally have been no more than a single term, e.g. "white," which proves to be internally defined by a hidden opposition we articulate by promoting the concealed pole "black" to visibility). I have suggested that other traditions may find this schema interesting if they entertain the hypothesis that it constitutes a virtual map of conceptual closure, or better still, of the closure of ideology itself, that is, ideology as a mechanism, which, while seeming to generate a rich variety of possible concepts and positions, remains in fact locked into some initial aporia or double-bind that it cannot transform from the inside by its own means.

However this may be, it seems appropriate to conclude this introduction with an outsider's observations on the multiple uses and interests of this mechanism. A few initial remarks ought to concern its "proper use," that is, to offer some warnings about what it can and cannot do. The square does offer, I believe, a kind of "discovery principle," but of a special type, and it cannot be guaranteed to replace intelligence or intuition. Indeed, insofar as it can often be called on simply to map thoughts and interpretations arrived at in other (seemingly less technical) fashions, it is appropriate at the outset to stress its initial pedagogical function: one can, in other words, very properly use this visual device to map out and to articulate a set of relationships that it is much more confusing, and much less economical, to convey in expository prose, and these humbler pedagogical capacities of the semiotic square may not be the least index of its importance.

As for its heuristic value, however, experience testifies that you must blacken many pages before you get it right and that a number of key decisions intervene in the process. One lists a variety of entities to be coordinated; it is a list that must never be considered final, nor should the nature and nomenclature of the entities be foreclosed. It is desirable (even, in my view, necessary) that seemingly aberrant or marginal, minor, eccentric entities be enumerated, since it is their place in the scheme of things, and their very presence, which is the most interesting of the problems the square can be called upon to solve.

As for operative decisions or moments, I will mention three that seem to me crucial. The first is the inaugural decision, not merely about the terms of the binary opposition to be expanded and articulated in the square as a whole, but also, and above all, the very order in which those terms are arranged; it makes a fundamental difference, in other words, whether the founding binary is ordered as white versus black, or as black versus white. The square is in that sense not symmetrical but "temporal" or positional, and the placement of the terms (obviously this initial formulation will already imply something like dominant/subordinate, center/margin, self/other), like that of mathematical equations (or the lobes of the brain, or right and left hand), is not indifferent but actively determinant in astonishing ways (that very astonishment playing its own part in the unexpected lessons we find ourselves learning in this process).

The second important recommendation is that the four primary terms ($S_1, S_2, \bar{S}_1, \bar{S}_2$) need to be conceived polysemically, each one carrying within it its own range of synonyms, and of the synonyms of its synonyms—none of them exactly coterminous with each other, such that large areas of relatively new or at least skewed conceptuality are thereby registered. Thus, for example, in Hayden White's conception of "metonymy" in *Metahistory*, two relatively distinct "semes" are encompassed—that of reduction (scientific or mechanistic explanation, determinism) and that of separation; this term thus includes a fruitful terrain for dialectical slippage, such that its "reductive" aspect may allow it to stand in opposition to the visionary and representational plenitude of "metaphor."[2] Its other "identity"—as sheer disjunction or separation—then allows it unexpectedly to be coordinated with (or against) "synecdoche" as the reintegration of the separated and the construction of new wholes. This will to embrace the slippage within terms is here a practical recommendation, like handicraft rules of thumb or inherited wisdom, but it also opens up a dizzying perspective of the subatomic universes, a prospect of what a very different semiotician, Umberto Eco, following Peirce, calls "infinite semiosis," in which each of the four primary terms of the square threatens to yawn open into its own fourfold system, down into the infinite divisibility of semiotic nature.

A final warning must be directed to the peculiar nature of the fourth term, the negation of the negation: $\bar{S}_2$. This must be (when the operation is successful) the place of novelty and of paradoxical emergence: it is always the most critical position and the one that remains open or empty for the longest time, for its identification completes the process and in that sense constitutes the most creative act of the construction. Once again, it is simply a matter of experience that the first three terms are relatively "given" and demand no great acts of intellection, but that the fourth one is the place of the great leap, the great deduction, the intuition that falls from the ceiling, or from heaven. Yet this is something that here can be only mythically conveyed, as in that system of apocalypses foretold by Mayan religion, which, fourfold in a relatively universal fashion, only springs apart from Western paradigms unexpectedly in its fourth moment. The world, for the Mayans, will end in fire, as for us; a second time around, the world will be destroyed by water, as for us; yet a third time, and it will be destroyed by air (hurricanes). And it will also be destroyed a fourth time . . . by jaguars! (which, formerly the stars in the heavens, take on their new carnivorous form and drop upon the earth to devour the human race). So also with J. G. Ballard's early and haunting end-of-the-world tetralogy: by

---

2 Hayden White, *Metahistory: The Historical Imagination in Nineteenth-Century Europe*, Baltimore: Johns Hopkins University Press, 1973. The interested reader will note some modifications of my own position on this classic work since the first publication, in 1976, of "Figural Relativism; or, The Poetics of Historiography," reprinted as a chapter of *The Ideologies of Theory*.

water (*The Drowning World*), by fire (*The Burning World*), by air or hurricane (*The Wind from Nowhere*), and then ... by turning into crystal (*The Crystal World*)!

The semiotic square is thus not static but dynamic: the significance of positionality within it is only one index of the way in which it can just as easily be considered to map a temporal process as to register a conceptual blockage or paralysis; indeed, the latter can most often be grasped as the very situation that motivates the former, namely, the attempt, by rotating the square and generating its implicit positions, to find one's way out of the conceptual or ideological closure, out of the old or given—into which one is locked—somehow desperately to generate the novelty of the event, or of breakthrough, or of the *Novum*. Yet to see the square as the very image of closure itself tends to encourage some pessimism about the possibilities of escaping from it in any other way than the Hegelian one: one does not resolve a contradiction; rather, by praxis, one alters the situation in such a way that the old contradiction, now dead and irrelevant, moves without solution into the past, its place taken by a fresh and unexpected contradiction (which may or may not be some advance on the older aporias or ideological imprisonment).

Yet the very gestalt properties of the square—its capacity to be indifferently static or dynamic—are what accounts for its powerful mediatory capacity: it can, in other words, "reduce" a narrative in movement to a series of "cognitive" or ideological, combinatory positions; or it can rewrite a cognitive text into a desperate narrative movement in which new positions are generated and abandoned, and in which terms ceaselessly amalgamate in order to achieve the release of this or that ideal synthesis and release from their warring and antagonistic, structural-fragmentary nature.

I have offered elsewhere illustrations of possible "applications" of the square to problems of narrative analysis: these unorthodox efforts may serve to suggest ways in which the two planes of narrative—"characters" or, better still, *systems* of characters, and cognitive complexes or contradictions—can be coordinated and transcoded into one another.[3] Here I will briefly sketch a sample of the analysis of a "cognitive" or theoretical

---

3   See Jameson, *The Political Unconscious,* Ithaca: Cornell University Press, 1981, 165ff. and 253ff.; or "After Armageddon: Character Systems in *Dr. Bloodmoney,*" *Science-Fiction Studies* 2, March 1975, 31–42.

text, Hayden White's *Metahistory*, which is to be sure in a way preprepared, insofar as this text is itself already organized around a fourfold set of categories: the four tropes of Metaphor, Metonymy, Synecdoche, and Irony. This first system of categories is then multiplied by three more: a typology of world views, drawn from Stephen Pepper (Formism, Mechanicism, Organicism, and Contextualism); Frye's "emplotments" (Romantic, Tragic, Comic, and Satirical); and finally Mannheim's categories of ideology (Anarchist, Radical, Conservative, and Liberal). In practice, it may be suggested that this set of, as it were, vertical layers in fact tends to amalgamate into two groups of coordinated features: the tropes and Pepper's "world hypotheses" function as alternate languages for the same characteristics, whereas the "emplotments" and the "modes of ideological implication" also tend to function synonymously. Yet within each of the two groups (which roughly correspond to the structure of a given history and to its metaphysical connotation, or reception, respectively), we already find that creative slippage I have referred to, the possibility of passing from one term to another by way of a shift in these levels (the earlier example of Metonymy illustrates a shift from the tropological sense of this "term" to its conceptual, or world-hypothetical, sense). What remains an open question is whether the two groups of categories need always function in unison, or whether one might not imagine a dissonance, that is, a contradiction, between say, the tropological mechanism and the emplotment or ideological message. This is something White seems to foresee, without, however, drawing any explicit conclusions from the possibility.[4]

White's book seeks to do (at least) two things: first, to reassert the historical and cognitive claims of the so-called philosophers of history (Hegel, Marx, Nietzsche), who have, in the traditional canon of historiography, been assigned a lower and more amateurish status by the historians themselves, in contrast to "real" or practicing historiographers, of whom this book deals with four (Michelet, Ranke, Tocqueville,

---

4   Thus, for example: "Certainly the greatest philosophers . . . resist reduction to the archetypes provided by Pepper. If anything their thought represents a mediation between two or more of the kinds of doctrinaire positions which Pepper outlines" (*Metahistory*, 13, note 7); or this: "The dialectical tension which characterizes the work of every master historian usually arises from an effort to wed a mode of employment with a mode of argument or of ideological implication which is inconsonant with it" (*Metahistory*, 29).

and Burckhardt). What *Metahistory* in fact achieves is a good deal less modest than this, since the thrust of the argument tends toward the assertion that in fact the philosophers of history are *better* historians than the historiographers. How the text generates this position will then be one of the questions an articulation by the semiotic square needs to answer.

The other function of *Metahistory* (which is specifically limited to the nineteenth-century "historical imagination") is to demonstrate not merely the relevance of the conceptual typologies already enumerated but their *cyclical* function, in a rhythm that begins in naive Metaphor or Romanticism, passes through the negative or Metonymic, Mechanistic stage of reduction, begins to reclaim a larger totalizing construction in the new unities of Synecdoche, and finally, in the moment of Irony, comes to a self-consciousness of its own linguistic or tropological procedures that signals a new crisis of the historical imagination and may be expected, by way of the great Viconian *ricorso,* to swing around again into a fresh belief, a fresh Metaphoric or Romantic moment with which the cycle can begin all over again on a heightened level. Indeed, it is this rebirth of historiographic belief that White calls for in his concluding pages, which speak out of the moment of Irony and its crisis. What is peculiar, however, is that the moment of Irony, *Metahistory,* takes two distinct forms: the crisis of the nineteenth century reaches as it were two distinct paroxysms simultaneously—the "bad" Irony of Burckhardt, serene and aestheticizing (the "philosophy" of Croce is in effect a more elaborate double of this position), and the "good" or strong Irony of Nietzsche from within which Hayden White clearly speaks (even though Hegel and Marx were to have been "rehabilitated" more or less on equal grounds with the author of the *Genealogy of Morals).* These intricate moves are, however, not random ones, nor are they in any way the "mere" results of the personal opinions or ideological predilections of the metahistorian; the pattern is indeed a very logical one, which can be clarified and articulated by the operation of the semiotic square as the various possible terms and positions of *Metahistory* are mapped onto it.

The diagram attempts to respect as much as possible the combinatory richness and intricacy of the text, very specifically including what I have called the slippage within the terms, that is their multiple semic content or the copresence of various levels and codes within each:

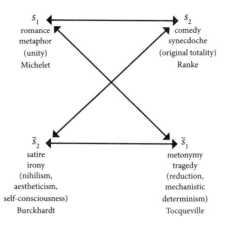

What should be clear from this initial mapping onto the semiotic square is that the four historians each present, in all their differences, the spectacle of unison between all the levels, and that indeed it is this very absence of inner tension or contradiction that accounts for the author's evaluations of them: itself a form of irony, not to say contempt, save in the case of Tocqueville, where a certain tragic honesty carries conviction, but where, it should be noted, this univocal position also ultimately disintegrates under its own momentum into a Burckhardt-type irony and nihilism, which itself—as yet another univocal ideological position—then is subjected to the full force of the metahistorian's Irony. This last must therefore be of a different type, and it is precisely the advantage of the semiotic square to hold open other conceivable positions, which have not yet been secured in our diagram, and which are the so-called compound terms, the complex and neutral terms S and $\bar{S}$, and the deictic axes in which the lateral sides of the square also designate possible syntheses. Before demonstrating those, however, it is worth noting the strategic function, already referred to, involved in the choice of an initial binary opposition. The story, as anyone would naturally tell it, and as Hayden White himself initially maps it in his diagram of the levels in *Metahistory*, is one in which an initial Metaphoric consciousness disintegrates into a Metonymic or negative moment of determinism and random mechanistic causality.[5] That negative crisis is then—on anyone's stereotypical narrative paradigm—slowly overcome by

---

5   Ibid., 29.

The Greimas Square

Synecdochic reconstruction, only to be sapped and vitiated by a new kind of disintegration and a new kind of crisis—that of Ironic self-consciousness, and of the sense that even the Synecdochic solution was itself only fictional and linguistic—at which point, as I have already said, the entire system turns over and swings back into a new cycle of Metaphoric reaffirmation.

But this corresponds neither to the order of the chapters nor to the combinatory logic of the work itself, in which Romance is followed by Comedy, and Metaphor by Synecdoche, rather than by Metonymy. Thus, we have mapped the semiotic square around a quite unexpected binary opposition, not the familiar one of Metaphor versus Metonymy, but some new constitutive tension between Metaphor and Synecdoche—a tension that must necessarily be conceptualized as the antagonism between two forms of *unity*, an initial Metaphoric or representational one (Michelet's great ecstatic moments of national unity in the Revolution and more specifically of the *"fêtes de la Fédération"* of June 1790) and a Synecdochic one, the construction of more "artificial" social unities, built up from their separate parts, in the form of Ranke's *institutions* (church, nation, and so on). The point I wish to stress is that the square *will not work* any other way (the reader may now wish to test this assertion by experiment) and that only this arrangement of the terms will generate the essentials of *Metahistory*, a book about which we have therefore learned something new, namely, that its deepest subject, the fundamental contradiction it is concerned to resolve, is not that of meaning versus nonmeaning, or belief versus causality (Metaphor versus Metonymy: the traditional way of mapping the nineteenth-century "crisis of faith"), but rather the tension between two incompatible visions of the social, neither of which (ecstatic revolutionary spontaneousness and the slow permanency of the great social institutions) seems satisfactory.

I must also add a word about the question of the "fourth term," also raised earlier. It is clear that, although the word itself is scarcely fresh or surprising, Irony is the great magical term on which the text turns and that its combinatorial mechanisms aim fully as much at *producing* this extraordinary "position" from across a wide range of meanings and uses (the slippage in this fourth term is far greater than in any of the others) as they simply register it as an object of study and one attitude among others.

We may now rapidly conclude the mapping of the square, whose complex and neutral terms can be loosely designated as historical Optimism and Pessimism respectively, a language whose slackness need not detain us long, since both are clearly logically impossible positions that the movement of the work rejects (S is a conceivable but impossible synthesis, $\bar{S}$ is merely the empty wiping out of that content and the place of the global, mechanical negations of both terms of the initial opposition). It is therefore to the lateral (or deictic) syntheses that we turn our attention. Here indeed the great "philosophers of history" find their positions, which have been generated by the inner logic of the square itself. Both Hegel and Marx, White tells us, achieved syntheses of Tragedy and Comedy: history is a comedy, all of whose individual moments are tragic. Nietzsche, meanwhile, begins with an identification of Tragedy and Comedy, which luminously eclipse each other and in their indistinction give rise to something else, which will be an Ironic sense of the powers of language that now once again releases the great Metaphoric energies. (Note how it is very precisely the semiotic slippage between Romance and Metaphor that enables this ultimate moment to be something more than a mere synthesis of Romance and Satire.) With this, the combinational movement of the book is exhausted and a message emerges: the priority of Hegel, Marx, and Nietzsche over the "univocal" historians, and after that, perhaps, the more tentative priority of Nietzsche over the other two positions insofar as Nietzsche "includes" their moments of Tragedy and Comedy and then projects further new and original possibilities, Metaphor and Irony (properly linguistic or reflexive moments), out of the earlier pair (Figure A3).

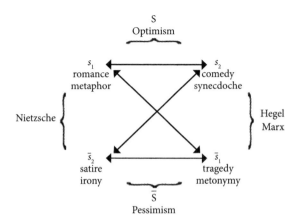

Returning now to the nature of the semiotic square itself, it seems clear that its emergence from the dynamic of Greimassian semiotics betokens some profound spatiality in the system in general. What interests me is not the viability of this enterprise, nor how one might resolve this persistence of the irreducibly spatial within semiotics in some new and enlarged philosophical system, but rather the historical fact of its emergence in our society, where it is by no means the only example or symptom of a period intellectually given over to space in a way radically different from the preceding generation of the modernists, in thrall to temporality. All the structuralisms are deeply spatial in one way or another, and not merely in their rhetoric or modes of presentation (although the fact, previously mentioned, that we find these diagrams today more pedagogically convincing and persuasive than the corresponding linguistic expressions and developments of them is surely not insignificant either). Alone of the great philosophers, Henri Lefebvre has posited a genuine new philosophy of space, and this on a historicist basis, namely, the tendential spatialization of late capitalism (and, one might wish to add, using a concept not foreseen in Lefebvre's work, of the *postmodern*). That Greimassian semiotics should be "true" in some sense (or at any rate, pragmatically, richly usable and full of practical development) and at the same time stand as a profound historical symptom of the nature of the age I find no difficulty in reconciling: the latter—the structure of the late capitalist global system—constituting something like the conditions of possibility for the conceptualizing and articulation of the new theoretical system.

Appendix B:
Consciousness Explained Allegorically

Let's try to surprise allegory *in medias res* in its effects, instead of beginning with definitions. Perhaps a relatively scientific or philosophical (or at any rate cognitive) text will be the most appropriate specimen for a counterintuitive demonstration. In any case, Daniel Dennett's now classic *Consciousness Explained* presents the additional advantage of dealing with a topic—subjectivity—where problems of representability intersect with ideologies of identity, and questions of literary representation and thematics cross paths with some of the oldest philosophical theories on the books.[1] His own theoretical context, if an outsider can grasp it, is torn by debates between Artificial Intelligence, computer models of the mind, neuropsychological explorations of the brain, and newer evolutionary theory, not to speak of the traditional history of philosophy as such. But I don't want to argue about the findings of this impressive book, but rather to examine it as a representation in its own right: indeed, as a kind of language experiment and perhaps as a conceptual narrative, with its own categories of completeness and its own rules for introducing new material or problems (as the novelist introduces new characters and disposes of old ones). Greimas indeed once famously declared that semiotics ought to be able to read a text like Kant's *Critique of Pure Reason* like a kind of novel, a proposal that might also lend confidence to the undertaking.

---

1 Daniel Dennett, *Consciousness Explained*, New York: Little, Brown, 1991. Page references in the text refer to this edition of the book.

Yet if in what follows we do not claim to evaluate the argument, we need at least to do it justice. By this I mean that I will try minimally to give a formal, not to say a formalist, account of the book. But what does it mean to "explain" consciousness? To give a theory of it, a new theory perhaps? Yet the book concludes with a more startling variant: "Look at what we have built with our tools. Could you have imagined [consciousness] without them?" (455) This now seems to change the dimensions of the problem. Is imagining the reader's acknowledgement of the validity of the explanation? But is not imagination a kind of picture thought, a satisfaction of conceptual needs in terms of the non-conceptual or preconceptual? And even if we decided to distinguish between *conceptualization*—the construction of a theory—and *imagination*—the rhetorical projection of an image—does not the significant introduction of the thematics of phenomenology in an early chapter of the book add yet a third possibility to this number, one we should not too hastily assume to be a kind of synthesis between the conceptual and the imagined? (Yet although phenomenology introduces the possibility of some identification with concrete experience in which intellection has its full share, it turns out that it will here be a question of "heterophenomenology"—that is to say, an eidetic construction based on other people's accounts, perhaps in some way vaguely comparable to "ethnomethodology.") We will return to these matters later on. Suffice it to add here that all three possibilities seem to fall under the general heading of representation as such. Yet not only must representation be a central theme of any approach to allegory, the issue of the representation of consciousness will necessarily loom large in any study of allegory. So perhaps our reading of Dennett will not be so purely formalist after all.

The starting point, and as it were the theoretical prerequisite against which all the stages of the argument can be checked, is the repudiation of dualism (associated with Descartes). Now as idealism is relatively inconceivable for modern people (despite the rather curious Bergson revival); and as materialism would seem to be equally inconceivable—a determination by the brain cells or whatever, dissatisfaction with all earlier versions of which can alone explain the project of this book itself—we seem to be in search of something else, the nature of which has already been queried and puzzled over in the preceding paragraph.

But at least the conceptual adversary is clear (or one of them). Dennett's opposition to Cartesian dualism is, however, only indirectly phrased in terms of the well-known mind/body split (or parallelism), something that famously made Descartes the father of modern idealism and of modern materialism alike and at one and the same time. Rather, he positions himself in any number of modern philosophical mainstreams by staging his conceptual objects in the form of a critique of what he calls "the Cartesian Theater of Consciousness" (33–39). The pineal gland is in other words the least of our worries. What this (non-Cartesian) characterization of Descartes makes unavoidable are a number of more basic philosophical issues: not merely the separation of the subject from the object, but also the static or contemplative function attributed to consciousness as its primary mode, as well as the perspectival unification of the scene or stage by the spectator in the audience (a theme that might draw us off into the considerations of camera vision deployed in film theory, as well as into the relationship posed by Guy Debord between commodification and the spectacle). A third fundamental theme is only implicit in the theater-of-consciousness model: it is that of personal identity, and it is easy enough to add it into the picture of the theatergoer. But one might also want to query the play itself: is it, as Dennett says in another context, a script "without an author" (12)? This is to repose the question of unification on the other or object side of the dichotomy, and also to raise the issue of narrative, which, transferred back to the subject or spectator, will become one of the fundamental explanatory schemata of Dennett's book, something which along with much else confirms, as we shall see, his family likeness with literary theory.

Cartesian "theaters," however, are not merely the theoretical models by various philosophers beyond Descartes himself: they also have relations with stubbornly held common sense views of the self (here called *folk psychology*), to the point where it is difficult enough to determine which comes first. One can at any rate "disprove" the philosophers, by adducing arguments and objections. Common sense, however—"la chose la mieux partagée au monde"—cannot exactly be said to be false, or rather its illusions must be acknowledged to be real and existing ones. Any theory that wishes to contravene common sense, therefore, must do more than point out fallacies: it must explain the illusion itself. At the limit this is a historicist enterprise: you not only have to show that your truth is true; you also, assuming that truth, have to show why no one has ever thought so before. So, more precisely, I will explain the various phenomena that compose what we call consciousness, showing how they are all physical effects of the brain's activities, how these activities evolved, and how they give rise to illusions about their own powers and properties. (16)

The formulation already allows us to note the expressions "composed" and "effects," which suggest that some account of synthesis will have to be offered (perhaps related to the "illusions") and also that, alongside narrative (already prematurely mentioned), we may also expect to receive an explanatory scheme organized around the term "evolved."

So perhaps for the moment we can redefine the troublesome term *explanation* as the construction of an alternative model of consciousness, whose function is to displace the commonsense (and traditional philosophical) one at the crucial points mentioned above: a separation of subject from object; a static, contemplative, epistemological definition of the subject; the unification of both subject—personal identity—and object world—a "reality" about which one formulates truths. The satisfaction supposed to accompany the "explanation" and to acknowledge its "truth" is then simply the feeling of completion that transpires when the new model has fully taken care of these flaws.

But we can go further in their enumeration, for it seems clear that Dennett has had to do some preliminary work or conceptual prepreparation in order to unify the various illusions. It would seem that this new and unified picture of the commonsense model (also sometimes still called the *Cartesian Theater*) turns precisely on unification itself, which can be considered dialectically in its two aspects: a manifold reduced to some kind of unity, and a center around which that new unity is constructed. Dennett's task will then be clarified: it is unification itself that needs to be discredited, at the same time that a substitute is proposed which can do the same work. That substitute will clearly enough initially be identified as the opposite of unification, a formulation which however only sets the direction of the investigation and has not yet done the real work.

Let's jump ahead to the concrete solution, in order to measure the distance we have to travel from the unification model to its more satisfactory substitute. The latter Dennett calls "Multiple Drafts": we have moved from a theater (a space) to a "process of production", indeed, a kind of writing project, in which various approximations are jotted down and then discarded in their turn. In fact, the literary reference is explicit here:

> In the world of publishing there is a traditional and usually quite hard-edged distinction between pre-publication editing, and post-publication correction of "errata." In the academic world today, however, things have been speeded up by electronic communication. With the advent of word-processing and desktop publishing and electronic mail, it now often happens that several different drafts of an article are simultaneously in circulation, with the author readily making revisions in response to comments received by electronic mail. Fixing the moment of publication, and thus calling one of the drafts of the article the canonical text—the text of record, the one to cite in a bibliography—becomes a somewhat arbitrary matter. (125)

Something like this is in fact Jerome McGann's proposal for a revision of literary criticism generally in the direction of a kind of "editorial materialism": drawing on the central example of Blake and the various home-made and hand-published "editions" of the latter's works, McGann constructs a model for which the term "Multiple Drafts is a very satisfactory name indeed, and one which would seem to me considerably to revise what happens on either side of the subject/object divide. On the object side, there is no longer any primary substance: there are simple successive versions of "something" about which our still Aristotelian prejudices are left to produce a kind of cubist vision; since no real object exists, no authoritative first intention or "vision" of the work to be elaborated (inasmuch the very process of linguistic elaboration modifies the starting point beyond recognition) and no "final" text except by the accidents of chronology and abandonment by the author. On the side of the subject, then, we rejoin one of the great themes of modern philosophy, from Sartre to Derrida: that of reification and temporality. If we want to be consequent about our life in time as subjects, we cannot privilege any present instant without reifying it and turning it into a stable thinglike reality: but could we endure (could we even imagine) a consent to temporality such that we are willing to relinquish all those temporal stabilities? Clearly, this is also Dennett's question, which he will answer by an appeal to narrative, or at least multiple drafts or versions of narrative (Sartre's "partial totalizations").

We should also note the insistent presence of history in this passage, in the form of the account of the computer. Is the computer here merely a useful metaphor, a submetaphor useful in the construction of the larger editorial and publishing metaphor? Certainly, from a static point of view. Yet the very historicity of the computer as an invention and an event suggests a perspective from which the computer was absent: what happened in the older slower mode of publishing? Did "final versions" and "canonical texts" exist then, or exist more strongly? Did that ontological category of the completed object have more validity before the word processor? And if the ontology of mutability was always valid, timelessly, even in the days of parchment or stone-carved hieroglyphs, can we say that it was nonetheless the historical "advent" of the new technology that enabled its deeper truth to be more adequately revealed, experienced, deconcealed, in postcomputer history? This is not some secondary matter, as we shall see, but has consequences for Dennett's book as a whole.

Back now to his Multiple Drafts: he has to show that the brain can function like this, on the one hand. But he also has to show that we can successfully reorganize our own experience of consciousness along the new lines. What has to be given up, then, is the impression that our conscious life consists in reliable messages from the outside world, which are transmitted to some (no doubt equally reliable) central witness or observer. But Multiple Drafts seems to suggest that such messages are not only fragmentary but very numerous indeed, and that the signals never stop coming in, on the heels of all the inadequately evaluated previous ones, which keep piling up somewhere. But couldn't that somewhere—a memory bank, perhaps—be the place in which someone sets all this information in order and produces at least a provisionally "final" version? Here the key critical concept turns out to be the idea of "filling in," attributed to the old commonsense or Cartesian theater model: obviously enough, faced with the "blooming, buzzing confusion" of the outside world, we fill in the gaps (94, 127, 344ff.). At the very least we "seem" to fill in the gaps (and the notion of "seeming" and subjective appearance is another Dennett target).

The problem is that we are "embarked," we are "thrown" into our "being-in-the-world," which is to say that we never have time to do the filling in, we're too busy with the next incoming signals. The provisional is certainly the crucial idea here, but what is its temporal connotation?

Consciousness Explained Allegorically

Are we to imagine that every so often we withdraw from embodied experience, and add up our findings, "provisionally" fill in the gaps? Even this compromise is not particularly conceivable: to be sure, it makes the Cartesian theatergoer over into a Brechtian spectator, smoking his cigar meditatively and evaluating the quality of the acting or boxing on offer to him. But this is perhaps the place of the philosophical problem of self-consciousness or reflexivity, to which we will return later on. For the moment, since there is no Cartesian theater in the first place (as Dennett so often likes to say), there can be no spectator either, Brechtian or otherwise. We are in real provisionality here, serious makeshift hand-to-mouth desperate crisis management, which is however the permanent situation of "consciousness" and from which there is no respite. Here reality never "comes together": "the brain does not bother 'constructing' any representations that go to the trouble of 'filling in' the blanks. That would be a waste of time . . . The judgment is *already in*, so the brain can get on with other tasks!" (128).

The brain is certainly faced with an overload of signals: "all varieties of perception—indeed, all varieties of thought or mental activity—are accomplished in the brain by parallel, multitrack processes of interpretation and elaboration of sensory inputs. Information entering the nervous system is under continuous 'editorial revision'" (111). But these "revisions" are as multiple and chaotic as the sensations they were supposed to interpret: moreover, the problem is temporal and chronological fully as much as it bears on some unimaginable simultaneity of all these sensations. For in that sense, just as there is no overarching Kantian form of empty space, so there is also no absolute grid of "linear" time upon which to organize this data. In the new dispensation, as Dennett suggestively observes somewhere, there is no "format in which 'time is used to represent time'" (153). Temporal sequence is as radically "provisional" a "construct" (if we can call it that) as everything else. At this point, Dennett interrupts himself to offer a brilliant illustration (and one in which the implicit persistence of the theme of communications technology is also to be noted): it turns on "the battle of New Orleans, [fought] on January 8, 1815, fifteen days after the truce ending the War of 1812 was signed in Belgium" (146). If you start to imagine the multiple repercussions of this temporal delay in Bengal, for example, or in Canada, a momentous and idiotic question begins to loom: "Exactly when did the British Empire become informed of the truce in the War of 1812?" (169). In this sense, the brain is as "far-flung" as that Empire (on which the sun never set), and the analogous question posed to it is equally meaningless.

But at least the British Empire had its Foreign Office in Whitehall and its seat of government in Buckingham Palace: can we do without some similar ultimate center when thinking about the brain? The answer is that provisionality still reigns absolutely and that even that "center," whatever it might be, must be thought to be radically provisional. I turn to another of Dennett's rhetorical illustrations:

> Orienting responses are the biological counterpart to the shipboard alarm "All hands on deck!" Most animals, like us, have activities they control in a routine fashion, 'on autopilot', using less than their full capacities, and in fact under the control of specialized subsystems of their brains. When a specialized alarm is triggered ... the animal's nervous system is mobilized to deal with the possibility of an emergency. The animal stops what it is doing and does a quick scan or update that gives every sense organ an opportunity to contribute to the pool of available and relevant information. A *temporary* centralized arena of control is established through heightened neural activity—all the lines are open, for a brief period. (180)

With this, I'm tempted to say, the construction of the model of Multiple Drafts is complete, and that of the Cartesian Theater (or of the common sense of "folk psychology") has been replaced. The latter's unification of the spectacle has been displaced by permanent radical provisionality; and the observing subject has been substituted by that "temporary centralized arena of control" mentioned above. Are we satisfied? Probably not, since a number of outstanding questions or problems have not yet been answered in the new mode: the model has not yet fully been put through its paces. For one thing, the issue of memory remains unexamined and is never fully addressed in this book: in other words, we might be willing to admit that our conventional picture of some larger "unification" of data by way of memory is part and parcel of the old system; but surely, and despite the repudiation of any overall organizing temporal grid, some place will have to be made in the new one for functional equivalent of what used to be called *memory*. And then there is the matter of thinking itself and of self-consciousness (let alone decision-making and the like). We need to separate this issue from the related issue of the centered subject, or in other words of personal identity. The last two topics are however fully treated here (at least to Dennett's satisfaction), and we need to note the terms of those treatments rapidly before going on.

What we call *thinking* is a function of the cerebral cortex (of which more later): but it is a second-degree function, and then naturally enough, thinking about thinking, or self-consciousness or reflexivity is a second-degree function of that second-degree function. For both are, in Dennett's view, effects of the emergence of language, something which happens relatively late in human evolution, after the cortex itself has been formed: "The innate specializations for language ... are a *very* recent and rushed add-on, no doubt an exploitation of earlier sequencing circuitry" (190): in other words, language is a form of software. How does language itself emerge? Dennett has a splendid and suggestive answer: by listening to ourselves speak—or cry, growl, mutter, shout (195). It is a theory that cuts across the impossible false problems that arise when one begins with "intersubjectivity" or "interpersonal" relations. And by the same token, once language has been elaborated, thinking is talking to ourselves, self-consciousness is a specific set toward that inner language (223) (not for nothing does Joyce achieve symbolic status in this book, alongside Von Neumann and his computer). Thoughts do not really preexist language, so that the operative principle must remain the immortal phrase E. M. Forster attributed to his fictional Old Lady: "How do I know what I think till I see what I say?" (193, 245), a formulation that has lost none of its suggestive power in full poststructuralism and postmodernity.

As for personal identity, here we touch on the alleged "mysteries" of consciousness, and the reader looking for some new theory or solution will probably be disappointed. But remember that what counts as a solution for Dennett is the replacement of the Cartesian model: the evaluation of his proposals for "personal identity" has thus rather to be made on a negative and critical basis and in terms of their adequacy as a substitute for the tradition (the soul, the self, and so on). Can the "temporary arena of control" really do the job personal identity used to do? Not without the positing of some new factor, as we shall see. Yet is not the neurological materialism of the brain and beyond it of the body, my body, "je mein Eigenes," as Heidegger might put it, enough to secure identity? In a sense: for the very concept of the body as an organism is at one with its boundaries, and already implies the solution to "the fundamental problem of recognition: telling one's self ... from everything else" (174). "This fundamental biological principle of distinguishing self from world, inside from outside, produces some remarkable echoes in the highest vaults of our psychology" (414). Clearly enough, once those borders are established, decision-making mechanisms are ready to hand, most notably the fundamental binary opposition between good and bad: self-preservation is then at least one indispensable feature of what will (in those "higher vaults of our psychology") be called personal identity, and its presence all the way down the organic ladder also suggests that Heidegger's supreme "Sein zum Tode," the death anxiety, is far from characterizing authentic human individuality alone.

But we have not yet tabulated all the "remarkable echoes." Let's reframe the question in philosophical terms, those for example so memorably formulated by Nietzsche:

> The "subject" is the fiction that many similar states in us are in the effect of one substratum: but it is we who first created the "similarity" of these states, our adjusting and making them similar is the fact, not their similarity.[2]

And to "similarity," which could easily turn into a basic category of Hegel's *Logic*, Nietzsche pointedly adds: "which ought to be denied." Will memory do? We remember William James's marvelous account of personal identity as the brand of private property we burn onto all our individual memories, so as to be able to round them like cattle when the need arises (when we hear the cry, All hands on deck! for example?). But as I have observed, Dennett here eschews an appeal to memory as some primary explanatory function.

Instead, he introduces that rather different "new factor" I have forecast, and this is narrative as such. All those "partial totalizations" and provisional unifications I have alluded to are in fact narrative ones (and we should remember that in that sense narrative in Dennett is always provisional, always partial, always coexisting with a host of other

---

2 Friedrich Nietzsche, *Writings from the Late Notebooks*, Cambridge: Cambridge University Press, 2003, 179.

narrative versions or drafts). The human being is thus here apparently a storytelling animal (79, 94), and an enormous amount of argumentation is made to rest on this apparently ungrounded or even metaphysical proposition, however satisfying it may be for the contemporary mind. Indeed, this is the moment in which the underwater reader suddenly bursts out of the depths of *Consciousness Explained* into the more familiar atmosphere of a completely different philosophical tradition, as Dennett wryly acknowledges, by quoting a passage from David Lodge's *Nice Work* (1988):

> According to Robyn (or, more precisely, according to the writers who have influenced her thinking on these matters), there is no such thing as the "Self" on which capitalism and the classic novel are founded—that is to say, a finite, unique soul or essence that constitutes a person's identity: there is only a subject position in an infinite web of discourses—the discourses of power, sex, family, science, religion, poetry, etc. And by the same token, there is no such thing as an author, that is to say, one who originates a work of fiction *ab nihilo* . . . In the famous words of Jacques Derrida . . . "*il n'y a pas de hors-texte*," there is nothing outside the text. There are no origins, there is only production, and we produce our "selves" in language. Not "*you are what you eat*" but "*you are what you speak*," or rather "*you are what speaks you*," is the axiomatic basis of Robyn's philosophy, which she would call, if required to give it a name, "semiotic materialism." (410–411)

Dennett draws the line at this name but agrees that "Robyn and I think alike—and of course we are *both*, by our own accounts, fictional characters of a sort, though of a slightly different sort" (411).

This is then the moment at which we must begin a critical analysis of *Consciousness Explained*, from which I must now admit that several very important "missing portions" have been withheld. These two missing portions are in fact explanatory mechanisms, which is why my account of the book will have seemed exceedingly thin to readers who have had firsthand contact with its richness and complexity.

The first of these is a feature we have already begun to observe in the discussions immediately preceding (and which, I might add, is significantly and originally present in Nietzsche himself). This is evolutionary theory as an explanatory principle. For one thing, I have omitted to mention that one enormous central chapter of the book is devoted to a seventy-page exposition of current evolutionary theory: not sociobiology exactly, no doubt, but which surely reflects the emergence of sociobiology and the historical need to come somehow to terms with it.

Evolutionist thought (of whatever kind) is certainly to be grasped as a variety of historicism generally: but its early form, Lamarckian teleology, prepares the way for full-blown historicist thinking, while its later or Darwinian version marks an advance on ordinary historicism, which it corrects and modifies in significant ways. Historicist thinking in general involves a mutation in what counts as the explanation of something (this is the sense in which it seems right to see its emergence as a paradigm shift or change—as for example Foucault does in *The Order of Things*). The change consists in this: that the historical coming into being of a thing, the narrative of its emergence, will now count as an understanding of it. To put it this way is to see how the evolutionist material in Dennett marks a supplement to the appeal to understanding we have described above, which required us to compare the new model with the old one (Multiple Drafts against Cartesian Theater) and seemed to be fulfilled when all of the constituent features wrongly dealt with in the latter were replaced by satisfactory equivalents in the former. Now, for some reason, we seem to need an additional kind of comprehension, which is to be supplied by narrative history.

Thus, where the structure of the brain is consulted in order to show that it was capable of housing the various mental processes posited by Multiple Drafts, we now in addition get the story of its emergence:

> Onto this substrate nervous system we now want to imagine building a more human mind . . . While chimpanzees have brains of roughly the same size as our common ancestor . . . our hominid ancestors' brains grew four times as large . . . When the ice ages began, about two and a half million years ago, the Great Encephalization commenced, and was essentially completed 150,000 years ago—*before* the development of language, of cooking, of agriculture. (189–90)

One can think of two reasons why this historical "supplement" is required. First, we can imagine a fairly complete philosophical account of the Multiple Drafts model of the mind that would not require any reference to the brain at all: it would not be an idealist account exactly, but not obviously a materialist one either (what it tries to be, of course, is monist, a somewhat different thing from either alternative). But Dennett wishes to position his theory at the crossroads of several traditions, very much including neurobiology and brain research (and their compatibility or incompatibility with computer models and simulations): the evolutionary story secures this materialist level of the content.

Meanwhile, it has not been pointed out that the twist or modification that evolutionism gives historicism generally, and that makes up its originality, lies in the notion of function. Evolutionism distinguishes itself from "mere" historicism by positing understanding or explanation as a grasping of the history of function. But told in terms of lower life forms, these stories become mere decorations or metaphors for human activity. To have the boundaries that make up human identity evoked in terms of amoebas, for example, is only to be offered a simpler and more vivid picture of the human situation: for the most part Dennett eschews the ideological consequences that define sociobiology, namely the conclusion that Ur-life offers us the authentic truth of what human life should be like and serves as an ethical and political model (in this case, incorporation, expansion, cyclical production of new entities, and so on). It is thus the history of human evolution that can alone convert the rich animal illustrations into a substantive argument about human consciousness.

In other words, the story of the cortex has to tell us something new, something that the life of the lower forms cannot convey. This "huge convoluted mantle that has swiftly burgeoned in the human skull and now completely covers the older animal brain underneath" (193) will allow an indispensable next step in what will in fact be a new story. (We have already seen how the general image of the cortex offered a kind of visual support to the model of the decentered mind, with its simultaneity of multiple signals and messages.)

But before outlining the new story, we have to show how its telling us was made possible; and this obliges us to return to the matter of evolutionist historicism in order to mark the originality and the distinctiveness of the Darwinian turn. It is often said that the older evolutionism was teleological insofar as, having told the history of the emergence of a function, it then had nothing more to say, thereby surrendering to the obvious next (metaphysical) question of the purpose of that function and that emergence. Darwinism's mechanism of natural selection then cuts this stage out and enables a radically nonteleological story of development and evolution to be told. Can this still be called historicism? People who have an interest in discrediting historicism by way of the accusation of teleology will certainly want to call Darwin something else (and it should be added that Marx's evolutionist view of society follows Darwin in this respect and in this respect is also nonteleological). But perhaps all this can be said in a more complicated Hegelian way: Darwinian evolutionism is a historicism that carries the negation of historicism within itself as a kind of counterpoison. It can thus seem either historicist (it tells the story of a historical emergence) or antihistoricist (it removes the teleology or invents a new kind of nonteleological storytelling): and this is an excellent polemic defensive position, which allows you to go on telling stories (as we see Nietzsche doing, for example), while at the same time attacking teleology and its historicisms and indeed in some cases using your own storytelling to discredit the older kind.

As for the remarkable mechanism of natural selection, however, we must observe that in Dennett it takes a different form, namely the crucial doctrine of multiple functions, or in other words the unforeseeable developments made possible when an organ developed for one specific function is now appropriated (or "parasitized") by one or several different ones:

> Human designers, being farsighted but blinkered, tend to find their designs thwarted by unforeseen side effects and interactions, so they try to guard against them by giving each element in the system a single function, and insulating it from all the other elements. In contrast, Mother Nature (the process of natural selection) is famously myopic and lacking in goals. Since she doesn't foresee any at all, she has no way of worrying about unforeseen side effects. Not "trying" to avoid them, she tries out designs in which many such side effects occur; most such designs are terrible (ask any engineer), but every now and then there is a *serendipitous side effect*: two or more unrelated functional elements interact to produce a bonus: multiple functions for single elements. (175)

This is a somewhat different way of continuing to be a historicist while roundly denouncing historicism: even if you thought, and tried to assert, that the Darwinian model of natural selection was still somehow secretly teleological and historicist, this new twist subverts even that larval teleology by positing the unexpected imposition of new parasitic multiple functions on top of the evolutionary function whose story Darwinism told. In fact, we have seen Dennett reap the benefits of the new second-degree story in his account of language: for he sees that as being a kind of software (221) added on to the evolved human cortex (whose functional reason for coming into being is apparently mysterious anyhow).

And as a matter of fact, the doctrine of multiple functions here stands as a kind of textual autoreferentiality: it models a process Dennett himself will replicate in the construction of his own text. Thus, the new theory of "connectionism"—specifically introduced at this point (175, note 3)—is an idea, a textual "function" if you like, which is here added on to the account of the evolution of the brain. The idea that "each node contributes to many different contents" will allow us to posit "whole systems having specialized roles but also being recruitable into more general projects" (175, note 3). But this is not exactly a neurological finding; rather, it is a mediation between the material description of the brain and the philosophical requirements of the Multiple Drafts model of the mind.

Indeed, the textual "parasitism" enabled by the doctrine of multiple functions will shortly have an even larger exemplification, whose account will complete our discussion of the evolutionist "addition" to the philosophical argument. For it turns out that the evolutionist historical narrative will also enable the superposition of a narrative of social history (in which the historicism of natural history "returns," as Hegel might put it, into its fundamental essence as the narrative of history *tout court*).

We have seen that the introduction of the theme of language was crucial for the first or philosophical model in Dennett, for it allowed him to develop a conception of thinking radically different from the old centered kind, based on a Cartesian point of consciousness (language offering multiple drafts of something that is not thinking until it is thus linguistically drafted, and so forth). Now that the fact of language has been drawn into an evolutionist account, however, we are rather unexpectedly able to confront a whole evolutionist story of the emergence of culture itself (in other words, of the nonmaterialist being of something which can no longer be considered natural history at all). This story is retold from Richard Dawkins's concept of the "memes" (199–208), or in other words specifically cultural entities that can be circulated from mind to mind and also stored up in large quantities:

> the sort of complex ideas that form themselves into distinct memorable units—such as the ideas of
> > wheel
> > wearing clothes
> > vendetta
> > right triangle
> > alphabet
> > calendar
> > the *Odyssey* etc. (201)

Am I right in feeling that here evolutionist thought has overstepped itself, and that such materials—which can be described in terms of Objective Spirit or in those of "cultural literacy" and attributed to the public sphere or to media culture—are out of place in an account of the evolution of physical organs and their functions? The discomfort comes from the sense of a vicious circle, in which the essentially cultural operations of the human mind are then "explained" by the illicit attribution of just such cultural materials to the physical structure of the brain as such.

Be that as it may, however, my purpose in raising the issue here is a somewhat different one: for I think that the theory of the "memes" now allows a secondary or parasitic historical narrative to be added on top of the first evolutionist one (which thus proves to admit of "multiple functions"). This second narrative is one of history itself, and in particular social history, and whatever it claims to say about the evolution of that history generally, I believe that its most obvious reference can be identified as our own contemporary postmodern society, oversaturated as it is with just such cultural information of this kind. I doubt if any earlier historical society would have described its culture in exactly this way, with the emphasis on the sheer multiplicity of the memes and their overpopulation. It is an intuition once again reinforced by the technological figure: for it will be remembered that language (which alone makes "memes" possible) was described as an add-on, a new software program: "the powers of this *virtual machine* vastly enhance the underlying powers of the organic *hardware* on which it runs" (210). Such figures cannot be altogether innocent, and in the present instance it is difficult to avoid the impression that such figurability has a historical content and logic. If we are dependent on the figure of the new information technology to convey our new sense of language and the memes, then surely in some other way the very state of language and the memes that is being characterized can be said to require the historical existence of that information technology in the first place. This is the sense in which I take both references as characterizing our contemporary situation and thereby as introducing some very contemporary connotations to what gave itself as a longer evolutionary narrative.

Let me try to sum this complicated situation up as follows: an evolutionary narrative is introduced into a nonnarrative argument. This narrative of natural history then seems to project a concurrent narrative of social history generally. But now that new dimension seems in its turn to project a far more concentrated story or narrative about contemporary social history (or in other words, the "postmodern condition"). Yet why should it do this, and what is the message of this new third-degree story?

I come therefore at some length to my second general excursus about *Consciousness Explained* and will now "restore" some other, rather different "missing portions" I have equally withheld until now. The curious reader, indeed, from time to time notes extended metaphors or similes in Dennett, which at first require no particular justification and stand or fall on their rhetorical merits. So it is initially merely amusing that he should deploy "Arthur Laffer's notorious Curve, the intellectual foundation . . . of Reaganomics" (109) to tarnish input–output theories of the mind and action on the grounds of the similarity of their graphs. Still, this might well trigger some feeble subliminal message about the relationship of the older mental theories to a certain conservative social order. One's attention perks up, however, when Stalinism and Orwell's *1984* enter the picture (116–17): these are meant to dramatize various unsatisfactory (old-fashioned) attempts to explain the alleged "filling-in" operations of consciousness as it rewrites the past—Orwellian "revision" of the past and the staging of Stalinesque "show trials, carefully scripted presentations of false testimony and bogus confessions, complete with simulated evidence" (117). Both are dialectically sent off back to back as versions of the same strategy, and they presumably contrast unfavorably with the new model of Multiple Drafts and perpetual revisions in which partial narratives engage in unending narrative unification of our current experience of consciousness and identity without requiring the act of "revision." Yet the allusions to the Cold War and its end in Reaganism do somehow begin to project a more specifically historical context of reference in which the emergence of Dennett's brand-new theory is associated with the new problems of some specifically contemporary situation of postmodernity.

What those new problems are can now be identified by turning to the far more central metaphorics that throughout the whole argument are called upon to characterize the fundamental model of the Cartesian Theater and its flaws and weaknesses. We have until now characterized the characterization of this "theater" in aesthetic terms: the theatrical spectacle itself, or the editorial and textual production of electronic mail. Nor would I wish to exclude some properly aesthetic "level" of the book in which a specifically aesthetic message is being conveyed, however faintly.

But the primary metaphorical rhetoric is political: Cartesian central consciousness is described as "dictatorial" (171), it is consistently referred to as a kind of simulation of the Oval Office (32, 429), as in the following:

> The pineal gland is not only not the fax machine to the Soul, it is also not the Oval Office of the brain, and neither are any of the other portions of the brain. The brain is Headquarters, the place where the ultimate observer is, but there is no reason to believe that the brain itself has any deeper headquarters, any inner sanctum, arrival at which is the necessary or sufficient condition for conscious experience. In short, there is no observer inside the brain. (106)

And by the same token, there is no "Boss" and therefore no "Boss agent of ominous authority" (261). And now the political figures take an interesting poststructuralist turn: for the Cartesian despot can also be understood as a Central Meaner or Conceptualizer (238), "an Author of Record, a Meaner of all the meanings" (228). Now a kind of Foucauldian power/knowledge swims into view and is denounced in the same spirit as the more general poststructuralist critiques of norm and authority, and in particular the authority of interpretation and of positing fixed meanings, alongside the political authority of the state.

For it is indeed a very contemporary, or even postmodern, conception of the state which has here via metaphorical repetition come to be associated with the Cartesian model. Centrality is finally also that: if you have a centered subject, a central observer, along with a point of consciousness at the very center, to secure a unified personal identity (not to speak of a unified world or a unified Truth), then you also at length confront the State.

What is the alternative?

> It is all very well to equip oneself with an "All hands on deck!" subroutine, but then, once all hands are on deck, one must have some way of coping with the flood of volunteers. We should not expect there to have been a convenient captain already at hand (what would he have been doing up till then?), so conflict between volunteers had to sort themselves out without any higher executive. (188)

The next immediate figure, that of Milton's Pandemonium, strikes a suitably revolutionary note, but the solution seems to remain that of what Dennett calls "an internal political miracle": the decentered brain

> creates a *virtual captain* of the crew, without elevating any of them to long-term dictatorial power. Who's in charge? First one coalition and then another, shifting in ways that are not chaotic thanks to good meta-habits that tend to entertain coherent, purposeful sequences rather than an interminable helter-skelter power grab. (228)

Is this satisfactory? Probably no more so than the model of consciousness that it is designed to represent (but no less so either). Yet the question of what counts as an "explanation" for consciousness has now strangely seemed to shift into the problem of what might count as a satisfactory or plausible political vision.

Indeed, I want to argue that such moments reveal the text to have been parasitized by a theoretical problem of an utterly different kind from that of philosophical or neurological models of consciousness. The philosophical function in other words has also and simultaneously been occupied by a political one; and Dennett (or his unconscious, or some crucial alliance of memes) has also found himself deploying one of the issues which crucially and centrally (if I may put it that way) has engaged postmodernity, the question of the state and that of some decentralized democracy, the question of unified power and multiple social difference, the old questions of political "representation" which have entered into crisis in a situation in which no one believes in the legitimacy of such representation any longer. That Dennett does not altogether solve his philosophical problem and project some fully satisfying new "explanation" of consciousness is then perfectly comprehensible, in light of the fact that political philosophy has been unable until now to provide any properly political models of "democracy" that do away with centralized state power altogether. Anarchism was the only true heroic effort to do so; and it was reactive against precisely those categories of centrality and state power in which the rest of us (no matter how well disposed) are still locked. This is a specific contradiction, I would now like to claim; and we cannot exactly get out of this historical and ideological contradiction by thinking new and better thoughts. Contradictions in that sense are never solved: they are made to deliver up new moments, new configurations, new contradictions indeed, in the light of which the old contradiction sinks into the past.

Thus I am perfectly willing to call the opposition between the State and democracy an ideological opposition: which does not mean that it is unreal, or that we can simply forget about it. On the contrary, it means that it is historically binding, and that we are locked into it without any Utopian vision of what might be possible if it were no longer in force.

Dennett's secondary narrative is ideological in precisely this sense, although it is difficult to determine whether it reflects the US anti-communist Cold War "liberalism" of the Reagan era (Stalinist despotism and so on) or the more anarchist displacement onto aporias about the state and "radical democracy" that followed the end of actually existing socialism. But I am not interested in passing judgments, even those implicit in such labels; I have been primarily interested in the structure of this work, which can now be seen to be complex and many-leveled. And at this (final) stage in my argument, I am also concerned to correct the misconceptions that may have been conveyed by my use of the term *metaphor* to characterize the delivery system of the political content described above. For to see this as "merely" metaphorical allows us to see all this as something purely rhetorical and to retranslate the political figures back into simple, if vivid, devices for conveying an idea or making a point.

Dennett himself raises a suggestive issue when, in his own conclusion, he tries to justify the kind of explanation his title promised, and which he feels himself to have offered:

> Only a theory that explained conscious events in terms of unconscious events could explain consciousness at all . . . This leads some people to insist that consciousness can never be explained. But why should consciousness be the only thing that can't be explained? Solids and liquids and gases can be explained in terms of things that aren't themselves solids or liquids or gases. Surely life can be explained in terms of things that aren't themselves alive—and the explanation doesn't leave living things lifeless. (454–55)

Perhaps the protest comes too late and is an admission of his own dissatisfaction. Yet the terms are most interesting indeed: you explain something in terms of something else, something that first thing is not, something different from it and radically other. But this also happens to be, not merely the meaning, but the very etymology, of the word *allegory*; and in fact I want to call the textual movement I have been describing an allegorical one, and I believe that I have shown *Consciousness Explained* to be a political allegory, whatever else it is. This is the sense in which the characterization of the crucial figures as metaphorical is really a competing explanation, which I cannot now refute, and it is a very damaging one indeed. To develop a convincing theory of the allegorical, therefore, requires a confrontation with the claims of metaphor itself.

In the absence of such a confrontation, however, perhaps an equally outrageous and unfounded claim can be made: one that has the whole weight of the tradition of the so-called "history of ideas" against it. The latter, indeed, affirms over and over again that the history of ideas is first and foremost the history of scientific ideas and that it is the latter which "explain" the emergence of other, parallel thoughts in realms as distant as the aesthetic and the political. But what if this were not so? What if, indeed, it was the emergence of new social forms and political experiences which came first, and allowed new forms of other thought—very specifically scientific thinking—to emerge? What if the conditions of possibility of those scientific "discoveries" lay in the apprenticeship of the mind to the new forms closest to its own concrete experience, in the social itself? In that case it will come as no surprise that Dennett needs his political allegory to express his "new" thoughts about consciousness and the brain: for he will have needed the social and political to conceive those new thoughts in the first place.

Appendix C:
Culture and Group Libido

For culture—the weaker, more secular version of that thing called religion—is not a "substance" or a phenomenon in its own right, it is an objective mirage that arises out of the relationship between at least two groups.[1] This is to say that no group "has" a culture all by itself: culture is the nimbus perceived by one group when it comes into contact with and observes another one. It is the objectification of everything alien and strange about the contact group: in this context, it is of no little interest to observe that one of the first books on the interrelationship of groups (the constitutive role of the boundary, the way each group is defined by and defines the other) draws on Erving Goffman's *Stigma* for an account of how defining marks function for other people: in this sense, then, a "culture" is the ensemble of stigmata one group bears in the eyes of the other group (and vice versa). But such marks are more often projected into the "alien mind" in the form of that thought-of-the-other we call belief and elaborate as religion. But belief in this sense is not something we ourselves have, since what we do seems to us natural and does not need the motivation and rationalization of this strange internalized entity; and indeed the anthropologist Rodney Needham has shown that most "cultures" do not possess the equivalent of our concept, or pseudoconcept, of belief (which is thus unmasked as

---

1   This appendix is an excerpt from Fredric Jameson, "On 'Cultural Studies'," *Ideologies of Theory*, London: Verso, 2009, 33–37.

something the translators illicitly project back into nonimperial, noncosmopolitan languages).

Still, it happens that "we" also often speak of "our own" culture, religion, beliefs, or whatever. These may now be identified as the recuperation of the Other's view of us; of that objective mirage whereby the Other has formed a picture of us as "having" a culture: depending on the power of the Other, this alienated image demands a response, which may be as inconsequential as the denial whereby Americans brush off the stereotypes of the "ugly American" they encounter abroad, or as thoroughgoing as the various ethnic revivals whereby, as in Hindu nationalism, a people reconstructs those stereotypes and affirms them in a new cultural–nationalist politics: something which is never the "return" to an older authentic reality but always a new construction (out of what look like older materials).

Culture must thus always be seen as a vehicle or a medium whereby the relationship between groups is transacted. If it is not always vigilantly unmasked as an idea of the Other (even when I reassume it for myself), it perpetuates the optical illusions and the false objectivism of this complex historical relationship (thus the objections that have been made to pseudoconcepts like "society" are even more valid for this one, whose origin in group struggle can be deciphered). Meanwhile, to insist on this translation program (the imperative to turn concepts of culture back into forms of the relationship between collective groups) offers a more satisfactory way of fulfilling the objectives of the various forms of a sociological Heisenberg principle than does the current individualistic recommendation to reckon back in the place of the observer. In reality, the anthropologist-other, the individual observer, stands in for a whole social group, and it is in this sense that his knowledge is a form of power, where "knowledge" designates something individual, and "power" tries to characterize that mode of relationship between groups for which our vocabulary is so poor.

For the relationship between groups is, so to speak, unnatural: it is the chance external contact between entities which have only an interior (like a monad) and no exterior or external surface, save in this special circumstance in which it is precisely the outer edge of the group that—all the while remaining unrepresentable—brushes against that of the other. Speaking crudely then, we would have to say that the relationship between groups must always be one of struggle or violence: for the only positive or tolerant way for them to coexist is to part from one another and rediscover their isolation and their solitude. Each group is thus the entire world, the collective is the fundamental form of the monad, windowless and unbounded (at least from within).

But this failure or omission of a plausible, let alone a "natural" set of attitudes whereby group relations might be conducted, means that the two fundamental forms of group relationship reduce themselves to the primordial ones of *envy* and *loathing,* respectively. The oscillation back and forth between these poles can at least in part be explained by prestige (to use one of Gramsci's categories): an attempt to appropriate the culture of the other group (which as we have already seen in effect means inventing the "culture" of the other group) is a tribute and a form of group recognition, the expression of collective envy, the acknowledgment of the prestige of the other group. It seems likely that this prestige is not to be too quickly reduced to matters of power, since very often larger and more powerful groups pay this tribute to the groups they dominate, whose forms of cultural expression they borrow and imitate. Prestige is thus more plausibly an emanation of group solidarity, something a weaker group often needs to develop more desperately than the larger complacent hegemonic one, which nonetheless dimly senses its own inner lack of the same cohesion and unconsciously regrets its tendential dissolution as a group as such. "Groupie-ism" is another strong expression of this kind of envy, but on an individual basis, as members of the dominant "culture" opt out and mimic the adherence to the dominated. (And after all that has been said, it is probably not necessary to add that groupies are thus already in this sense potential or proto-intellectuals.)

As for group loathing, however, it mobilizes the classic syndromes of purity and danger and acts out a kind of defense of the boundaries of the primary group against this threat perceived to be inherent in the Other's very existence. Modern racism (as opposed, in other words, to postmodern or "neo" racism) is one of the most elaborated forms of such group loathing—inflected in the direction of a whole political program; it should lead us on to some reflection on the role of the stereotype in all such group or "cultural" relations, which can virtually by definition not do without the stereotypical. For the group as such is necessarily an imaginary entity, in the sense in which no individual mind is able to intuit it concretely. The group must be abstracted, or fantasized, on the basis of discrete individual contacts and experiences, which can never be generalized in anything but abusive fashion. The relations between groups are always stereotypical insofar as they must always involve collective abstractions of the other group, no matter how sanitized, no matter how liberally censored and imbued with respect. What it is politically correct to do under such circumstances is to allow the other group itself to elaborate its own preferential image and then to work with that henceforth "official" stereotype. But the inevitability of the stereotypical—and the persistence of the possibility of group loathing, racism, caricature, and all the rest it cannot but bring with it—is not thereby laid to rest. Utopia could therefore, under those circumstances, only mean two different kinds of situations which might in fact turn out to be the same: a world in which only individuals confronted one another, in the absence of groups; or a group isolated from the rest of the world in such a way that the matter of the external stereotype (or "ethnic identity") never arose in the first place. The stereotype is indeed the place of an illicit surplus of meaning, what Barthes called the "nausea" of mythologies: it is the abstraction by virtue of which my individuality is allegorized and turned into an abusive illustration of something else, something nonconcrete and nonindividual. ("I don't join organizations or adopt labels," says a character in a recent movie. "You don't have to," replies his friend, "You're a Jew!") But the liberal solution to this dilemma—doing away with the stereotypes or pretending they don't exist—is not possible, although fortunately we carry on as though it were for most of the time.

Groups are thus always conflictual; and this is what has led Donald Horowitz, in the definitive study of international ethnic conflict, to suggest that although what he takes to be Marxism's economic or class account of such conflicts is unsatisfactory. Marx may have unwittingly anticipated a fundamental feature of modern ethnic theory in his notion of the necessarily dichotomous structure of class conflict as such: ethnic conflicts, indeed, are for Horowitz always tendentially dichotomous, each side ending up incorporating the various smaller satellite ethnic groups in such a way as to symbolically reenact a version of Gramscian hegemony and Gramscian hegemonic or historic blocs as well. But classes in that sense do not precede capitalism and there is no single-shot Marxian theory of "economic" causality: the economic is most often the forgotten trigger for all kinds of noneconomic developments, and the emphasis on it is heuristic and has to do with the structure of the various disciplines (and what they structurally occult or repress), rather than with ontology. What Marxism has to offer ethnic theory is probably, on the contrary, the suggestion that ethnic struggles might well be clarified by an accompanying question about class formation as such.

Fully realized classes, indeed, classes in and for themselves, "potential" or structural classes that have finally by all kinds of complicated historical and social processes achieved what is often called "class consciousness," are clearly also groups in our sense (although groups in our sense are rarely classes as such). Marxism suggests two kinds of things about these peculiar and relatively rare types of groups. The first is that they have much greater possibilities for development than ethnic groups: they can potentially expand to become coterminous with society as a whole (and do so, during those unique and punctual events we call revolutions), whereas the groups are necessarily limited by their own specific self-definition and constitutive characteristics. Ethnic conflict can thus develop and expand into class conflict, whereas the degeneration of class conflict into ethnic rivalry is a restrictive and centripetal development.

(Indeed, the alternation of envy and loathing constitutes an excellent illustration of the dialectic of class and group in action: whatever group or identity investment may be at work in envy, its libidinal opposite always tends to transcend the dynamics of the group relationship in the direction of that of class proper. Thus, anyone who observed the deployment of group and identity hatred in the 1992 Republican National Convention—the race and gender hostility so clearly marked in the speeches and the faces of characteristic "cultural counterrevolutionaries" like Pat Buchanan—understood at once that it was fundamentally class hostility and class struggle that was the deeper stake in such passions and their symbolisms. By the same token, the observers who felt that symbolism and responded to the Republican Right in kind can also be said to have had their smaller group-and-identity consciousness "raised" in the direction of the ultimate horizon of social class.)

The second point follows from this one, namely that it is only after the modulation of the ethnic into the class category that a possible resolution of such struggles is to be found. For in general, ethnic conflict cannot be solved or resolved; it can only be sublimated into a struggle of a different kind that *can* be resolved. Class struggle, which has as its aim and outcome, not the triumph of one class over another but the abolition of the very category of class, offers the prototype of one such sublimation. The market and consumption—that is to say, what is euphemistically called *modernization*, the transformation of the members of various groups into the universal consumer—is another kind of sublimation, which has come to look equally as universal as the classless one but which perhaps owes its success predominantly to the specific circumstances of the postfeudal North American commonwealth, and the possibilities of social leveling that arose with the development of the mass media. This is the sense in which "American democracy" has seemed able to preempt class dynamics and to offer a unique solution to the matter of group dynamics discussed above. We therefore need to take into account the possibility that the various politics of Difference—the differences inherent in the various politics of "group identity"—have been made possible only by the tendential leveling of social Identity generated by consumer society; and to entertain the hypothesis that a cultural politics of difference becomes itself feasible only when the great and forbidding categories of classical Otherness have been substantially weakened by "modernization" (so that current neoethnicities may be distinct from the classical kind as neo-racism is from classical racism).

But this does not spell a waning of group antagonisms but precisely the opposite (as can be judged from the current world scene), and it is also to be expected that Cultural Studies itself—as a space in which the new group dynamics develop—will also entail its quotient of the libidinal. The energy exchanges or ion formations of "articulation" are not, indeed, likely to take place neutrally, but to release violent waves of affect—narcissistic wounds, feelings of envy and inferiority, the intermittent repugnance for the others' groups.

Index

Abel, Lionel
  Metatheater, 91–92, 114
Abraham a Sancta Clara, 321
abstraction, 136, 194, 233, 284, 325, 386
  allegory and, 44–45, 307
  Greek discovery of, 44, 345
  personification and, 229, 231
Adorno, Theodor W., 32, 66, 114, 134, 139, 141, 152, 303
  breakthrough notion of, 144–47, 148, 149
  on Mahler, 135, 143, 145, 146–47
  on musical form, 130, 142, 149
  on narrative, 122–23
  on nature imagery, 305, 307
  on nominalism, 58–59, 136–37
  on *Threepenny Opera*, 321
aesthetics, 33, 46, 88, 98, 292, 312
  artistic autonomy in, 146
  beginnings and ending in, 125–26
  constructivism and, 35–36, 37
  Croce and, 13, 233, 261, 263
  Dante and, 232–33, 252
  philosophy and, 23–24, 34, 35
  Sartre on, 29, 243

  symbolism and, 24, 337
affect, 80
  language and, 94, 110, 321
  named emotions and, 44, 59, 66, 157, 200, 279, 280, 283, 310, 320, 325, 347
  theoretical conception of, 44, 59, 66, 200
affective allegory, 325
affect theory, 31, 76, 77, 80–81
Africa, 164–65, 180
  Ousmane Sembene depiction of, 179–85
agitation, 155–56
Ahmad, Aijaz, 187–88, 190
Albee, Edward, 76
Alewyn, Richard, 292–93, 295–96
Alexander, 12
alienation, 27, 56
  forms of allegorical, 38–39, 72
  nomination and, 54–55
  primal, 38, 55, 239
  reification and, 40–41, 346
allegoresis, 29, 278
  allegory's distinction from, 3, 10, 52, 140, 260

allegory's passage to, 26, 43
characteristics of, 310
Dante and, 260, 280
defined, 25
in postmodernity, 309–48
temptation of, 157, 260
allegorical frame, 10, 218–19
allegorical/mystical level of allegory, xiv, 18, 152, 213, 308
Hamlet and, 84, 117
in postmodernity, 310–11, 340, 343
allegory. *See* allegorical/mystical level of allegory; anagogic level of allegory; bad allegory; dual allegorical scheme; fourfold allegorical system; literal level of allegory; moral level of allegory; national allegory; one-to-one allegory; traditional allegory; tripartite allegorical scheme
Almen, Bryan, 122
Althusser, Louis, x, xii, xiii, 334
amplificatio, 4, 56, 58, 270
anagogic level of allegory, xvii, 117, 190, 213, 308
Dante and, 265, 267
level of meaning, 18, 20
Mahler and, 151–52
in postmodernity, 310–11, 328, 329, 332, 338–39, 340, 343
Spenser and, 234–35, 249
analogon, 258, 276, 297
concept of, 41–42
anarchism and anarchists, 206, 380
Anderson, Benedict, 193
anger, 75, 76, 94, 279
Aristotle on, 68–69, 73–74, 77
Greimas square and, 73–75
nature of, 66–67, 72
Anthropocene, 36, 37, 348
The Antinomies of Realism (Jameson), 44

Anti-Oedipus (Deleuze and Guattari), 96
Aristotle, 61, 101, 244, 269, 279
on emotions and passions, 65, 66, 67–69, 74, 76, 77, 155
on pairing of opposites, 50, 52, 67
on substance, 52–53
works
Nichomachean Ethics, 236
Rhetoric, 66, 67–68, 74
art for art's sake, 311–12
asabiyya, xvi, xix, 196–97, 198, 212
atonality, 133–34
Auerbach, Erich, 273–74, 277, 283
attacks on allegory by, 272, 273
figura doctrine of, 2, 18, 251–52, 253, 273
Mimesis, 273–75
Augé, Marc, 319n
Augustine, St., 58, 65–66
Confessions, 222
Austro-Hungarian Empire, 202, 328
autoreferentiality, 21, 27, 28–29, 375
Autos sacramentales, 294–95

Bachelard, Gaston, 52
bad allegory, xvii, 6, 9, 16, 64, 119–20, 148, 264
symbolism and, 270–71
bad infinity, 195, 314, 324
Badiou, Alain, 32, 45, 46–47, 48, 79
The Theory of the Subject, 46, 47
Bahro, Rudolph, 174
Bakhtin, Mikhail, 43, 115
Ballard, J. G., 352–53
Balzac, Honoré de, 271, 296–97, 312, 318, 338
Banfield, Ann, 8
Baroque
Benjamin on, 30–31, 90
Goethe and, 295–96, 299
Barthes, Roland, 128, 255, 312, 318, 341

Degré zéro de l'écriture, 26
Mythologies, xi, 386
base and superstructure, x, 210–12
Baudelaire, Charles, 31–32, 139, 208, 277, 318, 334
Bazin, André, 272
Becker, Paul, 144
Beethoven, Ludwig von, 127, 134, 146, 157, 290
    Wagner on, 119–21
Benjamin, Walter, 3, 21, 32, 33, 199n, 281, 294, 319
    allegory theory of, 22, 26, 30–33, 332
    on desirability of the symbol, 23–24
    on *Hamlet,* 111–12n, 114
    historical perspective of, 37, 45
    on *Trauerspiel* and *Tragödie,* 22, 87, 88, 90, 101, 111–12n, 114
Bennett, William, 162
Berg, Alban
    Wozzek, 321
Berger, Harry, 226, 239–40, 241
Bergson, Henri, 362
Bernstein, Leonard, 139
Bible, 21, 43, 273, 332–33
    allegories in, 3–4, 222
binary oppositions, 311
    body-mind, 65
    good-evil, 51, 242, 243–44, 245, 300
    individual-collective, xi–xii, xiii, xvi–xviii, 19, 310
    minimalism-maximalism, 249, 313–15, 316, 317, 324, 326, 327, 328, 341, 344–45, 355
    negative-positive, 65–66
    pain-pleasure, 65, 72, 78, 241
    private-public, 165
    subject-object, x, xi, xiii, 15, 80–81, 364, 365
    tragedy-comedy, 126, 358
Blake, William, 23

Bloch, Ernst, 44, 100, 190
Bloch, Marc, 85
Bloomfield, Morton W., 65
Boccaccio, Giovanni, 254, 278
body-mind dichotomy, 65
Bohr, Niels, 194
Bolaño, Roberto
    2666, 124
bourgeois revolutions, 2–3, 22, 289
Braudel, Fernand, 330
breakthrough notion, 144–47, 148, 149
Brecht, Bertolt, 37, 92, 105, 172, 297, 301
    on *Hamlet,* 84–85
    Mann ist Mann, 323
    The Threepenny Opera, 306, 321–25
Britain, 114, 203, 367–68
Browning, Robert
    "My Last Duchess," 255
Bruckner, Anton, 129, 145
Buchanan, Pat, 387
Bunyan, John, 10, 170, 271
    Pilgrim's Progress, 220–21, 222, 234
Burckhardt, Jacob, 354–55, 356
Burke, Kenneth, 74, 304
Byron, Lord, 292, 293, 294, 303

Calderon de la Barca, Pedro, 31
    La Vida es sueño, 114
Caligula, 7–8, 9
Camus, Albert, 7–9, 328
    L'Etranger, 7–8, 314
    The Myth of Sisyphus, 7
    The Plague, 7, 8, 9, 329
Can Grande della Scala, 236, 251, 253
Cantor, Georg, 46
capitalism, 21, 28, 184, 190, 205, 328–29
    emergence of, 84, 114–15, 130–31, 164, 188, 268
    globalization of, 26, 79, 137, 164, 309

Goethe on, 305, 307
late, 10, 25, 34, 37, 117, 153, 309, 314, 334, 335, 359
Marxism on, 25, 210, 252, 293
nation-state and, 25–26
superstructure of, 210–12
Cartesian Theater model, 363, 364, 366, 367, 368, 369, 372
The Castle (Kafka), 327328
castration complex, 96, 106
Cavalcanti, Guido, 261, 262, 264–65
Cazotte, Jacques
Diable amoureux, 103–4
centered subject, 15, 28, 161, 176, 369, 379
Cervantes, Miguel de, 217
Ceylan, Nuri Bilge
Winter Sleep, 76
Cézanne, Paul, 147
China, 10, 164–65, 188–89
Lu Xun allegories on, 167–75
national identity of, 207–9
Chrétien de Troyes, 217
Christian allegory, 21–22
Christianity, 3–4, 20, 64, 98, 239, 266, 268
theology of, 65–66, 283
typology of, 252
Cicero, 58, 74, 273
Cinema II (Deleuze), 99
Clark, Christopher
The Sleepwalkers, 201–5
class consciousness, xiv, 387
classicism, 295, 296, 299, 301–2, 303
class struggle, vii, 96, 188, 198
ethnic struggle and, 387–88
international, 190, 192
politics and, 190, 214
symbolism of, 23, 24–25
closure, 123, 133, 205, 305
in Dante, 222–23, 277
dualisms and, 94, 127
ideological, 350, 353
narrative, 173, 175, 206, 231

Cloud Atlas (Mitchell), 336–41
Coleridge, Samuel Taylor, 3, 22, 23, 92–93, 102, 170, 224
collectivity, 77, 200, 210, 213
conceptualization of, 194–95
group consciousness (*asabiyya*) and, xvi, xix, 196–97, 198, 212
ideology and, xi–xii, xiii, 197
individual and, xvi–xvii, 19, 310
unrepresentability of, 195, 214
Commedia. See Dante Alighieri—*Commedia*
commodification, 28, 66, 79, 146, 289, 346, 363
reification and, ix, 98, 239
simulacra and, 253, 310
common sense, 38, 52–53, 204, 207, 363
Dennett on, 364, 366, 368
communist parties, 267, 268
computers, 366
condensation, 240
Conrad, Joseph, 167, 168
consciousness
allegorical explanations for, 361–82
class, xvi, 387
group, xvi, xix, 196–97, 198, 212
impersonal nature of, 14–15
knowledge and, 14, 378
personal identity and, 363, 369–70
philosophy and, 14, 56
of self, xiii, 28, 53–54, 71, 126, 284, 355, 367, 368–69
situational, 185
tripartite allegory and, 15–16
unconscious and, xvii, 55, 57, 87, 88–89, 97–98, 104–5, 116, 202
Consciousness Explained (Dennett), 14–15, 361–82
as political allegory, 381–82
constructed subjectivity, 53–54, 238
constructivism, 341, 343, 346
aesthetics and, 35–36, 37

Index

Croce, Benedetto, 13, 233, 261, 263, 355
Cuba, 172, 173–74, 180, 334
cultural imperialism, 163, 181, 185n
cultural revolution, xi, 174
cultural studies, 163, 166, 388
culture
    evolution and emergence of, 375–76
    group relations and, 383–88
    identity and, 176
    ideology and, x
    politics and, 217–18
    religion and, x, 383–84
    third-world, 163, 165, 168, 185, 186

Dadaism, 29
Dahlhaus, Carl, 133–34
D'Annunzio, Gabriele, 217
Dante Alighieri, 52, 78, 280
    Cavalcanti and, 261, 262, 264–65
    language and style of, 222–23, 253, 273–75, 276, 300
    life of, 264, 269
    politics of, 265, 267
    theology of, 271–72, 283
    works
        De Monarchia, 253, 267
        De vulgari eloquentia, 274
        Letter to Can Grande, 236, 251, 253, 273
Dante Alighieri—*Commedia,* 251–85
    as allegory, 232–33, 251–52, 253, 255, 257, 265
    basic structure of, xx, 269–70
    books
        Inferno, 80, 229, 232–33, 245, 254–55, 257, 260–61, 278, 279, 283
        Paradiso, 80, 245, 270, 279, 284
        Purgatorio, 80, 232–33, 245, 257, 278–79
    closure in, 222–23, 277
    descent into Hell, 18, 256, 260, 282
    dualism of, 268–69, 278
    emotions in, 80, 255, 279–80
    force of gravity in, 257, 258, 260
    geography of, 256–57, 271
    Gramsci on, 263–64
    laterality in, 281–84
    literary tradition of, 217, 251
    Lukács on, 255–56
    memory as theme in, 258–59, 261, 264, 266
    named emotions in, 80, 255, 279–80, 283
    as narrative, 66, 253–54, 271, 280, 299
    personification in, 229, 260, 280–81
    picture thinking in, 270, 284
    political theme in, 262–63, 267–69
    on sins, 245, 258, 269–70, 278–79
    sublimation in, 258, 262, 265, 270, 271, 279
    sublime in, 284–85
    syntax of, 273–74, 275, 277
    temporality in, 223, 261, 263, 264, 266–67, 277, 278
    theme of love in, 48, 258, 262, 283
    three wild beasts in, 59, 229, 231–34
    transversality in, 255, 278, 285
    Virgil portrayal in, 253–54, 255, 258, 259, 265, 266, 271–72, 279, 299
    virtues and vices in, 245, 269, 279–80
Darcy, Warren, 122, 132
Darwin, Charles, and Darwinism, 62, 373–75
Dawkins, Richard, 376
death wish, 47, 100, 156, 293
Debord, Guy, 363
deconstruction, 32–33, 152, 323

Deleuze, Gilles, 35, 90, 125, 195, 196, 206, 317–18, 330
   on desire, 177–78
   on *Hamlet,* 98–99
   on time, 126, 319–20
   works
      Anti-Oedipus, 96
      Mille plateaux, xvi
Delius, Frederick, 337
de Man, Paul, 22, 32, 33, 42, 99, 241
   linguistics and allegory theory of, 26–28
democracy, 25, 113, 194, 252, 388
   state and, 380
demonic possession, 237–38
Dennett, Daniel, 14–15, 361–82
Derrida, Jacques, 28, 32–33, 99, 101, 365, 371
Descartes, René, 58, 60, 62, 63, 71, 114, 362–63
   Cartesian Theater model and, 363, 364, 366, 367, 368, 369, 372
desire
   Deleuze-Guattari conception of, 177–78
   and emotion classification, 64
   in *Hamlet,* 83–84, 100–101, 102, 106–7, 109, 110
   ideology and, xv–xvi
   Lacan on, 95–96, 98, 99–100, 104, 107, 109, 265
   of Other, 86, 99, 103–4
   tragedy of, 95–96, 109, 111
diagnostic function of allegory, 1, 45, 190
"Diary of a Madman" (Lu Xun), 167–68, 172, 175
Diaz, Lav, 314
Dick, Philip K.
   The Man in the High Castle, 222
Dickens, Charles, 223, 315
didacticism, 233, 272
difference, 168, 175, 223
   allegory and, 331–32
   cultural, 71, 160–61
   Greimas square and, 331–32, 380, 388
   identity and, xiv, xvii, 44, 109, 127, 132, 134, 276, 279, 310, 321, 331, 344–45, 347
   incommensurability and, 190, 332
   politics of, 388
   unity and, 19, 40, 126
   See also Others and Otherness
diplomatic allegory, 198, 201
Doctor Faustus (Mann), 144, 147–49, 289
Doderer, Heimito von
   Dämonen, 315
Dos Passos, John
   USA, 315
Dostoyevsky, Fyodor, 76, 160
doxa, xi, xii, 201
dreams, 1, 29, 41, 220
dual allegorical scheme, 4–5, 6–7, 9–10, 11, 45, 221
dualism
   allegorical, 9–11, 19
   Cartesian, 362–63
   closure and, 94, 127
   in Dante, 268–69, 278
Du Bois, W. E. B., 172
Duggan, Tony, 150
Dürer, Albrecht
   Melencolia, 31, 281

Eagleton, Terry
   Sweet Violence, 140
Eberhard, Wolfram, 169n
Eckermann, Johann Peter, 307
Eco, Umberto, 1, 29, 352
Ekman, Paul, 62
Elias, Norbert, 240
Eliot, T. S., 106, 223, 242
Elliott, Robert C., 178–79, 185
emotions
   allegorical, 76, 255

Index

anger as, 66–67, 68–69, 72, 73–75, 76, 77, 94, 279
Aristotle on, 65, 66, 67–69, 72–73, 74, 76, 77, 155
classification schemes of, xviii, 52, 59–64, 72, 82
communities of, 70–71
envy and loathing as, 387
experiencing of, 55, 75–76, 77
as historical concept, xvii, 50
James-Lange theory of, 52, 55, 62–63
love as, 46, 48, 57, 67
nomination of, 39, 50–52, 56–57, 347
passions and, 58, 59, 74
personification and, 63
pity as, 6, 67
reification and, 39, 52, 81, 236
sin and, 78, 79
theories of, 57–58
See also anger; desire; named emotions
empiricism, 58, 66, 136, 146
Empson, William, 90, 102, 112
Enlightenment, x, 213, 301
epic forms, 256, 319
epic theater, 297, 321
Epicureanism, 282
epigrams, 223, 300–301
episodes, 320, 324–25
ethnic theory, 386, 387
Evagrius Ponticus, 63, 78
evolutionary theory, 337–38n, 371–72, 373–76
existentialism, 92, 136, 167, 323–24, 344

fable, 173, 218, 239, 240, 303
  allegory and, 181–83
  in Kafka, 11, 328
The Faerie Queene (Spenser), 217–49, 299
  allegory in, 235–36, 242, 245, 247–49
  characters in, 225–26, 227, 228, 240–42, 244–45
  good-evil binary in, 242, 243–44, 245
  linguistic texture of, 227
  localities in, 224–25
  passions depicted in, 241–42, 243, 247
  personifications in, 229, 236–37, 240–42, 249
  political element in, 217–18
  temporal structure of, 245–47
  verse in, 223, 224
Fanon, Frantz, 174, 180
Faulkner, William, 315, 338
  Absalom, Absalom!, 186
Faust (Goethe), 287–308, 343
  as allegory, 289–90, 299–300, 303, 305–6, 308
  episodic nature of, 289, 302
  Faust I, 289–90, 291–92, 293
  Faust II, 223, 282, 287–91, 294, 295–300, 302, 303, 304
  gender theme in, 290
  Greeks' depiction in, 292–93, 302–3
  guilt and forgiveness in, 290, 291, 293, 294, 305, 308
  language and style in, 223, 296, 300–301, 302, 307
  Mephistopheles in, 288, 290–92, 294, 295, 300, 301, 304–6, 323
  moral of, 291–92
  nature images in, 307
  pageants in, 295–96, 297
  play within a play in, 302
  satire in, 288, 299, 300–301
  staging of, 287–88, 298–99
  temporal overlaps in, 292–93
  as tragedy, 289
feudalism, 114, 164, 269, 312
  Hamlet and, 85, 86, 89, 94
Fichte, Johann Gottlieb, 36
figura, 2, 18, 251–52, 253, 273

Fink, Bruce, 104, 116
Flaubert, Gustave, 151, 318, 327
  on nothingness, 311–12, 313
  La Tentation de Saint Antoine, 239, 298
Fletcher, Angus, 236–37
Fontanier, Pierre, 26
football (soccer), 191–93
Ford, Henry, 34, 206
Forster, E. M., 369
Foucault, Michel, 43, 64, 99, 124, 240
  The Order of Things, 372
fourfold allegorical system, 4, 11, 17, 42, 45, 117, 231, 251, 308
  described, 17–21
  Mahler and, 151–53
  modes of production and, 213–14
  in postmodernity, 328, 340, 342, 347
  transversality and, 231, 281, 282–83, 310
  See also allegorical/mystical level of allegory; anagogic level of allegory; Greimas square; literal level of allegory; moral level of allegory
France, 202–3
Franck, César, 124
Frankfurt School, 33
Franklin, Benjamin, 3
Freire, Paolo, 174
French Revolution, 26, 114, 146, 152, 189, 268
Freud, Sigmund, xvii, 47, 85, 100, 166, 240, 347–48
  on dreams as allegories, 1, 29
  on fantasies, xii–xiii, 104–5
  on *Hamlet,* 96, 101, 102, 115
  Marx vs., 165, 195
  and psychoanalysis, xii, 56
  on representability, 29, 35
  on the unconscious, 55, 57, 97–98, 104–5, 116
  works
    "A Child Is Being Beaten," 104–5
    "Creative Writers and Daydreams," xi–xiii
    The Interpretation of Dreams, 96
    "Mourning and Melancholia," 101
Frevert, Ute, 60
Fried, Michael, 31
Frye, Northrop, 43, 122, 126–27, 354
Fukuyama, Francis, 113
future-present relationship, 252–53
futurity, xviii, 168, 175, 179

Galdos, Benito Perez, 176–77, 215
  Fortunata y Jacinta, 177
Galileo, 114
Gay, John, 321–22
Geertz, Clifford, 280
  generic discontinuities, 183
Genette, Gérard, 230
George, Stefan, 145
Germany, 147–48, 202, 203, 296
Gestalt psychology, 75, 230
Girard, René, 70, 85–86, 88, 89, 102, 108
globalization, 26, 71, 191, 196, 197
  allegory and, 310, 344–45
Gödel's Law, 100
Goethe, Johann Wolfgang von, 12, 52, 301, 303
  absolutism and, xx, 291, 295
  classicism and, 295, 296, 299, 301
  comments to Eckermann by, 236, 307
  Hamlet interpretation of, 93, 102
  impulses of, 40, 300
  letter to Schiller, 289
  literary style of, 223, 295, 299, 305, 307
  as man of the theater, 298, 299
  on world literature, 25–26, 163, 293–94

Index   397

works
  Götz, 289
  Iphigenia, 302
  Werther, 289
  See also *Faust*
Goffman, Erving
  Stigma, 383
Goldmann, Lucien
  The Hidden God, 6
good-evil binary, 51, 242, 243–44, 245, 300
Goody, Jack, 122
Gracián, Baltasar, 8–9, 64
Gramsci, Antonio, 132, 174, 261, 385, 386
  on Dante, 263–64
  on Italian national divisions, 199
Grass, Günther
  The Tin Drum, 314, 316, 320, 336
Gravity's Rainbow (Pynchon), 314, 317
Greek philosophy, 13, 78, 346
  See also Aristotle; Plato and Platonism
Greeks, ancient, 5, 78, 296–97, 319, 345
  See also Homer
Greek tragedy, 5–6, 68, 302, 303
  Hamlet and, 91–93
Gregory the Great, 63
Greimas, Algirdas Julien, 349, 361
Greimas square, xiv–xx, 16–17, 20, 72–74, 330–32, 349–59
  relevance and advantages of, 72–73, 349–50
  usefulness of, 72–73, 350–51, 353–54
group dynamics, 383–88
consciousness (*asabiyya*) and, xvi, xix, 196–97, 198, 212
group identity and, xiv, 388
See also collectivity
Guattari, Felix, 96
  on desire, 177–78

transversality concept of, xviii, 42–43, 310
Guevara, Che, 21

habit, concept, 57–58
Hamlet (Shakespeare), 30, 83–117
  Adorno and Horkheimer on, 114
  Benjamin on, 111–12n, 114
  Claudius in, 88, 95, 102–3, 105–6, 107–9, 110, 113
  desire in, 83–84, 100–101, 102, 106–7, 109, 110
  as expression of modernity, 83, 114, 115, 117
  feudalism portrayal in, 85, 86, 89, 94
  Freud on, 96, 101, 102, 115
  ghost in, 105–6, 117
  Goethe on, 93, 102
  Hamlet's madness and obsession in, 92, 107, 109–10
  historical allegory in, 84–91
  Kyd original version of, 87, 92
  Lacan on, 96–104, 105, 106–11
  language of, 94–95
  literary style of, 90, 93–95, 262
  Ophelia in, 95, 100–101, 106–7, 110
  procrastination theme in, 89, 101–2, 108
  revenge ethics in, 89, 108
  Schmitt on, 87–88, 89, 106, 114–15
  as tragedy, 91–93, 114–15
Hammett, Dashiell, 160
Hardt, Michael, 196
Haydn, Joseph, 127
Hazlitt, William, 95
Hegel, G. W. F., 9, 30, 52, 74, 137, 214, 222
  on allegory, 7, 13
  on bad infinity, 195, 314, 324
  on Greek tragedy, 70, 303–4
  on identity, 277, 331
  on Master-Slave relationship, 185–86

on objectification, 40
as philosopher of history, 354, 358
on positing, 37, 57
on reality of the appearance, 201
on transformation, 41, 86
works
    Aesthetics, 70
    Logic, 13, 41, 370
    Phenomenology of Spirit, 70, 303
hegemony concept, 23, 386
Heidegger, Martin, 25, 33, 41, 66, 94, 103, 306, 369–70
    on "world pictures," 16, 24
Henry, Jules
    Jungle People, 86
Hepokoski, James, 122, 132
Heraclitus, 249
Hindu nationalism, 384
historical materialism, x, 45, 212–13
historicism, 307–8
    Dennett on, 372–75
history, 295, 319, 334
    allegory and, xi
    bourgeoisie and, 2–3, 325
    Cloud Atlas depiction of, 339–40, 341
    conventional framework of, 21
    Faerie Queene as vision of, 235–36
    Faust depiction of, 295
    Hamlet and, 84–91, 114
    narrative of, xvii, 205, 311, 376
    of ideas, 381
    philosophy and, 113, 196, 354–55, 358
    realism and, 2, 296, 305
    Schmitt on, 88–89
Hjelmslev, Louis, 73
Hobbes, Thomas, 52, 59, 60, 62, 80
    Leviathan, 114
Hobsbawm, Eric, 205, 318–19, 337
Ho Chi Minh, 172
Hölderlin, Friedrich
    Gedictete, 33
Holiday, Henry, 46

Homer, 273, 293
    allegory by, 3, 5–6, 11–13
    The Iliad, 5–6, 12, 66, 67, 292
    Odyssey, 325
homological allegory, 16
homology, 6, 9, 16–17, 43, 46, 148, 262
Hong Kong, 208–9
Horkheimer, Max, 114
Horowitz, Donald, 386
House of Leaves (Danielewski), 222, 315
Hugo, Victor, 315
humanism, 71, 124–25, 264, 288
    allegory and, xix, 9, 10, 11, 15–16
human nature, 9, 63, 124, 127, 213, 331
    nature and, 10, 11, 81–82, 100
Husserl, Edmund, 14, 53, 271
hypothetical music, 142–44, 155, 157
hysteria, 98, 103, 105, 109

Ibn Khaldun, xvi, xix
    Muqaddimah, 196
Ibsen, Henrik, 151
    Peer Gynt, 296, 298
idealism, 38, 62, 186, 212, 341, 362–63
    materialism vs., x, 80, 326
identity, 154, 278, 279, 307
    collective, 176, 197, 198–99
    cultural, 176
    difference and, xiv, xvii, 44, 109, 127, 132, 134, 276, 279, 310, 321, 331, 344–45, 347
    Greimas square and, 127, 351–52
    of identity and non-identity, 277
    national, 79, 176, 207–9
    personal, 28, 54, 57, 109, 153, 161, 323, 363, 364, 369–70
    political, 187, 189–90, 193
Ideologiekritik, xiii, xvi, 130, 147
ideology, 38, 130, 311–12, 346, 354

Adorno on empiricist, 58, 66, 136
allegory and, xi, 16, 331
centrality of, ix–x
closure of, 350, 353
collective, xi, xi–xii, 197
culture and, x
desire and, xvii–xix
"end of," 113
four levels of, xvi–xvii
of *Hamlet*, 83, 90
of humanism, 11, 124
ideologeme as unit of, xi–xii, xiv, xv, 102
individual-collective binary in, xi–xii, xiii
language and, 99, 124, 127
Marx on, xi
of modernity, 113, 114
narrativity and, xiii–xiv, xv, 17
religion and, 66, 71
subjectivity and, x, xiii–xiv, 112
of the symbol, 10
The Iliad (Homer), 5–6, 12, 66, 67, 292
Imaginary, 109, 110
  Lacanian theory of, 28, 111
  Symbolic and, 39, 47
imagination, 144, 242
  conceptualization and, 362
  in Dante, 271, 278
  historical, 86, 355
incommensurability, 30, 135, 137, 313, 326–27
  simultaneity and, 190, 193–94
  as term, 332–33
India, 164, 188
individual-collective binary, xvi–xvii, 19, 310
Infinite Jest (Wallace), 317, 336
intellectuals, 172, 173
intentionality, 53
international politics, 190
Iran, 267

irony
  in literature, 112, 143
  White's *Metahistory* on, 126, 354, 355, 356, 357, 358
Islam, xvi, 182, 196, 293, 316–17

Jakobson, Roman, 148
James, C. L. R., 172
James, Henry, 112, 336
  The Wings of the Dove, 112, 143
James, William, xiv, 40, 61, 370
James-Lange theory, 52, 55, 62–63
Jansenism, 6
Japan, 208
Jesus Christ, 20, 21, 42, 332–33
Jia Zhangke
  The World, 10
Joachim of Fiore, 79
Johnson, Uwe, 315
Jones, Ernest, 96, 102, 115
Jonson, Ben, 242
Joyce, James, 140, 147, 321, 369
  Finnegans Wake, 23
  Ulysses, 124, 207, 298, 325
Judaism, 3–4, 78
Jungianism, 23, 127

Kafka, Franz, 10, 11, 327–28
Kant, Immanuel, 56–57, 125, 146, 337
  categories of, 55, 141
  Critique of Pure Reason, 361
  on History, 2–3
  on mental functions, 14, 34
  on phenomenon and noumenon, 304–5
Kermode, Frank, 93–94
Kierkegaard, Søren, 125, 136
Kipling, Rudyard, 322
Klangfarbenmelodie, 44, 329
Kluge, Alexander, 139
Knapp, Stephen, 229–30, 231
Knight, Wilson, 262
knowledge, 12, 13, 24, 34, 88, 167, 213

consciousness and, 14, 378
power and, 378, 384
Spinoza on, 79–80
Kollontai, Alexandra, 172
Konstan, David, 69, 74
Kracauer, Siegfried, 272
Kuhn, Thomas, 46
Kyd, Thomas, 87, 92

Lacan, Jacques, 58, 194
on desire, 95–96, 98, 99–100, 104, 107, 109, 265
on *Hamlet*, 96–104, 105, 106–11
on Imaginary, 28, 111
on language, 99, 273
on modernity, 115–16
on Other and Otherness, 99, 100, 103–4, 239
on psychoanalysis, 28, 38–39, 47–48, 55, 56, 100
Seminars by, 100, 111, 115, 116
Sinthome theory of, 47–48
on structuralism, 99, 104
on subject and object, x, 57
Laclau, Ernesto, 332
Laffer, Arthur, 377
Lange, Carl, 55
language
affect and, 94, 110, 321
classification of, 128, 274
deception in, 1, 33
Dennett on, 369, 375, 376–77
of Goethe, 300–301, 307
ideology and, 99, 124, 127
Lacan on, 99, 273
learning and teaching of, 27, 72
linguistic turn and, 27
multiple, 23, 128
nomination and, 38, 55, 57, 346
poetic, 262, 263, 326
as primal alienation, 239
reification of, 98–99, 326
representations and, 14, 35
of Shakespeare, 90, 93–95

structure of, xiv, 98, 170
style studies on, 42
See also syntax
La Rochefoucauld, François de, 8, 64
laterality
concept of, 42–43
in Dante, 281–84
Lefebvre, Henri, 359
Le Goff, Jacques, 66
Le Guin, Ursula, 230
The Dispossessed, 218–19
Lenin, V. I., 21, 79, 173
Lessing, Gotthold Ephraim, 297
Lévi-Strauss, Claude, 44, 66, 284
Lewis, Wyndham, 81
libidinal investment, xvii, 83–84, 168, 198
Lin Biao, 188
linguistic reification, 98–99
linguistics, ix–x, 73, 104, 207
literal level of allegory, 2, 18, 21, 34, 42, 84, 152, 167, 328
as allegoresis, 26
Dante and, 283, 284
Faust and, 287–88, 308
Hamlet and, 84, 117
Marxian understanding of, 212, 213
in postmodernity, 326, 340, 343
literature, xii, xiii, 14, 28, 243, 342
content of, 311, 313
fantasy, 217, 252
irony in, 112, 143
lowbrow, 80, 312, 315
medieval, 217
national, 23
realism and, 276, 313
Third World, 159–86
western, 167, 176–77, 185
world, 25–26, 162–63, 187, 194, 223, 293–94
Lodge, David
Nice Work, 371

Loos, Adolf
  Ornament and Crime, 22
Lovecraft, H. P., 242
Luhmann, Niklas, 345
Lukács, Georg, 90, 195, 270, 319
  on Dante, 255–56
  on misunderstanding, 29
  on "second nature," 35, 81
  Theory of the Novel, 254, 255–56
Luther, Martin, 114, 221
Lu Xun, 166–73, 214
  Ah Q allegories of, 171–72
  "Diary of a Madman," 167–68, 172, 175
  "Medicine," 169–70
Lyotard, Jean-François, xvii, xviii, 27, 83, 113, 114

Machiavelli, Niccolò, 8, 64, 132, 196, 262
Mack, Maynard, 162
Mahler, Alma, 141, 150
Mahler, Gustav
  First Symphony of, 142, 145, 155
  life of, 148, 149–50
  musical style of, 134, 143, 157
  Sixth Symphony, 132–33, 135, 141, 151–56
  symphonic form of, 127–28, 137–38
  temporality in music of, 135–37, 139
Mahon, Alfred Thayer, 114
Malebranche, Nicolas, 61
Mallarmé, Stéphane, 36, 274, 347
  Livre, 23
Malraux, André
  La condition humaine, 7
Mann, Thomas, 327
  Doctor Faustus, 144, 147–49, 289
  Reflections of an Unpolitical Man, 147
Mannheim, Karl, 354
Manzoni, Alessandro, 281

Maoism, 173, 188–89
Marcuse, Herbert, 116, 174
Martí, José, 180
Marx, Karl, 21, 37, 334, 386
  on activity and productivity, 40, 41
  on capitalism, 252, 293
  Freud vs., 165, 195
  historical viewpoint of, 205, 212–13, 374
  on ideology, xi
  as philosopher of history, 354, 355, 358
  on reification, 346
  works
    Communist Manifesto, 205, 293
    Critique of Political Economy, 210–11
Marxism, xvi, 20, 25, 276, 288
  on base and superstructure, x, 210–12
  on class consciousness, 387
  on economic causality, 386–87
  historical framework of, 22, 37
  on modes of production, 163–64, 213–14
  psychoanalysis and, 47
  science and, x, 212–13
Master-Slave relationship, 185–86
materialism, 62, 102, 139, 185, 211, 273, 365, 371
  Cartesian dualism and, 362–63
  historical, x, 45, 212–13
  idealism vs., x, 80, 326
  mechanical and vulgar, 213, 341
matter and antimatter, 344
maximalism. *See* minimalism-maximalism binary
Mayans, 352
McCarthy, Tom
  Remainder, 341–44
McGann, Jerome, 365
McGinn, Colin, 14, 53
"Medicine" (Lu Xun), 169–70
mega-novel, 314–16, 317

melancholy, 76, 101, 120, 140, 241
    as concept, 6–7
    Dürer depiction of, 31, 281
melodrama, 242, 243
Melville, Herman, 321
memory, 45, 46, 135, 165, 334
    as Dante theme, 258–59, 261, 264, 266
    Dennett on, 368–69, 370
Metahistory (White), 351–52, 354–58
metaphor, 126, 378, 380
    allegory as different from, 148, 331
    Greimas square and, 352, 354, 355, 356–57, 358
    narrative and, 6, 148–49
    simile vs., 6
    symbol and, 10, 331
metaphysics, 10, 16, 45, 53, 63, 125, 213
metatheater, 93, 114, 117
Metatheater (Abel), 91–92, 114
metonymy, 351–52, 354, 356, 357
Meyer, Leonard, 124
Michel, Louise, 172
Michelet, Jules, 354–55, 357
Mickiewicz, Adam, 298
Midnight's Children (Rushdie), 316–17, 336
Mille plateaux (Guattari and Deleuze), xviii
Milton, John, 243, 379
    Comus, 294–95
    Paradise Lost, 59, 229, 236
Mimesis (Auerbach), 273–75
minimalism-maximalism binary, 316, 317, 335, 341
    antithetical nature of, 249, 326, 344–45
    in Kafka, 327, 328
    as relationship, 324, 326
    styles and techniques in, 313–15
mirror stage, 38–39, 86, 102, 104, 109, 111
misunderstanding term, 29–30

Mitchell, David, 336–41
Mitchner, James, 336
Mitscherlich, Alexander, 116
modal colorations, 285
modernism and modernity, 58, 135, 256, 284, 295, 327, 345
    allegory in, 9, 95, 309–10
    art and, 113, 312
    Faust and, 291–92, 295
    Hamlet as expression of, 83, 114, 115, 117
    ideology of, 113, 293
    Lacan theory of, 115–16
    literary, 28, 167, 207, 272, 328–29
    national, 79, 167, 272
    personification and, 48, 346
    temporality and, 139, 318, 330, 359, 365
    theories of, 71, 91, 115
modes of production, xi, 20, 21, 268, 269
    Asiatic, 164–65
    Marxism on, 163, 210–14
Monahan, Seth, 122, 132–33, 142, 145, 150–51, 155
The Money Order (Ousmane), 181–82, 184
Montaigne, Michel de, 156, 307
moral level of allegory, xvi, 9, 213, 234, 308
    Dante and, 233–34, 265, 267
    Hamlet and, 96–104, 117
    as level of meaning, 18, 19–20
    Mahler and, 151–52
    in postmodernity, 310, 328, 338–39, 340, 343
More, Thomas
    Utopia, 225
Mosca, Count, 57
Most, Glenn, 67
Mouffe, Chantal, 332
music
    allegory and, 119–21, 123, 130
    atonal, 133–34

beginnings and endings in, 125–26
breakthroughs in, 144–47
categories of modality in, 141–42
discontinuities in, 123–24
hypothetical, 142–44, 155, 157
irony in, 143
narrative and, 122–23, 126,
    128–29, 134–35, 152, 329–30
orchestration in, 138–39
philosophy and, 125
psychology and, 124–25
sonata form in, 123, 129–30, 139,
    145, 147, 152
sublime in, 145, 146, 323
symphonic form in, 123–24,
    127–28, 129–30, 137–38
temporality in, 125, 126, 135–37,
    139–40, 152
tonality in, 130–32, 152
See also Mahler, Gustav
Musil, Robert
Mann ohne Eigenschaften, 150

named emotions, 39, 51, 72, 76, 91
affect and, 44, 59, 66, 157, 200,
    279, 280, 283, 310, 320, 325, 347
allegory's organization of, 52
binary oppositions and, 64–65
in Dante, 80, 255, 279–80, 283
as term, 50, 54, 347
See also emotions
naming. *See* nomination
narrative
Adorno on, 122–23
allegory and, 21, 119, 127, 207,
    209–10, 309
closure in, 173, 175, 206, 231
constructional powers of, 265–66
Dante's *Commedia* as, 66, 253–54,
    271, 280, 299
Dennett on, 365, 377
futurity and, 175
generic transformation of, 184–85
"grand" category of, 113–14

Greimas square and, 353–54
of history, xvii, 205, 311, 376
ideology and, xiii–xiv, xv, 17
Jungianism and, 127
Mahler's Sixth Symphony as,
    153–54, 155
medieval, 217
metaphor and, 6, 148–49
music and, 122–23, 126, 128–29,
    134–35, 152, 329–30
philosophy and, xv, 342
postmodernity and, 309, 318,
    335–36
primal fantasy and, xii, 104–5
proto-narrative, 209–10
realism and, 276, 317–18
Sartre denunciation of, 206–7
as structure, 112, 113
temporality and, 221, 273
textuality in, 221–22
thick, 276
nation, 180, 197, 214–15
emergence of, 193, 199–201
national allegory, xix, 159–86,
    187–215
asabiyya and, xvi, xix, 196–97, 198,
    212
under globalization, 344–45
personification and, 194–95
as term, 165, 185n
in third-world culture, 185
western literature and, 176–77
national identity and character, 79,
    176, 201, 207–9
nationalism, 25, 159, 182, 195,
    297–98
national personification, 194, 201–5
Nattiez, Jean-Jacques, 122
natural selection, 168, 373–75
nature, 10, 81, 130, 198, 307
Needham, Rodney, 383–84
negation, 65, 136, 214, 301, 325, 344,
    374
definition as, xiv–xx

in fourfold system of allegory, 16–17
Greimas square and, 73–74, 331–33, 350, 352, 358
of the negation, 332, 352
negative-positive binary, 65–66
Negri, Antonio, 196
Neruda, Pablo, 172
Neto, Agostinho, 172
New Critical theory, 242, 262, 263
Ngugi wa Thiong'o, 181
Nielsen, Carl
Fourth Symphony (*The Inextinguishable*), 330
Nietzsche, Friedrich, 37, 69, 91, 168, 301, 371, 374
on God, xiii, 153
as philosopher of history, 354, 355, 358
on subject and object, xii, 53, 346, 370
nihilism, 300, 343, 356
nominalism, 58–59, 136, 139, 310, 313, 325
nomination, 194, 239
of emotions, 39, 50–52, 56–57, 347
identity and, 57
language and, 38, 55, 57, 346
personification and, 39, 346
reification and, 54–55, 346
nonsynchronous synchronicity, 190
nothingness, 156, 298, 324, 343
Flaubert on, 311–12, 313
noumenon, 34–35, 304–5
Novalis, 3, 22, 217
novel genre, 112, 123–24
history of, 115, 234, 254
mega-novel, 314–16, 317
postmodern novel, 221–22, 335
numerology, 16, 94, 127
Nussbaum, Martha, 64

Oates, Joyce Carol, 316
object. *See* subject-object binary
objectivity, 2, 195, 317
subjectivity and, 53, 334
obsessional neurosis, 98, 103, 105, 109–10
Oedipus complex, 98, 111, 168
Freud on, 101, 115
Lacan on, 96, 106, 116
Oedipus Rex, 97, 115
one-to-one allegory, 4–6, 9, 14, 86–87, 281
orchestration, 138–39
orientalism, 175, 201, 293
Origen, 17–18, 79–80
Origin of the German Traverspiel, 30
Orwell, George
1984, 377
Others and Otherness, 71, 175, 385
construction of, 64, 78
desire of, 86, 99, 103–4
as evil, 242–43
group dynamics and, 384, 388
Lacanian view of, 99, 100, 103–4, 239
positing of, 37–38
Ousmane. *See* Sembene, Ousmane
Ovid, 238–40, 278

pageants, 297, 299
pain-pleasure opposition, 65, 72, 78, 241
Pascal, Blaise, 6, 8
passions, 12–13, 61, 67, 221, 245
Aristotle's theory of, 67–69
emotions and, 58, 59, 74
Spenser depiction of, 241–42, 243, 247
See also emotions; named emotions
pastiche, 320–21, 335–36, 338, 341
Pater, Walter, 140
Paul, Saint, 4, 21, 64, 79
Paxson, James J.
Poetics of Personification, 230–31
Peck, Raoul, 334

Index 405

Peirce, Charles Sanders, 352
pensée sauvage, 44, 66, 284
Pepper, Stephen, 354
Pericles, 69
periodic sentence, 274, 275, 276–77
personal identity, 54, 57, 109, 153, 323, 364
   centered subject and, 28, 161, 176, 369, 379
   consciousness and, 363, 369–70
personification, 12, 51, 141, 230, 231, 236
   allegory and, 31–32, 39, 48, 140, 151, 153, 157, 194, 231
   in Dante, 229, 260, 280–81
   emotion and, 63
   national, 194, 201–5
   Paxson on, 230–31
   reification and, 198–99, 249, 346–47
   in Spenser, 229, 236–37, 240–42, 249
phenomena, 61, 125, 228, 273–74, 278
   allegorical, 52–53, 221, 325
   emotional, 61, 74
   noumenon and, 34–35, 304–5
philosophy, 14, 15, 32, 64, 92, 341–42, 359
   abstraction and, 44, 345
   aesthetics and, 23–24, 34, 35
   Greek, 13, 78, 346
   of history, 113, 196, 354–55, 358
   music and, 125
   narratives and, xv, 342
   numerology and, 16, 94, 127
   political, 253, 380
   postmodern, 335–36
   temporality and, 277, 365
   theology and, xv–xvi, 66
photography, 62
picture thinking, 270, 271, 284
Pilgrim's Progress (Bunyan), 220–21, 222, 234

Pinel, Philippe, 27
The Plague (Camus,), 7, 8, 9, 329
Plato and Platonism, 11, 33, 48, 265
poetry, 3, 188, 293, 303, 312, 341
   versification in, 222–24
point-to-point allegories, 10, 148, 260
   See also dual allegorical scheme
political unconscious, xvii, 87, 88–89, 202
politics of difference, 388
Pope, Alexander, 301
Popper, Leo, 29
positing, Hegelian, 37–38, 57
postmodernity, 34, 35, 83, 369, 378, 380
   as concept and term, 113, 318, 359
   narrative and, 309, 318, 335–36
   as pastiche, 335–36
postmodern novel, 221–22, 335
poststructuralism, 176, 221, 369, 378
Pound, Ezra, 262, 288n
present-future relationship, 252–53
primal fantasy, xii, 104–5, 108n
process allegories, 60
Propp, Vladimir, 129, 132, 207
proto-narrative, 209–10
Proust, Marcel, 57, 138, 147, 247, 275, 318
   on French national identity, 199–200n
   pastiches of, 338
   representation of self by, 53–54, 56
Prudentius, Aurelius Clemens, 13, 230
Psychomachia, 12, 67
psychoanalysis, 20, 266
   Freudian, xii, 56
   Lacanian, 28, 38–39, 47–48, 55, 56, 100
psychology, 13, 78, 124–25, 130, 240
   ancient Greek, 67–68
   Gestalt, 75, 230
   Jungianism and, 127

music and, 124–25
Stoic, 77
public-private split, 165
Puig, Manuel
   Betrayed by Rita Hayworth, 181
Pynchon, Thomas, 316

Rabelais, François, 43
Racine, Jean, 6
racism, xi, 79, 200–201
   neo-racism and, 385–86
Ranke, Leopold von, 354–55, 357
Ray, Nicholas, 178
reading play, 222, 296, 297–98
Reaganism, 377, 378, 380
realism, 22, 229, 253, 295, 297, 326, 338
   allegory's relation to, 2, 170, 346–47
   Auerbach on, 251, 253, 273, 275
   figural, 272
   Goethe and, 38, 305
   history and, 2, 296, 305
   naive, x, 38
   narrative and, 276, 317–18
   nineteenth-century, 22, 176, 181
   nominalism and, 59, 312–13
   rationalism and, 52, 327
   as slippery concept, 253
   speculative, 35, 80
redundancy, 262
Reich, Wilhelm, 174
reification, 310, 311, 320, 326, 365
   alienation and, 40–41, 346
   as allegorical figure, 346
   commodity world and, xi, 81
   emotions and, 39, 52, 81, 236
   linguistic, 98–99
   nomination and, 54–55, 346
   personification and, 198–99, 249, 346–47
   in Spencer, 237–39, 241, 243, 249
relativism, 24–25, 42, 71, 329, 335–36

religion, 62, 64, 98, 234, 339, 352
   allegory and, 1, 3–4
   culture and, x, 383–84
   as ideology, 66, 71
   new universal, 70, 77
   See also Christianity; theology
Remainder (McCarthy), 341–44
renunciation (ethical value), 291
representability
   allegorical systems and, 36–37, 233, 362
   as Freud term, 29–30, 35
   subjectivity and, 361
ressentiment, 168
revolution, 37, 268
rhetoric, field of, 4, 119, 230, 273
   allegory and, 22, 26–27
Ricoeur, Paul, xvi, 33
Rilke, Rainer Maria, 28, 42, 277
Ritchie, Guy, 339
Robbe-Grillet, Alain, 221
Robespierre, Maximilien, 21, 88
Roche, Thomas P., 248
Romains, Jules
   Hommes de bonne volonté, 315
Le Roman de la rose, 220–21, 222, 234, 271, 309
Romanticism, 2, 22, 24, 25, 355
Rosenwein, Barbara, 70
Rossellini, Roberto
   La Prise de pouvoir de Louis XIV, 85
Rossini, Gioachino, 134, 157
Rousseau, Jean-Jacques, 70, 194, 197
Rushdie, Salman, 320
   Midnight's Children, 316–17, 336

sacred texts, 3, 23, 25, 42, 84, 328
Said, Edward, 175
Sainte-Beuve, Charles Augustin, 312
Sartre, Jean-Paul, 27, 36, 40, 92, 172, 283, 327, 341
   on collective cohesion, 198
   on emotions, 57, 58

on literary aesthetics, 29, 243
Nausea, 206
on subjectivity and consciousness, 14, 53, 365
on temporality, 7, 206
satire, 171, 179, 184–85, 358
  in *Faust*, 288, 299, 300–301
Schelling, Friedrich, 3, 23
Schiller, Friedrich, 90, 91, 301
Schlegel, Friedrich, 22, 23
Schmitt, Carl, 198, 207, 270
  on Hamlet, 87–88, 89, 106, 114–15
  on tragedy, 101, 110, 114
  works
    Hamlet oder Hekuba, 87–88, 89
    Nomos der Erde, 114
Schoenberg, Arnold, 145
  atonal music of, 133, 134
  Klangfarbenmelodie idea of, 44, 329
  on Western tonality, 131
Scholem, Gershom, 33
Schopenhauer, Arthur, 55, 140
Schubert, Franz, 129
science
  Marxism and, xii, 212–13
  thematization of, 9, 11, 12–13
  tripartite allegorical system and, 11, 12, 17
  truth and, 17, 46, 48
  as worldview, 24–25
science fiction, 8, 27, 191, 219, 246, 339, 341, 345
scientism, 16, 46, 257
Scott, Walter, 296–97
self-consciousness, xiii, 53–54, 71, 126, 284
  Dennett on, 355, 367, 368–69
  of representational language, 284
  as term, 28
Sembene, Ousmane, 181
  films of, 182, 184
  The Last of the Empire, 180
  The Money Order, 181–82, 184

Xala, 179–80, 182–85
sentence structure, 273–75
  See also syntax
Sévigné, Madame de, 338
sexuality, 100, 106, 168
Shakespeare, William
  character portrayals by, 95
  life of, 90, 299
  literary style of, 31, 90, 93–95, 110, 262
  other plays by, 110, 116, 262
  See also *Hamlet*
Sharpe, Ella, 115, 117
Shaviro, Steven, 81
Shaw, George Bernard, 86, 102, 108
Sibelius, Jean
  Seventh Symphony, 329
Silberer, Herbert, 41
simile, 5–6
Simmel, Georg, 77–78, 256
sin
  Dante portrayal of, 245, 258, 269–70, 278–79
  emotions as, 78, 79
  Milton on, 59, 229, 236
  theorization of, 64
Singleton, Charles, 231, 259
Sisyphus, 7–8
situational consciousness, 185
The Sleepwalkers (Clark), 201–5
Sloterdijk, Peter, xviii, 197
social allegory, 185
sonata form, 123, 129–30, 139, 145, 147, 152
sonata theory, 122, 132
sovereignty, 86, 88, 108, 130, 267, 269–70
Soviet Union, 208
  Revolution of 1917, 79, 189
Soylent Green, 339
Spain, 177
spatial anomalies, 229, 231, 234
special effects, 297–98
Spengler, Oswald, 43

Spenser, Edmund
  allegory genre and, 12, 52
  culture and politics combined in, 217–18, 265
  The Letter to Raleigh, 227, 236
  life of, 249
  style of, 242
  See also *The Faerie Queene*
Spinoza, Baruch, 30, 61, 79
Spitzer, Leo, 277
Stalin, Joseph, and Stalinism, 189, 377, 380
state, 379–80
Stein, Gertrude, 117
Stein, Peter, 287–88, 299–300, 323
Steinberg, Michael, 129
Stendhal, 165, 247
Stoics and Stoicism, 11, 65, 71, 72, 74–75, 76, 77–78
storytelling, 206, 254, 297, 334, 371, 374
Strauss, Richard, 119
Strindberg, August, 76
structuralism, 6, 43, 51, 55, 96, 330, 359
  Lacan and, 99, 104
  linguistics and, 27, 104
  See also poststructuralism
Sturm und Drang, 289, 295, 296, 300, 301–2
subalternity, 110, 174
subjectivity, x–xi, 56, 153, 247
  centered subject and, 15, 28, 161, 176, 369, 379
  consciousness and, 53
  construction of, 19, 53–54, 64–65, 72, 222, 234–35, 238, 310
  Dennett on, 361, 369
  ideology and, x, xiii–xiv, 112
  objectivity and, 53, 334
subject-object binary, x, xii, xiii, 15, 80–81, 364, 365
sublimation, 4, 41, 107, 139, 221, 283, 305
  in Dante, 258, 262, 265, 270, 271, 279
  group conflict and, 387–88
  as term, 283
sublime, 299, 305
  in Dante, 284–85
  music and, 145, 146, 323
  verticality and, 270
substance, as category, 52–53, 346
substantialism, 38, 44, 141, 153
Sullivan, Louis, 313–14
surface reading, 42
Swift, Jonathan, 301
symbol and symbolism, 12–13, 39, 170, 281, 313, 387
  aesthetics and, 24, 337
  allegory and, 2–3, 9–10, 23–24, 25, 36–37, 170, 331
  in bad allegory, 270–71
  complex role of, 23–25
  Imaginary and, 39, 47
symphonic form, 123–24, 127–28, 129–30, 137–38
symptomatology, 334–35
synchronicity, 44, 190
synecdoche, 126, 352, 354, 355, 357
synonymity, 43, 332
syntax, xiv, 52–53, 94, 326
  allegory and, 273
  of Dante, 273–74, 275, 277
  periodic sentences and, 274, 275, 276–77

taboo function, 72
Tambling, Jeremy, 278, 279, 283
Tarr, Bela, 314
Tchaikovsky, Pyotr Ilyich, 129
temporality, 31, 65, 105, 223, 274, 367–68
  in Dante, 223, 261, 263, 264, 266–67, 277, 278
  Deleuze on, 126, 319–20
  dimensions of, 343, 344
  in Goethe, 223, 292–93, 299

Index   409

modernism and, 139, 318, 330, 359, 365
in music, 125, 126, 135–37, 139–40, 152
narrative, 221, 273
philosophy and, 277, 365
Sartre on, 7, 206
in Spenser, 217, 245–47
Tesky, Gordon, 229, 260
thematization, 9, 98, 99, 100, 245
theology, 24, 33, 71–72, 269, 282
   allegory and, 44–45
   Christian, 65–66, 283
   Dante and, 271–72, 283
   philosophy and, xv–xvi, 66
   as picture thinking, 284
   See also religion
thick narrative, 276
Third World
   allegorization in, 165, 214–15
   modes of production in, 164–65, 189
   as term, 162, 187–88
third-world literature, 159–86
   Lu Xun, 166–73, 214
   Ousmane Sembene, 179–85
   world literature difference with, 187
Thomas à Kempis, 19
Thomism, 251, 252, 273–74
A Thousand Years of Nonlinear History (DeLanda), xviii
The Threepenny Opera (Brecht), 306, 321–25
Thurber, James, 225
time image, 317–18, 319
The Tin Drum (Grass), 314, 316, 320, 336
Tocqueville, Alexis de, 354–55, 356
Tolkien, J. R. R., 217, 225
tonality, 17, 130–32, 152
   atonality and, 133–34
totality, 194–95
traditional allegory, 152, 170, 232, 276, 309–10

allegoresis and, 140–41
Dante and, 271, 273
isotopies in, 59, 220
personifications and, 48, 346–47
tragedy, 6, 115, 150, 301–2
   comedy and, 126, 358
   of desire, 95–96, 109, 111
   Greek, 5–6, 68, 91–93, 302, 303
   Schmitt on, 101, 110, 114
   Shakespearean, 31, 86, 87, 101–2, 105, 114, 157
   Trauerspiel and, 31, 87, 90, 91, 101, 110, 111–12n, 114, 321
transcoding, 43, 71, 201, 353
transversality, 340–41
   in Dante, 255, 278, 285
   Greimas square and, 331–32, 350
   Guattari concept of, xviii, 42–43, 310
   lateral, 231, 281, 282–83
Trauerspiel
   Benjamin on nature of, 31, 88
   human history and, 91
   Schmitt-Benjamin debate on, 87, 101, 114
   tragedy and, 31, 87, 90, 101, 110, 111–12n, 114, 321
The Trial (Kafka), 327–28
tribes, 56, 86, 310, 340
tripartite allegorical scheme, 19, 45, 119
   consciousness and, 15–16
   of Homer, 11–13
   science and, 11, 12, 17
tropes, 42, 93–94, 126, 148, 354
   de Man on, 26–27, 241
   tropological study of, ix–x
Trotsky, Leon, and Trotskyism, 21, 235, 265
Truffaut, François
   L'Enfant sauvage, 27
Tuve, Rosemond, 236, 245
Twain, Mark, 40
   Huckleberry Finn, 339

two-level allegories. *See* dual allegorical scheme

Ulysses (Joyce), 124, 207, 298
unconscious
  Freud on, 55, 57, 97–98, 104–5, 116
  political, xvii, 87, 88–89, 202
uneven development, 190
universality, 48, 71, 77, 296, 332
Utopian dimension and impulse, 179, 214, 305, 386
  allegory and, 215, 345

Valéry, Paul, 304
verse and versification, 222–24, 276
Vico, Giambattista, 44
Vierzehnheiligen, 30
Virgil, 223, 232
  allegory by, 5, 12
  Dante portrayal of, 253–54, 255, 258, 259, 265, 266, 271–72, 279, 299
Von Neumann, John, 369

Wagner, Richard, 147, 151, 297
  on Beethoven, 119–21
  Die Meistersinger, 121–22
  Parsifal, 217
Wallace, David Foster, 316, 317
Wallerstein, Immanuel, 177, 268
Weber, Max, 130, 345

Webern, Anton, 133
Weill, Kurt, 321
Wells, H. G.
  Time Machine, 347
Welsh, Alexander, 101
White, Hayden, 27, 126, 127
  Metahistory, 351–52, 354–58
Whitehead, Alfred North, 36, 80, 81
Whitman, Walt, 223
Who's Afraid of Virginia Woolf? (Albee), 76
Winckelmann, Johann Joachim, 293, 301
wish fulfillment, xiii–xiv, xvi, 147, 290
Wittgenstein, Ludwig, 56
Wolfe, Thomas, 315
Wordsworth, William, 2, 3, 22, 170, 229, 231
world literature, 162–63, 194, 223
  Goethe on, 25–26, 163, 293–94
  and Third-World Literature, 187
World War II, 7, 9, 25, 317

Xala (Ousmane), 179–80, 182–85
Xenien, 300–301

Yang, Edward, 334
Yeats, William Butler, 23, 42, 277

Žižek, Slavoj, 111n, 241
Zola, Émile, 275, 318